THE REVOLUTION IN EGYPT'S ECONOMIC SYSTEM

The Institute gratefully acknowledges the comments and suggestions of the following who read the manuscript on behalf of the Research Committee: David Henderson, Albert Hourani, and Elizabeth Monroe.

THE REVOLUTION IN EGYPT'S ECONOMIC SYSTEM

FROM PRIVATE ENTERPRISE TO SOCIALISM, 1952–1965

PATRICK O'BRIEN

Issued under the auspices of the
Royal Institute of International Affairs

OXFORD UNIVERSITY PRESS
LONDON NEW YORK TORONTO
1966

Oxford University Press, Ely House, London W.1

GLASGOW NEW YORK TORONTO MELBOURNE WELLINGTON
CAPE TOWN SALISBURY IBADAN NAIROBI LUSAKA ADDIS ABABA
BOMBAY CALCUTTA MADRAS KARACHI LAHORE DACCA
KUALA LUMPUR HONG KONG TOKYO

PRINTED AND BOUND IN GREAT BRITAIN BY
HAZELL WATSON AND VINEY LTD
AYLESBURY, BUCKS

FOR MY MOTHER AND FATHER

Contents

Tables

Preface

In July 1952 a group of young army officers seized power in Egypt and in just over a decade have transformed their country's productive system from a private enterprise market economy into a system where the most significant decisions concerning current production and almost all investment decisions are taken by agencies of the state. The direction of change could have been anticipated, because tendencies for the state to circumscribe the discretion of private producers could be perceived under the *ancien régime*. But the extent and rapidity of transformation is still surprising principally because it was carried through by a Military Junta, originally uncommitted to étatism in the economic field and who, in the early years of its rule, displayed every intention of trying to preserve and foster private enterprise.

To trace, explain, and evaluate the changes in Egypt's economic organization are the aims of this monograph. Unlike many studies of economic development its focus is not upon the performance of the economy but is concerned with the political, legal, and institutional framework within which economic enterprise has operated since the revolution. Where possible, changes will be measured. Where feasible, they will be accounted for and appraised in order to show when and why economic policy altered fundamentally.

Studies of economic institutions and the part they play in the allocation of resources provide a necessary background to understanding the process of economic change in countries with a cultural environment and legal system different from those normally encountered in Western Europe and the United States. Since Egypt's government proclaims its economic system as a model for the Middle East as a whole, a description of its broad features should help to clarify what would be involved in its emulation by other Arab states.[1] Finally, an attempt to delimit

[1] Iraq, to take a recent example, has adopted a pattern of ownership and control for its industrial sector closely based upon Egyptian experience and the

the stages and explain the transformation towards a centrally-controlled economy should add something to our understanding of the widespread rejection of private enterprise by other nationalist régimes in Asia and Africa. It might, for example, be instructive to compare the Egyptian case with Ceylon, Burma, Indonesia, and Ghana, countries which have passed through similar revolutions and emerged with comparable systems of economic control. Students of modern Egypt will be interested in these themes for their own sake.

The form of this monograph has been influenced by the questions I have raised but also by my wish to provide a background and historical perspective to its central theme. I have therefore included an introductory chapter on Egypt's economic problems as they appeared to the new government in July 1952. After all, the institutional and legal changes promulgated since then represent a response to these problems. Although I took 1952 as a starting point, I felt the need also to survey relations between government and economy before the revolution in order to supply not only perspective but also to reveal the real innovations in economic policy since the revolution. Too many studies begin in 1952 which, for the recent *economic* history of Egypt, is hardly a turning point at all. The years 1957 and 1961 are certainly much more significant dates as far as the reorientation of economic and social policy is concerned. Thus the early chapters are bounded by chronological divisions in the régime's economic and social policies: 1952–6, 1957–60, and 1960–4. My final chapters are really exploratory essays into the nature and efficiency of the economic system which now operates.[2] I have ventured to include a conclusion to some extent repetitive of the discussion contained in previous chapters, but which aims to bring together the threads of a diffuse argument and perhaps also to give busy people the opportunity to skip the body of the book more effectively!

While I was engaged on research for this study I was singularly fortunate to have been in the midst of a group of people at my university and at the Institute of National Planning in Cairo,

attempt to impose Egyptian economic institutions upon Syria during the period of Union was, to some degree, responsible for the break-up of the United Arab Republic.

[2] I hope to treat these subjects in greater depth in a subsequent monograph.

during my study leave in 1962–3, who were both knowledgeable about the Egyptian economy and interested in my work. They generously gave their time to discuss points with me, brought sources to my attention, and saved me from numerous mistakes. Looking back the book seems in many ways a collective rather than an individual effort. Its errors, of course, remain my own. I cannot mention everyone who helped me by name but I would like to record my gratitude to a few people. During the early days of my work I benefited more than they ever realized from the stimulating company of the Arab post-graduate community at the London School of Economics and I wish to thank Drs Galal Amin, Nour Farrag, Amr Mohiedden, and Aly Monafy for their forbearance and instruction to a novice in the economic affairs of their country. Dr Tom Johnstone of the School of Oriental and African Studies patiently taught me sufficient Arabic to read the sources on the Egyptian economy. Several friends, including Dr Anour Abdel-Malek, Dr Galal Amin, Professor Bent Hansen, Mr Albert Hourani, Dr Donald Mead, Mr Shane Olver, Professor Edith Penrose, Dr. Fakri Shehab, and Professor P. J. Vatikiotis kindly read and commented upon the original manuscript. The revised version owes a lot to their suggestions. Dr Guizine Rachid and Miss Madge Sahbi helped me with the arduous task of combing newspapers and Miss Valerie Lowenhoff and Miss Judy Howey skilfully typed successive drafts. To thank my wife is almost presumptuous. She spent long hours translating Arabic sources with me, correcting drafts, making the index, and above all encouraging me to finish.

I am most grateful to Miss Hermia Oliver of the Royal Institute of International Affairs for the forbearing and very efficient way she has edited my imperfect manuscript. Without her scrutiny it would have been marred by numerous errors.

P. O'B.

London,
February 1966

Abbreviations

Ann. stat.: *Annuaire statistique.*
ar.: Arabic.
Bank Misr, *Econ. B.*: Bank Misr, *Economic Bulletin.*
Basic Statistics: Central Statistical Committee, *Basic Statistics.* 1962.
BE: *Bourse égyptienne.*
CBE, *Econ. R.*: Central Bank of Egypt, *Economic Review.*
Census of Industr. Prod'n: Ministry of Finance & Economy, *Census of Industrial Production, 1945.* 1947.
Econ. J.: *Economic Journal.*
EEPR: *Egyptian Economic & Political Review.*
EG: *Egyptian Gazette.*
Ég. contemp.: *L'Égypte contemporaine.*
Ég. industr.: *L'Égypte industrielle.*
FIE, *Ann.*: Fédération des Industries Égyptiennes, *Annuaire.*
Gen. Frame of 5-Year Plan: Ministry of Planning, *General Frame of the 5-Year Plan for Economic and Social Development July 1960–June 1965.* 1960.
Industry after the Revolution: Ministry of Industry, *Industry after the Revolution and the 5-Year Plan.* 1957.
INP: Institute of National Planning.
Issawi, *EMC*: C. Issawi, *Egypt at Mid-Century.* 1954.
ME Econ. Papers: American University of Beirut, *Middle East Economic Papers.*
MEJ: *Middle East Journal.*
MRESE: Institute of National Planning, *Monthly Review of Economic and Social Events.*
Nasser's Speeches: Information Dept., *President Nasser's Speeches and Press Interviews, 1958, 1959, 1961, 1963.*
NBE, *Econ. B.*: National Bank of Egypt, *Economic Bulletin.*
NPC: National Planning Committee.
OES Egypt: GB, Board of Trade, *Overseas Economic Surveys: Egypt.* 1933, 1935, 1937, and 1951.
PCDNP, *Report 1955*: Permanent Council for the Development of National Production, *Report*, 1955 (ar.)

QJ Econ.: *Quarterly Journal of Economics*

Reports on Finances, Admin., &c.: GB, Parliamentary Papers: *Reports by the Consuls-General on the Finances, Administration and Conditions of Egypt, 1884–1921.*

Rev. éc. trim.: Banque Belge en Égypte, *Revue économique trimestrielle.*

Social Welfare in Egypt: Ministry of Social Affairs, *Social Welfare in Egypt.* 1950.

UAR Econ. Features: Federation of Egyptian Chambers of Commerce, *UAR; Some Economic Features.* 1958.

UN, *Dev. Manufacturing*: UN, *The Development of Manufacturing Industry in Egypt, Israel and Turkey.* 1958.

Note on Sources

THE sources used in this book were made available to me at the libraries of the British Museum, the London School of Economics, the Royal Institute of International Affairs, the School of Oriental and African Studies, and the United Arab Republic Embassy in London and the Institute of National Planning and Ministry of Planning in Cairo. I wish to thank the staff at these institutions for their kindness and courtesy.

Egyptian official publications are published at the Government Press, Cairo. Most of the laws and decrees quoted are taken from Ministry of Finance and Economy, *Economic and Financial Decrees issued between 23 July 1952 to June 1960* (2 vols in Arabic, 1957–60). I have preferred to translate Arabic sources in footnotes (where 'ar.' indicates that the work is in Arabic); but transliterated Arabic titles are included in the bibliography. I have not attempted to appraise the quality of the statistics used in the body of the work. Needless to say they are far from perfect, but I do not think any cited here are positively misleading. Where I have referred several times to a table I have located it in the Statistical Appendix; where the table is used to illustrate only a few points it is placed in the relevant part of the text.

Some memoranda of the National Planning Committee have duplicate numbers because they are divided into different sections, each numbered consecutively.

The following weights and measures have been used.

1 feddan = 1·038 acres = 4,201 sq. metres

£1E = £1.0.6 = $2·87 = 100 piastres

The symbol £ in the text refers to Egyptian pounds unless otherwise stated.

I

Egypt's Economic Problem at Mid-Century

ECONOMIC PROGRESS DURING THE TWENTIETH CENTURY

EGYPTIANS at mid-century were clearly a poor people. The country's per capita income, at around $118, was approximately a tenth of the average British income, and its distribution was very unequal.[1] At the top of society stood a small minority of families who owned most land and other productive assets, and whose incomes were far above the national average, yet at the same time they formed such a significant proportion of the total, as to make comparisons between average real income of Egypt with that of other societies almost meaningless.[2] Food intake figures are a much less ambiguous comparison of international welfare and they reveal that the consumption standards of the average Egyptian, while markedly below those achieved in western Europe and the United States, were nevertheless above the meagre diets of many Asian and certain African societies.[3]

Disease, sickness, and early death characterized the existence of almost all who inhabited the Nile valley and life expectancy for an Egyptian male at birth was only 36 years while an American could expect to live 69 years. Just about a quarter of the population over ten years old could read and write compared with almost complete literacy among the world's wealthy societies.[4] Aggregated statistics conceal much of the real quality of poverty experienced by the mass of Egyptians. Probably the most vivid and certainly the best documented description of their meagre existence is contained in a study by the International Health Division of the Rockefeller Foundation of the village of Sindbis, just thirty kilometres north

[1] UN, *National and Per Capita Income in Seventy Countries* (1949), p. 14.

[2] One estimate for 1955 indicated that 55 per cent of national income was received by 20 per cent of the population while 60 per cent of the population enjoyed only 18 per cent of national income (see GB, Board of Trade, *Report of the United Kingdom Trade Mission to Egypt, Sudan and Ethiopia* (1955), p. 55).

[3] FAO, *Yearbook 1956*, table 80.

[4] UN, *Demographic* and *Statistical Yearbooks*.

of Cairo. Conditions there cannot have been untypical of the rest of rural Egypt. Most likely they were better; but after careful measurement of the income, health, literacy, accommodation, and nutritional level of the people the report reaches this cold conclusion.

In general the village population is one with an extremely low economic status, with low but improving literacy rate, and with a pressing need for social and community development. The burden of disease carried by the population is heavy. Nutritional deficiencies, epidemic and chronic eye diseases, enteric fevers and dysenteries, tuberculosis, syphilis, and bilharzia are all found at extremely high levels in the village population.[5]

Nor, looking back, is it possible to detect many signs that the welfare of the average Egyptian had improved much during the first half of the twentieth century. Literacy obviously advanced, because, with rising government expenditure on education, the proportion of the Egyptian population who could read and write was roughly nearly three times the ratio for 1917.[6] But the statistics of real income and consumption indicate no similar progress. On the contrary, from 1913 to 1950 real income per person not only showed no tendency to rise but fell sharply in the Great Depression of the 1930s and again during the Second World War,[7] while the average consumption of an array of necessities including cereals, meat, textiles, and coffee was probably slightly higher just after the Great War than at mid-century. No perceptible alteration occurred in the health of the population before 1945–9 when the death rate fell 4 points, to 23 per 1,000, and the trend continued downwards during the 1950s.[8]

Reasons for the poverty and economic stagnation of Egypt at mid-century are not difficult to find. For approximately forty years national production barely managed to keep pace with a relatively modest rise in population (averaging about 1½ per cent

[5] J. Weir, 'An Evaluation of Health and Sanitation in Egyptian Villages', *J. Eg. Public Health Ass.* (1952), p. 109.

[6] Dept. of Statistics, *Census of Population*. For 1917, vol. ii and for 1947 chs 4 and 5 respectively.

[7] A. Sherif, *General Trends of Egyptian Economic Growth over the Last 25 Years* (1959), NPC Memo. 121 (ar.), and B. Hansen & D. Mead, *The National Income of Egypt, 1939–62* (1963), INP Memo. 335.

[8] Issawi, *EMC*, pp. 55, 85–86.

a year), so that by 1952 real output per head was not appreciably above the level attained just before the Great War.[9] In addition, for most years (compared with 1910–14) the movement in the terms of trade was very definitely adverse and so depressed average real income below average real product.[10] During the Second World War, which cut off Egyptian agriculture from imported supplies of fertilizers, when industry was unable to replace depreciated equipment and the terms of trade worsened considerably, real income and production per head fell to their lowest levels this century.[11] After the war Egypt's terms of trade improved markedly, and as fertilizers and industrial equipment became importable again, production and real income per head moved rapidly upwards, despite a marked acceleration in the rate of population growth, from about 1½ to 2½ per cent per annum. But when the Korean boom in primary products had ended Egypt's terms of trade moved in an adverse direction once again, and on the eve of revolution both output and real income per person were merely at their 1913 level.[12]

At this juncture the death rate had fallen sharply and showed every sign of continuing to decline, while the birth-rate remained high and stable.[13] Egypt was passing through a population revolution and output per head showed no further tendency to rise. Looking backwards or forward from 1950, the economy seemed to be capable of little more than keeping output apace with the increasing number of people, but appeared incapable of realizing real economic progress.

THE AGRICULTURAL SECTOR

To discover why economic stagnation had prevailed and might continue involves examining the components and development of Egyptian output in some detail, beginning with agriculture which was then and remains now the dominant sector of the economy. At mid-century farming provided approximately a third of the national product and employment for two-thirds of the labour force.[14]

[9] NPC Memo. 121 & INP Memo. 335.

[10] A. Tanamli, 'L'Évolution de l'économie rurale égyptienne dans les cinquante derniers années', *Ég. contemp.*, Oct. 1960, app. 3.

[11] M. Anis, *A Study of the National Income of Egypt* (1950), pp. 690–700.

[12] INP Memo. 335.

[13] *Ann. stat. 1955–6* (1957), sect. 3.

[14] See tables 10 & 11, pp. 325–6 below.

Almost all land is cultivated with the aid of river water or, in that oft-quoted phrase, 'Egypt is the gift of the Nile'. Agricultural progress over the nineteenth century resulted on the whole from additions to the extensive margin and the reallocation of farmland to crops which yielded higher monetary returns rather than from improvements to the physical productivity of the land itself. Techniques of cultivation did not, however, remain static. Towards the end of the century farmers had begun to utilize selected seeds and chemical fertilizers and to participate in campaigns organized by the Ministry of Agriculture to combat pests and plant diseases, while yields per feddan of cotton, wheat, beans, and barley increased considerably between 1879–83 and 1907–11.[15] But the very impressive growth of agricultural output in the century before 1914 originated principally from the extension of the area cultivated by farmers and additions to the number of crops grown on that given area of cultivable land.

Before the time of Mohammed Ali the bulk of Egyptian farmland was cultivated by means of a system of basin irrigation: that is during the flood season, when the level of the Nile ran high, farmers trapped river water in fields or basins along its banks and allowed the water to soak into the soil. In November, when the water had subsided, they planted a winter crop in the silt and harvested the following April. From May to October the land remained fallow. Over the nineteenth century the basin system was gradually replaced by perennial irrigation. Continued and massive investment by the state under Mohammed Ali, Ismail, and the British administration in canals, drains, dams, barrages, and pumping stations had the effect of bringing into cultivation land farther and farther away from the river and made water available to more and more farmers throughout the year.[16] Extra land meant more farms, and with extra water farmers could then grow another crop on land formerly left fallow during the months of summer. Vast areas of the Nile valley became perennially irrigated and were cropped more than once a year. As table 1 shows, between 1820 and 1914 the cultivated area

[15] Yield figures for crops other than cotton are available for state domains only (Min. Finance, *Monthly Return on State & Prospects of Cotton Crop* (1913), pp. 14–15.

[16] A. Crouchley, 'A Century of Economic Development', *Ég. contemp.*, Mar. 1939, pp. 138–42.

increased by 74 per cent, and in 1880 the cropped area probably exceeded the cultivable area by 25 per cent. Thirty years later the latter had increased by a further 1·2 million feddans and exceeded the cultivated area by 44 per cent.

TABLE I

Agricultural Development, 1820–1954

Year	Total population (000)	Cultivated area (000 feddans)	Cropped area (000 feddans)	Cotton output (000 cantars)	Wheat output (000 ardebs)	Maize output (000 ardebs)	Rice output (000 ardebs)
1820–4	2,514	3,053	3,053	51	1,151	912	141
1825–9	—	—	—	—	—	—	—
1830–4	2,500–3,500	3,342	—	147	1,186	995	117
1835–9	—	—	—	229	—	—	—
1840–4	—	3,764	—	196	—	—	—
1845–9	4,463	—	—	236	—	—	—
1850–4	—	4,160	—	475	—	—	—
1855–9	4,402	—	—	515	—	—	—
1860–4	—	4,106	—	944	—	—	—
1865–9	4,841	4,500	—	1,329	—	—	—
1870–4	5,203	4,765	5,433	2,041	—	—	—
1875–9	5,251	4,776	—	2,402	3,780	6,113	127
1880–4	6,806	4,758	5,754	2,733	—	—	—
1885–9	7,491	4,886	5,972	3,026	—	—	—
1890–4	8,654	4,967	6,350	4,396	—	—	—
1895–9	9,681	4,943	6,725	5,577	6,226	11,250	817
1900–4	10,484	5,334	7,361	6,372	7,422	13,097	662
1905–9	11,232	5,374	7,595	6,751	6,616	13,800	1,020
1910–14	11,998	5,285	7,644	7,499	5,960	13,960	1,035
1915–19	12,752	5,309	7,729	5,060	5,831	13,808	1,230
1920–4	13,516	5,305	8,049	6,531	6,649	14,154	764
1925–9	14,280	5,544	8,522	7,965	6,769	16,344	1,172
1930–4	15,106	5,485	8,555	7,555	7,249	14,915	1,773
1935–9	16,032	5,312	8,302	8,692	8,334	14,706	2,441
1940–4	17,113	5,351	8,942	4,640	8,411	15,358	3,418
1945–9	19,086	5,761	9,133	6,370	7,752	14,055	3,992
1950–4	21,469	5,715	9,416	8,074	8,060	13,984	2,187

Notes & Sources

1. *Population*

No population census was taken in Egypt until 1882 and that census is regarded as unreliable. The first reliable population census was conducted in 1897.

The estimates before 1882 are usually based upon tax data or the application of birth and death rates (collected for particular sample areas) to previous estimates. The registration of births and deaths even within these particular areas was usually incomplete. All figures before 1882 are no more than rough estimates.

2. *Cultivated area*

The estimates for the period before 1895 are in general not based upon cadastral surveys but upon land subjected to tax. Cadastral surveys were, however, conducted in 1813 and 1852. The series provides us with a fairly good estimate of the cultivated area up to 1895 and the estimates thereafter are reliable.

3. *Cropped area*

No estimates for cropped area exist before 1895. The figures cited are my estimates which are based upon the plausible assumption that the cropped area was equal to the cultivated area plus the area devoted to summer crops. After 1895 official estimates are available for the cropped area.

4. *Output of cotton, wheat, maize, & rice*

These are the principal crops grown in Egypt over this period. Before 1895 the figures are rough estimates, after that date they are official estimates and are more or less reliable.

5. *Sources*

A full list and discussion of the figures presented in table 1 appears in my essay 'The Long-Term Growth of Agricultural Production in Egypt, 1821–1962', in P. Holt, ed., *Political and Social Change in Modern Egypt* (to be published in London, 1966).

The extension of and improvements to the irrigation system were accompanied by public and private investment in facilities for transporting, financing, storing, and selling agricultural produce. Egyptian farmers responded fully to the opportunities presented to them by public investment in the infrastructure and expansion of world demand for cash and food crops by reallocating land to rice, fruit, vegetables, and above all to cotton.[17] Farm out-

[17] Issawi, 'Egypt since 1800', *J. Econ. Hist.*, Mar. 1961, pp. 8–13.

put rose approximately twelve times between 1821 and 1880 and doubled again by the Great War. Egyptian agriculture became transformed from a traditional subsistence sector into a highly commercialized and responsive enterprise which proved to be capable of employing and feeding at a higher standard of living a population which probably increased four times over the course of the nineteenth century.[18]

By 1914 the government had completed all the more obvious irrigation projects, and investment to expand the area of cultivable and cropped land continued thereafter upon a reduced scale. As a result, between the Great War and the revolution of 1952 the cultivated area increased by 16 per cent and the cropped area by a third, but, given the accelerated growth of population, this slower rate of expansion in the extensive margin was not sufficient to prevent the ratio of cropped land per head of the population, and also per head of the rural labour force, from declining quite sharply. Thus for 1910–14 the cropped area per Egyptian was 0·64 feddans; by 1950–4 the ratio stood at 0·44 feddans.[19] In 1907 each person employed in agriculture worked on average 3·18 feddans, but forty years later the average area of land per worker had fallen to 2·51 feddans. During the twentieth century irrigated land clearly became a much scarcer factor of production.

Some further reallocation of land towards the cultivation of crops yielding higher monetary returns per feddan (such as cotton, rice, and vegetables) helped to obviate the shortage in the inter-war period. Farmers also attempted to compensate for the shortage of land by utilizing more chemical fertilizers and improved varieties of seeds, but for most of the period the substitution of new factors of production did not occur at a rate sufficient to offset the scarcity of land and the decline in soil fertility due to salination and multiple cropping. Up to 1936 the average yield of cotton per feddan remained consistently and appreciably below the level attained for 1900–4, but thereafter it rose slightly.

Investment along the intensive margin after 1914 did not achieve anything like the spectacular results which accrued from the investment in irrigation facilities during the nineteenth century. Given the more rapid growth of population, fertilizers, scientific drainage, the reallocation of farmland and selected seeds

[18] O'Brien, in Holt. [19] See table 1.

did not prove capable of offsetting the overall shortage of land and water. Although total output continued to rise for about four decades, the trend of per capita farm output and product per head of the rural working force definitely moved downward. Egyptian agriculture had clearly run into diminishing returns, with output per man employed and output per inhabitant of the Nile valley well below the level of 1915.[20]

In 1950, after a half century of virtual stagnation, the Egyptian agricultural sector exhibited many of the characteristics commonly associated with farming in poor countries as well as several unique features of its own. Every available feddan in the Nile valley was cropped with cotton and cereals (the principal products), and to a more limited but growing extent with vegetables, fruit, and clover. The bulk of raw cotton was sold abroad, and realized around 80 per cent of the country's earnings of foreign exchange.[21] As local farmers had produced cotton for international markets for well over a century, agriculture had been thoroughly commercialized and utilized transport, credit, and marketing facilities on a scale and of a calibre not often found in poor countries. Agricultural development was not, therefore, conspicuously impeded by the common obstacles to improved farming found in the backward primary production of many other low-income societies.

On the other hand Egyptian agriculture shared many of the deplored characteristics of unprogressive agricultural sectors. Ownership of land was very unequally distributed and underemployment endemic.[22] Several observers argued that with relatively small increases in investment or minor alterations to productive organization, a large proportion (possibly up to a third) of the agricultural working force could have been withdrawn without affecting output, but where the underemployed rural workers could have found alternative work does not seem to have concerned them over much.[23]

[20] A. Imam, *A Production Function for Egyptian Agriculture, 1913–55* (1962), INP Memo. 259, and O'Brien, in Holt.

[21] Tanamli, in *Ég. contemp.*, Oct. 1960, app. 9.

[22] *Ann. stat. 1949–51* (1951), sect. 10 shows that 5.8 per cent of all owners owned 64.5 per cent of all cultivable land.

[23] M. Quni, *The Economic Development of Egypt in the Modern Age* (1944, ar.), p. 178 and W. Cleland, 'A Population Plan for Egypt', *Ég. contemp.*, May 1939, p. 471.

As in many poor countries, the labour force had adapted its mode of production to the amount of work available and Egyptian agriculture, to quote a popular saying, 'had become like gardening'. Egypt's agrarian problem was not, however, to increase productivity per man (the abundant factor) but output of her scarce factor, land; yet for several crops cultivated in the Nile valley returns per acre were already among the highest in the world.[24] Such returns, unusually high for a poor society, suggested further progress would be difficult, but high yields are not the same as optimum yields, and scope certainly existed for further additions to the productivity of Egyptian farmland.

To begin with, tenurial arrangements and institutions did not appear conducive to efficiency. Unfortunately available measures of the extent of tenancy in Egyptian agriculture are difficult to interpret, but it appears that probably well over half of the cultivated area around 1950 was farmed by owner-operators. Although tenant farmers were not typical, tenancy nevertheless was sufficiently important to have a significant influence on agricultural productivity.[25] Leases usually ran for very short periods and afforded the tenant very little security. Although rents normally took their most efficient form, namely fixed cash payments, they had risen precipitously with the increased pressure of population on the land. Thus between 1940 and 1950 cash rents had risen nearly five times, while the elevation in the cost of living was only about 300 per cent. Rent amounted frequently to half the total cost of production, and average cash rents per feddan attained levels well above the net returns per feddan on owner-operated farms.[26]

Short insecure leases discouraged tenant farmers from taking a long view and they tended to allocate their land to cash crops yielding quick returns, such as cotton, grain, and rice, instead of more profitable, but longer gestating, investments, in animal husbandry and horticulture. Moreover their contracts of tenure gave them no interest in the fecundity of the soil or in improve-

[24] FAO, *Yearbook 1952*, sect. 4.

[25] *Basic Statistics*, p. 63.

[26] M. Ghonemy, *Resource Use and Income in Egyptian Agriculture* (unpubl. thesis, 1953), pp. 50, 56, & 94; Inst. Nat. de la Statist. et des Études Écon., *Égypte* (1950), p. 54.

ments to their farms and their concern with short-run returns often impoverished land, depreciated farm capital at a rapid rate, and impeded long-run agricultural growth. High rents prevented farmers from accumulating sufficient cash to buy farms, and thus retarded evolution to the more efficient tenurial system of owner-cultivation. High rents often became associated with indebtedness to the landlord which prevented tenants from moving to farms where their efficiency might have been higher.[27] It also seems that a large proportion of agricultural rent was paid to absentee landowners: persons who, with a rising population, received a growing share of agricultural output, not for their part in production or investment in agriculture, but because they happened to own a factor of production in inelastic supply.[28]

How far the efficiency of Egyptian agriculture fell below its optimum level because of an inappropriate scale of farming is impossible to ascertain. Four-fifths of all farms were less than 5 feddans in size, but they accounted for only a fifth of the total cultivated area.[29] Several commentators have suggested that farms below 20 feddans (covering about 60 per cent of the cultivated area) were not able to take advantage of mechanized techniques of production, but the assumption that, with its resource endowment, factor prices, and structure of production, Egyptian agriculture should have been more mechanized is itself very dubious.[30] But economies from enlarging the unit of cultivation might well have been reaped in relation to irrigation, crop treatment, and harvesting.

Egyptian farms consisted of several strips of land scattered over three or more fields, and within a given field the individual strips might grow separate crops, while the field was irrigated and drained as a whole. Certain plants became watered too intensively, others insufficiently, while the drainage of surplus water off the fields to prevent salination of the soil was badly conducted by open drains which also wasted land.[31] The National Planning Com-

[27] Ghonemy, pp. 56–58 & 95 and Issawi, *EMC*, pp. 128–9.

[28] *Basic Statistics*, pp. 60–63, and Issawi, *EMC*, pp. 128–9.

[29] *Basic Statistics*, p. 63.

[30] G. Amin, *The Food Problem and Economic Development in Egypt* (unpubl. thesis, 1964), pp. 142–50.

[31] A. Ammar, *A Demographic Study of an Egyptian Province* (*Sharqiya*) (1942), p. 54.

mittee estimated that about 10 per cent of food production was lost through insects and plant diseases, but at the same time only a small proportion of crops was treated against these natural hazards. Pests and plant diseases could certainly have been more easily and efficiently controlled over large monoculture fields than on small farms. Similarly, at harvest times the seasonal labour shortage was undoubtedly accentuated by the inefficient application of labour time over a large number of small production units. Finally, the consolidation of scattered strips of land not only economized scarce land and water, but was a precondition for the application of more scientific systems of crop rotation.

Egyptian farmers, unlike those of more traditional societies, were already familiar with a good deal of modern agrarian technology such as chemical fertilizers and selected seeds, but the utilization of nitrogenous chemicals and hybrid seeds was certainly not optimal. Scope for further increases in yields certainly existed both by introducing more conservative farmers to the modern inputs already employed on progressive farms and also by disseminating more knowledge among farmers at large about seeds appropriate to particular soils and climatic conditions and by the provision of information about the correct rates of fertilization and water input for different crops.[32]

Egyptian farming in 1950 cannot really be called backward or traditional but it had certainly not achieved optimum efficiency: field drainage remained in a primitive state and the unequal distribution of landownership, the separation of ownership from control, and local tenurial institutions were far from conducive to maximum economic efficiency. Consolidation of holdings would have created the conditions for improved systems of rotation and the application of new techniques to cultivation. Nevertheless the backlog of techniques and scientific methods which could be adopted by Egyptian farmers was not nearly so great as was often the case for other underdeveloped countries. With given technology and social organization, Egyptian agriculture already stood close to the margin of intensive cultivation. Appreciable rates of

[32] This discussion of the scale and techniques of Egyptian farming is based upon reports by the Agricultural Sub-Committee of the NPC, Memos 249–63 (1959, ar.). I assume that the points raised by the Committee in 1959 apply to 1950–2, and see Quni (ar.), pp. 170 & 180–3.

progress might be achieved in the short run by further investment in irrigation facilities. But even along the extensive margin the evidence suggested that the rapid rate of population growth was liable to outstrip any feasible rate of addition to the cultivable area, so that the amount of land available per head of the population if not of the rural labour force seemed bound to fall still farther.[33] Thus as far as the national economy was concerned, output needed to be diversified and opportunities created for production and employment outside the agricultural sector.

THE INDUSTRIAL SECTOR

As Egypt is not well endowed with mineral wealth, the country's development strategy was inescapably pointed towards industrialization. Industry in 1950 made but a small contribution (15 per cent) to national output and employed only a tenth of the labour force.[34] Although the origins of most manufactures then carried on in Egypt can be traced back possibly to antiquity, the establishment of an industrial sector was a much more recent event. Setting aside Mohammed Ali's unsuccessful attempt to create a range of manufacturing enterprises during the early decades of last century, industry appears to have been a twentieth-century development.[35] Precise measurement of its long-term growth is unfortunately impossible but if we accept the change in registered capital of industrial joint-stock companies as a rough indicator of development, then it seems that the 'take-off stage' probably occurred during the first two decades of this century when their capital almost doubled. Industrial growth must have been very rapid in the Great War when Egypt was cut off from her suppliers of manufactured imports, and local entrepreneurs set about meeting the demand created by the presence locally of foreign troops and the rise in domestic incomes associated with the war-time inflation of cotton prices.[36]

[33] H. Hurst, *The Nile* (1952), pp. 314–15.

[34] See tables 10 & 11 (pp. 325–6 below).

[35] M. Fahmy, *La révolution de l'industrie en Égypte, 1800–50* (1954).

[36] R. Barawi & M. Ulaish, *The Development of the Egyptian Economy in the Modern Era* (1945, ar.), pp. 197–8 and *Report on Finances, Administration &c. 1914–19* (Parl. Papers, 1920), pp. 1–5.

TABLE 2

Registered Capital of Egyptian Industrial Joint-Stock Companies, 1902–40 (£000)

Industry	*1902*	*1921*	*1930*	*1940*
Cotton and sugar processing	2,750	4,017	4,124	4,571
Building materials	82	138	949	1,388
Food industries	554	1,440	1,327	1,561
Other industries	458	2,384	3,321	7,728
Total	3,844	7,979	9,721	15,248

Source: A. Gritly, *The Structure of Modern Industry in Egypt* (1947), table 1.

After the war, when Egyptian enterprises had again to face the full rigour of foreign competition, development slowed down and between 1921 and 1930 the registered capital of industrial joint-stock companies increased by only 21 per cent. Much of this investment went into the so-called sheltered industries, such as building materials, furniture, and food processing, where profits were higher because the bulk and weight of the product relative to its value rendered it difficult for foreign substitutes to compete in local markets.[37]

In 1930 Egypt, for the first time since Mohammed Ali, secured tariff autonomy and the government immediately revoked the country's traditional free trade policy and imposed duties of between 15 and 20 per cent *ad valorem* on a wide range of consumer goods likely to compete with domestic commodities. As a number of surveys by the Board of Trade noticed, the Egyptian government became uncompromising in protecting local industry and over the following decades tariffs were raised several times and extended to all competing foreign goods.[38] Further, during the 1930s prices of raw cotton slumped heavily on world markets, and Egyptian landowners found agriculture a less remunerative outlet for their capital and began to diversify their investments by financing industrial enterprises.[39] Considerable impetus was also

[37] M. Hamdi, *A Statistical Survey of the Development of Capital Investment in Egypt since 1880* (unpubl. thesis, 1943), pp. 283–5.

[38] OES, *Egypt, 1953*, p. 41; *1935*, p. 50, & *1937*, p. 89; Quni, pp. 180 & 185.

[39] Hamdi, pp. 157–8 and Barawi & Ulaish (ar.), pp. 200–1.

afforded to the development of large-scale manufacturing firms by Bank Misr. The Bank was founded by a group of Egyptian capitalists in 1919 to promote local industrial and commercial enterprise. Banks which combine the functions of an investment trust with deposit banking often emerge in underdeveloped countries where savings are scarce and do not flow easily into industry. Thus Bank Misr floated companies together with foreign and Egyptian industrial promoters. The Bank's good name and popularity, as a purely national institution, attracted private capital away from the more traditional channels of land, commerce, and buildings. If particular share issues were not fully taken up by the public, the Bank was prepared to absorb them temporarily into its own portfolio, and sold the shares later when their value and security were more established. In addition, Bank Misr provided working capital, managerial and technical advice for all its affiliated companies.[40]

Protection, the agricultural depression, the efforts of Bank Misr to promote and finance new enterprises, as well as the availability of a fairly mature infrastructure all helped to make the 1930s a decade of impressive advance. Egyptian industrialization did not proceed stage by stage from handicraft production to small factories and then on to large-scale mechanized enterprises; it is rather a textbook example of development through import substitution. By 1930 foreign products had already pioneered the local market; an internal distribution and credit organization was available and mechanized production had demonstrated its efficiency for other countries; thus large-scale national firms could and did establish themselves behind tariff barriers with relative ease. Unfortunately there is no production index which measures the overall rate of growth before 1939, but progress can be traced through import statistics, employment data, and scattered totals of physical output for particular industries. The decline after 1930 in the import of such foreign manufactures as shoes, cement, furniture, flour, cotton yarn, and processed foods is very striking. In little more than six years the proportion of Egyptian consumption of cotton piece-goods satisfied by local producers rose from 3 to 24 per cent.[41] By the

[40] A. Soliman, *L'Industrialisation de l'Égypte* (1932), pp. 183–96.
[41] OES, *Egypt 1937*, p. 115.

eve of the Second World War the country was already self-sufficient in sugar, alcohol, cigarettes, salt, and flour, and almost independent of foreign suppliers for cotton yarn, shoes, cement,

TABLE 3

Statistical Indicators of Egyptian Industrial Production, 1920–50

Product & unit	*c. 1920*	*c. 1930*	*c. 1940*	*c. 1950*
1. Textiles				
Cotton consumed by local spinning mills (000 cantars)	55	177	868	1,400
Cotton yarn & thread (000 tons)	—	3	25	52
Mechanically woven cotton cloth (m. sq. yd)	9	20	159	—
Woven cotton (m. metres)	—	—	138	249
2. Food, drink & tobacco				
Refined sugar (000 tons)	79	109	224	287
Cotton seed oil (000 tons)	—	—	50	87
Milled rice (000 tons)	—	244	470	842
Beer (m. litres)	—	7	16	13
Cigarettes (m.)	—	—	6,000	9,800
3. Chemicals				
Soap (000 tons)	—	38	45	65
Sulphuric acid (000 tons)	—	—	8	33
Paper & cardboard (000 tons)	—	—	7	21
Alcohol (m. litres)	—	—	5	13
4. Building materials				
Cement (000 tons)	24	190	370	994
5. Minerals & power				
Petroleum (000 tons)	—	287	938	2,324
Crude phosphates (000 tons)	—	313	281	449
Electricity (m. kwh)	—	—	288	609
Commercial consumption of energy, coal equivalent (000 tons)	—	—	2,059	4,728

Notes: Where possible the figure quoted is a three-year average. If not the nearest total to the above years has been selected.

Sources: NPC, *Industrial Development over the Last 25 Years* (1958), (ar.); *Ann. stat.*; FIE, *Ann.*

soap, furniture, matches, beer, and vegetable oils; a situation in sharp contrast to 1913.[42]

The development of production and employment associated with this decline in imports can perhaps be most eloquently described with the aid of tables 3 and 4, which bring together the rather scarce information now available on the progress of Egyptian industry before the revolution.

For example, table 3 reveals that the rate of growth of output for all sectors of industry for which information is now available ran well ahead of the growth of population. Textile output (yarn and mechanically woven cotton) rose approximately seven times;

TABLE 4

Employment in Manufacturing Industry, by Sector (000)

Sector	*1927*	*1937*	*1947*	*1952*
Food processing	14.3	32.5	59.9	49.6
Beverages & tobacco	9.1	10.3	13.1	14.6
Textiles	21.3	40.5	134.4	116.1
Clothing & footwear	4.7	9.6	3.3	6.1
Wood & products	9.2	4.2	3.8	7.5
Paper & products	0.6	2.5	4.5	5.3
Printing & publishing	5.2	6.9	5.4	7.5
Leather & products	1.5	1.4	2.7	2.1
Rubber products	—	—	1.0	1.0
Chemicals	2.9	6.4	15.8	11.2
Petroleum & products	—	0.2	3.6	4.3
Non-metallic mineral products	4.5	7.7	13.0	14.3
Metals & products	10.5	11.5	13.5	11.4
Transport equipment	—	—	2.3	1.4
Miscellaneous	0.4	5.9	1.1	2.6
Total	84.2	139.6	277.7	255.0

Notes: The figures relate to manufacturing industry only and the figures for 1927, 1937 and have been adapted from *Census of Industrial and Commercial Establishments* for 1927 and 1937. The figures for 1947 and 1952 are from the *Census of Industrial Production.*

Sources: UN, *Dev. Manufacturing*, table xiv and *Statist. Pocket Yearbooks, 1952* & *1954*, ch. 9.

[42] I. Levi, 'Le Commerce extérieur et l'industrialisation de l'Égypte', *Ég. contemp.*, Dec. 1939, pp. 595–632 and NBE, *Econ. B.*, iii (1948), p. 113.

processed food production, as measured by refined sugar, milled rice, and beer, doubled in output, as did cement, while soap production increased by 20 per cent at a time when the population rose by only 16 per cent.[43]

The Second World War imparted an impetus to Egyptian industry very similar in character to that of the Great War. Demand for local commodities became inflated by allied military expenditure on such things as sweets, chocolates, canned fruit, beer, cigarettes, furniture, and textiles. And the incomes paid by the British army to the 200,000 or so additional civilians employed on the construction and maintenance of military installations also increased local expenditure upon manufactured products. Finally, Egyptian consumers were impelled by wartime shortages of imported manufactures to purchase domestic products, and since she possessed the most highly developed industry in the area, Egypt also benefited by exporting to other countries in the Middle East afflicted by similar shortages.

Prices rose faster than wages and the huge profits made in manufacturing prompted merchants and landowners to invest in industry or even to become industrial entrepreneurs. Their attraction towards industry was also enhanced by the lower remuneration on investment in agriculture which arose from the inability of Egypt to export her most profitable crop (cotton) or to obtain essential supplies of fertilizers.[44] Moreover Egyptian entrepreneurs were encouraged and assisted to meet wartime demands by the British military authorities. For example, the training in skills and industrial discipline provided by the British army for thousands of Egyptian workers at least helped to mitigate the labour bottleneck which emerged after 1939, and the Middle East Supply Centre procured raw materials for firms and helped them in numerous ways with technical and managerial advice to overcome production problems.[45]

Not all industries benefited equally from hostilities; some, cut off from imported supplies of raw materials, stagnated and many firms suffered from a shortage of equipment which was almost

[43] Barawi & Ulaish (ar.), pp. 204–7.

[44] This section is based on A. Prest, *War Economics of Primary Producing Countries* (1948), ch. 4; Anis, ch. 2; and Barawi & Ulaish (ar.), pp. 278–88.

[45] M. Wilmington, 'The Middle East Supply Centre', *MEJ*, Spring 1952, pp. 144–66.

invariably obtained from outside Egypt. But for the major branches of manufacturing (textiles and food processing) the war was undoubtedly a boom period.

As real industrial output rose by approximately 37 per cent and total population by 11 per cent between 1939–45, per capita industrial production appears to have grown by just under 4 per cent per annum during the war.[46] Unlike the previous decade this development was also reflected in employment figures which reveal that the number of persons in 'industrial occupations' increased by 50 per cent between the Census enumerations of 1937 and 1947, and table 5 (p. 20) shows the very marked increase in the numbers employed in food processing and textiles.[47] Employment rose because the very unusual demand conditions of the war years produced a situation where thousands of small-scale handicraft producers could survive and prosper alongside their capital intensive rivals, who deprived of possibilities for importing machinery could only expand production up to capacity output.[48]

Many elements of the wartime situation persisted into the post-war era. Prices went on rising and manufactured goods continued to be scarce on world markets, while pent-up wartime demand within Egypt sought outlets in the purchase of manufactured goods. In addition, when cotton was exported again, its price, stimulated by inflated international demand, moved rapidly upward and gave Egyptian farmers additional income to spend on processed foodstuffs, textiles, and household equipment. For about five years after the war Egyptian industry continued to operate in a seller's market and firms responded by replacing their obsolete and depreciated equipment with new foreign machinery. Industries such as wood and rubber products, which had suffered from war-time shortages of their raw materials, resumed production and promoters inaugurated several new lines of manufacturing, particularly in chemicals and metallurgy.[49]

Thus every year the increment to industrial production was

[46] The estimate of industrial output is that of Anis, p. 685.

[47] Dept. Statist., *Population Census 1937 & 1947*, ch. 1.

[48] Anis, pp. 772–84.

[49] NBE, *Econ. B.*, iv (1951), pp. 250–1; OES, *Egypt 1951*, pp. 56 & 63; Issawi, *EMC*, pp. 142–3.

large and the growth rate for 1947 to 1949 established a record for the post-war period. Overall per capita industrial production was about a third higher in 1952 than it had been at the end of the war, but for the final years of the old régime (1950–52) output showed no further tendency to rise.[50] However, after two decades of fairly impressive development, at mid-century Egyptian industry still made only a small contribution to national output and employment.[51] The rate of growth of industrial production had not been sufficient to offset the stagnation of per capita agricultural output and thereby provide Egypt with real economic progress. Its deceleration after 1949 was a bad sign for a poor society so obviously dependent on industrialization as the solution to its economic problems; particularly as the relatively poor performance of manufacturing from 1950 to 1952 was not accidental and temporary but reflected the closing of a stage in the industrialization of Egypt. For over two decades local enterprises assisted by tariffs and war had been actively engaged in replacing foreign consumer goods in mass demand. Industries which had developed readily were those for which the country also possessed comparative advantages, usually in the form of agricultural raw materials (such as cotton and foodstuffs), or alternatively the minerals for the manufacture of such products as salt, soda, and cement. And Egyptian entrepreneurs had chosen to produce commodities where the amount of capital required per unit of output was relatively low, where productive techniques were less complicated, and where fuel and transport charges did not form a substantial proportion of the cost of the finished product. Thus around 1950 Egypt had acquired an industrial structure dominated by the manufacture of simple consumer goods. As the table on p. 20 shows, whether measured in terms of net output or employment, food processing and textiles were of overwhelming importance, while the manufacture of consumer durables, metallurgical products, inputs utilized by other industries, and capital equipment was of little significance.

[50] See tables 19 and 21 (pp. 334 & 336).
[51] See tables 10 & 11 (pp. 325 & 326).

TABLE 5

Industrial Production for 1952

Industry	*Gross output* (£000)	*Cost of raw materials* (£000)	*Net value added* (£000)	*No. of employees* (000)	*Wage bill* (£000)
Cotton ginning & pressing	18,495	14,094	4,401	26	1,128
Mining & quarrying	1,620	473	1,147	4	364
Food processing (incl. beverages)	71,206	57,653	13,533	50	3,075
Tobacco manufacturing	43,057	37,573	5,484	11	835
Spinning & weaving	64,938	44,617	20,321	90	7,310
Apparel & footwear	3,390	1,990	1,400	6	548
Furniture & fixtures	2,757	1,729	1,028	6	510
Paper & products	2,852	1,876	976	5	318
Printing & publishing	4,680	2,621	2,059	7	601
Chemicals & products	18,178	12,608	5,570	11	826
Non-metallic minerals	8,233	5,057	3,176	14	1,237
Basic metals	7,240	4,723	2,517	11	1,011
Transport equipment	3,663	1,327	2,336	9	944
Unclassified	20,545	8,853	11,692	18	2,209
Electricity, gas, & water	4,957	1,813	3,144	4	555
Total	275,811	197,007	78,804	237	21,471

Source: Basic Statistics, p. 90.

By 1950 the replacement of imports of simple consumer goods by domestic substitutes had been almost completed. Further and impressive rates of expansion in the output of processed food and textiles could only be achieved either if local demand for manufactured goods grew rapidly, if the efficiency of industry improved substantially, or via exports. But prospects for expansion through domestic demand did not appear too bright. As industry was a small sector of the economy the multiplier effects of industrial investment upon the overall demand for manufactured commodities continued to be small. The mass market remained in rural areas but for reasons outlined above real output per capita in agriculture was virtually stagnant, and further diversion of rural income towards manufactured products appeared implausible. Real incomes in rural areas could go up if cotton prices increased on international markets or if agricultural prices in general rose faster than the prices of manufactured goods, but in 1950, movements of the terms of trade (internal or external) favourable to the agricultural sector also appeared unlikely. Some increase in the propensity to consume manufactured products could reasonably be expected from increasing urbanization, but this fillip to demand would probably be more than counteracted by the rising population with the diversion of expenditure by larger families towards basic foodstuffs.

As for exports, international demand for textiles and processed food was not expanding rapidly and in a highly competitive situation Egyptian products appeared to have no overwhelming cost, quality, or other advantages to attract large numbers of foreign buyers. Less than 10 per cent of manufactured output was sold abroad and the rapid development of Egyptian industry via world markets was never seriously envisaged.

Given the potential rate of growth of domestic and world demand, by cutting prices firms could still expand sales, but any survey of Egyptian industry at mid-century was bound to be sceptical about its ability to achieve significant reductions in costs, at least in the short run. Real information about present or past efficiency of Egyptian industry is, however, extremely scarce; almost anything said about it is merely tentative and impressionistic.

The Census of Industrial Production for 1950 reported that 19,527 establishments manufactured commodities in Egypt. Just over one-third of all establishments produced an output valued at less than £500 a year and 60 per cent produced annual outputs of less than £1,000; one-half had registered capitals of less than £200 and three-quarters employed less than 10 workers. Probably the majority of these small firms were operated by the 18,304 owners and their families enumerated by the Census.[52] Thus the typical manufacturing enterprise was a small-scale owner-managed venture.[53] But the representative enterprise was far from being the most important, because in terms of output and employment the larger-scale incorporated firms appeared overwhelmingly more significant. Unfortunately precise measures of the contribution made by these firms to output and employment are difficult to find, but if we use the three categories of establishment distinguished by the Census (enterprises with an output valued at more than £1,000 a year, termed 'large'; enterprises with production of between £500 and £1,000 a year, termed 'medium'; and 'small' enterprises with annual outputs of less than £500) then it appears that a *gross* product of £276·9 million emanated from large firms, £3·1 million from medium enterprises, and £1·9 million from small firms.[54] Moreover Dorra noted for 1937 that the 312 largest establishments with capitals of £10,000 and above accounted for 84 per cent of the total 'declared' capital of industrial establishments.[55] Larger firms, employing ten or more workers, again predominated in terms of employment and for 1950 had engaged roughly 83 per cent of the industrial working force.[56]

Although the figures and descriptive categories are imprecise and ambiguous for purposes of measurement, they do show that Egyptian manufacturing activity was dominated by relatively

[52] *Census of Industr. Prod'n 1950* (1953). The Census separated industrial establishments engaged upon maintenance, repair, and services from those producing commodities. The above total refers to the latter category. It includes mining, gas, electricity, and water. Throughout this account I will utilize this definition of productive establishments. Alternative definitions employed by the *Census of Industrial Commercial Establishments* for 1927, 1937, and 1947, and used by Gritly and Anis, embrace thousands of repair, maintenance, and service establishments (including garages, shoe repairers, dry cleaners, hairdressers) and give a misleading impression of the extent of *manufacturing* activity in Egypt. On the other hand to use the *Census of Industr. Prod'n 1952* and subsequent years, which enumerated only establishments employing 10 workers and above, underestimates industrial activity.

[53] A. Dorra, 'L'Industrie égyptienne', *Ég. contemp.*, Nov. 1943, pp. 423–4.

[54] *Census of Industr. Prod'n, 1950*, table 5.

[55] Dorra, p. 424.

[56] *Statist. Pocket Yearbook 1953*, table 31 & *Census of Industr. Prod'n 1950*, table 2.

large incorporated enterprises.[57] In legal organization at least Egyptian industry in 1950 appeared not dissimilar to the structure of enterprise manufacturing in more developed economies with a pre-eminence of bigger firms, operated by salaried managers who owned only a fraction of the assets they controlled.

Thus the expansion of existing manufactures depended, to an important degree, on those who controlled a very small group of firms, but beyond deducing that the difficulties of industrial management in Egypt were greater than those normally encountered in developed economies, I can say very little about this managerial élite or how it operated. The shortage of technicians, personnel officers, accountants, workshop supervisors, and sales managers meant that managers were less specialized than considerations of efficiency demanded. Authority was centralized and top administrators impelled to engage in a variety of tasks properly delegated to subordinates. Over time industrial growth itself generates skilled personnel, but in the short run the educational and social system appeared unlikely to alleviate the shortage. Few institutions for management training existed in Egypt and arts graduates, who dominated the universities, gravitated towards higher prestige occupations in public service or the professions. Nor were the structure of industry and the attitudes of its controllers conducive to widening the managerial élite. Thousands of small family firms contributed little to the training of the administrative and technical class needed to run large-scale industry, while the larger firms had not made proper use of graduates from the faculties of commerce or extended their support to the feeble and inefficient efforts of the government in vocational education. Further, they had not consistently adopted a policy of promoting promising personnel from the shop floor, and several firms were dominated by the 'tycoon' type of director whose failure to delegate further inhibited the growth of a managerial élite.[58]

The direction of industry in a poor country was certainly difficult and administrators were scarce, but how competently

[57] *Census of Industr. Prod'n 1954* (table 5) reported that 53 per cent of all enterprises employing more than 10 workers were joint-stock companies and a further 3 per cent were private limited liability companies.

[58] F. Harbison & I. Ibrahim, *Human Resources for Egyptian Enterprise* (1958), pp. 41–44, 51, 65, 104–6, 112–16, 119 & 121, and UN, *Dev. Manufacturing*, pp. 83–84.

Egyptian managers performed the tasks of purchasing raw materials, recruiting workers, raising finance, combining capital and labour, supervising the process of production, and marketing the finished product can be described but unfortunately not measured.

For example, although some commentators have hazarded assertions that 'some Egyptian firms have passed well beyond the size needed to secure economies of scale' or on the contrary that 'a number of manufacturing establishments appear to be below the minimum size required for economical operations', the complete absence of figures of costs of production at varying levels of output makes it impossible to reach any definite conclusions about how far Egyptian firms had departed from an optimum scale.[59] But both statements are probably correct. A few firms accounted for the bulk of the output of particular industries, such as sugar and salt refining, cotton yarn spinning, rayon, cement, and chemical fertilizers, not apparently because considerations of efficiency dictated large-scale production, but because their owners were concerned to reap monopoly profits.[60] Moreover Dr Gritly claims that the desire to find outlets for retained profits had produced vertical and lateral integration in several sectors of Egyptian industry, and the persistence of excess capacity throughout the post-war period supports the suggestion that some Egyptian plants were beyond their optimum scale.[61] On the other hand the controllers of Egyptian industry were often precluded from establishing firms at the most efficient scale because of the smallness of the local market and the uncertainties of international markets. And firms below a certain size, even though efficient and adaptable to local conditions, found it difficult to borrow the long-term capital and short-term credit required to support their operations.[62]

Finance for industrial needs was expensive and difficult to obtain. Capital costs depended upon the supply of investible funds to industry. Of course, the overall rate of saving and the

[59] Issawi, *EMC*, p. 158 and UN, *Dev. Manufacturing*, p. 38.

[60] Naggar, *Industrialization and Income* (1951), pp. 256–66 and Gritly, pp. 489–90, 502–7, & 525.

[61] Gritly, p. 499; G. Said, 'Productivity of Labour in Egyptian Industry', *Ég. contemp.*, May 1950, p. 504; UN, *Dev. Manufacturing*, p. 81.

[62] UN, *Dev. Manufacturing*, p. 37.

willingness of persons and institutions to lend money to manufacturing establishments were factors largely beyond the competence of industrial managers. Compared with developed economies, the overall ratio of savings to national income, running at approximately 12 per cent per annum, remained low, and with other things equal the preferences of the investing class certainly displayed no tendency to favour industry compared with more traditional outlets for their savings, such as land or real estate.[63] On the contrary, their antipathy, coupled with the reluctance of commercial banks to lend to industry, either long or short term, had prompted Egyptian industrialists in 1919 to found Bank Misr in order to channel investible funds towards manufacturing enterprises. Over time industrial development came from necessity to be financed mainly from retained earnings, but small and medium-scale enterprises continued to encounter such difficulties in obtaining funds that in 1949 the government founded the Industrial Bank to cater for their needs.[64] Even though industrial corporations financed expansion very largely from internal sources, the ratio of dividends to paid-up capital for large firms remained high during the post-war period. In other words, shareholders continued to receive handsome returns on their money while industry experienced difficulty in attracting long-term capital; a situation which suggests that private investment may have been highly sensitive to distributed profits. Part of the difficulty was, however, of industry's own making. While fairly developed facilities existed for marketing titles to property, shares tended to be of high denomination and of a single type, namely equity shares, and most firms made insufficient use of preference or debenture stocks. Moreover the legal framework within which limited liability companies operated afforded too much power and privilege to directors and not enough protection to the interests of shareholders; a situation which undoubtedly added to the general antipathy towards industrial investment.[65]

Managers could minimize capital costs by purchasing the

[63] B. Hansen, *The National Outlay of the UAR* (1963), INP Memo. 377 and Hamdi, pp. 157, 162 & 258.

[64] A. Eman, 'Le Financement de l'industrie en Égypte', *Ég. contemp.*, Mar. 1945, pp. 250–6 and Industrial Bank, *The Development of Industrial Credit in Egypt* (1956), pp. 11–13.

[65] Gritly, pp. 405–17.

equipment appropriate to particular production functions as cheaply as possible and also by combining capital and labour in optimally efficient proportions. A recent sample study of large-scale firms considered that Egyptian firms were certainly aware of and took full advantage of, the technical possibilities open to them.[66] On the other hand many smaller firms, according to a United Nations report, tended to use obsolete and unsatisfactory machinery.[67] How far the particular combinations of capital and labour employed by Egyptian firms departed from the optimum is impossible to say, but the descriptive evidence suggests that managers had not been particularly adept at exploiting the potentialities of an unlimited supply of cheap unskilled labour, but appeared biased in favour of modern capital-intensive techniques used by more developed economies.[68]

Over several inputs included in the costs of manufactured commodities, managers of industrial firms exercised little control. Thus prices of raw materials, transport, power supplies, and distribution services had to be taken as given. Although the cost of transporting certain minerals was high, the Egyptian economy was not nearly so deficient in social capital as many other developing economies. It possessed 14 km. of railway for every 100 square km. of inhabited area and 25 km. of road for every 100 square km. of cultivated area: ratios approaching those found in Europe. And a network of rivers and inland waterways covered the Nile valley.[69] Similarly, its long involvement in the international cotton trade had given Egypt marketing and distribution facilities of a wide range and high competence.[70] Deficiencies were more clearly evident in the cost and availability of power. Egypt was not adequately covered with a grid system, so that some 34 per cent of the installed capacity of industrial firms represented electrical-generating equipment, but costs per unit of power were not appreciably above those paid by British firms and lower than charges met by French industrial enter-

[66] Harbison & Ibrahim, p. 52. [67] UN, *Dev. Manufacturing*, p. 80.

[68] P. O'Brien, 'Industrial Development and the Employment Problem', *ME Econ. Papers 1962*, pp. 99–100.

[69] Issawi, *EMC*, pp. 181 & 185.

[70] But for a criticism of Egyptian compared with American marketing facilities see A. el Sherbini & A. Sherif, 'Marketing Problems in Egypt', *Ég. contemp.*, July 1956, pp. 5–85.

prises.[71] Of course, considerable room for improvement existed in the range and efficiency of power supplies, transport, distribution, and financial services used by manufacturing firms, but, in contrast to many other developing economies, it does not appear reasonable to maintain that the pace of Egyptian industrialization had been seriously retarded by the quality of the country's infrastructure.

But from all accounts the high price and low quality of raw materials, which formed the largest proportion of the cost of manufactured commodities, exercised the most significant impediment to the reduction of industrial prices. For example, wool was of poor quality; hides for the leather industry were often spoiled by inefficient slaughtering techniques; prices of milk and sugar used by the food-processing industries were way above the cost of those products in Europe; and canning firms found it difficult to obtain regular deliveries of fruit and vegetables of the required grades and specification. Finally, Egyptian textile firms were compelled by government edict to utilize high quality and expensive long-staple domestic cotton, which militated against their attempt to capture both local and domestic market in cheap yarns and cotton-piece goods.[72] On examination a significant share of the high cost of industrial products made in Egypt, as well as in other developing countries, reflects the low productivity of their agricultural sectors.[73]

Wages and the quality of the labour force rank after raw materials as components of industrial costs and were also, more or less, beyond the control of the managers of Egyptian industry. But with rising population on a relatively fixed area of land and a high rate of migration from rural to urban areas, the supply of labour offering itself for employment to manufacturing firms had risen steadily. Labour organization was underdeveloped because of difficulties of organizing a mass of illiterate unskilled workers, and also because the legal and social environment had been hostile to trade unions. Unions contained only a minority of the working force, usually skilled men, and their overall influence on wage

[71] UN, *Dev. Manufacturing*, pp. 77–78.

[72] Ibid. p. 79 and Issawi, *EMC*, pp. 163–164.

[73] Table 5 (p. 20) reveals that nearly 70 per cent of total costs for industry was accounted for by raw materials.

rates was probably very slight.[74] In this situation it is hardly surprising to find that wages in Egyptian industry were among the lowest in the world and that, with the lag of money wage rates behind industrial prices, wages costs per unit of manufacturing output had fallen for over a decade.[75] The falling share of wages in the gross value of industrial output between 1945 and 1950 also reflected declining labour costs.[76] For the post-war period at least Egyptian industry, unlike its counterpart in some developed countries, had experienced the very opposite of wage push inflation.

Wages were low but in large part their level reflected the poor quality of labour. Labour productivity cannot, however, be meaningfully measured, as some writers imagine, by comparing output per man in Egyptian industry with comparable workers in the United States or Western Europe, because the differences may often reflect little more than different capital-labour ratios.[77] The productivity of labour *per se* can only be measured by comparing workers operating with the same equipment within a similar productive organization. In this sense the overall efficiency of Egyptian labour has never been measured, but a United Nations study commented of one sector that 'the number of looms per worker in the cotton textile industry was 2 to 4 in Egypt and 4 to 8 in Turkey compared with 24 to 28 in Japan and 75 to 100 in some American plants producing coarse fabrics'.[78] Moreover there are good reasons to suppose that Egyptian workers were likely to have been much less effective as producers than their counterparts in developed economies. Certainly their general level of health and education and their amenability to the demands of industrial discipline would *prima facie* have produced quite wide disparities in efficiency. To some extent the poor health of Egyptian workmen reflected the inadequate diet, housing, and medical care they could afford on low wages, but some larger firms had appreciated the relationship between productivity and health and had provided their employees with medical care and improved accommodation.

[74] Gritly, pp. 550–3.

[75] UN, *Dev. Manufacturing*, pp. 46, 51, 75 & 120.

[76] *Census of Industr. Prod'n, 1945 & 1950.*

[77] Naggar, *Industrialization & Income*, p. 256.

[78] UN, *Dev. Manufacturing*, p. 85. See also Harbison & Ibrahim, p. 136 and NBE, *Econ. B.*, xiv (1949), p. 188 & ii (1950), p. 100.

However, most firms operated on too small a scale to offer fringe benefits of this kind.

Deficiencies were also apparent in the education and training of industrial labour. Most labourers were illiterate, which made the communication of instructions relating to their work and initial training protracted and difficult. Moreover illiterate workmen are usually less receptive and display less initiative than those who have received even a modicum of education. Apart from the low level of literacy, shortages of skill, both technical and managerial, existed at all levels of the productive process. With its narrow base and non-scientific orientation the education system had not provided industry with anything like the number of technicians and managers required.[79] While the state had recognized the need, its effort remained negligible and less than 10 per cent of all pupils undertaking secondary education received any form of vocational training, and the universities remained dominated by arts faculties.[80] Thus training had usually to be given on the job and although some larger corporations, such as the Misr Group, had established training facilities, most firms were reluctant to invest in personnel who might very well move on to alternative employment.

Finally, the whole character and tradition of the industrial working force made it less amenable to industrial discipline than efficiency demanded. Many labourers were inexperienced migrants fresh from rural areas, with low aspirations, who maintained strong links with the village. While such ties provided security to the workers, they rendered them less dependent on and subordinate to their immediate employment. In turn, the rural link led to demands upon the industrial workers which induced absenteeism and frequent resignations in order to go back to the countryside. Turnover rates were further raised by the predilection of workers with some experience and training to seek higher pay and status. Here management was often at fault for not creating systems of promotion and incentives which retained experienced personnel. Even so, the agrarian character of the labour force with its lack of expertise and experience rendered firms vulnerable to losses from

[79] Said, in *Ég. contemp.*, May 1950.

[80] I. H. Abdel-Rahman, *Planning for Balanced Social and Economic Development* (1961), pp. 63–67, INP Memo. 63.

faulty workmanship as well as day-to-day bottlenecks from absenteeism and high rates of turnover. Once again the larger firms appreciated the problem and attempted to engender loyalty by providing their employees with fringe benefits in the form of pensions, housing, and medical care, but the effort was far from widespread.[81]

Any survey of Egyptian industry at mid-century can only conclude that while opportunities existed for quite substantial reductions in costs, the probability that they would be made in the short run and on a scale sufficient to promote further rapid expansion in production was not high. Over the prices of raw materials, labour, finance, power, transport, and marketing facilities those who supervised the manufacture of industrial commodities exercised very little influence. The costs and quality of the labour force and the nation's infrastructure would improve only with industrial development itself, or alternatively with a massive programme of public investment in education, health, roads, railways, and power supplies. Raw material prices could decline with rises in agricultural productivity, but, for reasons already outlined, this seemed unlikely to occur.

Nor could immediate and very positive improvements in the efficiency of inputs more directly controlled by industrialists be expected. Changes in scale, capital-labour ratios, productive organization, personnel management, and methods of raising finance were unlikely to be carried out to a degree sufficient to force down industrial prices, particularly as most Egyptian firms were not subject to the pressures of operating in competitive markets. Thus prospects for the continued growth of Egyptian manufactures already existing in 1950, either through increases in demand with constant industrial prices, or via reductions in costs, did not appear auspicious.

THE ECONOMY ON THE EVE OF REVOLUTION

At mid-century the Egyptian economy might be described as stagnant. Stagnation in this case does not mean that total product remained stationary. On the contrary, agricultural and industrial

[81] H. Saaty, *Industrialization in Alexandria* (1959), pp. 66, 78, 80, 82 and Said, in *Ég. contemp.*, May 1950, pp. 501–2.

output continued to rise at far from unimpressive rates of growth which were, however, not rapid enough to raise real per capita income, and in this sense the economy appeared stagnant. If material progress was to be achieved in face of a population growing at the rate of 25 per 1,000 every year, the country needed to make more efficient use of all available supplies of land, labour, and capital and also to expand its resource base by much higher rates of fixed capital formation.

With land and water as the scarce resources in the agricultural sector, capital formation there needed to be directed towards extending the area of farmland. While possibilities for investment in the irrigation system were not so obvious as they had been in the nineteenth century and liable to prove more costly per unit of output, they certainly existed, and blueprints had been drawn up by engineers of the Ministry of Public Works. These ambitious schemes called for government support, organization, and finance. But even though Egypt farmed less than 10 per cent of her area, possibilities for additions to the margin of cultivation were not unlimited. Hurst had estimated that the waters of the Nile could never irrigate more than 10 million feddans of farmland, and his estimate was confirmed by surveys made since the revolution.[82] Given the limited area of potentially cultivable land, agricultural output could still be increased by the reallocation of land to more valuable produce such as meat, fruit, vegetables, and rice and by raising yields per feddan for all crops grown in Egypt. To raise productivity required reforms to tenurial institutions and changes in the scale of farming as prior conditions for the application of new techniques. But in the unlikely event that all suggested improvements were undertaken by local farmers, the results were not likely to be spectacular. Yields per hectare of most crops cultivated in Egypt were already among the highest in the world, which suggested that further progress along the intensive margin would be both difficult and modest. Thus opportunities for production and employment had to be created outside the agricultural sector.[83]

As informed Egyptian opinion had recognized, to obviate stag-

[82] Hurst, p. 287 and A. Meguid, *The Economic Significance of the High Dam* (1959), NPC Memo. 68.

[83] O'Brien, in *ME Econ. Papers 1962*, pp. 90–97.

nation required rapid industrialization, but by mid-century industry itself had reached a kind of impasse. Local firms had already replaced the more simple kind of imported consumer goods on the domestic market.[84] Opportunities for further expansion at the expense of foreign products appeared somewhat limited. At the same time the accelerated growth of population did nothing to raise expenditure on manufactured commodities, and the overall efficiency of Egyptian industry seemed unlikely to improve sufficiently to encourage growth via world markets or through lower prices in the domestic market. By 1950–2 it seems to have been widely acknowledged that manufacturing output was not growing at a desirable rate and that industrial firms had begun to encounter real difficulties after the unprecedented expansion of the war and post-war years. In fact bank reviews and surveys by the Federation of Egyptian Industry characterized 1950–2 as a period of crisis, and pointed to excess capacity, unemployment, and falling profits experienced by certain sectors of manufacturing, particularly textiles.[85]

A variety of explanations were offered for industry's failure to grow more rapidly. The chairmen of the Federation of Egyptian Industries and the National Bank correctly stressed the height of industrial prices, which the latter explained in terms of 'the low efficiency of specialist staff, the high costs of raw materials and low output of manpower'.[86] The shortage of hard currency and the difficulties of utilizing available sterling reserves to buy machinery overseas were offered, with some merit, as excuses for the slowness at which industrialists re-equipped their factories after the war.[87] But in a later report the president of the National Bank blamed industry's problems on 'the reluctance to invest in stocks and shares' which he considered 'one of the principal causes of the slow development of our economy'. Apparently landowners and merchants who had gained from rising cotton prices during the post-war years had chosen to invest their additional earnings

[84] *Report by Financial Committee of Parliament* quoted in *EG*, 24 Feb. 1949; NBE, *Reports of President*, 1947–51.

[85] Introd. to FIE, *Ann. 1951–2* & *1952–3*; *Rev. éc. trim.*, Jan. 1951, pp. 2–4, & Apr. 1951, p. 5, & July 1951, p. 21; *EG*, 15 May 1949 & 25 Sept. 1951.

[86] Introd. to FIE, *Ann. 1951–2* & NBE, *Ann. Rep. of President 1949; EG*, 14 Apr. 1949.

[87] NBE, *Econ. B.*, iv (1951), p. 250; *EG*, 14 Apr. 1949.

in land and middle-class housing.[88] Here the president merely added his lament to a frequently observed and persistently deplored facet of the Egyptian investing class, namely their preference, in Dr Hamdi's words, 'for the ownership of real estate as against industrial and commercial stocks and shares and securities in general'. As a group they were not easily persuaded to depart from traditional and deeply entrenched patterns of investment.[89]

A great deal of the blame for the deceleration of industrial progress also came to be placed at the door of the government for not improving the nation's infrastructure. After the war parliament had accepted a Five-Year Plan for augmented public expenditure on the irrigation system, roads, railways, postal facilities, technical education, public health, &c., but apparently by 1950 only about half the agreed appropriations for new 'public works' had been spent.[90] As usual, industrialists claimed they were subjected to bureaucracy, over-taxed and under-protected from foreign competition.[91] More fundamentally, the government came in for strong criticism for failing to comprehend the problems of industry and several authors called for a constructive and positive state policy for the industrialization of Egypt.[92] As the next chapter will show, the call for further government intervention came at a time when the state, under the pressure of war, cyclical depression, and public opinion, had modified the operation of the free market economy in several important respects and already played quite a positive role in production.

[88] NBE, *Ann. Rep. of President 1950* & *Rev. éc. trim.*, Apr. 1951, p. 5.
[89] Hamdi, p. 157.
[90] NBE, *Ann. Rep. of President 1947, 1950* & *1951* & *Econ. B.*, xxi (1949) p. 82.
[91] *EG*, 14 Apr. & 14 June 1949, 31 Aug. 1951.
[92] FIE, *Ann., 1951–2* & *1952–3; Rev. éc. trim.*, Jan. 1953, p. 5; *EG*, 24 Feb. 1949; NBE, *Econ. B.*, i (1952), p. 31 & *Rep. of President 1948*.

II

Government and the Economy before the Revolution

THE TOTALITARIAN ECONOMY OF MOHAMMED ALI

FOR any society the degree of control exercised by the state over production can be anything from near-complete to tenuous and economies may be classified on a spectrum with *laissez-faire* at one extreme and totalitarianism at the other. But just as *laissez-faire* is the 'one great untried Utopia', central command over all aspects of economic life has never existed anywhere. Rather we can observe tendencies towards or away from centrally directed economic systems. Direction from the centre may or may not be accompanied by state ownership of the means of production, and the ratio of public property to aggregate national wealth is not an index of governmental control over production. Decisions about allocations of resources, the composition of output, and how to conduct the process of production may remain highly decentralized even when a large proportion of the nation's resources is publicly owned. Nor is the private possession of wealth incompatible with a high degree of direction by the state over its employment in production.

Looking back over the history of Egypt during the nineteenth and twentieth centuries it is possible to trace a swing away from a centrally directed towards a free market economy, and recently an abrupt swing back again. The reversal is by no means complete because the degree of economic control exercised by Mohammed Ali at the height of his reign during the 1820s and 1830s appears to have been stronger than that wielded by the Military Junta today. His power over industry, to begin with the sector which contributed only a small proportion of total output, was almost absolute. Traditionally Egyptian industry had been carried on in the houses of artisans and villagers, or in small urban workshops. Mohammed Ali proclaimed manufacturing a state monopoly and forbade any industrial production outside the public sector. The government assumed sole responsibility for providing workmen with their raw material and for collecting and selling their finished products. The state also laid down specifications as to the type and quality of commodities which might be produced and established an inspectorate to see standards were met. As far as we know the government did not normally attempt to direct the process or determine the pace of production in the handicraft sector, nor did it provide weavers, spinners, and other craftsmen with equipment or credit. It simply assumed the functions usually provided by merchants under more primitive forms of the 'putting-out system'.[1]

In addition to monopolizing both the provision of raw materials to workers and the sale of their finished products, Mohammed Ali attempted to expand industrial output by setting up mechanized factories for the manufacture of textiles, glass, iron products, armaments, and ships. He usually imported the requisite machinery, engineers, and managerial staff, while skilled labour from among urban artisans and small masters found themselves directed to work in government factories and unskilled peasants were likewise conscripted for the new industries.[2] Unfortunately we do not know the proportion of output and employment accounted for by these mechanized enterprises; probably the greater part continued to emanate from the handicraft sector, which was not subject to such complete central control.[3]

But industry contributed very little to national product and Mohammed Ali's Egypt remained an agricultural country. Despite all his efforts to foster manufacturing, the vast majority of his subjects continued to till and live from the soil of the Nile valley. Central control over the agricultural sector during his reign certainly appears stronger and more extensive than it was under the Mamelukes or has been ever since. The government directed agriculture in order to provide the revenues required to pay for a rising volume of military and bureaucratic expenditure. For this end Mohammed Ali attempted to raise both farm output and the share expropriated by the state. He regarded agriculture not as the

[1] Gritly, pp. 28–32; Quni (ar.), pp. 45–47.

[2] G. Douin, *La Mission du Baron Boislecomte en Égypte et la Syrie en 1833* (1927), pp. 79–89.

[3] Fahmy, pp. 10, 14, 57, & 58; Gritly, pp. 38–41.

means of sustenance for the majority of Egyptians but as a vast domain for the support of soldiers and public officials. To increase output the government made more land and water available to cultivators and also attempted to raise the productivity of the soil. Both methods involved the institution of an extensive system of controls over the land and the peasantry.

For any given year the area cultivated depended upon the volume of Nile water carried on to the fields. In years of high flood naturally more water became available than in years of low water when less land was farmed. Given natural variations in the level of the river, the flow of water on to and off the fields was regulated by an elaborate system of dikes, banks and canals, barrages and primitive machinery for lifting water on to the land. Unless somebody maintained the irrigation system at peak efficiency the area of land cultivated fell below the optimum, and for many centuries the state had exercised overall responsibility for the maintenance of and extension to the irrigation system. Net investment consisted in adding to the existing network of canals and dikes and barrages so that less accessible land might be farmed and also of excavating canals to a depth sufficient to transport water on to and off the fields during the summer season of low flood or during periods when the overall flow of the Nile declined below average.

All investment (gross and net) in the irrigation system was labour intensive. Excavating and pumping machinery was unknown to the Egypt of Mohammed Ali, and while his civil engineers made use of the scientific principles and experience developed in Europe, actual construction was normally undertaken with primitive implements and dikes and barrages built with local rudimentary materials. Labour, the principal input, was recruited and organized by government officials; perhaps conscripted is the more appropriate term because peasants were compelled to work on the irrigation system whether they agreed or not.[4] According to Dr Rivlin, the government forced about 400,000 men from a population of about 4 million to join corvées every year and each man worked on average about forty-five days. Sometimes the government furnished tools and food, particularly on new public works, but more often the labourer himself had to provide his own implements, and his family remained responsible for his suste-

[4] A. R. Rafi, *History of the National Movement* (1930, ar.), iii, 540–4.

nance. At the end of a working period he received a wage of 1 piastre a day from the state. Obviously the system worked best when the peasants renovated or constructed irrigation facilities which benefited their own farms. They could be fed more easily and worked more willingly, but the government remained interested in the overall level of output, not the welfare of a particular locality, and a corvée was always liable to be dispatched, under guard, to villages far from home where labour was short or where the state was executing a new large-scale project.[5] Under Mohammed Ali net investment in the irrigation system appears to have risen considerably, and unless underemployment among the agricultural force increased proportionately, the real costs of corvée to the peasantry (in terms of output foregone by not cultivating their own lands) probably increased. Certainly the meagre and often long-delayed payment of 1 piastre per day represented an insufficient recompense for removing peasants from work on their farms. On the other hand with a rising population the total time passed by any given fellah on conscripted labour presumably fell.[6]

The state not only directed the efforts of the agricultural working force towards extending the margin of cultivation but under Mohammed Ali it assumed a large measure of responsibility for increasing the productivity of the land as well. It could assume such responsibility without too much difficulty because legally all land belonged to the state. During the eighteenth century public ownership had, however, implied only a nominal amount of central control over Egypt's principal productive asset. Overall supervision of agricultural production remained vested in a small group of tax farmers or *multazims* who had been granted extensive estates or provinces to manage on behalf of the state. They were responsible for maintaining the irrigation system, collecting taxes for remittance to Cairo, and administering law and order in the countryside. The government remunerated *multazims* with grants of land for their personal domain, and by giving them the right to collect taxes from the peasants on their own behalf. The land

[5] H. Rivlin, *The Agricultural Policy of Mohammed Ali* (1961), pp. 117, 237; L. Brehier, *L'Égypte, 1798–1900* (1903), p. 112.

[6] A. Boinet, 'L'Accroissement de la population en Égypte', *B. l'Inst. ég.*, vii (1886), pp. 278–9.

was cultivated by the fellahin who, provided they paid taxes and worked the area allotted to them, remained in control of their family farms. Beyond raising corvées to maintain local irrigation facilities and to work their personal domains, *multazims* appear not to have interfered very much with those who actually cultivated the land.[7]

Mohammed Ali devoted a great deal of time and energy to reasserting the power of the central government over all cultivable land and to ending the divorce of ownership from control which had grown up during past centuries. He succeeded by expropriating estates of the Mamelukes and adding them to his personal domains; by restricting, and in many instances cancelling, the rights formerly enjoyed by beneficiaries of endowed or *waqf* land, and finally by terminating the system of revenue farming and appointing an entirely new class of tax officials to administer the countryside directly on behalf of the state. His success in abolishing tax farming remained only partial and the system survived under new names over considerable areas of the countryside, but the evidence suggests that in the early decades of the nineteenth century the bulk of Egyptian land and the Egyptian peasantry passed under central control, and the fellah came into a face-to-face relationship with officials responsible directly to the government in Cairo.[8]

Although Mohammed Ali expropriated the *multazims* and circumscribed the rights of beneficiaries to *waqf* land, he left the peasantry in nominal possession of their family holdings, on condition that they paid taxes and obeyed government instructions. His problem appears to have been that of keeping cultivators bound to the land. So harsh were state exactions that the peasantry frequently retaliated by abandoning their farms; but flight invariably proved hazardous and detection almost certain because peasants were forbidden to travel beyond the confines of their villages, and anyone harbouring fugitives risked very severe punishment.[9]

Nominally a peasantry, in practice the status of Egyptian culti-

[7] I. Amr, *The Land and the Peasants* (ar.), pp. 65–68.

[8] G. Baer, *History of Landownership in Modern Egypt* (1962), pp. 1–8, and M. F. Lahitah, *The Economic History of Egypt* (1944, ar.), pp. 111–24.

[9] Rivlin, pp. 90–91, 116, 134–5.

vators during the early decades of the nineteenth century rose very little above that of paid state labourers. All available farmland had to be worked and failure to cultivate was punishable by beating and continued failure by eviction. Given the technological possibilities, the allocation of land among alternative uses was determined to a considerable degree by the state. With taxes normally paid in kind, the state decided the composition of its revenue from the land by compelling various provinces of the Nile valley to contribute quotas of particular crops. The government used these crops to provision the army or supply local industry with raw material, or sold them either at home or abroad. Provincial quotas were translated by local officials into tax liability for departments, villages, and ultimately for particular farms.[10]

In addition to the land which had to be set aside to meet taxes, the state compelled cultivators to allocate part of their farms to the production of crops designated public monopolies. Under Mohammed Ali, the government monopolized the sale and supervised the cultivation of several cash crops which were relatively novel to Egyptian farmers of the early nineteenth century and were produced mainly for export. Thus when it compelled farmers to grow cotton, rice, sugar, indigo, and silk the government assumed the role of innovator. Moreover the state issued detailed instructions on how these new crops should be planted, tended, and harvested, and provided the farmers with seed and animal power necessary for their cultivation. Often farmers worked directly under an agronomist imported by the government from Europe to train cultivators in new techniques. Inspectors visited villages to ensure that official instructions were properly carried out and meted out physical punishment to obdurate or inefficient peasants.[11]

With certain minor exceptions the government attempted to monopolize the distribution of all farm produce grown in Egypt. Crops destined for export had to be delivered immediately after harvest to public warehouses at prices fixed by the state. Later

[10] Rivlin, pp. 90, 93, 95, 96–98, 115–16, and F. Mouriez, *Histoire de Mehemet Ali* (1958), pp. 34–36.

[11] F. Mengin, *Histoire de l'Égypte sous le gouvernement du Mohammed Ali* (1823), pp. 345–74.

government agents sold the crops at higher prices to foreign merchants for sale overseas. The private sale of exportable crops by the farmers was forbidden and discouraged by heavy penalties and an elaborate system of measuring and checking cash crops while under cultivation. Nevertheless compulsion often proved not a sufficiently effective method of eliciting the quantities of exportable crops required by the state and officials found it expedient to offer the peasants fairly high prices for novel crops like cotton and rice; prices which declined once the crop became established.[12]

At various times throughout his rule Mohammed Ali also attempted to control and monopolize *internal* trade in agricultural products. After paying taxes a peasant might have a surplus over and above his own consumption of wheat, barley, or legumes, and the government required him to deliver this spare produce to public warehouses, again at fixed prices. Occasionally, when the government needed additional revenue, an entire crop of wheat or beans had to be sold to the government for resale at higher prices to the original cultivators. Naturally, the peasants resisted such incursions into their freedom to subsist from their farms and to sell produce locally on free markets, and, even with his army officials checking and searching for illegal disposal or consumption of crops, Mohammed Ali encountered insuperable administrative difficulties in his endeavour to monopolize internal trade. On the other hand external trade both for imports and exports proved so much more easy to regulate because commodities traded internationally were limited in number and passed through well defined and fairly centralized channels of distribution. It remained only for the ruler to forbid direct trading between Egyptians and the small community of foreign merchants resident in Cairo or Alexandria for state regulation of international trade to be immediately and almost completely effective.[13]

Mohammed Ali at the apex of his power operated an economic system which warrants the adjective totalitarian. Under him the state owned nearly all the means of production such as land, the irrigation system, roads, storage facilities, river and sea transport,

[12] Rafi, *Hist. of National Movement* (ar.), iii, 609–11 and P. Arminjon, *La Situation économique et financiére de l'Égypte* (1911), pp. 32–36.

[13] Amr (ar.), pp. 78–83 and Rivlin, pp. 112–15, 140, 146–7, 164–5, 168–80.

industrial machinery, and factories. It also exercised almost sole responsibility for net and gross domestic capital formation. Not only did the state own, maintain, and add to the nation's productive assets, but to a considerable extent their employment in production was centrally directed. Thus public servants managed mechanized industry while handicraft manufacturers operated within a tight and wide ranging system of controls which allowed craftsmen virtually no economic initiative. Similarly, the amount of discretion allowed to the mass of the Egyptian labour force who cultivated the soil appears to have been severely limited. The state compelled peasants to allocate a considerable proportion of land and labour time towards satisfying its requirements for revenue, which took the form of payments in kind or compulsory deliveries at fixed prices of exportable cash crops. External trade was a complete public monopoly and the government made several attempts, only partially successful, to monopolize internal trade as well. Finally, all labour was liable to state direction: it was either conscripted for the army, organized into corvées for work on the irrigation system, or made to work in the government's new factories.

THE TRANSITION TO FREE MARKETS, 1844–1914

At no time since Mohammed Ali has the power of the state over the economic life of Egypt been so absolute. As the nineteenth century wore on the system he established gave way to a decentralized private enterprise economy, and the economic functions of the state gradually withered. However, one important function retained by the state was its overall responsibility for the irrigation system. Almost all additions to the area of land or the volume of water made available to Egyptian farmers resulted from state investment in barrages, dams, pumps, canals, and drains to control the flow of the river Nile. And both under the Khedives and the British the construction of roads, railways, bridges, telegraphs, docks, harbours, lighthouses (in short all social capital) continued to be built and managed by the central authority.[14] Ismail's efforts between 1863 and 1879 to furnish Egypt with a modern system of communications are frequently cited by his defenders

[14] D. Cameron, *Egypt in the 19th Century* (1898), pp. 228, 232, & 257.

as something to be balanced against the inexpert way he borrowed money abroad and his more profligate expenditure of public revenues.[15] Under British rule public expenditure on telegraphs, postal services, railways, and above all upon irrigation facilities continued, but probably at a diminished rate, so that by the end of the century the infrastructure probably represented the bulk of Egyptian fixed capital.[16] Houses were generally rudimentary structures while manufacturing and farm equipment probably totalled only a limited sum, thus it seems reasonable to conclude that the bulk of Egyptian capital formation up to the Great War continued to be undertaken by the state. Unlike their British or American contemporaries, Egyptian farmers, merchants, and manufacturers depended upon the government to provide them with water, transport, or marketing facilities within which their productive activities could flourish, and as a consequence the central government remained intimately involved in the country's economic development.

With the exception of some sugar refineries, printing works, bakeries, and clothing factories constructed by Ismail (which were in any case after a brief but unsuccessful experience as state enterprises sold to private capitalists), the government made no further efforts after Mohammed Ali to establish publicly operated industry.[17] Nor is there evidence that the state attempted to foster private manufacturing; on the contrary, the complete absence of protection against foreign competition, together with the imposition of an excise duty of 8 per cent on local products, discouraged domestic enterprise. Mohammed Ali's controls were dismantled by his successors and the state left entrepreneurs to develop manufacturing and to utilize methods of production or raw materials in whatever directions they found profitable. For industrial activity the period from Mohammed Ali to the Great War might well be characterized as one of *laissez-faire*.

For the agricultural sector emancipation from state control developed more slowly, and throughout the period the rural economy continued to be less free than industry or trade. First,

[15] A. R. Rafi, *The Reign of Ismail* (1932, ar.), pp. 4–10 & 15–19; P. Crabitès, *Ismail the Maligned Khedive* (1933), pp. 130–5; J. McCoan, *Egypt under Ismail* (1889), pp. 51, 53, 71, 129 f., 282.

[16] *Reports on Finances, Administration &c.* (Parl. Papers, 1884–1914).

[17] Lahitah (ar.), pp. 284–5 & Rafi, *Reign of Ismail* (ar.), pp. 12–13.

because although the evolution towards the private ownership of land proceeded rapidly under Said's rule (1854–63), not until 1891 could those who held title to land be described as indisputable masters of their personal property.[18] The maintenance and regulation of the irrigation system kept farmers always in close contact with the officials and directives of the central authority. Right up until the last decade of the nineteenth century peasants continued to be conscripted for excavating canals, strengthening dikes, or erecting dams and barrages along the Nile. The government further compelled them to work on other public projects such as railways, harbours, and the Suez canal. While the real burden of the corvée may well have decreased as the population grew and as the government opted to employ more voluntary paid labour, corvée remained a liability until 1885. On the other hand the real cost of corvée in terms of the decreased output which followed from the absence of labour increased when water became available in the summer months. Barrages prevented canals and drains from silting up and made the corvée less necessary, but peasants continued to be directed to keep watch for Nile floods, damage to dikes, and burst banks right up to 1936. Presumably with the development of private ownership the laws binding peasants to the land were also gradually rescinded, but the evidence suggests that for most of the nineteenth century agricultural labourers were not free to choose their occupation or place of work.[19]

Free markets for farm produce developed more quickly than for land and labour. Already during the last years of Mohammed Ali's reign, when the Ottoman Porte opened Egypt to penetration by foreign merchants, farmers began to enjoy the right to sell at least part of their output on open markets to the highest bidder. Under Said the state monopoly system for agricultural crops gave way gradually to free markets for all farm produce whether for domestic or external sale.[20] With the end of compulsory deliveries of crops to government warehouses peasants systematically con-

[18] Baer, pp. 7 f., 11 f.; Y. Artin, *The Right of Landed Property in Egypt* (1885), pp. 30–71.

[19] J. Nahas, *Situation économique et sociale du fellah égyptien* (1901), ch. 5; McCoan, pp. 53–54.

[20] A. Crouchley, *Economic Development of Modern Egypt* (1937), pp. 63, 73, 87, 107, & 111 and A. Mustafa, 'The Breakdown of the Monopoly System in Egypt after 1840', in Holt.

verted their tax liabilities from payments in kind to monetary contributions. This transition proceeded most rapidly in Lower Egypt, where farmers found ready outlets for the sale of their food and export crops in the urban centres like Cairo and Alexandria, but with the spread of its cultivation to all parts of the Nile valley and the growing international demand for cotton, by 1880 almost the entire payment for the land tax both in Lower and Upper Egypt had been monetized.[21] Egyptian farmers thus became free from the restraints which compelled them to allocate part of their lands to crops designated by tax officials of the central government. Tobacco remained, however, the one exception to their unfettered initiative to plant anything they liked, for a decree of 1876 forbade the growing of tobacco and declared its import a government monopoly.[22]

At the beginning of the First World War the Egyptian state had retreated further from interference with production than at any time since 1800. With free trade as its commercial policy and an absence of restrictions on capital movements across its frontiers; without a central bank or controls on the money supply; with very little social welfare legislation, minimal public expenditure on health and education, no taxes on income or wealth except the land tax, and free markets in land, labour and capital, Egypt appears almost as the archetypal *laissez-faire* Utopia of classical liberals. Yet government had not been quite relegated, in Lassalle's famous phrase, to 'the job of night watchman', principally because agriculture in the Nile valley demanded strong centralized control over the irrigation system. Furthermore the shortage of private capital and initiative had prompted the government to create a modern system of communications, and the subsequent profitability of railways, roads, and harbours to the revenue had ensured their retention as public enterprises. Thus a high, but probably declining, share in capital formation maintained for the state a place in Egyptian economic life of more importance than that usually found in most free-enterprise countries.

Why the state abdicated from the commanding position it held over the economy at the time of Mohammed Ali is a question not yet adequately explored by historians of modern Egypt, but the greater part of the explanation must surely be political rather than

[21] Artin, p. 145.

[22] Barawi & Ulaish (ar.), p. 38.

economic or ideological. Mohammed Ali's attempts to control agriculture and to foster domestic industry were ultimately frustrated by treaties between the Porte and the powers opening the Ottoman empire to free trade; although the question whether he could, in the long run, have succeeded in establishing mechanized industry or in maintaining agriculture as a vast state farm remains very much open.[23]

Abbas and Said, the rulers who followed Mohammed Ali, displayed little desire to emulate the totalitarian policies of the founder of their dynasty. To some extent Ismail did, and his reign was marked by a more active participation by the state in economic affairs, but his programme of large-scale public investment, designed to modernize communications and extend the cultivable area, foundered on his inept dealings with foreign creditors, the ill-conceived nature of many of his projects, and the endeavour to combine a rapidly growing rate of public investment with a comparable rate of public consumption. Ismail's ambitious policies to extend the power of the state both internally and abroad were financed largely by foreign loans, and eventually his failure to meet the demands of his European creditors involved the occupation of Egypt by a foreign power and the subsequent withdrawal of the state into a more circumscribed sphere of activity.[24]

The *raison d'être* of British rule was to restore order to Egypt's finances and to give priority to the payment of interest and the amortization of the national debt. Public policy naturally became one of retrenchment on all items of expenditure except investments which clearly benefited public revenue. Ismail's programme of enforced and hurried modernization gave way to cautious expenditure on irrigation projects, guaranteed to yield return either from the land tax or from duties upon additional imports which, as Lord Cromer repeatedly argued, inevitably followed the expansion of cultivable land and cotton exports. Under British administrators, who were in any case predisposed from their own political experience to confine the economic functions of the state, the activities of the government became contained within limits

[23] E. T. Penrose, 'Economic Development and the State', *Economic Development & Cultural Change*, Jan. 1963, pp. 196–202.

[24] Rafi, *Reign of Ismail* (ar.), pp. 11–26, 307–32 and G. Gindi & G. Tajir, *Ismail d'après les documents officiels* (1946), p. 24.

prescribed by the availability of taxes. Moreover their policy sought to alleviate and rationalize the burden of taxation on Egyptian citizens, and tax rates were rarely increased. Tax revenue, in other words, determined expenditure rather than the more common reverse. After Ismail borrowing was seldom utilized, and an understandable but strong prejudice existed against further heavy expenditure by the central authority.[25] Apart from maintaining the infrastructure and making some slight attempt to protect small farmers from the uncertainties and rigours of the free market, the state left economic development to private enterprise.

THE SLOW RETREAT FROM THE FREE MARKET SYSTEM, 1914–52

Between the Great War and the revolution of July 1952 the Egyptian economy proceeded slowly but discernibly to revert towards a centrally-directed system again. Impetus for this movement came from several directions including: two world wars and their attendant problems of control over production; the international depression of the 1920s and 1930s; the gradual transfer of political power from the British administration back to the hands of native Egyptians; and finally, a growing, but far from widespread, appreciation among Egypt's rulers that the development of the economy and the protection of citizens from some of the more deleterious consequences of uncontrolled private enterprise demanded action by the state.[26] Government measures either to influence the structure and pace of production or to curb the initiative of private producers may accordingly be divided into welfare legislation and decrees designed to promote economic growth. Perhaps the body of legislation promulgated by the old régime in order to ameliorate poverty, prevent exploitation, and mitigate the effects of cyclical depression upon its citizens forms the most noticeable contrast with the previous period and provides us with the best examples of increased government concern with economy and society after 1914.

[25] *Reports on Finances, Administration &c. 1884–1914* and Earl of Cromer, *Modern Egypt* (1908), ii, 443–5.
[26] Quni (ar.), pp. 140 & 170–8.

The more active intervention by the state in the agricultural sector during the inter-war period stemmed from its concern to reduce the effects of rapid secular decline and sharp fluctuations in the prices of farm products, particularly cotton, on world markets during the Great Depression. Some insight into the vulnerability of Egyptian agriculture to the international conditions had already been provided at the outbreak of the Great War which disrupted world commodity markets and prevented the sale of the Egyptian cotton crop. Fortunately disruption proved only temporary and was succeeded by a sharp elevation of cotton prices until 1920 but, nevertheless, pressured by landowners and cultivators to do something 'to avert the catastrophe', the government reacted by purchasing part of the cotton crop and depositing public money with the National Bank for advances to farmers to enable them to hold crops in anticipation of more normal market conditions by reducing farm rents by one-quarter, and, finally, it imposed restrictions upon the acreage devoted to the cultivation of cotton during the following season.[27]

Confronted by the far more serious problem of the international business depression of the 1920s and early 1930s, the state, in an often hesitant and futile endeavour to stabilize cotton prices and agricultural incomes, continued to intervene along precisely the lines initiated at the outbreak of war.[28] In addition, it imposed tariffs on foreign wheat to cushion domestic grain prices as farmers transferred land from cotton to wheat, and for two years the government even subsidized grain exports and attempted to reduce dependence on cotton by a policy of diversification. Sugar cultivators also suffered severely from the slump in prices for their crop on world markets, and the government alleviated their distress by means of import controls and by compelling local refineries to purchase their crops at fixed prices.[29] Parliament in 1931 and 1933 also voted to pay off the mortgage debts of landowners who had suffered sharp falls in income from the depression.[30]

[27] *Reports on Finances, Administration &c. 1914–19 & 1920*, pp. 37–41; *1921* (xliii), pp. 19–21, and Barawi & Ulaish (ar.), p. 192.

[28] NBE, *Econ. B.*, i (1950), p. 12 and Barawi & Ulaish, pp. 193, 224–6, 229, & 281.

[29] Quni (ar.), pp. 182–3.

[30] Said, in *Ég. contemp.*, Oct. 1951, pp. 3 & 8–9.

The Second World War engendered a far more prolonged and extensive interruption to international trade than the Great War. After the fall of France and the entry of Italy into the conflict, Egypt became deprived of nearly all its overseas markets for cotton. Cultivators urgently needed protection from the vicissitudes of war and the government, represented by the Egyptian Cotton Commission, offered to buy all cotton not sold privately at a fixed price. For five seasons the Commission purchased cotton, but to prevent stocks accumulating to unmanageable proportions and also to reserve land for critically short food supplies, very strict limitations were imposed on the area which farmers might allocate to the cultivation of cotton.[31]

All those who derived income from agricultural production (landowners, farmers, and agricultural labourers) benefited to some extent from the government's stabilization policies, but the poverty of the mass of cultivators, small tenant farmers, and owner-occupiers came to be regarded as requiring special amelioration. Most of the policies designed to protect this group for the uncertainties and harshness of the free market economy originated under British rule. At the turn of the century the imperial government had taken the first steps to establish banking facilities which would provide small farmers with loans at much less than the usurious rates of interest charged by village moneylenders. Lord Kitchener's administration tackled the same problem of indebtedness by passing a law protecting farms of under 5 feddans from seizure against debt. Before the Great War the Ministry of Agriculture established *halakars* or cotton markets, in several provincial centres and also supplied peasants with good quality seed on credit in order to alleviate the exploitation of small farmers by seed and cotton merchants. Officials in charge of *halakars* kept peasants informed of market prices in Cairo and Alexandria and also purchased their crop from them at 'fair' prices. British administrators sought in fact to redress the balance of bargaining power between small illiterate farmers on the one side and middlemen (cotton merchants, seed dealers, and moneylenders) on the other. Although they operated on far too small a scale to make serious inroads into the problem of rural poverty,

[31] Anis. pp. 692–6 and Institut National de la Statistique, *L'Égypte*, pp. 65–66.

they at least laid the foundations and established the broad lines of future agrarian policy.[32]

But the principal policy designed to tackle rural poverty consisted of the promotion of co-operatives and the provision through them of credit for smaller farmers. As early as 1907 co-operatives had been formed by two wealthy landowners but they did not spread beyond a few model societies until the government began actively to encourage the movement during the agricultural depression. By 1948 roughly half of all Egyptian farmers appear to have joined co-operatives; although it must be emphasized that co-operative societies varied enormously in the range of their activities and the services they performed for members.[33] But nearly all supplied credit on conditions and at rates of interest more favourable than those obtainable from commercial sources. Indeed, the provision of cheaper credit formed a *raison d'être* for most co-operatives and was *the* function most actively encouraged by the state as being an appropriate method of relieving farmers from their burden of debt accumulated during the Great Depression. Thus at the onset of the downturn in 1923 the government deposited a fund with Bank Misr for short-term loans to small farmers and to co-operatives. Bank Misr paid the government 2 per cent interest and charged societies 4 per cent, who in turn collected a small additional premium from their members. Four years later public funds deposited with Bank Misr reached £250,000 and continued to rise until, at the height of the depression in 1931, the state found it expedient to form and support a specialized institution, Le Crédit Agricole d'Égypte, in order to supply poorer farmers with credit and to foster co-operatives.[34] Half of the initial capital for the Crédit Agricole emanated from the treasury and the government guaranteed a dividend of 5 per cent on the remaining moiety of shares. In addition, for 1931 £3 million of public money was deposited with the Bank for

[32] Lahita (ar.), pp. 556–8; A. Fikry, *The Economic Development of Egypt since 1876* (1918), pp. 61–73, and *Report on Finances, Administration &c. 1914–18*, pp. 21 & 34–37.

[33] This proportion has been calculated from figures cited in Issawi, *EMC*, p. 133 and *Basic Statistics*, p. 63.

[34] Z. Shabanah, *Co-operative Agricultural Economy* (1961, ar.), pp. 116–20; J. Heyworth-Dunne, *Egypt; the Co-operative Movement* (1952), pp. 8, 27, & 28 and *UAR Yearbook 1959*, p. 272.

agricultural credit, and for the next three years the government deposited a further £1 million annually. Generally speaking the Crédit Agricole loaned money for the purchase of implements, seeds, and fertilizers and to tide farmers over the waiting period between planting and harvest. In order to encourage the formation of co-operative societies it charged higher rates of interest to individual borrowers and, as a result, even quite large landowners formed themselves into co-operatives to take advantage of cheaper interest rates.[35] But up to the revolution the Crédit Agricole loaned all but 25 per cent of its funds to individuals. Apparently the government was disappointed with the small scale of its lending to co-operatives, and when the Crédit Agricole was reformed into the Agricultural Credit and Co-operative Bank in 1948, its revised statutes stipulated that the Bank was 'to render services of all kinds to co-operatives, using favourable practices whereby they may be reinforced and spread and whereby the co-operative system is best served'.[36]

As well as providing credit, co-operatives also purchased farm supplies on behalf of their members. This function also enjoyed government support through sales of seeds, fertilizers, and eventually implements from the Crédit Agricole to co-operatives and small farmers.[37] Collective arrangements for marketing seem to have been fairly rare, but many co-operatives set aside part of their funds for welfare services. Yet expectations that co-operatives would gradually establish a system of social security throughout the countryside were too optimistic, and by the Second World War the state decided to institute its own programme of rural welfare in the form of Combined Centres. These centres contained in a single building, under a centralized administration, doctors, teachers, agronomists, and social workers who provided a given area with their respective services—public and personal health, adult and part-time education, agricultural extension (including veterinary services), infant and child welfare, &c.[38] In 1946 the

[35] Quni (ar.), pp. 182–4.

[36] A. Tanamli, 'Agricultural Credit and Co-operative Organization', *Ég. contemp.*, Oct. 1962, pp. 22, 23, 27, & 29–31. On the other hand most of the credit utilized by co-operatives came from the Crédit Agricole (I. Rashad, 'The Co-operative Movement', ibid. May 1939, p. 489).

[37] Tanamli, pp. 25 and Quni, pp. 183–4.

[38] Min. Soc. Aff., *Social Welfare in Egypt* (1950), pp. 12 f. & 17.

government committed itself to providing a Social Welfare Unit for every village, but at mid-century only 126 had been constructed and they served a population of only 1½ million. The shortage of experts available and willing to staff village centres emerged as the most obvious bottleneck to their rapid extension over the Egyptian countryside.[39]

Egyptian co-operatives failed to develop into village organizations for health and mutual welfare; moreover the Egyptian movement did not arise as a spontaneous and voluntary response among farmers. Right from the start government encouragement and financial assistance was accompanied by quite strong measures of public control. Thus the co-operative movement received 'guidance' from the Ministry of Social Affairs operating through a hierarchy of provincial advisory councils and general unions of local societies. All co-operatives had to register with the Ministry of Agriculture. Their accounts were inspected and audited by its officials. The minister possessed the right to veto decisions taken by local societies and dissolve them if necessary.[40]

Concern for the welfare of the fellah represented only one reason for government interference with the agricultural sector; another and perhaps more pressing motive arose during the Second World War when the state sought to ensure that sufficient food continued to be available for the local population. The state in addition wished to ameliorate the consequences upon the living standards of the poorer classes, particularly those dwelling in towns, of the very serious inflation which accompanied the war in Egypt. Both motives prompted the government to institute a far-reaching system of controls over the production and distribution of food (between 1939 and 1944).[41]

Various policy instruments were employed in order to protect the living standards of poorer consumers. For example, the government imposed price controls upon a whole range of foodstuffs regarded as necessities, such as wheat, maize, rice, sugar,

[39] B. Mattison, 'Rural Social Centres in Egypt', *MEJ*, Autumn 1951, pp. 464–7.

[40] Shabanah, *Co-operative Agric. Econ.* (ar.), pp. 122–214; Min. Soc. Aff., *Social Welfare*, pp. 45 f. & 49–50.

[41] To a much more limited extent the government had also intervened to protect urban consumers from inflation during the Great War (*Report on the Finances, Administration &c. 1914–19*, pp. 3–4).

meat, tea, coffee, vegetable oil, &c. For most commodities the penalties prescribed by law seem to have been erroneously considered a sufficient deterrent to evasion of official prices, but some rough equity was achieved in the distribution of sugar and vegetable oil by rationing these particular products. Bread, however, was thought too vital a food to be left simply with the prescription of a fixed price. To maintain supplies of cheap bread the state ordered farmers to devote one-third of their holdings to the cultivation of wheat and decreed that a specified proportion of the grain harvested should be surrendered to the Ministry of Supply at fixed prices. However, the price was normally set at a level which gave farmers little incentive to evade the official injunction. Subsequently the Ministry sold the grain to millers at a lower price, thus effectively subsidizing the price of bread. While wartime and post-war policies failed to exert much influence upon the cost of living of the urban working class, they do represent the beginnings of fairly extensive interference with the price mechanisms and an intrusion by government into the freedom normally enjoyed by cultivators to allocate land and sell farm produce as they chose.[42]

Although affecting a much smaller part of the population, policies to protect industrial workers from the more obvious evils of unregulated capitalism afforded them a more thorough safeguard against urban poverty than similar measures to alleviate rural poverty. Administratively it proved less difficult to regulate employment conditions in a few thousand highly localized factories than for farms scattered over the whole Nile valley. Scale made all the difference between enforcement and non-enforcement, as the Ministry of Social Affairs discovered when it attempted to apply welfare legislation to workshops, small family firms, and the myriad units operating in the service sector. Moreover the big corporations were sometimes in advance of government in the range of the welfare facilities they provided for their workmen. Although it was by no means adequately enforced, between the wars the Egyptian government built up a whole code of legislation governing the conditions of employment for industrial workers.

[42] E. Lloyd, *Food and Inflation in the Middle East* (1956), pp. 122, 130, 133, 181, 225 ff.; Prest, pp. 135, 137, 147, 150 f., and Barawi & Ulaish (ar.), pp. 279–87.

As was often the case in other countries, the laws related initially to minors and women and were later extended to adult males. By 1936 employees had to be compensated for certain categories of industrial injury and their working hours had been legally limited. During the war years comprehensive rules governing the contract of employment, including mode of remuneration and discharge, indemnity, holidays, and sick leave, became law. Companies were obliged to educate illiterate workers.[43] Finally, in 1944, to safeguard workers against the soaring cost of living, the government prescribed a statutory minimum wage of 10 piastres a day, and six years later the minimum became $12\frac{1}{2}$ piastres a day.[44]

Thus by 1950 the discretion of owners and managers of larger factories over their labour force had been definitely circumscribed, at least legally. On the other hand the state had not displayed the same readiness to permit workmen to organize for their own protection and welfare. Towards the formation and operation of trades unions official attitudes persisted in being unsympathetic and intimidatory. Thus during the 1920s penalties against strikes stiffened and the judiciary could be relied upon to interpret laws relating to labour in a repressive manner. Collective bargaining was not legally recognized until the Trades Union Act of 1942. But as with co-operatives, once it became official policy to encourage the formation of unions, the state at once subjected their activities to 'guidance' from the Ministry of Social Affairs. Thus under the act of 1942 ministerial permission was required to form any union. Government employees and agricultural labourers were, however, expressly forbidden to organize, and general federations of unions were likewise prohibited. Notice had to be given to the authorities of all meetings and strikes and contending parties to an industrial dispute could be subjected to compulsory arbitration.[45] As the Ministry of Social Affairs naïvely admitted, 'it may seem as if the line of demarcation between intervention and guidance cannot be clearly defined'.[46]

Whereas on the one hand a concern for social welfare had led

[43] Min. Soc. Aff., *The Labour Department* (1951), pp. 12–17.

[44] M. Audsley, 'Labour and Social Affairs in Egypt', *St Antony's Papers*, iv (1958), p. 102.

[45] W. Handley, 'The Labour Movement in Egypt', *MEJ*, July 1949, pp. 279 f. & 283 and Gritly, pp. 552 f. & 554.

[46] Min. Soc. Aff., *Social Welfare*, p. 69.

the state to limit the initiative of private producers, its desire to promote economic development on the other hand took the form of creating conditions within which free enterprise might flourish, but even here the Egyptian government bestowed a more positive interpretation upon this traditional role. As early as 1922 a special council had been established to make proposals for the economic development of the country, and no doubt the transfer of power from British to native hands, together with the emergence of nationalist aspirations among certain sections of the Egyptian middle class, prompted more active participation by the state in economic affairs. After the Great War closer attention appears to have been paid to possible improvements to the infrastructure, and the government studied proposals for the generation of electricity from the Aswan Dam.[47] In 1935 a Five-Year Plan of public expenditure on roads, railways, and irrigation facilities received parliamentary approval.[48] But war and the preparations for war delayed the construction not merely of new projects but also impaired the renovation and maintenance of existing social capital. After the Second World War the Council of Ministers drew up another Five-Year Plan, again concentrating on improvements to the railways, new roads, drainage, drinking water, the Edfina and Esneh barrages on the Nile, the generation of electricity at Aswan, schools, hospitals, &c.[49] Unfortunately, the plan remained largely on paper, and by 1950 less than half the appropriations set aside by the budget for 'new works' had in fact been spent. Egyptian businessmen frequently criticized the government for delays, yet tardiness was not entirely due to government lethargy but arose also from the great difficulties in buying almost all kinds of capital equipment on international markets during the early post-war years.[50]

More direct and positive government action to increase either agricultural or industrial output was seldom employed. For

[47] Quni (ar.), pp. 170–1.

[48] H. Khallaf, 'Financing Economic Development in Egypt', *ME Econ. Papers 1955*, p. 31, and *OES Egypt*, 1935, p. 7.

[49] Planned expenditure was as follows: hydro-electricity £6 m., agriculture and irrigation, £4.5 m.; industry and commerce, £3 m.; transport, £11 m.; social services, £21 m.; and education, £5 m. (see UN *Economic Development in Selected Countries* (1947), pp. 191–4).

[50] NBE, *Ann. Reports of President, 1947, 1950, & 1951*.

example, throughout the inter-war years the problem of yields from the land received considerable publicity from writers on agricultural problems, who frequently pointed out that the productivity of Egyptian land was not merely below some hypothetical optimum but that average yields for several crops had fallen below the level achieved before the Great War. The policies of the Ministry of Agriculture sought to increase productivity mainly through extension services. The Ministry ran experimental farms and its research department produced useful reports on seeds, fertilizers, water intake, plant and animal diseases. As usual the real difficulties arose with the propagation of new techniques, but the total amount of resources devoted by the government to persuading farmers to adopt more refined methods and inputs appears pitifully small compared to the magnitude of the problem.[51] Apparently the government hoped to attach an agronomist to each new Social Welfare Centre, but by 1950 only 126 centres had been constructed and by no means all had secured the services of an agricultural specialist.[52]

After the Committee on Industry and Commerce of 1917 had proposed the active encouragement of local industry, the government employed a full range of policy instruments to give effect to its numerous recommendations.[53] Rebates on freight charges for domestic manufactures were allowed by the nationalized railways; incentives were afforded through the tax system; two cotton firms received subsidies; public departments where possible gave preference to local manufacturers in the placing of government contracts; and, finally, the two most significant state supports for industry were protective tariffs and the provision of cheap credit.[54] The total amount of government-sponsored loans to industry should not, however, be exaggerated because the bulk of that sector's finance continued to emanate from commercial sources. Government participation in the supply of credit to industry dates back to 1922, when the Ministry of Finance deposited £50,000 with Bank Misr for loans to small newly-established firms which

[51] Min. Agric., *Agricultural and Advisory Work in Egypt* (1945, ar.) and Quni (ar.), pp. 170 & 180–2.

[52] Min. Soc. Aff., *Social Welfare*, pp. 13, 16–17.

[53] Industrial Bank, *The Development of Industrial Credit in Egypt* (1956), p. 6 and Barawi & Ulaish (ar.), p. 198.

[54] Quni, pp. 180 & 184–5 and Barawi & Ulaish, pp. 200, 203, & 231–2.

found difficulties in obtaining short-term finance elsewhere. Later the government decided not to restrict public credit to this particular category of enterprise or to confine its offer only to short-term loans. By 1936 approximately £1 million of public money was being allocated every year to local firms at lower than market rates of interest. This policy led to the idea of creating a specialized institution to handle industrial credit, but the war delayed its foundation until 1949, when the government provided just over half the capital for the foundation of the Industrial Bank; most of the remainder came from insurance companies. Members of the board and the managing director were nominees of the state charged to support Egyptian industry by providing existing companies with long- and short-term loans and also to participate in the foundation of new enterprises. The government deposited £2 million with the Bank and guaranteed its shareholders an annual dividend of $3\frac{1}{2}$ per cent.[55]

Protection from foreign competition represented by far the most important stimulus afforded by government to manufacturing. Before 1930 the Egyptian tariff remained fiscal in character, but after the country had attained fiscal autonomy its traditional free-trade policy was soon abandoned and uncompromising protection afforded to local industry. Pressured by the powerful Federation of Egyptian Industries, the government revised import duties whenever domestically-manufactured products suffered from foreign competition.[56] Dr Gritly noticed that the protection afforded to industry in 1947 was for all intents and purposes prohibitive.[57] The government also gave every encouragement to the amalgamation of rival domestic producers. Certainly it had no policy to strengthen efficiency by fostering competition behind the tariff barrier but favoured larger combines by granting them differential freight rebates on state railways.[58]

State interference with the discretion of Egyptian producers and merchants to trade freely with the outside world passed well beyond the imposition of protective tariffs and included a rela-

[55] Industrial Bank, *Dev. Industrial Credit*, pp. 7–19.

[56] Levi, in *Ég. contemp.*, Dec. 1939, pp. 601–2 and *OES Egypt 1933 & 1935*, pp. 41 & 50.

[57] Gritly, pp. 556–64.

[58] Naggar, *Industrialization & Income*, p. 255. But for government relations with the sugar monopoly see Barawi & Ulaish (ar.), pp. 237–8.

tively far-reaching system of commercial regulations, both direct (i.e. relating to the flow of commodities) and indirect (relating to the flow of funds). Controls upon foreign trade originated from the war years when Egypt as a member of the sterling area was subject to all the rules of the area with respect to receipts and payments in foreign currencies. Under these regulations members of the sterling area maintained their currencies at a fixed parity with one another, the free movement of funds was allowed within the area, but rigid controls were imposed with respect to trade with non-sterling countries. The enforcement of these controls involved licensing both imports and exports: exports to ensure the repatriation of the proceeds of sales abroad, and imports to distinguish essential from non-essential purchases coming from outside the sterling area. Currency reserves had in addition to be surrendered to a central pool in London. Although trade controls were administered by the National Bank of Egypt, in co-operation with the Egyptian Customs Service, the sterling area regulations provided for the needs of the member countries as a bloc, and when Egypt in 1947 found it no longer in the national interest to remain a member and left the area, its government found it necessary, for the first time in the country's history, to establish independent exchange and commercial policies.[59]

Of course, the new commercial policy and system of laws and regulations which embodied it related intimately to the Egyptian balance-of-payments situation and to the state of the country's foreign currency and gold reserves on leaving the sterling area. The balance-of-payment accounts for the post-war period reveal a persistent deficit on current account which resulted from a rising volume of imports accompanied by a very much slower rise in the volume of exports. Imports of foodstuffs and capital goods increased faster than other categories of purchases from abroad because Egyptian agriculture failed to provide the food demanded by the rising population, while capital goods were imported to replace equipment which had depreciated or become obsolete during the war years. Egypt's deficit on income account was met largely by drawing on the country's accumulated reserves of foreign currency, but the continuous disequilibrium in the balance

[59] Inst. National, *L'Égypte*, pp. 159–62.

of payments called for correction.[60] By regulating transactions and payments with the rest of the world, the government hoped to reduce the deficit, to maximize receipts of foreign exchange, and to provide the country with the means for buying food, raw materials, and capital goods not produced locally but needed in ever increasing quantities for the long-term development of the Egyptian economy. Foreign exchange, the government recognized, was difficult to obtain and had a social opportunity cost, and where feasible the state imposed tariffs to actively encourage the production of domestic substitutes for imported foreign products.

Apart from tariffs, the policy instruments utilized to correct the balance-of-payments deficit included measures operating directly on the flow of goods and services to and from the outside world, backed up with controls over all transactions in foreign exchange. Thus exports continued to be licensed to ensure the repatriation of the proceeds and to preserve certain locally-produced commodities for domestic consumption. Licences were issued freely for cotton flax and salt, but exports of wheat and livestock were forbidden. Exports of yarn and onions were restricted to fixed quotas while shoes, leather goods, and hides could only be sold abroad if paid for in hard currencies.[61]

Raw cotton as the dominant export naturally provided the focal point of commercial policy. Egyptian farmers produced the bulk of extra long-staple cotton sold on world markets and the government assumed that restrictions on supply would raise its price. Hence the state attempted to control the acreage Egyptian farmers devoted to cotton growing and prescribed a minimum area to be devoted to the cultivation of grain. This policy aimed at one and the same time to stabilize agricultural incomes by reducing the farmers' dependence on cotton, and also to maximize receipts of foreign exchange. The cultivation of grain provided an alternative to cotton and also to the import of wheat as well. Furthermore the Egyptian Cotton Commission tried to regulate the rate at which raw cotton was released on to world markets by purchasing and holding stocks. When the acreage limitation on raw cotton was

[60] *Analyses of Egypt's Balance of Payments* (1957–9, ar.), NPC Memos 9, 11, 29, 44, 61, 62, & 86.

[61] E. Nasif, 'Le Problème des prix en Égypte', *Ég. contemp.*, May 1947, p. 271. Regulations regarding exports for 1951 can be found in FIE, *Ann. 1951–2*, pt. 4.

lifted during the Korean boom the government imposed an export tax on the raw material which they assumed would be paid by foreign buyers.[62]

Monetary devices did not appear among the instruments open to the government for regulating transactions with the outside world because until 1951 the National Bank of Egypt (nominally the country's central bank) lacked authority and most of the techniques of control necessary to influence either the volume or direction of lending by local financial institutions.[63] But the Bank maintained responsibility for administering the laws relating to all receipts and payments in foreign exchange.

From 1947, when Egypt left the sterling area, to 1952 the government considered sterling reserves sufficient to allow unrestricted imports from sterling countries. On the other hand Egypt experienced an acute shortage of dollars and other hard currencies required to purchase machinery and raw materials essential to its economic development. The government therefore directed its exchange policy to conserving hard currency and allocating it for the more essential purchases abroad. All imports other than those from the sterling area were licensed. Permits to import were issued more or less liberally for 'essentials' but 'luxuries' were prohibited. Other foreign goods could be bought in restricted quantities determined by the Ministry of Economy, and quotas for these commodities were allocated by licence among individual importers.[64]

Permits for almost all imports were, however, issued freely if the foreign exporter agreed to accept as payment Egyptian pounds, at the official rate of exchange, credited to his account at a bank in Cairo. Export pound accounts, as this device was termed, could be directly repatriated only in the form of Egyptian commodities. Alternatively export pounds could be sold on the free market to anyone interested in importing from Egypt. This rule circumvented the official fixed rate of exchange by allowing the Egyptian

[62] M. Radi, *The Structure of the Cotton Market in Egypt* (unpubl. London Univ. thesis, 1957), pp. 147–56; Said, 'The Cotton Problem', *Ég. contemp.*, Oct. 1951, pp. 3–7; Barawi & Ulaish (ar.), pp. 224 f. & 287.

[63] NBE, *National Bank of Egypt, 1898–1948* (1948), pp. 91–94 and *Econ. B.*, ii (1951), pp. 121–3.

[64] Foreign exchange regulations are summarized annually in *Rev. ec. trim.*, in April 1948–52.

pound to depreciate and thus introduced *de facto* multiple rates of exchange. Its object was to promote exports.[65] Another device with similar aims and effects was the system of allocating import licences to exporters of Egyptian commodities to the United States who succeeded in selling amounts in excess of the quotas imposed upon them by the American government.[66]

On the eve of revolution the direct part played by government in the economic life of the country still appeared relatively insignificant. Consumption and capital expenditure by the state represented about an eighth of national outlay.[67] The state's contribution to national output amounted to a mere 16 per cent of gross domestic product, most of which can be included under the heading of historical public services: defence, justice, fiscal and social administration. Only 2 per cent of local production came from state enterprises (railways, postal services, the gas and electricity undertakings of the Cairo municipality and a petroleum refinery at Suez).[68] As for employment, in 1947 just 8 per cent of the working force was engaged by public authorities, central and local.[69]

Government participated more actively in adding to and maintaining the stock of fixed assets upon which future production depended. Approximately one-quarter to one-fifth of gross domestic fixed capital formation for the years 1945 to 1952 was accomplished by the state, but most public expenditure on capital account was concentrated in fields of traditional interest to the government such as the upkeep and extension of the irrigation system, provision of health and education facilities, investment in railways or electrical power supplies.[70] Moreover the part played by the state in fixed capital formation had diminished over time as new and more productive forms of investment became quantitatively more significant than the upkeep of and additions to the infrastructure. Thus the provision by private enterprise of in-

[65] NBE, *Econ. B.*, i & ii (1948), pp. 36 & 75; iv (1949), p. 218; iii (1950), p. 182; iv (1951), p. 265.

[66] Ibid. i & iii (1953), pp. 29 & 204.

[67] INP Memo. 377.

[68] Statist. Dept., *National Income of Egypt for 1953* (1954), and see also table 10 (p. 325).

[69] See table 11 (p. 326 below).

[70] H. Abdel-Rahman, *Statistics of Trade, Income, Production and Capital Formation* (1959), NPC Memo. 86.

dustrial equipment and factories, farm buildings and machinery, and permanent improvements to the soil, transport by road, river, sea, and air exceeded in value the efforts made by the government to add to the nation's wealth. Nor, finally, had the state assisted very much in the finance of investment undertaken at private initiative. On the contrary, after 1950 the flow of savings happened frequently to be in a reverse direction, because the budget surplus on current account was insufficient to cover expenditure on public development projects.[71]

Thus around 1950 Egyptian private enterprise provided employment for 92 per cent of the labour force, produced 84 per cent of the nation's output, and was responsible for three-quarters of gross fixed capital formation. But the Egyptian state had not confined itself entirely to defence, security, justice, and the provision of an infrastructure. Since the Great War statesmen had come to realize that the nation's economic and social problems were too overwhelming and urgent to be left to businessmen. By mid-century the government's response to the Great Depression and the inflationary conditions of the war and post-war years had engendered a body of regulations designed to temper the effects of a harsh and rapidly changing economic environment upon the welfare of the poorer classes. The state attempted, albeit with partial success, to stabilize first agricultural incomes in face of severe instability in world primary commodity markets and to protect the real incomes of the urban working classes in the face of a serious and persistent inflation,[72] while rural poverty was alleviated by state encouragement for the co-operative movement, through cheap credit and, from 1946, a commitment to build a Social Welfare Centre in every village. Plans for the redistribution of land had been put forward by intellectuals but, under a landowning parliament, never came anywhere near being translated into law.[73] However, the Fellah Department of the Ministry of Social Affairs was supposed to be engaged in studying proposals on how to regulate landlord-tenant relations, rent, agricultural

[71] Compare government development expenditure in table 4 with the annual budget accounts published in the *Ann. stat.*

[72] For post-war policies see NBE, *Econ. B.*, i (1950, p. 6); & i, ii (1952), pp. 33 & 220, and *EG*, 25 Feb., 13 Apr., & 7 June 1949.

[73] Baer, pp. 202–19.

wages, and village housing.[74] For the urban poor minimum wage legislation already operated, and in 1951 the dependants of certain categories of industrial workers were granted assistance and pensions from the state if and when the wage-earner became sick and disabled or died. It was the beginnings of social security.[75]

Although most state interference with the economy had been prompted mainly by welfare considerations, the government showed awareness that poverty and the population explosion demanded positive policies for the promotion of economic development. Some statesmen appreciated the need to create alternative opportunities for production and employment outside agriculture and recognized the importance of extending the area and raising the productivity of cultivable land. Thus during the post-war era plans had been made and partially implemented for improvements to the infrastructure.[76] The Ministry of Agriculture propagated new crops and techniques of production among the rural population. Calls for an industrialization policy had been answered by the establishment of an Industrial Bank to supply firms with cheaper credit, by adjustments to tariffs and tax incentives.[77] Although the Five-Year Plan of 1947 contained no provision for direct expenditure on manufacturing, the Department of Commerce and Industry had initiated a series of studies by foreign experts on the feasibility of manufacturing steel, fertilizers, and other commodities locally.[78] Here lay the hint of a industrialization policy based upon the premise that industry had to proceed, not by further expansion of consumer goods, but via the creation of entirely new lines of production such as metals, chemicals, and engineering.

My survey of economic legislation and policy suggests that after the Great War, there was a definite trend away from a free-enterprise system and indicates that the state had begun to reclaim the position it possessed under Mohammed Ali. But since the movement remained only just perceptible, it still seems apt to

74 Min. Soc. Aff., *Social Welfare*, pp. 35–39.

75 Ibid. p. 109.

76 Expenditure on new works in the budget had risen from £7.8 m. in 1944–5 to £33.5 m. in 1949–50 (see NBE, *Econ. B.*, i (1951), p. 48).

77 NBE, *Reports of President*, 1947–51.

78 A. Galotoli, *Egypt in Midpassage* (1950), pp. 154–5 and *EG*, 1 Feb. 1949 & 30 Sept. 1951.

characterize the relationship which had persisted between state and economy for about a century before the Revolution as being one of *laissez-faire. Laissez-faire* is, however, a popular but somewhat inept description initially applied to relations between state and economy during the Industrial Revolutions in Western Europe and the United States. Inept because almost from the beginning of industrialization governments everywhere intervened to ameliorate some of the worst consequences to its citizens of unregulated capitalism. Thus public authorities, both central and local, regulated the conditions under which workers could be employed in the new factories, controlled the urban and later the rural environment in order to preserve public health, established rules for the operation of collective bargaining in the interest of public order, provided free education, and finally intervened to protect workers against the uncertainties of modern economic life, such as accidents, unemployment, sickness, and old age.

Egyptian development over the past century certainly seems *prima facie* to provide a better example of *laissez-faire*. For most of its modern history the rules established in Western Europe and the United States to temper and regulate capitalism have either not existed or have been enforced in a desultory manner. Reasons for this contrast are not difficult to find. Egypt was and has remained an agricultural country, and regulations about working conditions and public health or measures to mitigate economic uncertainty are not usually considered so urgent and essential as they are for urbanized industrial societies. Moreover in more recent times when some social regulation of the agricultural sector was perceived to be necessary, the Egyptian government of landowners proved not amenable to promulgating laws contrary to their immediate interest, although they were usually less averse to legislating in the interests of urban industrial workers. Furthermore, if the experience of other countries is relevant, the state has tended to control capitalism at points in time when a certain general level of affluence has already been attained and 'black spots' become more visible, but average living standards remained too low in Egypt to set up pressures for extensive regulation of private producers. Those with most to gain from state intervention, the industrial and agricultural proletariat, remained both without political power or an acute sense that their conditions were intolerable and might be improved. Life for them had always been harsh and Islam engendered acquiescence or channelled their protests into futile movements like the Muslim Brothers.[79] Even where pressures did exist and became transformed into legislation, the Egyptian state did not command an administration capable of enforcing legislation upon a multitude of small enterprises, and state control is invariably easier where the economic institutions involved are large-scale concerns. Small family-operated enterprises posed administrative problems quite beyond the competence of the Egyptian civil service and inspectorate. Moreover many of the larger production units both in commerce and industry were owned and managed by foreigners, who operated in a position of legal privilege granted to them under the Capitulations, and until 1936 were not subject to Egyptian law.[80] It seemed incongruous and unfair to impose rules upon Egyptian enterprises not applicable to their foreign rivals.

On the other hand, in contrast to the industrialized nations, the Egyptian government had always participated more actively in the process of capital formation. For Western Europe and the United States private capital proved sufficient and resourceful enough not only to create directly productive enterprises but also to build the greater part of the infrastructure as well. Egypt's fixed capital on the other hand was dominated by irrigation facilities, and as Nile water was too vital a resource to be distributed among cultivators according to private-ownership principles, public ownership and centralized control of the irrigation system remained the only viable way of organizing agricultural production. As for other parts of the infrastructure—railways, roads, docks, and marketing facilities—they were seldom built, as in Britain for example, by entrepreneurs as extensions to their enterprises or by groups of private shareholders in anticipation of profits. They were instead frequently constructed by the state in order to open up or stimulate development in the Nile valley. Egyptian transport was built to create rather than to serve productive activity. Moreover the heavy cost, long gestation period, and very uncertain yield made such investment an unattractive proposition to the tiny class of domestic capitalists and difficult to achieve for a country with a low level

[79] N. Safran, *Egypt in Search of a Political Community* (1961), pp. 194–205.
[80] J. Anderson, 'Law Reform in Egypt', in Holt.

of saving. In the early stages of Egyptian development only the government of Ismail had the resources and the vision to invest in transport facilities, but later on, when such outlays had proved profitable, foreign capital became attracted particularly into light railways and bus services.

Although it assumed the prime role in the creation of a modern transport system, only rarely after Mohammed Ali had the state participated directly in production. Why in the face of such widespread poverty the Egyptian government refrained for so long from at least supplementing the efforts made by private capital seems difficult to understand from our present vantage-point, so difficult that many historians account for the lack of government participation in economic affairs after the deposition of Ismail in terms of a deliberate British policy to keep Egypt an agricultural country.[81] They furthermore explain the reticence of native Egyptian régimes to intervene more positively after the achievement of independence in 1923 as a failure of will on the part of the landowning and conservative ruling élite. According to this view, the *ancien régime* possessed neither the desire nor the capacity to modernize and industrialize Egypt.[82]

Looked at in historical perspective both arguments appear somewhat myopic. Not until the second half of the twentieth century did the conviction become general that it was the task of governments in underdeveloped countries to accelerate economic advance by direct participation in production. One should not, however, exaggerate this point. British administrators might certainly be excused for not formulating more ambitious policies for developing the economy; their view of economic policy remained restricted by their own tradition and temperament. Britain had progressed satisfactorily without the active participation of the state. Given the efficient administration of law and order, external security, and an improved infrastructure, they naturally expected similar success in Egypt.[83] Britain had not occupied Egypt to develop the economy but to restore order to her tangled finances and to rationalize the tax structure. Moreover, the experience with

[81] F. Girgis, *Studies in the Political History of Egypt* (1958, ar.), pp. 112–16 and Issawi, in *J. Econ. Hist.*, Mar. 1961, pp. 11–12 & 17.

[82] A. Abdel-Malek, *Égypte; société militaire* (1963), pp. 33–36 & 42–46.

[83] Cromer, pp. 555–63.

Mohammed Ali and Ismail strongly suggested that the Egyptian people would be better off if the state restricted its activities as much as possible: that way their tax burdens would be light, and profligate or useless public expenditure would be avoided.

On the other hand the native Egyptian governments which at least had charge of domestic policy after 1923 need not have been quite so committed to *laissez-faire*. After all, it was not in their tradition, and nationalist régimes elsewhere in the Middle East, particularly Turkey and Persia, used the state to promote the economic development of their countries. Hassan Riad's argument that the old Egyptian ruling classes were in fact not nationalist but cosmopolitan and had imbibed the attitudes and ideology of a complacent European bourgeoisie is not without point.[84] Successive Egyptian governments from 1923 to 1952 displayed no strong disposition to force the pace of economic advance. Those years are certainly not marked by large and imaginative public projects, or by very positive governmental attempts to take the lead in the promotion of economic development.[85] But in defence of the old régime it should be said that much of the energies of politicians came sadly to be diverted into a protracted struggle with the king and British embassy over sovereignty. Men struggling to establish a viable political system seldom have time for anything else, but they were in any case rarely given sufficient credit for the efforts they did make to push Egyptian society out of its prison of poverty or to make that prison more habitable. For much of the time conditions outside Egypt, the international depression and the Second World War, reacted seriously and adversely on the local economy, so that government attention became further distracted with short-term palliatives rather than being focused on long-term economic advance. Finally, the precise lines along which the state could have intervened with real effect were not so obvious. Egypt already possessed a fairly mature infrastructure which no doubt required extension and improvement, particularly in relation to power supplies, while higher levels of expenditure on technical education might well have raised productivity. But further public investment on roads, railways, power, and marketing facilities probably would not have made

[84] H. Riad, *L'Égypte nassérienne* (1964), pp. 77–81.

[85] But for a more favourable view of the government see Quni, pp. 170–91.

that much difference to the overall rate of growth. Private enterprise seemed to be developing the more obvious consumer-goods industries at an impressive pace. Criticism might be levelled at the government for failing to promote heavier industry, such as metals, chemicals, and engineering, but until light industry had attained a certain level of development, it seemed doubtful if markets, skilled labour, managerial talent, and other resources required to establish more sophisticated forms of manufacturing were then available to Egypt. The strategy of proceeding stage by stage seemed a reasonable one to adopt for a country so deficient in resources and with so short an industrial tradition. But the charge of lethargy might be more easily substantiated against the government's agricultural policies. Here projects to extend the area of cultivable land had been proposed and a backlog of new methods and techniques of cultivation were available for propagation among farmers. Yet the government did very little except consider the plans for raising agricultural productivity, and it rejected all suggestions for reforming the institutional framework of agriculture. The additions to the cultivable area were minor and public expenditure on agricultural extension services seems pathetically inadequate. The government of landowners appear to have been strangely negligent towards the nation's most important resource.

Faced with growing and vociferous demands for the amelioration of poverty, and during its latter years with a serious population explosion, when all the qualifications have been offered, Egypt's former rulers cannot be excused from the charge of having displayed an incapacity to act and an unrealistic faith in the virtues of *laissez-faire*. It probably needed a profound change in the political system to push the state farther and faster along the path towards positive and far-reaching intervention in the economic affairs of the nation.

III

The Revolution and the Economy, 1952-6: The Free-Enterprise Phase

WHEN the Free Officers seized power in July 1952 they were without an economic ideology, and apart from land reform not even the most general ideas relating to economic organization had formed part of their pre-revolution discussions on the future of Egypt.[1] Moreover their statements referring to relations between state and private enterprise during the early years of the revolution seem calculated to assuage any doubts businessmen may have entertained about the intentions of the new régime. 'We are not Socialists', insisted Gamal Salem, Minister of National Guidance; 'I think our economy can only prosper under free enterprise.'[2] 'The state', said Dr Kaissouny, 'encourages private enterprise and aids it in every way'. His aim, as Minister of Finance, was to 'create a favourable atmosphere for the investment of national and foreign capital'.[3] Although it is difficult to gauge the reactions of the business community to the change of government because their journals rarely commented upon economic policy, repeated stress by members of the Revolutionary Council on the need for 'stability, quietude and security' evoked some response at least in the public remarks of business leaders.[4] 'During 1954', claimed the president of the National Bank, 'feelings of anxiety in the business world have been dispelled', and his reports for 1955 and 1956 commended the government for creating a favourable atmosphere for industrial investment.[5] Chairmen of the Cairo and Alexandria Stock Exchanges, spokesmen from the French Chamber of Commerce in Cairo and the president of Bank Misr also waxed eloquent in their praise for the economic policies of the

[1] G. Abdel Nasser, *The Philosophy of Revolution* (1954); A. Sadat, *Revolt on the Nile* (1957), and P. Vatikiotis, *The Egyptian Army in Politics* (1961), pp. 67–68.

[2] *BE*, 26 Jan. 1954.

[3] Ibid. 15 & 20 Dec. 1954 & 9 Aug. 1955.

[4] *EG* & *BE passim* for 1954 & 1955.

[5] NBE, *Ann. Reports*, 1954, 1955, 1956.

military régime.[6] If there was even a glimmering of a new ideology in the minds of Free Officers, it remained hidden or diffused under the régime's nationalism which insisted that the new government was the government of

> the whole nation, the Government of farmers and workers, of officials and students; of financiers and businessmen; of the rich and the poor; of the weak and the strong; of beginners and those who have attained success. It is a government that looks on all Egyptians as one big family and is working for their common good.[7]

Thus little surprise need be evoked by the conclusion that, during the early years when the officers remained very preoccupied with consolidating power and expelling the British from the canal zone, no very clear departure can be observed from the kind of economic policies pursued by the old régime. Men so overwhelmingly concerned with a struggle for political power naturally found little time to consider the long-term future of their country. Excluding land reform, up to the Tripartite Aggression, continuity seems more evident than change.

Our stress on continuity does not, however, intend to minimize the more positive role played by the new government in economic development. It replaced the defunct Economic Advisory Committee by a new institution, the Permanent Council for the Development of National Production, in order 'to synchronize economic and social policy on sound principles, and to examine the country's resources and exploit them fully.[8] Members of the Council included ministers, engineers, industrialists, agriculturalists, and bankers. Their function was to study and recommend policies and projects which would promote economic development.[9] The Council was not a mere advisory body but possessed powers which allowed it to participate actively with ministries and the private sector in the formulation, execution, and finance of projects. It represented the prime example of several similar institutions created to facilitate co-operation and consultation between govern-

[6] *BE*, 28 Mar., 4 May, 9 Aug., & 30 Dec. 1955.

[7] Speech by Col. Nasser, 23 July 1954, published in Information Dept., *Goals of the Egyptian Revolution* (1955), pp. 86–87; F. Bertier, 'L'Idéologie sociale de la révolution égyptienne', *Orient*, ii (1958), pp. 61 & 62, quotes other speeches on the same lines by Col. Nasser for 1955.

[8] *PCDNP Report 1955* (ar.), p. 3.

[9] Ibid. *1954*, pp. 3–4.

ment and the private sector; as its second annual report emphasized, 'a cornerstone of the new régime is a definite plan of compromise between private and state efforts to achieve the desired economic and social objectives'.[10] What precise influence the Council's numerous recommendations had upon the private sector is impossible to say, but by July 1953 it produced a plan for an expansive four-year programme of public investment. Unlike the plans of the old régime, this one was acted upon immediately and capital formation by the state proceeded on a much enlarged scale after the revolution, but continued to be the type of investment normally undertaken by government or centred in projects which private enterprise was content to leave to public risk. According to figures compiled by the National Planning Committee, government investment increased from an annual average of £28 millions for 1950–2 to £34 millions in 1953, £53 millions in 1954, £62 millions in 1955, and £66 millions in 1956.[11] Most of the investment proposed by the Council remained traditional public expenditure; for example, 61 per cent went into irrigation, drainage, and land reclamation and the bulk of the remainder was divided between electricity and transport.[12] Public investment by the new régime appears designed, as indeed it had been since the time of Ismail, to create a more efficient infrastructure within which private enterprise could develop more rapidly and efficiently.[13]

While economic development did not receive the highest priority or urgency during the early years of the revolution, nevertheless the speeches and manifestos of the Free Officers demonstrate that they fully appreciated the need to industrialize.[14] The whole emphasis of their economic policy became directed towards affording industry help to expand and, more specifically, to giving private investors every possible incentive to place their savings with manufacturing firms. Investors included foreigners

[10] Ibid. *1955*, pp. 1–3. The other major institutions of this type were the Permanent Councils for Public Services, for Industrial Training, and for Land Reclamation.

[11] UN, *Economic Developments in the Middle East 1956–7* (1957), p. 13. The figures cited in table 4 of 'developmental expenditure' by the government are compiled on a different basis but show the same upward trend.

[12] *UAR Econ. Features*, p. 16 and *Budget Analyses 1954–64* (1959, ar.), NPC Memo. 149.

[13] INP Memo. 63, pp. 16–17.

[14] *BE*, 9 Jan., 12 Feb., 15 & 27 May 1954, & 26 May 1955.

as well as nationals and, in order to attract more private capital from overseas, the Officers partially reversed the Egyptianization policy of the old régime by allowing foreign shareholders to possess a majority interest and control in any domestic company. Under law 138 of 1947 at least 51 per cent of the shares of a joint-stock company had to be set aside for Egyptians, while the new law of July 1952 proclaimed that only 49 per cent had to be so reserved and further stipulated that if the required proportion was not taken up by native citizens within a month, then the share issue became open to public subscription regardless of nationality.[15]

Private foreign capital was not, however, easily enticed into Egypt during the politically uncertain years following the revolution and the Free Officers realistically importuned their own domestic capitalist class. Apart from providing it with ideological reassurances and placing businessmen on the Councils for National Development, the new government usually avoided intervention in the industrial field without consulting the Federation of Egyptian Industries. Changes in the law relating to foreign capital had emerged from such co-operation and the new régime acceded to the Federation's frequently reiterated demand for lower taxes and higher protection.[16] Thus tariffs were raised and customs duties on raw materials and capital goods lowered. The government granted new joint-stock companies a seven-year exemption from profits tax and released profits accruing from new share issues by existing companies from the same tax for five years, while all undistributed dividends were exempted from 50 per cent of the profits tax.[17] Further, companies found it easier to obtain finance needed for development because, when the government raised its guarantee of the loans by the Industrial Bank to £5 million, the Bank became more venturesome in lending. It participated directly in founding new firms, covered subscriptions for extensions of plant, and guaranteed loans made to businessmen by commercial banks.[18] Finally, the Federation of Industry found itself strengthened by a government decree compelling all firms above a certain

[15] R. Barawy, *The Military Coup in Egypt* (1952), p. 226 and *UAR Econ. Features*, pp. 18–19.

[16] FIE, *Ann. 1952–3 & 1953–4*, introd.

[17] Laws 324, 1952; 251 & 430, 1953; 418 & 502, 1955; 151, 1956; & 5 & 54, 1957.

[18] Industrial Bank, *Dev. of Industrial Credit*, pp. 21–27.

size to affiliate to industrial chambers which were the constituent parts of the Federation. As firms even within the same industry had often failed to co-operate in matters of mutual concern, the government empowered certain Chambers of Industry to impose a levy on their members in order to inaugurate technical and market research programmes of interest to all affiliated enterprises.[19]

By no means all advice from the Federation of Egyptian Industries became government policy. Its admonition against direct state participation in the creation of manufacturing enterprises and its appeal for guaranteed profits on all new industrial investment were largely ignored.[20] When it came to implementing the recommendations made by foreign consultants to the former régime, who proposed to extend the industrial sector into several novel lines of production, the government, almost for the first time since Mohammed Ali, became directly involved with the initiation and running of manufacturing enterprises. Civil servants designed industrial projects, negotiated with foreign firms for the supply of the necessary equipment, technicians, and credit facilities, and sat on the boards of the new companies. But the government acted, so the Officers repeatedly insisted, as the partner of private enterprise and deliberately confined itself to the area of heavy or basic industry. The rest of manufacturing the state explicitly reserved for private endeavour, aided and encouraged, of course, by tax incentives, and cheaper public credit, transport, and power supplies.[21] Thus during the early years of the revolution the state participated in the foundation and finance of several pioneer industrial ventures of a heavy or basic type. Half the capital for an iron and steel plant at Helwan came from the government, the remainder from private firms including the Demag Steel Company of Germany.[22] Egyptian State Railways contributed 20 per cent of the money required to establish a company to make railway equipment.[23] Fertilizer and cement plants were financed in large part by the National Production Council. The Council also designed the projects and encouraged

[19] NBE, *Econ. B.*, iv (1953), p. 291. [20] FIE, *Ann. 1952–3*, introd.
[21] PCDNP, *Report 1955* (ar.), pp. 174–6.
[22] Inform. Dept., *The Egyptian Revolution in Three Years* (1955), p. 67.
[23] *UAR Yearbook 1959*, p. 162.

the formation of two private companies to make electrical cables and rubber tyres. To one company the government gave land, to the other a contract to supply all tyres for the public service for a five-year period. For other firms the state guaranteed profits over an interim period or paid interest on their loans.[24]

But the industrial policy of the new government did not stop short at the mere encouragement of investment in manufacturing; it also imposed some additional controls over the discretion of those who managed industry. The controls were almost entirely of a protective character, designed to ameliorate the disadvantages suffered by two social groups—shareholders and industrial workers—although the additional protection afforded to investors was also directed towards stimulating the flow of private savings into industry. Before the revolution long discussions had occurred, both in parliament and the press, about the reform of company law. The need for change arose with the growing divorce of ownership from control throughout industry and the subsequent strengthening and misuse of powers by those who managed assets for other people. Advocates of legal reform maintained that boards of companies contained far too many directors, most of whom were either functionless or, because they occupied directorships of several firms concurrently, had no time to attend properly to the specialized affairs of any single concern. They further argued that directors in general received too much remuneration, and that the present legal position afforded inadequate protection to the rights of shareholders. They concluded that, as a result of such defects in the law relating to corporate firms, the boards of companies had become overstaffed and investors were inhibited from risking money in enterprises over which they exerted virtually no influence.[25] Given the emphasis placed by the new régime upon industrialization, the new government was naturally anxious to remove any obvious obstacles to the flow of savings into industry and also to improve the efficiency of management.[26] It therefore took up the proposals of reformers and translated them into extensive amendments to company law. Law 26 of 1954 lowered

[24] PCDNP, *Report 1954* (ar.), p. 14.

[25] Gritly, pp. 409, 412, 415 & 416.

[26] Min. Econ., *Economic Progress in the UAR* (1960), p. 9 and *UAR Econ. Features*, pp. 22–24.

the denomination of a minimum share from £4 to £2. At the same time, and in order to strengthen the powers of shareholders *vis-à-vis* the boards of joint-stock companies, it compelled directors to retire at 60 and fixed their remuneration at a maximum equal to 10 per cent of final profits after a dividend of 5 per cent had been distributed. The maximum could not in any case exceed £2,500 for one or more directorships. No man was henceforth allowed to be a director of more than six companies or a managing director of more than two companies, and each director had to assume responsibility for a particular aspect of company policy.[27] This part of the law was amended again in 1957 when the number of directorships was limited to two and managing directorships to one.[28] Shareholders' rights to inspect accounts, to call extraordinary meetings, and to vote on matters of policy became more sharply defined, thus strengthening their influence over boards of directors.

The prerogatives of management became limited still further by the substantial amendments introduced by the new government to the existing body of labour and social welfare legislation. But labour policy, like industrial policy, was not formulated unilaterally. In an endeavour to gain political support from urban workers, the Officers reconstituted the defunct Advisory Council for Labour to include stronger representation from trade unions and sought the Council's advice on most matters pertaining to the welfare of industrial workers.[29] Unions, the new government realized, need not be a disruptive influence; they could promote stable industrial relations and help to raise productivity.[30] The Officers therefore encouraged their formation, and amended the Trades Union Act of 1942 in order to permit additional categories of workers, including agricultural labourers, to organize. The new law also allowed for confederations of unions and stipulated that if 60 per cent of employees in any given company belonged to a union, then the remainder could be compelled to join. Union membership rose rapidly during the years after 1952 and, with their rights to organize and bargain more positively protected by law, challenged

[27] Min. Commerce & Ind., *The Companies Law* (1954).
[28] Law 114, 1957.
[29] US Dept. of Labor, *Summary of the Labor Situation in Egypt* (1955), p. 8.
[30] Inf. Dept., *The Permanent Council for Public Welfare Services* (1955), pp. 35–36.

management more militantly over a wider front. Confrontation between both sides of industry did not, however, develop into the kind of free collective bargaining which obtains in Europe and United States, and the government continued to guide and direct industrial relations in the same paternal way as it had under the monarchy. Strikes, however, became illegal. If parties to an industrial dispute failed to agree they were subjected to compulsory arbitration. Unions remained debarred from political activity and even stricter public control was exercised over the allocation of their funds.[31]

Thus, although the new government encouraged industrial workers to organize, it retained overall responsibility for almost all matters pertaining to their welfare, and they appear to have derived more benefits from direct state interference with the prerogatives of their employers than from union activity. But no doubt unions performed the vital task of ensuring that companies obeyed the law.

Under a series of substantive amendments to the Law of Individual Contracts of Service, 1944, the government raised the level of employees' sick pay, holidays, medical care, and indemnities for dismissal. Employers found their rights to sack workers more strictly circumscribed and their discretion to fix wage rates limited by a law raising the minimum legal daily wage they could pay from 12½ to 25 piastres.[32]

Finally, in 1955 the government introduced a scheme for social insurance, prepared by the Advisory Council on Labour, in order to replace the inoperative Act of 1950, which had provided public assistance for the dependants of sick or deceased industrial workers. The new scheme covered workers in Cairo or Alexandria employed by firms with more than fifty workers. It was financed not by the state but by compulsory contributions from employers and employees, whose premiums were collected and invested by an autonomous public body, the Institute for Workers' Savings and Insurance. Out of the accumulated fund pensions were payable

[31] Audsley, in *St Antony's Papers*, iv (1958), pp. 104–6; cf. Handley, in *MEJ*, July 1949, pp. 279–83, for the legislation of 1942.

[32] Inf. Dept., *Social Development under the New Régime* (1954), p. 19 and Audsley, in *St Antony's Papers*, iv (1958), pp. 103–4. Law 41 of 1944 is explained in Handley, in *MEJ*, July 1949, p. 287.

to the wives and children of sick, disabled, and deceased workers.[33] Although the new scheme added to the wage bill of larger companies, it aroused no great opposition because in many cases they already operated similar private insurance funds of their own.[34]

While the new government emphasized industry, rural Egypt was by no means neglected, but its agricultural policy departed in only a single, albeit a highly significant, way from the kind of measures promulgated by the old régime. The departure was of course, the now famous land reform, long advocated, but given the highest priority by the Free Officers and implemented just three months after their coup d'état.

By legislation of September 1952 the government placed a ceiling of 200 feddans on the ownership of land. Land possessed by an individual in excess of that amount was expropriated and gradually redistributed by the new Ministry of Agrarian Reform to landless tenant farmers in plots of 2–5 feddans. The state fixed rents for all agricultural land at levels much lower than previous payments and prescribed minimum daily wages for agricultural workers.[35] Land subject to expropriation represented, however, no more than 10 per cent of the total area and only a minority of agricultural families gained or lost land. Legal provisions for fixing agricultural wages proved unenforceable, while the prescribed rents were evaded on all but the larger estates.[36]

Although the stated purpose of land reform was simply to bring about immediate redistribution of rural income, policy as it evolved gave the government a strong measure of control over agricultural production on expropriated estates. For example, farmers who gained land were compelled to join a co-operative.[37] Land reform co-operatives vary in size. All are run by a board elected by the members, but each board includes a supervisor

[33] Inst. de l'Assurance de l'Épargne des Travailleurs, *Rapport 1956* (1957).

[34] Min. Soc. Aff., *Social Welfare*, pp. 16–17.

[35] This summary simplifies a complex law. Details concerning categories of land exempt from expropriation and the ceiling of 200 feddans as well as provisions for fixing rents and wages can be found in E. Garzouzi, *Old Ills and New Remedies in Egypt* (1958), pp. 80–87.

[36] D. Warriner, *Land Reform and Development in the Middle East* (1962), pp. 13 f., 34 f., 38 f., 193 f.

[37] Barawy (*Military Coup*, pp. 234–6) gives a full account of the legal provisions with respect to the formation of co-operatives.

who is directly responsible to the Ministry of Agrarian Reform.[38] What the exact role of the supervisor was or became is difficult to say. Eva Garzouzi considers that he operates merely in an 'advisory capacity'; Professor Warriner that he 'effectively runs' the co-operative.[39] Probably his degree of control varies from place to place, but during the winter of 1963, I visited three villages in Lower Egypt where the supervisor enjoyed the right to veto decisions reached by other members of the board. Even the older co-operatives fostered to channel public credit to farmers had found themselves under definite government tutelage, so it is not surprising to discover that the new organizations founded by decree to farm lands redistributed by the state should remain under some kind of public control. Moreover the Officers were most anxious that output and productivity should not fall. Hence the continued presence of expert supervisors attached to all land reform co-operatives.

From their co-operatives farmers purchase seeds, livestock, implements, and fertilizers; through it they market their crops and obtain credit.[40] Co-operatives performing some of these tasks had existed in Egypt since the First World War, but the new organizations went beyond bulk purchase, credit provision, and marketing. As the government emphasized: 'It is not enough to assign to the peasant a plot of land leaving him to himself: he should learn the best method of cultivation and should be offered technical and material help.'[41] To this end land reform co-operatives organize production: thus ploughing and harvesting are undertaken collectively. Crop rotation and seed selection, investment in machinery, improvements to the field irrigation system, or social welfare amenities are also co-operative decisions and are financed by deduction from sales of cash crops.[42] Within this institutional framework farmers are free to sow and tend crops on their own land; and receive income proportionate to its yield.

As the first major policy measure of the new régime, land

[38] S. Marei, *UAR Agriculture Enters a New Age* (1960), pp. 53–54.
[39] Garzouzi, p. 92 and Warriner, pp. 42–43.
[40] Marei, *UAR Agriculture*, p. 53. [41] *UAR Yearbook 1959*, p. 263.
[42] Min. Agrarian Reform, *Statutes of Zaafaran Co-operative* (1955 ar.); G. Saab, 'Rationalization of Agriculture and Land Tenure Problems in Egypt', *ME Econ. Papers 1960*, pp. 74 f. & 78; Higher Committee for Agrarian Reform, *Replies to UN Questionnaires relating to Egyptian Agrarian Reform* (1955), pp. 72–90.

reform may well have disquieted the entire Egyptian capitalist class. Farmers probably wondered if the new co-operatives were the beginnings of a more general curtailment of their discretion to utilize land. Merchants and industrialists may have considered the expropriation of land as the initial expression of an attack upon the rights of private property. But as time passed it became apparent that the reform, affecting less than 10 per cent of total area and only a small minority of wealthy landowners, was not part of a wider programme for the redistribution of wealth and the extension of state control over agriculture.[43] In reality agrarian reform, as initially conceived by the Free Officers, was perhaps little more than a political device designed to break the power of Egypt's old ruling families.[44] Moreover many landowners were relieved to find that the redistribution of land was less radical than some advocates of reform had hoped, and rejoiced that the attempts to fix rents and wages proved unenforceable over a wide area.[45]

The remainder of the new government's agricultural measures appeared far less radical than land reform, being for the most part a vigorous and often more imaginative application of activities or ideas initiated under previous governments. Policy remained firmly focused upon agriculture's extensive margin although some additional resources were allocated towards soil surveys and basic research directed towards the improvement of yields per feddan.[46] For example, plans for a massive extension to the cultivated land of Egypt had been under discussion for nearly a decade, and the early stages of one scheme designed to add about a million feddans to the Egyptian cultivated area, the Century Storage Plan, was already under way when the Officers obtained power. They replaced it, however, by the more ambitious High Dam project, which aimed to increase the cultivable area by 1½ million feddans. Although Egyptian and foreign engineers completed preliminary designs for the High Dam by the end of 1954, work at Aswan did not really begin until four years later, after long negotiations with

43 J. & S. Lacouture, *Egypt in Transition* (1958), p. 166 and Warriner, p. 13.

44 Baer, 'Egyptian Attitudes towards Land Reform', in W. Laqueur, *Middle East in Transition* (1958), pp. 90–94.

45 Ibid. pp. 95–99. The President of the National Bank praised the government for proceeding slowly with land reform (see NBE, *Ann. Reports 1953–5*).

46 Marei, *UAR Agriculture*, pp. 78, 80, & 81–84.

Sudan over the distribution of Nile water, and when Russia had agreed to finance the project.[47] As well as initiating the spectacular High Dam, the government also continued to survey Egypt's expanse of unused desert land and to design projects for its reclamation. Plans for the irrigation of nearly half a million virgin feddans in such areas as the New Valley, Fayoum, Beheira and Tahrir Province existed on paper by 1954, and by the Suez war work had already begun on the latter projects.[48]

Aside from plans, the amount of land actually reclaimed during the early years of the revolution was not nearly so impressive as additions made to the cropped area as a result of continued improvements to the irrigation system. By deepening existing drains and installing pumping equipment, and from extensions to irrigation and drainage canals, the Ministry of Public Works made water available perennially to more and more farmers and enabled them to add considerably to the aggregate cropped area by 1957.

Under the new régime farmers and landowners continued to operate within a wide ranging system of price controls, subsidies, and area restrictions, introduced long before the revolution. Continuity prevailed because the Officers condoned all the substantial modifications made by previous governments to free markets in agricultural produce. They too appreciated the need to restrain rises in the cost of living for urban consumers, and therefore continued to control and subsidize the prices of foodstuffs regarded as necessities. They also compelled farmers to devote a minimum proportion of their land to wheat and to deliver part of the crop to the Ministry of Supply for sale at fixed prices to millers.[49] The new government certainly also wished to insulate agricultural incomes from the effects of fluctuations in the price of cotton on world markets and to maximize the country's receipts of foreign exchange.

Between 1950 and 1952 both these latter problems became more acute, as raw cotton prices tumbled from the heights attained during the Korean boom and as the elevation in export incomes from the boom and the government's investment programme

[47] High Dam Authority, *Report on the High Dam* (1955, ar.), pp. 6–7 and Hurst, pp. 304–20.

[48] Marei, *UAR Agriculture*, pp. 105, 110–14, 120–1 and PCDNP, *Report 1955* (ar.), pp. 92–174.

[49] NBE, *Econ. B.*, ii & iii (1952), pp. 105 f., 109, & 220.

generated a rapid increase in imports. The new government inherited a situation of rapidly declining cotton prices, mounting stocks of raw cotton in the hands of the Egyptian Cotton Commission, and a balance-of-payments deficit larger than for any year since the war.[50] Although Egypt still possessed ample reserves of foreign currency, the government realized that it had a high opportunity cost and immediately instituted measures to restrain the deficit within narrower limits and to protect local farmers from the effects of the downturn in cotton prices. Thus restrictions on the area which could be devoted to cotton, in abeyance since 1949, were immediately reimposed. Support prices for grain were raised in order to encourage farmers to grow more wheat and to discourage excessive concentration on cotton which had mined the soil.[51] The Egyptian Cotton Commission continued to operate buffer-stock policies, but the government closed the cotton futures market at Alexandria because, the Officers argued, its speculative activities had exercised a destablizing influence upon cotton prices.[52]

The new government supported its interference with agriculture by further controls on the flow of international trade and upon transactions in foreign currency, but the regulations promulgated in October and December 1952 could be described as a much more stringent and extensive application of the type of controls already introduced by the old régime. For example, all imports except fuel and those on government account were made subject to licence, and more restricted definitions of essentials and luxuries were applied by the Officers, with top priority given to capital goods required for development and a sharper discrimination against commodities purchased with hard currencies. Since reserves of sterling had been badly depleted between 1948 and 1952, the policy of unrestricted imports from the sterling area was discontinued.

To encourage exports, the system of payment through export pound accounts was widened wherever possible to include more commodities and countries. The government also extended the device of allowing exporters to the United States to retain and sell

[50] H. Tadross, 'Recent Developments in Egypt's Balance of Payments', *ME Econ. Papers 1957*, p. 122.

[51] NBE, *Econ. B.*, iii (1954), p. 3.

[52] Radi, pp. 151–3.

part of their dollar earnings. Thus under the Import Entitlement System, introduced in 1953, Egyptian exporters to Germany, the sterling area, and Scandinavia also received permission to retain part of their receipts of hard currency for purposes of importing or for sale on the free market at premiums above the official rate of exchange. These two devices for promoting exports (which in effect sanctioned depreciation and multiple exchange rates) were, however, abolished in September 1955 when Egypt reverted to a fixed rate of exchange; but discrimination against imports from hard-currency areas continued to be practised through licensing of imports.[53]

To sum up or characterize the early years of the revolution is difficult, particularly as the new régime brought no coherent or radical philosophy to the tasks of government. On the political level it seems, however, possible to go beyond conventional descriptions of the Free Officers as authoritarian rulers with an uncommitted or unformulated ideology, and to argue that they leaned more perceptibly to the right than to the left. Indeed, the political actions and speeches of the Officers did everything to allay suspicion that their coup was left wing. They purged their ranks of leftish elements, imprisoned most of Egypt's 'communists', and appeared intent on maintaining good relations with the western bloc, especially the United States. The new system of government certainly proved more authoritarian than the old, and the Officers resisted demands from the Egyptian bourgeoisie for a return to party politics, although they consulted businessmen on most matters directly affecting their interests, and representatives of the Federation of Egyptian Industries or Misr Group sat on nearly all the newly created National Councils of Development. The middle classes must have been relieved that a much more radical group had not seized office. At least the military obviated the danger of a communist government or rule by the Muslim Brothers. Furthermore, by destroying both these movements of the extreme left and the extreme right, and by persuading Britain to evacuate troops from the canal zone, the Officers successfully terminated a long period of violent strife in Egyptian public and political life. After 1954 the country possessed the law and order

[53] *Rev. éc. trim.*, ann. suppl. on foreign trade & exchange regulations, Apr. 1953, 1954, & 1955.

it so conspicuously lacked during the closing years of the old régime.[54]

Lastly, apart from the small minority of very wealthy landowners affected by land reform and some minor amendments to the income tax, the new government made no direct attacks on property, in fact very little redistribution of wealth or income occurred during the early years of the revolution.[55] The Marxist observation that the coup of July 1952 represented a bourgeois revolution may not do justice to the complexities of recent Egyptian history, but at least it points to certain important attitudes of the Free Officers, such as their support for private enterprise, their willingness to protect property rights, and their apparent lack of sympathy for socialism.[56]

Politically the coup d'état of July 1952 engendered a new set of questions about sovereignty, the system of government, the goals of society, &c., but economically the same old difficulties remained, and thus the economic policies of the new régime were simply designed to solve or remedy certain persistent problems related to the prevalence of widespread poverty in the Nile valley. Moreover the situation produced by the population explosion demanded immediate action to make more land available to farmers, to increase its yield, and above all the creation of opportunities for production and employment outside agriculture. Yet by mid-century industry itself had also reached a kind of impasse. Industrial efficiency had not attained standards sufficient to make Egyptian firms formidable competitors upon world markets. Instead the bulk of manufactured commodities were sold on the highly protected home market. Further advances, it appeared, could only be achieved by the continued replacement by domestic substitutes of such sophisticated imports as chemicals, metals, and engineering products.

As might be expected from men possessed of no coherent ideology, and anyway preoccupied with the struggle for power and Egypt's relations with the outside world, the elements of

[54] Vatikiotis, chs. 2 & 4 and K. Wheelock, *Nasser's New Egypt*, ch. 2.

[55] Up to 1956 only about 6 per cent of the total cultivated land had been redistributed. For changes in direct taxation see laws 146 & 159 of 1952, 417, 424, & 448 of 1953, and 56 & 254 of 1954.

[56] Riad *Égypte nassérienne*, pp. 220–3.

continuity in their economic policy are very marked. They took familiar kinds of action and promulgated laws which more often than not represented extensions and additions to the existing body of legislation rather than definite innovations. For example, their response to the balance-of-payments crisis and the accumulation of cotton stocks was the traditional one of restricting the cotton area, clamping down on luxury imports, and depreciation of the currency. Their actions to improve crop yields centred around the kind of extension services operated for many years past. Outside the small area occupied by land reform co-operatives, the new government made virtually no attempt to interfere with the discretion of farmers to cultivate land as they pleased, and the degree of influence exercised by the Ministry of Agriculture upon the scale and techniques of local farming changed hardly at all after 1952. Land reform certainly represented a radical departure from traditional agricultural policy, but the overall effects on output of redistributing such a small area of cultivated land, as well as the partially successful attempt to regulate landlord-tenant relations throughout the countryside, should not be exaggerated. The Officers furthermore hardly thought of land reform as a measure to promote growth, but rather as a political device to break the economic power of the former ruling élite, to effect an immediate redistribution of agricultural income, and thus to win the support of the fellah. As reform proceeded, the problem was not one of improving but of maintaining yields on expropriated lands. The Officers certainly supported imaginative and ambitious plans for extensions to the area of cultivable land, but apart from some minor additions to the cultivated and, more noticeably, the cropped area, up to 1956 the High Dam and the New Valley remained paper projects largely because of difficulties encountered by the government in their negotiations to obtain foreign finance and technical co-operation.

More radicalism and innovation is perhaps apparent in the new régime's industrial policy. As their speeches so frequently emphasized, the Officers accepted wholeheartedly the case for rapid industrialization and also embraced the strategy outlined in the Little[57] and other reports which maintained that the structure of

[57] Arthur D. Little, Inc., *Final Report* (Cambridge, Mass., 1954).

industry needed to be diversified.[58] Where former governments had commissioned studies on the feasibility of new lines of manufacturing, the Officers acted and initiated several projects in metals, chemicals, and engineering products during the early years of the revolution. Despite opposition from the Federation of Egyptian Industries, the government became directly involved in the finance and management of these projects, but it gave the private sector every encouragement to participate as well. In addition, every conceivable incentive, from higher protection and tax concessions to reform of company law, was afforded for higher levels of investment in industry. On the other hand the Officers took little direct action to raise the efficiency of industry but preferred to leave such problems as scale, capital-labour deployment, pricing and sales policies to the discretion of industrialists. But they did curtail the prerogatives of management in just two respects. Their reform of company law reduced the privileges of directors; apparently to their chagrin,[59] while amendments to the Law of Contracts and Services and the encouragement given to the formation of trade unions diluted the power of management over personnel in a manner which reacted adversely, so managers argued, on industrial efficiency.[60] But on the whole the Officers preferred to encourage investment in industry rather than interfere to improve its efficiency.

After the change of régime in July 1952 the critics of government had virtually no reason to complain about a lack of will to develop the country or no further occasion to jeer at the 'agrarian mentality' of the ruling élite. For the first time since Mohammed Ali, the Egyptian economy experienced the imprint of firm government and the state moved farther along the spectrum away from *laissez-faire*. Even so, the years 1952–6 might appropriately be described as the 'free-enterprise phase of the Egyptian Revolution', that is the years when the Free Officers attempted to achieve development by employing traditional methods and techniques, recommended by those who believe in the efficacy of private entrepreneurs in poor countries to respond to incentives and so set their economies along paths of sustained growth.

[58] See leader in *BE*, 26 May 1955, called 'Principles of the Revolution to encourage Industry' and Permanent Council of Public Services, *The Population Problem in Egypt* (1955), p. 21.

[59] *EEPR*, May 1955, pp. 37–38.

[60] Harbison & Ibrahim, p. 164.

IV

Guided Capitalism, 1957–60

INVESTMENT AND INDUSTRIALIZATION

PRESIDENT Nasser's term 'controlled capitalistic economy' is an apposite description of the next phase of the revolution during which state control over private enterprise was considerably extended both in range and intensity.[1] Ideologically the move away from previous policy was anticipated in the new constitution, promulgated at the beginning of 1956. Although constitutions are normally only vague pointers to action, the document of 1956 expressed in more or less accurate terms, the direction of future developments in the economic field. Article 3 recognized private ownership and private economic activity. Private economic activity was guaranteed to be 'free from state interference provided that it does not prejudice public interests or endanger the people's security, or infringe upon their freedom or dignity' (art. 8). The constitution promised that development would be planned (art. 7); 'capital should be at the service of the national economy' (art. 9); and that 'the reconciling of public and private economic activity' was 'guaranteed by law in a manner which ensures social aims and public welfare' (art. 10).[2] Most of its articles are open to divergent interpretation, but looked at together they represent an advance in clarity over the vagueness of earlier ideological pronouncements by the military régime contained, for example, in such manifestos as *Goals of the Revolution*.[3]

They also provide a general but accurate anticipation of future economic policies. Thus presidential decree 78 of January 1957 set up a National Planning Committee to 'prepare a long-term plan for social and economic development which would mobilize public and private effort'. Measures for 'comprehensive planning' had received presidential sanction before but proved abortive.[4] This time the government were serious. Two hundred officials formed themselves into a technical secretariat and foreign experts came

[1] *Nasser's Speeches 1958*, pp. 362 & 403.
[2] 'The Egyptian Constitution, 1956', *Mideast Mirror*, suppl. 16, Jan. 1956.
[3] Inform. Dept., *Goals of the Egyptian Revolution*. [4] Law 141 of 1955.

over to assist from Holland, East Germany, and Norway. Work began immediately on an interim investment programme for 1958 and 1959, while materials were gathered and studies undertaken for a long-term plan scheduled to begin in 1960.[5] Given their emphasis on industrialization, the Officers were not prepared to wait three years before attempting to elevate the rate of industrial growth. Discussions began in October 1956 on a separate plan for manufacturing, and by summer 1957 officials of the newly formed Ministry of Industry had prepared a Five-Year Plan which became operational the following year.[6] In a foreword the Minister, Dr Sidky, held that 'the ingredients for industrialization are abundant in Egypt. We must realize that our lack of experience in the industrial field may drive us into exaggerated hesitation and cause us to refrain from taking positive steps.'[7]

Certainly his Plan was anything but hesitant. It aimed to increase the annual rate of growth of industrial production from about 6 per cent (the average rate for the preceding five years) to 16 per cent per annum over the Plan period. This would raise the share of national income originating in the industrial sector from 11 to 19 per cent in five years.[8] To achieve such a startling acceleration of industrial growth required, so the Ministry had calculated, *net* investment in industry of £45 million a year between 1957 and 1961, but over the previous quinquennium *gross* industrial investment had averaged only £34 million a year.[9]

While the Plan proposed 'to establish industry on a well planned basis and to direct it in the correct economic and technical path', it merely catalogued a lengthy and often contradictory list of priorities which does not inspire confidence that the 150 projects which formed the core of the Plan had been carefully chosen.[10] The Ministry published no information about how the Plan would be financed, or how projects would be executed.[11] Apparently the intention was to provide 61 per cent of the finance from public

[5] J. Tinbergen, *Draft Reports on Egyptian Planning* (1957), NPC Memos 164 & 165.

[6] *BE*, 28 Oct. 1956.

[7] *Industry after the Revolution*, pp. 89 & 198.

[8] Ibid. p. 101 and table 7. [9] Ibid. p. 165 and see table 8.

[10] Ibid. pp. 93 & 102–4 and *UAR Yearbook 1959*, p. 150.

[11] The Plan was criticized for neglecting finance by NBE, *Econ. B.*, iii (1957), p. 230.

sources, for projects mainly in heavy or pioneer industries, leaving light and more profitable manufacturing to private investment.[12] Achievement of targets, the Minister recognized, depended on attracting capital into industry and co-operating with businessmen.[13] Yet they had not been consulted in designing the Plan. Nor were any institutions established to facilitate co-operation between the public and private sectors for the construction and timing of projects. On the contrary, both the Councils for the Development of National Production and Public Service (consultative bodies on which private business had hitherto been represented) were replaced by a purely public organization, the National Planning Committee, thereby terminating what one Egyptian economist described as 'the years of partial planning'.[14]

Egyptian leaders constantly re-emphasized the need for co-operation between public and private enterprise but their actions, and occasionally their more frank utterances, indicate how determined they were to achieve a higher rate of industrial growth by means of closer control over the flow of the nation's investible funds.[15] The government had already noticed that the response to tax and other incentives introduced after 1952 in order to attract private savings into industry had proved disappointing. Most investors apparently preferred to place their money in real estate, and total investment in buildings rose from £40 millions in 1954 to £59 millions in 1958.[16] Their preference represented to some extent an 'irrational' antipathy to industrial equities but was mainly a natural response to higher returns on investment in housing engendered by the population explosion and ever-increasing urbanization of Egypt. Nevertheless the government in September 1956 took firm steps to curb the real-estate boom by making the erection or improvement of buildings, costing £500 and above,

[12] These proportions relate to the preliminary estimates of 1957 (see S. Amin, 'Le Financement des investissements dans la Province égyptienne de la RAU', *Ég. contemp.*, Jan. 1960, p. 7; *UAR Econ. Features*, p. 75; *EG*, spec. issue on industry, July 1957.

[13] *Industry after the Revolution*, p. 93.

[14] A. Morshidy, *Planning Economic Development in the UAR* (unpubl. report to UN, 1963), p. 24.

[15] *BE*, 31 Jan., 31 May, 2 & 22 June, 4 July 1956.

[16] Total investments in 'buildings' recorded by the FIE, *Ann.* rose from £40 m. in 1954 to £42.5 m. in 1955, £51.4 m. in 1956, £53.4 m. in 1957, and £59 m. in 1958 but dropped to £43 m. in 1959.

subject to official licence.[17] To discourage such 'anti-social' investment still further, law 55 of 1958 reduced rents by 20 per cent on all accommodation erected after September 1952.[18]

Building licences might be used to arrest the flow of resources in disapproved directions, but they provided the government with no powers to push savings towards industry. Tax incentives had proved a weak stimulus, and in their search for ways of raising the rate of investment in industry the Officers, for sound technical reasons, turned to the organized, or corporate, sector of Egyptian business. When the National Planning Committee studied domestic resources available for development, it found savings by households constituted only a small proportion of total Egyptian savings and were directed mainly towards housing and bank deposits.[19] Retained profits of the non-organized business sector (individuals, partnerships, and small-scale private companies) contributed more to domestic savings than households, but these funds were normally ploughed back into business. Further, because of administrative difficulties in dealing with a multiplicity of small-scale business units, they could not be utilized for purposes decided by the state.[20] There remained the retained profits of organized business. In 1954 these profits provided about half of total Egyptian savings and they could, in the opinion of the Planning Committee, be easily mobilized.[21]

Although the ratios cited by the National Planning Committee are only a very rough guide to the relative importance of different sources for investible funds, the government's decision to focus attention upon organized business seems to have been based upon a realistic appraisal that it could, if necessary, compel corporate enterprises to retain and invest more profits in projects listed in the Industrial Plan, whereas the savings of households and family firms were probably beyond public control.[22] Thus law 7 of 1959 fixed the amount of dividends corporate enterprises were allowed

[17] Industrial Bank, *Ann. Report 1956* (ar.), p. 15.

[18] NPC Memo. 185, *Ways of Financing the Plan* (1959, ar.).

[19] NPC Memo. 113, *Estimates of Savings for 1959–63* (1958, ar.) and table 18 (p. 333).

[20] NPC Memos 138 & 173, *Estimating Savings in the Non-Organized Sector* (1959, ar.) and table 18.

[21] NPC Memo. 113.

[22] Bank Misr, *Econ. B.*, Mar. 1959, p. 101 and *UAR Yearbook 1960*, pp. 113 & 114.

to distribute at not more than 10 per cent above their level for the previous year and compelled firms to invest in government bonds a proportion of their net profits equal to 5 per cent of the amount paid to shareholders.[23]

The government's commitment to plan industry not only led to the imposition of controls over the flow of investible funds but it presaged that only manufacturing projects approved by the state would be countenanced in future.[24]

The Minister of Industry spoke clearly and frankly about the implications of the Plan, which he recognized 'paved the way towards government interference directly and indirectly in industrial activities'.[25] Those concerned would 'be directed towards collaboration if necessary'.[26] Moreover he did not equivocate over the question of initiative for enterprise but admitted candidly:

> If capitalists were left free to invest their capital in the industries they liked or were able to determine the place, volume and object of their projects in the manner they desired without control or supervision or guidance from the Government, whose task is to see that they avoid ways leading to risks and to protect them from the consequences of bad investment great harm would befall the public welfare. It has been observed that this absolute liberty most often leads to the existence of industrial projects not needed in any way for the national economy.[27]

At the beginning of 1958 the Minister introduced a law which made the establishment, expansion, change of purpose or location of any industrial plant subject to licence by his Ministry.[28]

Promulgating laws was easy, actual enforcement was another matter, but control over the operations and investment policies of corporate enterprises already partly owned by the state could obviously be exercised with least difficulty. Making all such enterprises responsible to a single public authority ensured that a unified policy would be more efficiently implemented. Thus in January 1957 the government placed nearly all industrial and commercial property possessed by the public under the manage-

[23] *UAR Yearbook 1959*, p. 137. [24] *BE*, 7 & 18 Oct. 1956.
[25] Bank Misr, *Econ. B.*, June 1959, p. 5.
[26] *Industry after the Revolution*, p. 93.
[27] Ibid. app. 4.
[28] Law 21 of 1958 for Organizing and Encouraging Industry.

ment of a single institution, the Economic Organization, which became, during its brief existence of four years, the most important government agency for promoting industrial expansion.[29]

Just how widespread the influence of the Economic Organization upon industry was between 1957 and 1961 is, however, difficult to gauge. Thirty-one industrial firms were affiliated to it in 1958. Some were old-established public enterprises, such as petrol refineries. Others had been founded more recently in combination with private capital. A third group represented former British and French assets sequestrated during the Suez war. The Economic Organization embraced a complex of industrial property covering steel, minerals, chemicals, and textiles. But the production of these firms amounted to under 12 per cent of total industrial output, nor did they provide employment for more than 10 per cent of the industrial labour force.[30] At first glance the Economic Organization appears fairly insignificant, but by placing its activities within the context of total industrial production, its importance is definitely underestimated. As has already been pointed out, the area of production amenable to public control was represented by organized business. Family firms, repair and workshops are part of the industrial sector and swell the total of industrial output, but they are, by and large, outside the province of an industrial policy. If we exclude small firms from view and concentrate upon the area of production encompassed by organized business, then the importance of the Economic Organization can be assessed in a more relevant way.[31] Within this more restricted sector of industry the firms affiliated to the Economic Organization produced roughly a third of aggregate output and employed about 20 per cent of the labour force.[32] The companies affiliated to the Economic

[29] Economic Organization, *Yearbook 1958–9* (ar.), pp. 259–71 and A. R. Ali, *Commercial Banking in Egypt* (1961, ar.), pp. 90–92.

[30] These ratios have been calculated from gross output figures published in *Gen. Frame of 5-Year Plan*, tables 50 & 92, Min. of Treasury, *Budget Project 1961–2* (1961), p. 61, and Dept. of Statist., *Census of Industrial Production 1959*, publ. in *Statist. Pocket Yearbook 1960*, table 34.

[31] Firms employing 10 or more workers accounted for 56 per cent of *net* industrial output and employed 46 per cent of the labour force.

[32] I have assumed, not quite accurately, that the output from 'organized' industry is equal to the output of firms employing more than 10 workers. The proportion of output again refers to gross output. Net output figures are not available.

Organization were, therefore, fairly important within that sphere of industry amenable to centralized authority.

How legally and actually the government exercised that authority is again by no means obvious. Where the state owned 25 per cent and more of the shares of a company, the Organization possessed the power to appoint a majority of directors to its board and the Managing Director. Most companies affiliated to the Economic Organization came into this category; even if the state's shareholding was less than 25 per cent, the Organization was still entitled to be represented on the board of directors.[33] Policy decisions of all companies had to be reported, and where the state owned 25 per cent of the capital the Organization could demand revisions of policy.[34]

Although its legal powers were certainly extensive, it is difficult to make an assessment of the kind and degree of public control the Economic Organization in fact exercised over affiliated companies. One journal considered the Organization appointed representatives to their boards of directors in order 'to ensure operations are directed to public benefit';[35] another that it functioned as a 'managing centre for the State as entrepreneur and investor'.[36] Official statements invariably emphasized that relations between the Organization and the management of constituent companies was one of partnership, and in 1960 the Department of Information was at pains to refute 'prejudiced elements' who had rumoured 'the relation was one of control, domination and exclusivity' by stating categorically, 'relations have been one of co-operation and participation in these companies orientation with a view to ensuring harmony between public and private economic activity'.[37]

While the evidence published so far does not form a sufficient basis for an appraisal of the degree of actual control exercised by the Economic Organization, the government had certainly provided it with sufficient authority over the investment and produc-

[33] At the end of 1959 57 companies were affiliated to the Economic Organization in all, but 10 of the state's shareholding was 25 per cent and above (*UAR Yearbook 1959*, p. 182).

[34] Economic Organization, *Yearbook 1958–9*, pp. 17–18 and Bank Misr, *Econ. B.*, Sept. 1957, p. 7.

[35] *EEPR*, Feb. 1957, p. 29. [36] NBE, *Econ. B.*, ii (1958), p. 103.

[37] Min. Fin. & Econ., *Budget Report 1957–8*, pp. 13 & 16; *UAR Yearbooks 1959* & *1960*, pp. 93 & 181, and statements by Min. of Treasury in *EG*, 28 Aug. 1957.

tion policies of companies in which the state owned shares to ensure that they participated in plans for industrial expansion.

The other area of organized industry amenable to government authority and pressure was the giant complex of industrial and commercial assets controlled by Bank Misr. The Bank, together with Egyptian capitalists, had promoted companies since its foundation in 1920. It also sponsored new capital issues by established concerns and provided credit, both long and short term, to firms in which it held shares. The Bank retained, in its own portfolio, only a part of the share capital of subsidiary companies but had an important say in their management, and directors of Misr companies were frequently directors of the Bank as well.[38]

Bank Misr had established shipping, publishing, hotel, and insurance firms. The Misr Group produced chemicals, pharmaceutical products, edible oils, cement, and above all textiles.[39] Textiles, as has been shown, dominated Egyptian industry.[40] Misr spinning and weaving firms produced about 60 per cent of the output and employed 53 per cent of the labour force engaged in the organized sector of textile production.[41]

Links between the state and Bank Misr had been close almost from its inception. In 1922, when the Ministry of Finance began offering loans to industrialists, Bank Misr was chosen to administer the scheme. In fact most industrial finance supplied by the state went to Misr companies.[42] At the beginning of the war when a run on the Bank occurred the government stepped in and guaranteed its deposits, repaid £2 million of its debts, and avoided a bankruptcy which could have had serious repercussions on the whole of industry. In return the Ministry of Finance reorganized the administration of Bank Misr, took over some of its share capital

[38] Bank Misr, *Econ. B.*, Dec. 1959, pp. 36–37 & Jan. 1960, pp. 46–49 and Gritly, pp. 433–40.

[39] Min. of Treasury, *Budget Project 1960–1*, p. 74 and *UAR Yearbook 1959*, p. 134.

[40] Textiles provided 43 per cent of the net output, 41 per cent of the employment, and nearly two-thirds of the earnings in foreign exchange for Egyptian industrial firms employing more than 10 workers (Dept. of Statistics, *Census of Industr. Prod'n 1957*, in *Statist. Pocket Yearbook 1958*, table 34).

[41] Bank Misr, *Econ. B.*, Jan. 1960, p. 43.

[42] Industr. Bank, *Dev. of Industr. Credit*, pp. 7–8 and Gritly, p. 433.

and assumed the power to veto appointments to its board of directors.[43] After 1956 the Officers made more and more use of such powers and impelled the Misr group to participate in their plans for industrial expansion.[44] According to estimates published by the Ministry of Industry in 1959, the Misr group were made responsible for nearly half of all activity undertaken by private enterprise as part of the Industrial Plan.[45] Misr textile companies certainly played the dominant part in executing spinning and weaving projects; out of an investment expenditure of £23 million on such projects in 1959, £18 million came from the group.[46]

Given the Free Officers' determination to influence the flow of investible funds, it is not surprising to find that the state attempted to regulate the allocation of credit by local banks. Monetary controls are, after all, among the most available and readily implemented devices open to governments concerned to influence the pattern of investment. Before 1957 control over the Egyptian banking system had been conducted under law 57 of 1951. Under that statute a privately-owned institution, the National Bank of Egypt, exercised all normal functions of a central bank. It enjoyed, for example, a monopoly of note issue and operated as the government's bank and a lender of last resort. The National Bank had charge of implementing monetary policy and foreign-exchange regulations. With that charge went legal powers to compel commercial banks to maintain fixed cash reserve and liquid asset ratios and to conduct open-market operations as well as authority to vary the bank rate and ration accommodation to commercial banks. Although the National Bank was privately owned, its constitution gave the government powers of control over its operations. Monetary policy was made by the Supreme Committee of the Bank presided over by the Minister of Finance. The committee consisted of 7 members, 5 of whom, including the Governor, were government appointees. On the other hand overall responsibility for the implementation of monetary policy rested with the board of 13 directors, elected by shareholders of the Bank. The board

[43] Gritly, pp. 442–4.

[44] This statement summarizes the views of economists and officials with whom I discussed this question in Cairo in the winter of 1962–3.

[45] Amin, in *Ég. contemp.*, Jan. 1960.

[46] Bank Misr, *Econ. B.*, Jan. 1960, p. 34.

included, however, the Governor and his deputy, both appointed by the state.[47]

By 1957 the government was evidently dissatisfied with the existing system of state control over the money supply and the allocation of credit, because the new and comprehensive Banking and Credit Law of that year strengthened both the power of the state over its central bank and the power of the central bank over commercial banks. Thus both the making and administration of monetary policy came to be centralized in a single committee chaired by the Minister of Finance and dominated by state nominees. The government required the Bank 'to regulate the availability and cost of credit in such a way that the *real* requirements of the commercial, industrial and agricultural sectors are met'. It empowered the Bank to fix interest rates for all banks; to control not merely their reserve and liquid asset ratios, but also to prevent commercial banks from holding assets in lines of investment which were not officially permitted and to ensure that banks observed the ceilings placed by the government on certain types of loans. Control was made more effective by compelling banks to register with the National Bank, to publish detailed statements about their credit operations, and to submit their accounts to a public audit. [48]

Egyptian banks are of two types: specialist institutions involved mainly with the finance of particular types of economic activity, and commercial banks of a British model. In terms of total credit transactions the latter are much more important, and in 1959 their total advances amounted to about eight times the loans by specialist banks. Before 1956 most of the capital of commercial banks operating in Egypt was owned by British and French nationals while the ownership of specialist banks was pretty well confined to Egyptians or to the Egyptian government, who owned the Crédit Hypothécaire (a real estate bank) and held half the shares of the Industrial Bank and the Agricultural and Co-operative Bank.[49]

[47] H. Fahmy, 'The Technique of Central Banking in Egypt', *ME Econ. Papers 1954*, pp. 57, 63, & 71–72, NBE, *Econ. B.*, ii (1957), pp. 245–52 & ii (1958), pp. 121–4, and Ali, pp. 103–7.

[48] Law 163, 1957.

[49] Economic Organization, *Yearbook 1958–9*, pp. 59–78 and Tanamli, in *Ég. contemp.*, Oct. 1962, pp. 16–18.

When the Free Officers sequestrated British and French assets during the Suez war, the government emerged as the owner of a majority interest in 7 commercial banks, 2 specialist institutions—the Crédit Foncier and the Land Bank—and 5 insurance companies. All sequestrated property, together with the Industrial Bank, the Agricultural and Co-operative Bank, and the Crédit Hypothécaire, already partly owned by the government, were placed under direct supervision of the Economic Development Organization.[50] Thus by 1958 the state, through the Organization, controlled all specialist banks in Egypt, 7 commercial banks whose loans represented just under half of all lending by commercial banks in Egypt, and 5 insurance companies, whose activities accounted for well over 68 per cent of all insurance business transacted in Egypt.[51] Insurance funds did not, however, contribute very much to the finance of domestic capital formation.[52]

Initially the sequestration of enemy property represented a reaction to the Anglo-French attack, but the impetus grew into 'Egyptianizing the main arteries of the national economy'.[53] All foreign banks, insurance companies, and commercial agencies were compelled to convert themselves into domestically-owned joint-stock companies within five years. This policy was described by the government as a nationalist measure designed to rid the country of foreign influence over the investment policies of Egypt's financial institutions.[54] Egyptianization, it claimed, had 'given back to the citizens the right to direct their own capital' or 'the right to manage their own funds', and foreign banks and insurance companies were simply transformed into Egyptian institutions.[55]

But whatever their main motive or origin, the Egyptianization laws placed the state in a perfect position to control the main

[50] Econ. Organization, *Yearbook 1958–9*, pp. 59–78 & 89–91 lists the assets of sequestrated banks and insurance companies. The 7 foreign banks were amalgamated to form 4 companies and renamed Bank Alexandria, Republic Bank, Cairo Bank, and Union Bank.

[51] Min. of Treasury, *Budget Report 1960–1*, pp. 69–70 and *UAR Yearbook 1959*, p. 97.

[52] NPC Memo. 79, *The Activities of Insurance Companies* (1959, ar.).

[53] Min. of Treasury, *Budget Report 1956–7*, p. 10.

[54] Min. Econ., *Economic Progress in the UAR*, pp. 89–93; *UAR Yearbooks 1959 & 1960*, pp. 101–3 & 89.

[55] Ali, pp. 84–90; *Budget Report 1956–7*, p. 11 and *UAR Yearbook 1959*, p. 101.

channels of finance. In reality there seems to have been no question of turning over financial institutions of such strategic importance to private entrepreneurs: a course which seemed implied by the term 'Egyptianization' as well as by government statements explaining its policy. Instead the principal banks and insurance companies came under the Economic Organization, which conducted their operations 'in conformity with the national interest' or 'put the banking system on the right track towards the economic benefits of the country'.[56]

Dr Kaissouny's budget speech of 1957 recognized that 'the functions of government are no longer restricted to the classical ones of achieving security, justice, and defence, but have come to be varied and extended far and wide'.[57] Certainly the government abandoned the former policy of merely encouraging investment in industry in favour of a much more positive approach. Its ambitious plan for industrialization led to direct interference with the flow of investible funds. First of all the law checked investment in real estate. Then, through the Economic Organization and Misr Group, the state compelled the organized sector of industry to retain more profits and invest them only in approved ways, and the major companies virtually lost the power to initiate their own investment projects.

Finally, the nationalization of foreign banks and insurance companies, together with the existing system of control over foreign exchange, gave the government sufficient powers to regulate and determine the allocation of finance throughout most of the economy. By 1958 the state had, it seems, attained a position where investment could be planned.

AGRICULTURE

The government had not, however, obtained anything like the same powers over the agricultural sector. Farmers, as in so many other societies, eluded central authority. Agricultural policies are classified in Egypt into horizontal and vertical. Horizontal policies are concerned with adding to the area of land and with the

[56] *EG*, spec. issue, July 1957, p. 12; *Budget Report 1960–1*, p. 72, and *UAR Yearbook 1959*, p. 101.

[57] *Budget Report 1957–8*, p. 49.

quantity of irrigation water made available for agricultural production, matters which have, generally speaking, traditionally been left to the state. Vertical policies are related to the productivity of land and the men who work it, and in the past efficiency was overwhelmingly the province of private enterprise. Although the main emphasis of policy since the revolution continued to be directed towards land reclamation and improvements to the irrigation system, the government had also increased its interest in yields from the land; a concern which became reflected in rising public expenditure on projects for vertical expansion in agriculture. Public money was allocated to the kinds of projects long recommended by those who have studied Egyptian agricultural problems. Much of it appears to have gone into basic research designed to discover seeds, livestock strains, pesticides, and animal medicines appropriate to the Nile valley. Soil surveys were initiated to find out the particular crops and fertilizers most suitable for different parts of the valley, and experiments conducted to determine optimum amounts of moisture necessary for various crops and how best to drain off surplus water. Public funds were also spent on propagating new discoveries and methods among farmers. Improved strains of cotton, wheat, and rice seeds were distributed free over wide areas. To demonstrate the efficacy of modern agricultural inputs the government built extension centres in many villages and the Ministry of Agriculture mobilized special campaigns in order to introduce farmers to techniques for combating animal and plant diseases.[58]

Of course, the introduction of innovations proceeded most easily on lands already controlled (in some way) by the state. For example, on land reform co-operatives fragmentation of holdings had been avoided by allowing beneficiaries three strips of land distributed among three large fields over which the co-operative enforced a common rotation. This system avoided the diseconomies of scattered strips growing a multiplicity of crops, often intermingled; and also prevented farmers from impairing soil fecundity by unscientific crop rotations.[59] The co-operative purchased seeds

[58] PCDNP, *Report 1955* (ar.), pp. 66–78; Marei, *UAR Agriculture*, pp. 78–84; *UAR Yearbook 1959*, pp. 237–53.

[59] M. Darling, 'Land Reform in Italy and Egypt', *Yearbook of Agricultural Co-operation 1956*, p. 18.

and fertilizers, and the fight against pests and plant and animal disease was also undertaken collectively.[60] The Ministry of Agrarian Reform usually appointed agronomists as managers of the new co-operatives in order to facilitate the dissemination of new methods among farmers, and in the last resort these managers had sufficient power to compel their members to adopt whatever methods of cultivation the ministry thought advisable.[61] But land reform co-operatives covered only a fraction of Egyptian agriculture. Although the redistributed area had increased somewhat by the inclusion of *waqf* land and by compelling reclamation companies to sell a quarter of their lands to the state, not more than 12 per cent of the total cultivable area had been subjected to control by the Ministry of Agrarian Reform at the end of 1959.[62]

Co-operative farming was also practised on land newly reclaimed by the government. Farmers in Liberation Province, for example, were carefully selected and closely regulated even though they legally owned the land.[63] Presumably the million feddans reclaimed by the High Dam will be made subject to some similar system of supervised cultivation, but even when the dam is complete, the area of cultivable land under direct government control would still be only approximately a third of the total area.[64] In 1957, when the benefits from the dam appeared to be at least a decade away and something had to be done immediately in order to increase yields, particularly on smaller farms outside land reform areas, the government decided to extend co-operation to cover all farmers throughout the countryside.

No doubt the brief experience with the agrarian reform co-operatives, as well as the longer experience with credit co-operatives, convinced the government that it could influence the process of cultivation more easily if peasants were organized into groups. At the very least co-operatives facilitated communication between the Ministry of Agriculture and the thousands of small farmers

[60] Marei, *UAR Agriculture*, p. 57.

[61] Under Law 554 of 1955 beneficiaries of land reform could be evicted for mismanagement of their holdings.

[62] *EG*, 18 July 1957 and Saab, in *ME Econ. Papers 1960*, pp. 73–74.

[63] Warriner, pp. 49–52.

[64] There are a number of estimates of land area which will be reclaimed when the Dam is in operation. I used the figure of 1 million feddans cited in a report of the High Dam Authority, *Economic Aspects of the High Dam* (1962 ar.), p. 3.

scattered along the Nile valley The articles of association within which co-operatives were formed and had operated in Egypt likewise presented the government with opportunities to 'guide' their activities. For example, the law obliged co-operatives to register with the Ministry of Social Affairs and to submit their accounts to public audit, and the Minister possessed the right to veto decisions taken by local societies.[65]

Before the revolution the state encouraged the formation of co-operatives by offering their members cheap credit and, to a more limited extent, supplies of seed and fertilizers at reduced prices. Public funds had been channelled to peasants through the Agricultural Credit and Co-operative Bank, founded on the initiative of the state in 1931, to meet the needs of small farmers for short-term loans at reasonable rates of interest. By 1956 nearly 2,000 co-operative societies had been formed to take advantage of the facilities offered by the Bank and to realize economies from bulk buying and, less commonly, marketing on behalf of their members.[66] Thus when the government decided to organize all Egyptian farmers into co-operatives it found the Agricultural Credit and Co-operative Bank a most useful institution for its purposes. From 1957 the cheaper credit offered to farmers by the Bank became available only to members of co-operatives. Similarly, co-operatives alone became eligible for purchases of seed, fertilizers, and farm implements sold by the Bank at reduced prices. Co-operatives also received state grants for educational and social welfare amenities provided on behalf of their members.[67] Farmers were not compelled to join co-operatives, but the government offered them every inducement to become members.

At the same time co-operatives and agricultural credit changed from being the means for ameliorating the poverty of small farmers into instruments of state policy for raising yields throughout agriculture. All co-operatives were linked to the Agricultural Bank, which became responsible for supervising their activities and appointed staff for their management. As Dr Tanamli observed: 'The system of co-operative credit has been established in Egypt

[65] See Shabanah, *Co-operative Agricultural Economy* (ar.), pp. 130–4.

[66] Garzouzi, pp. 42–43 and Tanamli, in *Ég. contemp.*, Oct. 1962, pp. 29 f., 30, 34 f.

[67] *EG*, 13 Oct. & 25 Dec. 1957 and Garzouzi, pp. 38–43.

with the understanding that the Crédit Agricole is to supervise the use to which loans are put.'[68] Thus the farmers' need for credit on reasonable terms encouraged them to form co-operatives and provided the state with the opportunity to see that loans were used in ways approved by the Ministry of Agriculture. The provision of cheap credit thus went hand in hand with strong influence by the Bank over land use, crop rotation, and seed and fertilizer selection.[69] To ensure that his loan is 'correctly' utilized the farmer frequently received not cash but seeds, fertilizers, and implements selected for him by government officials.[70]

CONCLUSION

After 1956 the Free Officers moved away from their previous policy for the development of the economy through the encouragement of private investment in favour of higher rates of public capital formation, distributed partly among spheres of traditional interest to the state such as power supplies and irrigation facilities but also allocated to ambitious projects designed to accelerate the growth of industry.

By 1959 almost a complete reversal of roles had occurred in responsibility for the country's capital formation. The figures are crude but they reveal rough orders of magnitude and indicate that, for the years 1952 and 1953, 72 per cent of gross capital formation was carried out by the private sector.[71] By 1959–60, 74 per cent was undertaken by the state.[72] The government's share of investment had grown steadily since the revolution until it became dominant.[73] In 1959 private enterprise still built most of the houses erected in Egypt. It played an important part in the provision of motorized and marine transport, storage facilities, equipment for small-scale manufacturing, and the assets required

[68] Tanamli, p. 34.

[69] Marei, *Agrarian Reform in Egypt* (1957), pp. 121–2.

[70] Min. Agric., *Towards a Socialist Agriculture* (1962, ar.), pp. 301–15; *UAR Yearbook 1959*, pp. 272–5; *Budget Report 1956–7*, pp. 19–20.

[71] See table 14 (p. 329 below).

[72] This ratio has been calculated from the figures in tables 12 & 13 (pp. 327–8).

[73] According to one series of statistics compiled by the NPC, the government's share of gross domestic fixed capital formation rose from 34 per cent in 1953 to 49 per cent for 1954, 54 per cent for 1955, and 63 per cent for 1956 (UN, *Econ. Developments in the Middle East 1956–7*, p. 13).

for financial, commercial, and trading services. But the new fixed capital required for the country's electrical power supplies, for agricultural and for the major part of industrial production was being provided by the government.

As a result of the state's increased investment activity, significant inroads had been made into the autonomy of private enterprise in order to prevent investible funds going into projects not approved of by the government and also to avoid competition between private and public sectors for scarce resources which could easily lead to inflation. Thus the government asserted its control over all companies in which it held shares, tried to regulate the distribution of dividends in organized business, and through its special relationship with the Misr group managed to manœuvre into a position where it could exercise strong influence over the profits and investment policies of several large corporations.

Controls over investment had not, however, been accompanied by much additional regulation of production itself. The Minister of Industry's powers to define specifications for industrial products and raw materials and to fix prices and profit margins for organized business seem to have been held in abeyance. Those who managed or owned non-corporate enterprises, which dominated production in agriculture, commercial services, internal trade, and construction, probably remained almost unaware of any additional constraints upon their discretion as producers. Legally, house owners could no longer charge whatever rents they could obtain. Some producers found the government refused to make foreign exchange available for the purchase of particular kinds of 'unnecessary' imports; others may have experienced difficulties in obtaining bank credit to finance activities not sanctioned by the government; while farmers certainly found officials of the Agricultural Bank more ready to interfere with the way they cultivated their lands. But on the whole the prerogatives of private producers had not been significantly curtailed since the revolution, although they may well have been uneasy at the more positive part played by the state in Egyptian economic affairs, and may also have resented the fact they were being compelled more and more to manage their concerns within the framework of some overall system of priorities for the development of the economy.

While the state had assumed almost complete responsibility for investment and Egyptian leaders had committed the economy to comprehensive planning, up to the nationalizations of 1961 they appeared uneasily suspended or even ambiguous as far as their economic ideology was concerned. Even the most enthusiastic planners, like the Minister for Industry, repeatedly insisted that development could only be achieved with the co-operation of the private sector.[74] Dr Kaissouny assured businessmen that the government had not established the Economic Organization to compete with them but merely to stimulate private investment.[75] On the other hand President Nasser told the Third Co-operative Congress at the end of 1957 that Egypt was now moving towards a 'Socialist, Democratic, and Co-operative Society' and the Egyptian press publicized this slogan most enthusiastically. The speech also contained several words of warning against 'opportunistic individualism and exploitation of the people by a profiteering minority', and the President promised the state would watch over capitalists to see that resources were employed for the service of the country. 'Economic initiative', he considered, 'must be the state's, which protects the interest of all classes'. His government intended to study production possibilities and co-operate with private capital towards their realization.[76] A month later, on the eve of Union with Syria, the President refused to go farther in defining the Egyptian economic system and denied that he had an economic doctrine, but in the course of a press interview talked revealingly about controlled capitalism.[77]

No doubt a 'Socialist, Democratic, and Co-operative Society' seemed a somewhat inept political slogan upon which to build union with a country like Syria, where the virtues of private enterprise had always been so strongly lauded. The provisional constitution of the United Arab Republic, promulgated in March 1958, was certainly less explicit on questions of economic organization than its Egyptian counterpart of January 1956. Part 2 of the constitution, called 'Basic Constituents of the Society', states

National economy is organised according to plans which conform to the principles of social justice . . . private property is inviolable; the

[74] Min. Industry, *Industry after the Revolution*, p. 93; *EG*, 7 July 1957; Bertier, in *Orient*, ii (1958).

[75] *Budget Report 1957–8*, p. 13 and *EG*, 7 July 1957.

[76] *EG*, 6 Dec. 1957.

[77] *Nasser's Speeches 1958*, pp. 362 & 403.

law organises its social function. Property may not be expropriated except for purposes of public utility and in consideration of just compensation in accordance with the law.[78]

For most of 1959 the press published very little about the 'Socialist, Democratic, and Co-operative Society' so readily vaunted at the end of 1957, while the President's speeches and interviews usually contained assurances and encouragement for private enterprise. 'Under no condition and in no circumstance would we look with envy or rancour upon national capital.' 'Private capital is free so long as it works for the general welfare of society.' 'Our aim is not to . . . control private factories. But it is important for us that private factories should continue with their working for public interest.'[79] No doubt M. Bertier is correct in insisting that the term 'socialism' as used in Egypt in 1958 and 1959 implied something like association or co-operation for the common good and had little of the content normally associated with it in a European context.[80] Some change in the attitude of Egyptian leaders towards private enterprise was, however, perceptible for, as Professor Vatikiotis points out, 'to read President Nasser's speeches of 1958 and 1959 is to recognize the apparent shift in emphasis'.[81] The introduction of a comprehensive Five-Year Plan in 1960 pushed the Egyptian leaders into more specific statements about the kind of economic system they wished to create and also revealed more sharply certain incompatibilities between central planning and private enterprise.

[78] The Provisional Constitution of the United Arab Republic (*Nasser's Speeches 1958*, app. 1).

[79] *Nasser's Speeches 1959*, pp. 185, 357, & 358.

[80] Bertier, in *Orient*, ii (1958).

[81] Vatikiotis, p. 137.

V

Private Enterprise and the First Five-Year Plan

THE PROCESS OF PLANNING

NOWHERE does the ambivalent attitude of Egyptian leaders towards private enterprise appear more obvious than in the formulation of the Comprehensive Five-Year Plan, drafted during the second half of 1959. Most capital formation planned for 1960 to 1965 was to be undertaken by the state: a fact which confirms and clarifies the subsidiary role private enterprise had come to play in the long-term development of the Egyptian economy. Nevertheless, official publications and speeches nearly all insist or imply that the Plan, as originally formulated, represented an effort of co-operation between government and private business. Both in his speech introducing the Plan to the National Union and in a foreword to the Plan itself, the Minister of Planning made this point explicitly. 'Co-operation, collaboration and integrated efforts between the various groups and the private and public sectors are among the fundamental principles on which this plan is founded.'[1] 'Thus the proposed plan', Vice-President Boghdadi also said, 'was not laid out by a few experts, it is rather the fruit of continuous efforts and long experience on the part of the technical departments in all Ministries as well as public and private organizations.'[2]

Morshidy (a Director-General of the Minister of Planning) has described in some detail in his report to the United Nations the way the Plan was built up. Apparently the government established six main committees, for industry, agriculture, irrigation, transport, public services, and economic and financial problems. About 500 persons sat on these committees and their sub-committees representing 'all government departments and agencies, all private business social and labour institutions, and well as private indi-

[1] *Gen. Frame of 5-Year Plan*, p. viii.

[2] A. Boghdadi, *Speech to the National Union*, 4 July 1960 (1960), p. 14.

viduals'. Their function was to study resources and recommend programmes for the particular sector covered by the committee. Throughout the construction of the plan, insists Morshidy,

a spirit of close co-operation has prevailed between the National Planning Committee, the various Ministries, Public and Private Organizations. Above all there existed the common wish to realise the objectives and to prepare the national plan in the best possible manner and within the time fixed for it.[3]

Mixed Committees certainly met in the early months of 1959, but just how far they represented the private sector is impossible to say without a very detailed study of their personnel. Nor is the relationship between their reports and the Plan Frame at all clear. As far as manpower, consumption, and foreign trade projections are concerned, a comparison of reports from Mixed Committees with the Plan Frame does seem to justify calling the relationship tenuous,[4] although the government included many of the projects recommended by the Committees on Industry, Agriculture, and Transport in the Plan.[5] But on the very crucial question relating to the potential volume of resources available for the achievement of a higher rate of growth, a definite difference of opinion arose between the Mixed Committee on Economic and Financial Problems and the National Planning Committee. On the basis of their studies and projections of domestic savings and foreign exchange likely to be available, the Mixed Committee argued that the growth rate suggested by the National Planning Committee was too optimistic.[6] Both committees must, therefore, have been somewhat confounded by the President's decision to select a growth rate even higher than either of their original recommendations. As the Ministry of Information explained, 'economists have estimated a period of 20 years for the execution of the plan. It has been decided to amend the plan so as to ensure the execution of

[3] Morshidy, pp. 31, 58, & 60 f.; see also I. Abdel-Rahman & N. Dief, *Social Aspects of Development Planning in the UAR* (1961), INP Memo. 76.

[4] NPC, Memos 219, 245 & 246, *Reports of Committees on Foreign Exchange. Manpower Potential, and Consumption* (1959, ar.).

[5] NPC, Memos 201–10, 221–40, & 249–61, *Reports of Committees on Transport, Industry, and Agriculture* (1959, ar.); cf. with the projects listed in Comité de Planification Nationale, *Cadre du Plan 1960–5* (1960), pp. 195–265.

[6] This controversy is covered by NPC Memos 113, 124, 134, 163, 216–17, 218–20, & 292 (1959, ar.).

the programme on a revolutionary basis in a period of 10 years'.[7] Thus a comparison of the Mixed Committee reports with the Plan Frame supports the conclusion that for most of the crucial decisions about planning the advice of the private sector, in so far as it was represented by these committees, was probably ignored.

Yet the participation and active co-operation of private business was vital to the success of the Plan. Since the revolution the state had certainly eroded the autonomy and reduced the overall importance of the private sector, but on the eve of planning the Egyptian economy still retained the appearance of a free-enterprise system. The Officers' commitment to plan *comprehensively* appears somewhat ambitious in the face of the large areas of production which remained outside government control. Just how ambitious can be appreciated from the social accounts included as part of the Plan Frame. These accounts distinguish between the private and public sectors and, furthermore, divide the public sector into 'Government Administration' and 'Government Business'. The former contained 'public organizations which undertake to furnish collective services to society either of the classical type such as security or justice or of the type the Government provides for the benefit of the people and not for profit'.[8] Government business, on the other hand, was defined as 'commodity producing activities, transport and communications services, economic housing and financial business undertaken in pursuit of profits either as a substitute for the private sector or as a supplement to it'.[9] Government business included all establishments subject in some way to public control. They encompassed three types of enterprise: first, establishments owned and controlled by the government since their inception, for example railways, telecommunications, postal services, and some military factories; second, establishments owned by the state as a result of the Egyptianization of alien property, such as the Suez canal, banks, and insurance companies; and third, firms entirely and partly owned by the state, placed under the control of the Economic Organization.[10] The Plan accounts for government business in

[7] *UAR Yearbook 1959*, p. 82. The NPC recommended doubling *per capita income* in 20 years but the Plan aimed to double *gross national product* in a decade.

[8] *Gen. Frame of 5-Year Plan*, p. 183.

[9] Ibid. p. 149.

[10] Ibid. pp. 150 & 183–5.

1959–60 did not include Misr companies, over which some sort of public influence was exercised through the special relationship between the state and Bank Misr, but the inclusion of these companies would have made no important difference to the overall division of the national output between public and private sectors, although it would have altered distribution within the organized industrial sector.

The national income account for the base year of the Plan, 1959–60, shows that 18 per cent of the gross domestic product originated in the public sector, as defined above, compared with about 16 per cent at the beginning of the revolution.[11] Still a minority of the working force (12 per cent) were employed by the government.[12] At first sight, and in view of the high rate of government investment since 1952, the small addition to the share of national output and employment emanating from the public sector may appear surprising. The restricted definition of 'public sector' employed by the National Planning Committee certainly underestimates the real significance of the state's contribution to output for 1959–60. To begin with the Committee excluded the Misr group from the public sector despite the fact that their investment policies were regulated by the state.[13] Furthermore, the Committee defined land reform farms as private sector; a part of agriculture which, it could be argued, might be more appropriately classified as government business. But the main reason for the surprisingly small public contribution to total output is probably that most public capital formation since the revolution had taken the form of irrigation facilities, transport, or power supplies, that is investment which was characterized by high capital output and capital-labour ratios and which, moreover, had the effect of elevating output and employment in the private sector more than it yielded directly in revenue to the state. Many of the government's industrial projects, particularly those in heavy industry, were also characterized by high capital-output ratios and long gestation periods. By 1959 very few of the projects contained in the Industrialization Plan of 1957 actually operated at capacity

[11] See table 10 (p. 325). [12] See table 11 (p. 326).

[13] In February 1960 Bank Misr was in fact nationalized in order to bring Misr Companies under more direct and definite public control (*BE*, 13 Feb. 1960).

output and most were still under construction. Significant changes had, however, occurred in two sectors of the economy: industry, where a number of state-controlled enterprises had come into operation since 1952, and transport, where nationalization of the Suez canal accounts for two-thirds of the increase in value added by this sector.[14]

THE CONTROL OF INVESTMENT

When all the qualifications have been offered for ambiguities in the definitions employed by the National Planning Committee for private and public sectors, it remains true that in 1959 the Egyptian government proposed to plan comprehensively an economy with a relatively small public sector and where at least two-thirds of national production took place outside its immediate control. The government's somewhat shallow confidence that it could go ahead even without the positive co-operation of the private sector may have been engendered by a narrow concentration on the Plan's investment targets. Since the revolution the state had appropriated more and more responsibility for capital formation, and by 1959 nearly three-quarters of gross investment was undertaken by the government. Moreover when the Plan was inaugurated in July 1960, the government had at its disposal a canopy of controls over private investment. For example, the expansion or establishment of industrial plant required permission from the Ministry of Industry. No building could be erected or improved without a licence from the Ministry of Municipalities. Any capital formation requiring imports became subject to regulation through the foreign-exchange budget, managed by the Central Bank.[15] Since the state owned most of the banking system, it was in a position to encourage or discourage investments which needed bank credit for their execution.[16] It can reasonably be concluded, from a survey of the relevant laws in operation at the beginning of 1960, that only investments which involved no building and required no bank credit or foreign exchange could have legally

[14] *Gen. Frame of 5-Year Plan*, p. 67.

[15] Morshidy, pp. 74–76.

[16] During 1960 and 1961 the government extended its control over the banking system still further by the nationalization of the National Bank of Egypt, Bank Misr, and Bank Belge (Laws 39, 40, & 288 of 1960).

escaped state control. The government could, therefore, expect not to be hampered by competition from the private sector for scarce investible resources.

Thus the draft Plan confirmed and clarified the subsidiary part private enterprise had come to play in the long-term development of the Egyptian economy and its investment projections explain, at least to some extent, the government's cavalier treatment of private business. Unfortunately the figures for total planned investment, 1960–5, contained in the Plan Frame are not divided between public and private sectors. However, the annual plans for 1960–1 and 1961–2 (formulated before the nationalizations of July 1961) make government intentions clear by showing that approximately four-fifths of all net investment during the first two years of the Plan was to be undertaken by the public sector.[17] Evidently the National Planning Committee expected that the share of investment undertaken by the private sector would rise, because by the closing year of the Plan only 61 per cent of gross capital formation was allocated as the responsibility of the state.[18]

It seems fairly clear from the figures that the government expected to organize and execute the bulk of projects contained in the Plan, but not all, and for certain parts of the economy the achievement, or even near achievement, of investment targets definitely depended on the private sector. Thus in building and construction private investors remained paramount because the Plan designated approximately 60 per cent of construction as their responsibility. Another sector in which private producers were allotted a minor but important role was in the creation of fixed assets required for trade and commercial services. Planners also left nearly a quarter of net industrial investment during the first two years of the Plan to private initiative. Outside these three sectors, in agriculture, irrigation, transport, and power supplies the achievement of investment targets was overwhelmingly a matter for government.[19]

Although the state had clearly assumed responsibility for the major part of planned investment and the Plan presaged a higher

[17] See table 16 (p. 331).

[18] Calculated from *Gen. Frame of 5-Year Plan*, tables 80–81, 85, & 89. The figures refer to gross investment. Investment figures for the target year of the Plan are, however, unreliable and ambiguous. [19] See table 16.

rate of growth for the public sector, this did not mean that the importance of the private sector had diminished to the point where it could be virtually ignored. After all, planners had blandly assumed that private industry and agriculture would grow at much faster rates and that the private sector would provide approximately 80 per cent of the planned rise in output between 1960 and 1965.[20] To plan without the active co-operation of private business does seem unrealistic because in such circumstances the ability of the state to execute projects depended very much on the achievement of output and savings targets by manufacturers, households, and farmers. Public enterprise did not and could not operate in isolation; its whole performance was linked ultimately with the rest of the economy. The National Planning Committee had, moreover, revealed these relationships in a series of commodity-flow and input-output tables appended to the Plan. The tables illustrate perfectly the interdependence of the economy and show how investment and production in the public sector depended upon the deliveries of planned quantities of intermediate goods, mainly from abroad, but to an important degree from domestic suppliers as well. If local enterprises failed to meet production targets, the government would immediately encounter supply bottle-necks and its own investment and production programme would be frustrated. Again, if private firms failed to export at the planned levels, foreign exchange would not be available for the purchase of capital goods on government account. Lastly, if manufacturers and farmers did not realize the output of consumer goods projected for them by planners, the additional incomes created by public investment would set up strong inflationary pressures which might jeopardize the success of the Plan. For example, the pressure of local demand on the available supply of consumer goods would probably reduce the sales of Egyptian commodities overseas and at the same time increase imports, thus diverting scarce foreign exchange away from planned uses. Alternatively public resources could be switched from the production of capital goods, upon which overall achievement depended,

[20] The Plan posited an annual growth rate of about 12 per cent for the public sector and 7 per cent for the private sector. The annual rates of growth for private industrial and agricultural production were planned to be approximately 7 per cent and 1 per cent higher than for the previous quinquennium (*Gen. Frame of 5-Year Plan*, tables 39–43 & see tables 10 & 19 below) (pp. 325 & 334).

towards the satisfaction of consumer demand. The government could, of course, attempt to narrow the inflationary gap through taxation or by the encouragement of further domestic saving. But for an underdeveloped country like Egypt the limits to manipulation of tax rates were quite narrow, while for reasons outlined below the government seemed unlikely to be able to stimulate higher rates of private saving.

The failure of private enterprise to achieve the production targets formulated for it by the government could in numerous direct and indirect ways seriously jeopardize the whole success of the Plan. Yet just how private firms were to be impelled or encouraged to fit in with the investment and production designs of the National Planning Committee were left rather vague, although members of the Committee had published lengthy memoranda about the administrative problems of plan implementation for the public sector.[21]

While the government could prevent the investment of funds in almost any but its own projects, it was in a very much weaker position when it came to persuade private industry and commerce to take positive measures to realize investment and production targets. Here ministers could rely on very little except political appeals, tax and other financial incentives. In his report to the United Nations Morshidy mentioned inducements from the 'revenue side of the budget and tax laws which give an incentive in those economic activities that enjoy tax exemptions'.[22] His examples were, however, limited to exemptions from the profits tax and lower import duties on capital goods and essential raw materials; the kind of concessions employed by governments before and since the revolution, but which by 1960 had already attained levels where further concessions represented no more than minor incentives to private entrepreneurs.[23] The facility of obtaining cheap credit probably provided a stronger inducement to businessmen to invest along officially approved lines, and when the state raised its guarantee on loans offered by the Industrial

[21] INP Memo. 63; N. Dief, *The System of Follow-up of the First 5-Year Economic and Social Plan* (1962), INP Memo. 141; I. Abdel-Rahman, *Comprehensive Economic Planning in the UAR* (1962) and *Development Programming and Public Budgeting in Egypt* (1961), INP Memos 238 & 167.

[22] Morshidy, p. 75 and Min. of Planning, *Ann. Plan 1960–1* (1960, ar.), p. 1.

[23] Morshidy, p. 83 and Bank Misr, *Econ. B.*, Mar. 1959, p. 101.

Bank to £10 million, the Bank's management actively promoted small-scale enterprises in manufacturing.[24]

THE FINANCE OF CAPITAL FORMATION

Nor was the Plan Frame explicit on how capital formation between July 1960 and July 1965 would be financed, but once again figures published in the annual plans for 1960–1 and 1961–2 help to elucidate government intentions.[25] These figures show that whereas for the execution of investment projects the role of the private sector can correctly be described as minor, planners expected the savings of households and private firms to form a major part of the finance required for capital formation.

The government expected that nearly one-fifth of total savings required to finance the construction and replacement of fixed assets during the first two years of the Plan was to come from abroad in the form of loans and grants, but 70 per cent of the required domestic finance was expected to emanate from local private savings. By the end of the Plan private sources had to provide only 55 per cent of the required domestic finance. Presumably, planners had calculated that by 1964–5 the retained profits of government business would have increased sufficiently to provide the remaining 45 per cent of domestic savings.[26] Private savings were defined as disposable income not consumed by households and retained business profits. The latter were expected to rise absolutely with the rise in turnover and to increase proportionately to gross profits as well.[27] Very optimistic assumptions appear to have been made by the Ministry of Planning about household savings. The statistics reveal that for the first year of the Plan (1960–1) planners expected a rise in household saving

[24] Law 223, 1960 and *BE*, 26 June 1961. Under Law 392 of 1957 the guarantee had been raised to £7 m.

[25] The Plan Frame merely tabulated the proportion of investment expenditure to be made in foreign exchange and specified targets for 1959–60 and 1964–5 (*Gen. Frame of 5-Year Plan*, tables 1, 74, & 75). Savings targets recommended by the Mixed Committee on the Means of Finance were ignored by the National Planning Committee (NPC Memo. 220, *Final Estimates of the Committee on the Means of Finance*, 1960, ar.).

[26] See table 18 (p. 333 below).

[27] 84 per cent of gross profits were retained by the organized business sector in 1959–60 and 91 per cent were expected to be retained in 1964–5 (calculated from *Ann. Plan, 1960–1*, p. 204 and *Gen. Frame of 5-Year Plan*, tables 79 & 88).

greater than the net addition to disposable income. Or, in other words, they assumed the marginal propensity to save was greater than unity.[28] Some arithmetical error is undoubtedly concealed in such figures. Even so, a comparison of the savings targets for households between base and target years reveals the further optimistic assumption that the Egyptian marginal propensity to save was 0·178, a ratio above that normally achieved in developed economies.[29]

Despite the importance of private savings, neither the Frame nor any of the memos prepared as a background to the Plan pass beyond generalities in discussing how the desired rate of private saving might be realized.[30] State influence could obviously be most easily exercised over the undistributed profits of larger-scale and organized firms, and in order to facilitate more widespread control over business profits in general one economist recommended the replacement of partnerships and family business by corporate forms of enterprise which would be registered with the Ministry of Economy.[31] At the beginning of 1959 the government had promulgated a law limiting the amount of dividends distributed by corporations to a maximum of 10 per cent above their level for 1958. As originally enacted the law prescribed a maximum of 10 per cent above dividends declared in 1958, but protests from investors were so strong that the minister was persuaded to raise the maximum to 20 per cent.[32] Stringent dividend limitation might have proved a viable method of compelling the private sector to save more, but it ran counter to other policies designed to attract the savings of households and small firms into industrial projects. The government could not reasonably expect to restrain the distribution of profits and to attract an increased share of non-corporate savings into planned projects at one and the same time. Moreover, through its possible effects on the confidence of potential investors, the policy of dividend limitation might well have reduced the overall volume of private savings.

[28] *Ann. Plan, 1960–1*, table 88.
[29] *Gen. Frame of 5-Year Plan*, tables 74 & 88.
[30] The memos I have read which might be expected to deal explicitly and in detail with questions of finance are NPC Memos 71, 75, 82, 99, 185, & 186 (1959 & 1960, ar.).
[31] A. Hosny, *Financing Capital Formation in UAR* (1962), INP Memo. 211.
[32] *EEPR*, Feb. 1959, pp. 38–40.

How the savings of unorganized business and households which represented 32 per cent of local finance required during the first two years of the Plan could be raised to the planned level and then mobilized was never specified in any detail, and both the budget reports for 1960–1 and for 1961–2 simply lapse into platitudes about 'spreading savings consciousness among various classes'.[33] One positive step was, however, taken in 1960, when the government established a National Investment Fund to 'combat hoarding, to increase national savings to render small savers a safe and profitable means for the investment of their savings, to reduce the risk to which small investors might be exposed when they try to invest their savings individually without much technical knowledge and experience.'[34] Morshidy in his report tabulates the following techniques to stimulate voluntary saving: 'fiscal and financial incentives, commodity taxes, social insurance policies, high interest rates on postal savings, graduated interest rates on time deposits and issues of new bonds, stocks and shares of small face value to be within reach of low income groups.'[35]

Similar measures had been taken almost since the revolution began, and as early as 1957 the Minister of Treasury had pointed out that 'voluntary savings are the most important source for investment funds and the government gives much attention to increase the capacity for saving and the creation of a suitable environment for its growth'.[36] To this end the rate of interest on post office savings had been raised ½ per cent at the beginning of that year and a further ½ per cent in 1961.[37] At the same time profits on funds loaned to investment trusts were exempted from taxation in order to encourage the small saver, and the amendments to company law undoubtedly facilitated and made more secure the investment of small sums in the shares of joint-stock companies.[38] Finally, the Economic Organization had made strenuous efforts to attract private savings into its industrial projects.[39]

[33] *Budget Reports 1960–1* & *1961–2*, pp. 63 & 57.

[34] *BE*, 16 Feb. & 14 May 1960 and *Budget Report 1960–1*, pp. 64–65.

[35] Morshidy, pp. 75–76.

[36] *Budget Report 1957–8*, p. 15.

[37] Min. Econ., *Economic Progress in the UAR*, p. 80 and NBE, *Econ. B.*, iv (1961), p. 34.

[38] Law 95, 1957 and Min. Comm. & Industr., *The Companies Law*.

[39] *UAR Yearbook 1960*, p. 114.

No conspicuous success attended these manifold endeavours and it could well be argued that their possible effects had been more than counteracted by several political actions which probably reduced private saving. Although the Officers had made only minor additions to direct taxes since the revolution, their policies of land reform, rent controls on land and accommodation, their strongly enforced wage legislation and controls over conditions of employment undoubtedly redistributed income from property owners to tenant farmers, householders, and wage-earners: that is away from those with a high propensity to save towards groups with a higher propensity to consume.[40]

The trend since 1956 towards closer control of the economy together with the espousal of socialism and planning could hardly be said to provide a suitable environment for the growth of private savings, particularly the retention and reinvestment of profits by small-scale family firms. Not all state directives are inimical to private enterprise but the attempts of the government to regulate, for example, private investment in houses or to restrain dividends may well have had a dampening effect on incentives to save and invest throughout the private sector.

THE CONTROL OF AGRICULTURE

While nearly a third of the planned increase in commodity production was expected to come from the agricultural sector, the National Planning Committee expected all but a tenth of investment expenditure for agriculture to be undertaken by the government; the great bulk in projects designed to add to the area of land and volume of water made available to farmers.[41] According to the *Yearbook* for 1962, 885,000 feddans would be reclaimed between July 1960 and July 1965.[42] Assuming the average productivity of reclaimed land to be equal to land currently

[40] Laws 177, 1952; 417, 423, & 448, 1953; 254, 1954; 153, 1957, & 91, 1959.

[41] See tables 10 & 17 (below, pp. 325 & 332) and *Gen. Frame of 5-Year Plan*, table 18. The proportion, 10 per cent, relates to the first two years of the Plan, 1960–1 and 1961–2, but there is no reason to suppose the distribution of investment between public and private sectors would be any different in later years of the Plan.

[42] *UAR Yearbook 1962*, pp. 94–95.

cultivated (an optimistic assumption), then by 1965 the government's projects for horizontal expansion would add 15 per cent to total agricultural output for 1960.[43] But, according to the Plan Frame, agricultural production should be 28 per cent higher in 1965. It therefore appeared that planners expected approximately half of the planned increase in farm output to come from a rise in the productivity of land cultivated at the beginning of the Plan. Yet only £52 million from a total investment expenditure of £392 million would be devoted to projects designed to raise yields.[44]

Part of the planned addition to yields between 1960–5 would come from the reallocation of land to more valuable crops for export, and the Ministry of Agriculture intended to continue with the policy of encouraging farmers to produce more fruit, vegetables, meat, and dairy produce.[45] This policy involved the ministry in breeding on its own farms improved strains of cattle, sheep, and poultry and in the development of better varieties of vegetables and fruit. Carefully selected plants, seeds, young trees, and animals were then distributed among farmers at subsidized prices. In addition, the government planned to meet the needs of farmers who opted for horticulture and animal farming by setting up a network of veterinary stations, packing units, and facilities for marketing and processing fruit and vegetables.[46]

But planners clearly expected most of the increment to agricultural production to arise from an increase in output per unit of land cultivated in 1959–60. Proposals as to how yields might be raised had been well analysed and explored upon an experimental scale before the Plan opened. In fact many were recommendations of the Permanent Council as early as 1955, and included the familiar catalogue of selected seeds, pest control, reformed crop rotations, and the scientific application of fertilizers and water to particular crops. For example, the experimental farms of the Ministry of Agriculture had produced novel and better varieties of seed for almost all grain crops and cotton fibres, distinguished

[43] *Basic Statistics*, p. 62 places the area cultivated in 1960 at 5.9 m. feddans.

[44] *Gen. Frame of 5-Year Plan*, tables 2 & 4.

[45] PCDNP, *Report 1955* (ar.), pp. 28, 40–41, 59, & 62.

[46] NPC, Memos 251 & 252, *Report of Committee on the Diversification of Production* (1959, ar.) and *UAR Yearbook 1959*, pp. 192–7.

by their favourable effects on yields and resistance to plant diseases. During the Plan period the ministry intended to spend more upon research into seeds and to distribute them widely among local farmers.[47]

The National Planning Committee estimated that losses through plant and animal diseases amounted to 10 per cent of food production and pests reduced cotton output by as much as 25 per cent.[48] In order to reduce these losses the government planned to divide the countryside into regions and establish local units to counteract pests and plant diseases and veterinary centres to combat animal diseases throughout a given region.[49] Pest-control units would be equipped with the appropriate machinery and chemicals. Their tasks were to introduce farmers to modern methods of pest control and to spray crops over wide areas of farmland, while veterinary stations offered farmers free advice and treatment for their sick animals.[50]

Agronomists had also worked out the type and quantity of fertilizers appropriate for particular crops and soils, and they considered that the application of nitrogen and phosphorous upon local farms fell below the optimum. Thus between 1960 and 1965 the Ministry of Agriculture planned to induce farmers to employ more fertilizers and to use them systematically. Similarly with water: experts had shown that some crops were watered too intensively, others insufficiently and at the wrong times. Part of the problem was that many fields were deficient in drainage canals, and as a result the salinity of the soil had risen over the years. Yields would rise if farmers could be persuaded to regulate the flow of water on to and off their lands scientifically.[51]

Egyptian agriculture did not require to be intensively mechanized, but for certain tasks machines could raise yields and the government planned to encourage co-operatives and individual farmers to buy tractors, diesel pumps, and drilling equipment by

[47] Marei, *The Agricultural Development Programme* (1962), pp. 12–14, 16, 22, & 31 and *UAR Agriculture*, pp. 165, 167, 170, 172, & 178.

[48] NPC, Memo. 263, *Report of Committee on Measures to Counteract Plant Diseases* (1959, ar.) and Marei, *UAR Agriculture*, p. 187.

[49] NPC Memo. 263.

[50] Marei, *UAR Agriculture*, pp. 192 & 194–7.

[51] NPC Memo. 260, *Report of Committee on Irrigation & Drainage*, and Memos 250 & 258, *Reports of Committee on Ways to Improve the Soil* (1959, ar.); Marei, *UAR Agriculture*, pp. 81–94.

establishing a network of maintenance and repair stations for agricultural machinery throughout the countryside.[52]

One suggestion adopted enthusiastically by planners, the consolidation programme, was both novel and radical, and a prerequisite for almost all improvements to techniques of cultivation. Experiments by the Ministry of Agrarian Reform at Nawag and Sultan had demonstrated that yields per feddan could be raised if farmers consolidated their small scattered plots into a single holding, located in one large field which followed a uniform system of rotation.[53] Under traditional methods of strip farming the proximity of different plants affected each other adversely. For example, cotton planted adjacent to clover often became infected with pests peculiar to the fodder crop, and when cotton stood next to rice it suffered damage from excess water. On the other hand monoculture fields could be watered scientifically, they were more easily treated against pests and plant diseases, fertilizers could be applied with greater facility, and labour could be utilized more efficiently.

But the reform of a field layout which had prevailed for generations was obviously difficult to implement, particularly as consolidation brought government officials into a face-to-face relationship with a suspicious and conservative peasantry. The whole programme required a close working relationship between the agronomists sent out by the ministry and representatives of the farmers concerned. Where a village co-operative existed officials dealt with the elected board, if not, their first task was to form a co-operative or committee to represent the interests of farmers. Given the existence of a body which in some way served to reflect the various interests in a particular village, the agronomist's next task was to redesign the entire field layout in order to bring about improvements in efficiency. Private ownership remained inviolable and no peasant lost a square yard of land, but all his separate plots were gathered together and relocated in one particular field. Next the committee, guided by the advice of the agronomists, selected an appropriate rotation for each field. Finally farmers, who con-

[52] NPC, Memo. 253, *Report of Committee on the Mechanization of Agriculture* (1959, ar.).

[53] M. Fawzi, *Nawag, a Pilot Experiment for Solving the Problem of Fragmentation* (1958, ar.).

tinued to till their own soil, were encouraged to utilize selected seeds, fertilizers, and pesticides and to adopt improved watering of crops by the offer of these inputs on credit at subsidized prices. Cheap and in some cases free inputs and services represented the major incentive offered by the government to farmers who co-operated in the consolidation programme.

For any given time period a farmer's entire land would be devoted to a single crop, whereas under the traditional system his several plots would be divided among a diversity of crops according to his needs. Thus the problem emerged as to how a farmer would meet his requirements for food, when his land grew, for example, cotton, or for cash while all land remained under wheat, maize, or clover. In practice this problem was left to the villagers themselves to solve by exchange, either within the village boundaries or upon a wider market, conducted in money terms or as barter.[54] Originally the government expected to introduce the new field layout and rotation into all villages by 1970, but it subsequently announced that the consolidation programme would be completed by 1965.[55]

The Plan as it related to the agricultural sector presupposed that the government could persuade thousands of small farmers to consolidate their tiny plots into more efficient holdings for cultivation and adopt improved systems of rotation, use selected seeds, and apply fertilizer and water more scientifically. It further assumed that the establishment of veterinary centres, stations for the repair of agricultural machinery, packing and marketing facilities for fruit and vegetables would induce farmers to diversify output towards horticulture and animal farming. If farmers failed to comply and targets for primary output fell below the planned level, the entire investment programme could be frustrated by supply bottlenecks in the form of food and raw materials. But knowledge of how yields might be raised was one thing, the task of persuading farmers to depart from traditional crop patterns and techniques of production was quite another, and posed administrative problems for the Egyptian government which had defied solution in many other underdeveloped countries.

[54] M. Hindi, 'The Regulation of Agriculture and its Economic Effects on the Increase in Yield', *Agricultural Economics*, Sept. 1962 (ar.) and Min. Agric., *Towards a Socialist Agriculture*, pp. 42–47.

[55] *al-Ahram Econ. Suppl.*, 1 Oct. 1963 (ar.), p. 18.

Yet when planning began not more than a tenth of cultivable land (the areas of agrarian reform) came under direct state control. Members of the land reform co-operatives could be told what to grow and more or less directed how to cultivate land nominally in their possession.[56] Outside reform areas Egyptian farmers were subjected only to limited amounts of pressure from the central authorities. They were forbidden to devote more than a fixed proportion of their land to cotton and were compelled to grow wheat, and the government further influenced the pattern of agricultural output through its control of food prices. But the National Planning Committee realized that if the state wished to bring stronger pressure to bear upon the mass of cultivators, it had to operate through co-operatives, otherwise the administrative problem of dealing with thousands of small, atomized production units would prove intractable.[57] Between 1956 and 1960 public policy had been directed towards persuading all farmers to associate together in co-operatives. The inducements offered by the government were certainly tempting. Members of co-operatives alone became eligible for cheap (and from 1961 free) public credit channelled through the Agricultural Bank. Seeds, fertilizers, and other inputs were also supplied by the Bank at subsidized prices. Co-operatives enjoyed tax exemptions and received grants for the purpose of providing social welfare for members. It paid to join, and as a result by 1960 nearly all farmers had become members of co-operatives.[58]

The question then emerged how could these voluntary associations of farmers, formed to buy and sell in bulk and to negotiate credit, help to raise average yields throughout the countryside? Their traditional function had been to redistribute agricultural income away from middlemen (the purveyors of seed and fertilizers, moneylenders and cotton merchants) back to producers by uniting small farmers into groups with stronger bargaining powers, able to reap economies of scale from buying and selling in quantity. Co-operatives had been only marginally concerned with production itself. As early as 1957 the then Minister of Agrarian Reform,

[56] See above, p. 98.

[57] NPC Memo. 255, *Report of Committee on Agricultural Institutions* (1959, ar.).

[58] CBE, *Econ. R.*, ii (1963), p. 168 and *UAR Yearbook 1960*, pp. 443, 448, & 453; Shabanah, *Agricultural Co-operative Economy*, pp. 126–30.

Sayed Marei, suggested that they should be transformed into the kind of producers' co-operatives found on land-reform estates.[59] While the Five-Year Plan was under discussion there were further suggestions for sending an agronomist to every village and enlarging the functions of agricultural co-operatives, but the government made no definite plans to alter the existing institutional framework of farming.[60] In 1960 the government established a General Organization for Co-operatives, attached to the Presidency, and a year later the Ministry of Agriculture replaced the Ministry of Social Affairs as the ministry responsible for co-operatives.[61] This step could be interpreted as a recognition by the government that the role of co-operatives should be wider than the provision of social welfare, but the precise significance of these changes at the top did not become clear until later. Meanwhile the government continued to influence farmers through the means open to it.

Agricultural credit stood at the forefront of techniques of persuasion available for raising yields. Since 1956 the Agricultural and Co-operative Bank, through the medium of supervised loans, had exercised an influence on the inputs and methods of cultivation used by many farmers.[62] The Plan opened with the offer of more and cheaper agricultural credit to those farmers who used public loans in ways approved by the government, and in August 1961 a presidential decree declared loans from the Agricultural and Co-operative Bank interest-free.[63] In free and supervised credit the government possessed a useful instrument for bringing its influence to bear on the process of cultivation.

The government also controlled the distribution of two other important agricultural inputs, seeds and fertilizers. To assist the Ministry of Agriculture in the propagation of seeds of the approved quality and type, the production and sale of seed had been subjected to increased control. Full technical supervision had been secured over large and medium producers of seeds, and the best grade of seeds from the ministry's own farms were distributed at

[59] Marei, *Agrarian Reform*, p. 121. [60] NPC Memo. 255.

[61] Law 267, 1960 and Shabanah, *Agric. Co-operative Societies*, p. 122.

[62] Min. Agric., *Towards a Socialist Agriculture* (ar.), pp. 301–15; *Budget Report 1961–2*, pp. 63–66; *BE*, 30 Mar. & 29 Sept. 1960.

[63] CBE, *Credit and Banking Developments* (1962), pp. 19–20 and *Budget Report 1961–2*, pp. 63–66.

low prices. In addition, the government promoted the formation of companies for the production of highly fertile hybrid maize and subsidized producers of good-quality cotton seed.[64] The distribution of all imported nitrogen and phosphates was controlled by the Agricultural Bank, and through its influence on farmers who purchased fertilizers on credit, the Bank attempted to bring practice into line with the recommendations made by soil scientists.[65]

Once planning began it soon became obvious that the instruments then available to the authorities for ensuring that farmers complied with the Plan were inadequate, and by 1962 several suggestions for further extensions of central control over the agricultural sector received publicity in the press.[66]

CONCLUSION

The formulation of Egypt's First Five-Year Plan in 1959–60 revealed clearly most of the difficulties inherent in attempts to plan any economy with a large private sector. Central planning and a mixed economy are certainly not incompatible provided the state is able to obtain positive support from businessmen and farmers. Such co-operation is, however, by no means easy to secure, and involves protracted negotiation and compromise at almost every stage in the construction and execution of a national plan. To some extent the Egyptian government had appreciated the need to work with the private sector, and hence had established mixed committees to draft the Plan. Furthermore, politicians frequently and publicly emphasized their support for a mixed economy and close co-operation between public and private enterprise. But on the whole the endeavour appears as form without substance. Those same political leaders continued to make ambivalent references to the evils of capitalism and the virtues of socialism, while the Mixed Committees had very little influence on the content of the Plan. Targets for production, investment, and saving were in the end simply handed down from above, and

[64] Marei, *Agric. Development Programme*, pp. 12–13, 16, 18–22, & 31–32.

[65] *Budget Report 1961–2*, pp. 63–66; *Towards a Socialist Agriculture*, pp. 326–7; *BE*, 22 Nov. 1960.

[66] *BE*, 7 Dec. 1960, 28 Aug., 22 & 29 Jan. 1962.

the private sector was expected to comply with central directives.

Although the government had assumed major responsibility for the execution of the projects included in the Plan, the co-operation of the rest of the economy still remained vital if its investment aims were to come anywhere near realization, for if the private sector failed to achieve the targets established for it by the National Planning Committee, the success of the Plan would be seriously jeopardized. Yet in July 1960 the government committed the economy, with a fanfare of publicity, to doubling the national income over the following decade. In other words the state had committed households, managers, entrepreneurs, and farmers, who it had not seriously consulted and over whom it possessed only limited powers of control, to ambitious production, saving, and investment targets. Moreover the techniques of persuasion and inducement open to the government had already been severely tested and found wanting. Thus when the Plan opened, to the Egyptian government the problem of how it could fulfil its promise and comprehensively plan an economy with so large a private sector must have seemed to be the overwhelming question.

VI

The Demise of Private Enterprise

THE EXTENSION OF PUBLIC OWNERSHIP AND CONTROL

WHEN comprehensive planning began in July 1960, Egyptian private business had witnessed not only a steady expansion of the public sector and annexation by the government of more and more responsibility for economic development, but since 1956, an extension and tightening of controls over the freedom of private business itself. Private enterprise, which had not, in any meaningful sense, been consulted about the form and content of the Five-Year Plan, was nevertheless expected to play an important part in its implementation by fulfilling investment and savings targets laid down by the state. By the end of 1959 remarks by politicians about the need for 'co-operation' between government and private sector had nothing behind them tangible enough to allay the growing uncertainty of the business community. And when union with Syria became consolidated, President Nasser and his ministers felt free to air more radical views about the place of capitalism in the United Arab Republic. State ownership of industry was justified, to paraphrase the President, because it represented the people, created a balance with private ownership, and avoided the domination of industry by private capital.[1] Arguments of quite this kind had not been expounded before, and a perceptive capitalist may have asked if such a balance required interference with his property. Neither the President's repeated remarks about a policy to eliminate 'corrupt capitalism' and 'monopolies' nor persistent press discussion on rent control, wage policies, or progressive fiscal systems appeared likely to assuage fears of investors and businessmen about the then vaguely defined place of private enterprise within the planned economy.[2]

Their apprehension was soon vindicated. Just three months after the President's pronouncements, the first of a long sequence

[1] *Nasser's Speeches 1959*, pp. 400–1.

[2] Ibid. 1960, p. 135 and *BE*, 25 Jan., 1, 8, & 9 Feb. & 11 Apr. 1960.

of nationalization measures became law. On 13 February 1960 Bank Misr was taken into public ownership. This act gave the government control, not merely over the largest commercial bank remaining in private hands, but over a considerable part of corporate industry as well.[3] Bank Misr held shares throughout the organized sector of industry and, according to one paper, companies affiliated to the Bank accounted for 20 per cent of Egypt's industrial output, including half of all textile production.[4] The nationalization of the Bank did not bring all the shares of Misr companies into direct public ownership, but these firms came immediately and more firmly under government control because the state acquired powers to appoint nominees to their boards of directors. Links between the state and Bank Misr had remained close since the consolidation of 1941, but the relationship evidently allowed the Bank too much autonomy, because the Minister of Treasury admitted in a press interview that Misr companies could have refused to participate in the plan.[5] In his Budget Report, presented the following July, Dr Kaissouny dilated even more explicitly on 'the pressing necessity to nationalize this Bank within which a huge concentration of power was concentrated and any misuse of such power would have had a destructive reaction on the economy'.[6]

From the Minister's remarks and press comments at the time, it appears that some kind of conflict had arisen between the government and directors of Bank Misr, possibly over the targets allocated to Misr companies under the Plan. The Bank was accused of threatening to unload its portfolio of shares on to the Stock Exchange and thereby disrupting the capital market; thus according to some accounts, the state had stepped in to avoid 'a catastrophic fall in share prices'.[7] But one editor noted more candidly that 'the régime cannot allow abuse of freedom of ownership' and in his view 'attempts to secure co-operation from the overprivileged business group had failed'.[8]

Whatever the precise reasons for the measure, four months

[3] Law 39, 1960. [4] *BE*, 13 Feb. 1960. [5] Ibid.

[6] *Budget Report 1960–1*, p. 89.

[7] *EEPR*, Mar. 1960, p. 18. Under Law 163 of 1957 the Bank was legally required to divest itself of its industrial shareholdings, but both Bank and government had ignored the law.

[8] Ibid. Apr. 1960, pp. 17–19 and Ali (ar.), pp. 107–9.

before the Plan opened the government found it expedient to assert further control over the organized sector of industry, and the nationalization of Egypt's largest holding company represented a most convenient way of extending authority over the economy. Thus Bank Misr and its companies subsequently became the Misr Organization, 'a national-socialist institution', which formed part of the 'machinery side by side with the Economic Organization, the Five-Year Industrial Board, and the General Board for Military Factories, working for the realization of the economic and social objectives of the state'.[9]

In June 1960 all Egyptian newspapers became state owned. Although censorship already operated, President Nasser accused the press of frivolity and slanting news in ways hostile to the revolution.[10] Almost the same week, Cairo bus services were municipalized for failing to provide the city with an adequate service, while another reason, this time the charge of 'profiteering', was offered by the Minister of Supply when both internal and external trade in tea and pharmaceutical products were removed from private hands in July.[11]

Share prices fell rapidly in 1960. According to foreign correspondents resident in Cairo, the business community existed in 'a state of gloom wondering where the axe would fall next'.[12] *La Bourse Égyptienne* published an editorial to reassure them that the government did not, contrary to rumour, contemplate further sweeping nationalizations.[13]

Meanwhile, when planning began, ministers publicly reminded private enterprise of the important role it had still to play and, in his speech to the Congress of the National Union, President Nasser presented the Plan 'as an instrument of encouraging private capital and for guiding this capital away from exploitation and monopoly'.[14] The Minister of Education did his best to define socialism in a way palatable to businessmen. 'It is a type of

[9] Decree 249, 1961; *UAR Yearbook 1960*, p. 187, and *Budget Report 1960–1*, p. 75.

[10] C. Cremeans, *The Arabs and the World* (1963), p. 37.

[11] *BE*, 14 June and 18 July 1960.

[12] See *Guardian* and *Christian Science Monitor*, 4 & 11 Aug. 1960.

[13] *BE*, 2 July 1960.

[14] Information Dept., *Reports and Statements by Ministers to the Congress of National Union* (1960), pp. 151–2.

socialism', he told delegates, 'that protects individual ownership, upholds the freedom of individual economic enterprise and reconciles public and private economic activity.'[15] On the other hand private enterprise was warned about 'deviation' by Abdel Latif Boghdadi.

If we are to assume [said the Minister of Planning] the public sector will follow the Plan in all its dealings, we may find the private sector, which covers an extensive sector in our Republic, may deviate from this trend to realize personal interests regardless of the serious results which may befall the country. . . . A prompt and conscious response to the directives of the authorities [he concluded] will save the trouble of taking stronger and more drastic measures, which the State will reluctantly resort to, to maintain and preserve the major objectives which the Plan aims at and has decided to achieve and from which it expects great results.

The minister went on in an uncompromising manner to attack free competition for heading to a waste of capital, and capitalists for not entering certain fields because profits were not high enough.[16]

Boghdadi's speech implicitly raised the whole problem of comprehensive planning in a mixed economy, and he is the only minister who attempted to bully the private sector into compliance with the régime's economic policies, but throughout the first year of the Plan his threat of 'stronger and more drastic measures' remained veiled. Ministers reverted to familiar exhortations and appeals, urging private enterprise to co-operate with the government for the public good.[17] Dr Kaissouny during a press interview in May 1961 denied strongly that the government contemplated further nationalization measures and his Budget Report submitted to the National Assembly before the nationalizations of July 1961 is perhaps the classic statement of the revolutionary government's economic doctrine before much of Egyptian property passed into public ownership.[18]

This country [he said] is determined that its policy will spring from its own pure soil fashioned by its own circumstances and serving

[15] Ibid. p. 64.

[16] Boghdadi, pp. 8 f., 72–73 and *EG*, 11 July 1960.

[17] See statements by President Nasser and Dr Kaissouny in *BE*, 25 Jan. & 12 Apr. 1961 and the report in the *Financial Times*, 30 May 1961.

[18] *BE*, 6 May 1961.

its own interests. It is built on three pillars: socialism, co-operation and democracy. The socialist aspect resides on three foundations. The belief that both private ownership and private enterprise should exist and be protected within those limits necessary to prevent the re-emergence of feudalism, exploitation and monopoly. Assuring a reasonable standard of wealth for whoever works, produces and contributes to the development of the national income. Wholehearted collaboration in production under whose impulse the efforts and investments of the public sector are combined with those of the private sector. Our co-operative system aims at putting a limit to the middleman's profits and at the reduction to a minimum of production costs as well as to supply consumers at a time when the State is encouraging small production in the fields of agriculture, industry and commerce by ensuring the supply of the implements and needs of production. Economic democracy as we perceive it means we respect individual economic liberty with this provision that should this individual liberty run counter to the economic interests of society as a whole we will give weight to society's will and give priority to its economic interests over the interests of the individual.

It is these principles that cause us to adopt a guided economy for our society. Guidance and supervision do not imply domination or dictatorship. We intend to ensure that capital shall remain free as long as it contributes to the general welfare. The illegitimate domination of capital will be abolished. It is incumbent upon the State to intervene and direct investments along the correct path of exploitation. To consolidate the socialist, democratic and co-operative system, public and private capital combine in the implementation of the investment projects planned for economic development. Public capital goes into certain basic industries and participates with private capital in other industries. The Government takes charge of industries which individuals are unable to establish either for the lack of technical experience, great risks, or the large volume of capital required. The Government may also intervene to stop exploitation and undue price manipulation of certain products. Otherwise the Government leaves other industries especially the processing industries to individual initiative. We have to pursue a policy of achievement. We must see that our plans do not remain just ink on paper and our aspirations merely wishful thinking.[19]

Dr Kaissouny's statement is perhaps the most explicit formulation of the vague doctrine of 'guided capitalism' ever propounded by

[19] From *Budget Report 1961–2*, pp. 41–45. The quotation is not reproduced verbatim but consists of selected sentences.

an Egyptian minister, but he also skirts the problem of how in detail the private sector could be compelled to participate in the government's plans for economic development.

Although ministerial assurances and the cessation of nationalization measures after July 1960 should on the face of it have allayed the fears of the business community, according to foreign correspondents it continued to be as gloomy as ever, and in an atmosphere which included daily press articles about socialism, exploitation, monopoly and planning, their apprehension is certainly understandable.[20] Controls had tightened and incursions were made even into retail trade by the Ministry of Supply, which announced a programme to build a chain of co-operative stores to compete with existing shopkeepers in order to reduce prices of foodstuffs to the poorer classes.[21] The Minister of Economy obtained powers to inspect the accounts of any joint-stock company to ascertain if it was being efficiently managed.[22] In the Northern Province of the United Arab Republic the state steadily extended control over private enterprise and so limited the almost classical freedom previously enjoyed by Syrian capitalists.[23]

Furthermore, private business could not have derived reassurance from the foreword to the second annual plan which affirmed the government's aim to push on with industrialization and its determination 'not to allow private capital to place obstacles in the way of its execution'.[24] It is impossible to find out what obstacles (if any) businessmen had placed in the way of the industrialization programme. Perhaps the Minister of Planning simply implied that the private sector had failed to fulfil targets for the first year? Unfortunately reliable figures upon which an assessment of its performance could be made have not been published, but given ambitious aims and an unfavourable political environment, it would be surprising if the goals set for private business had been fully achieved.

[20] Moreover Belgian property was nationalized in December 1960 as a reprisal for the behaviour of the Belgian government in the Congo (Bank Misr, *Econ. B.*, Mar. 1961, p. 85; *New York Times*, 10 Jan. 1961, and *Financial Times*, 30 May 1961).

[21] *BE*, 3 Jan. & 9 Feb. 1961.

[22] Ibid. 9 May 1961.

[23] This study will not deal with legislation promulgated for the Syrian Region. Developments there can be traced in the columns of the *Beyrouth Express*.

[24] *Ann. Plan 1961–2* (ar.), pp. 3–4.

Thus it may be more than coincidence that the third sequence of nationalization measures came at the beginning of the second annual plan, that is at a point when the government had had time to take into account the overall performance of the private sector during the first year of comprehensive planning.

Towards the end of June 1961 there began what is now referred to in Egypt as the 'Social Revolution'. First, the entire cotton trade passed into government hands. The Alexandria futures market was closed and the Egyptian Cotton Commission assumed responsibility for buying and selling all raw cotton at fixed prices.[25] Concurrently houses exporting cotton had to assume the form of joint-stock companies with a government participation of no less than 35 per cent in their share capital.[26] Four firms which pressed and baled raw cotton (an integral part of the organization for the export of cotton) were nationalized outright on 9 July.[27] The same week the law compelled all export-import houses to exchange 25 per cent of their share capital for an equivalent amount in public bonds bearing interest at 4 per cent and redeemable after fifteen years.[28] By bringing all firms engaged in external trade under the jurisdiction of the Ministry of Economy, the government strengthened control over supplies of foreign exchange. Officials also argued that the huge profits made by these firms which accrued as a direct result of public policy ought to be appropriated by the state.[29] The government nationalized only one other company (the Khedivial Shipping Line) at the beginning of July. Apparently some capitalists proved difficult to 'guide' because this particular firm had refused to execute wage legislation and had suspended operations without official permission.[30]

Coinciding with the ninth anniversary of the revolution, the state nationalized a massive share of Egypt's industrial and commercial property. Banks and insurance companies which had remained in private hands were taken over completely; so were

[25] Laws 69 & 70, 1961. Laws relating to the nationalization measures of 1961 have been summarized in NBE, *Econ. B.*, iii (1961), pp. 323 f.; INP Memo. 137, *Social Laws and Decrees issued in July 1961* (1962), and Information Dept., *Socialist Laws 1961* (1961).

[26] Law 71, 1961. The proportion was later raised to 50 per cent by Law 120, 1961.

[27] Law 110, 1961.

[28] Law 107, 1961.

[29] NBE, *Econ. B.*, ii (1961), pp. 117–18.

[30] Law 109, 1961 and *Beyrouth Express*, 15 July 1961.

44 companies from such basic industries as timber, cement, copper, electricity and motorized transport.[31] The state expropriated half the capital of 86 companies, mainly in commerce and light manufacturing.[32] The owners of a further 147 companies were dispossessed of their assets by law 119, which limited individual shareholdings in the firms to a market value of £10,000. All shares in excess of that amount passed into state ownership.[33]

Following the nationalization measures of late July 1961, which officially laid the foundations of a 'Socialist, Democratic, and Co-operative Society', the prevarication and ambiguity which had characterized the attitude of Egyptian leaders towards private enterprise since 1957 ceased, and they vigorously supported the extension of public ownership with a whole battery of slogans drawn largely from socialist ideology. Thus according to their speeches the aims of the new laws were:

> to turn all citizens into owners; to permit people to control the means of production; to orient production in the public interest, to reduce class differences, to eliminate feudalism, monopoly and the dictatorship of capital; to give society assurances which would enable it to prevent exploitation or domination by a minority.[34]

President Nasser described the enlargement of the public sector in industry and commerce as the 'application of socialism in its real meaning'.[35] Even after the nationalization measures ministers continued to try to reassure private business by saying that 'our socialism doesn't involve complete nationalization'; 'is not communism', or that the new policy 'respects individual ownership and economic freedom so long as it works in line with the welfare of society'.[36] Words were not enough to satisfy the propertied class in the Syrian region of the United Arab Republic, who reacted to the application of similar measures to their country by supporting a military coup d'état which effectively dissolved the nascent union between Egypt and Syria and reversed all steps taken towards socialism in Syria.[37] In Egypt the politically much

[31] Law 117, 1961. [32] Law 118, 1961. [33] Law 119, 1961.

[34] INP Memo. 137, pp. 1 f. & 19; *BE*, 20–23, 25, & 29 July 1961; M. Kerr, 'The Emergence of a Socialist Ideology in Egypt', *MEJ*, Spring 1962, pp. 133 f., 139, & 142.

[35] *Nasser's Speeches 1961*, pp. 135–6, 146, 341–6, & 379–95.

[36] *Dawn*, 23 July 1961 and *BE*, 22 July 1961.

[37] Abdel-Malek, *Égypte, société militaire*, pp. 156–9.

weaker bourgeoisie responded by petitioning the Commander-in-Chief of the military forces, General Amr, to end the dictatorship. The régime's response to this 'threat of counter-revolution' was harsh and swift. The government immediately imprisoned representatives of many of the old ruling families and sequestrated the property of several hundred people from the wealthy classes.[38] Of course these attacks on the old bourgeoisie may simply reflect the government's need to find a scapegoat for its own political failure to consolidate union with Syria. Or on the other hand 'a capitalist plot' against the régime may have existed. Inside Egypt the government's ruthless reaction certainly paralysed all further opposition and had the effect of bringing yet more private property into the public sector.

After February 1962 the wave of nationalization and sequestration measures subsided, and at that time the government seemed content with a position which gave the state complete ownership and control over the infrastructure, financial institutions, and heavy industry and part-ownership and direct control over external trade and all large-scale corporate industry. Nationalization had been considerably less than wholesale. Nearly all land, houses, motorized transport, small-scale industrial and commercial enterprises, and the assets required for internal trade remained outside the public sector. In fact the bulk of national wealth, dominated by land, was still in private ownership, although all managers and owners of productive assets operated within a wide ranging and tight system of controls over many aspects of their economic activities.

In May 1962 President Nasser offered to the Congress of Popular Powers the now famous Charter[39] which defined the economic system in some detail. Of course, the Charter contained very much more than an outline of the new economic organization. It attempted in fact to supply a comprehensive doctrine or ideology to serve both as an explanation for all the changes promulgated since the revolution of 1952 and as a foundation for future developments throughout the whole area of political, economic, and social life in modern Egypt. The focus here will be, however, upon the system of production, and other aspects of the document will be

[38] Ibid. pp. 156–8 and *BE*, 19 & 29 Oct. & 8 Nov. 1961.

[39] Information Dept., *The Charter* (*Draft*), *21 May, 1962* (1962). All quotations throughout this book are from this version.

analysed in the next chapter. The Charter described the economic system which emerged as a result of the July decrees and the sequestration measures as socialist. But socialist organization in Egypt did not, it maintained, 'necessitate the nationalization of all means of production or the abolition of private ownership'; rather the 'creation of a capable public sector that would lead progress in all domains and bear the main responsibility of the development plan' (p. 54). For this purpose the Charter defined the public sector to include the infrastructure, heavy and medium industry, and the institutions and companies responsible for foreign trade and financial operations.

On the other hand the Charter defined the sphere of private ownership and enterprise as land, buildings, construction, light industry, and internal trade. It assumed that the bulk of Egyptian property would remain in private hands and justified the exclusion of land from public ownership on the grounds that 'the Arab application of socialism in the domain of agriculture does not believe in nationalizing the land and transforming it into the domain of public ownership. . . . The right solutions to the problem of agriculture . . . necessitate the existence of the individual ownership of land' and support for such 'ownership by means of agricultural co-operation, along all the stages of the process of agricultural production' (pp. 63–64). Buildings could be privately owned because their rents were now controlled and subjected to progressive taxation. Similarly light industry would be excluded from state ownership provided it accepted guidance from the public sector. Finally, the Charter promised private enterprise the ownership and control of most internal trade as long as it did not exploit consumers, but even in this area of economic life 'the public sector must have a role' and should 'take charge of at least one-quarter of the internal trade' over the following eight years (p. 57).

More directly the Charter warned the private sector 'to renovate itself and strike a new path of creative effort not dependent, as in the past, on parasitic exploitation' (p. 60). It hoped private enterprise would encourage free competition within the framework of economic planning thereby invigorating the public sector; further, that private business would 'promote the process of development . . . only restricted by the socialist laws now in force, or by steps deemed necessary by the popular authorities elected in future' (p. 73).

In summary, the Charter defined the new socialist economic system as one where the commanding heights (financial institutions, social capital, and heavy industry) would be owned by the state. It allowed for mixed ownership in light and medium industry and external trade; confirmed private ownership in the spheres of land, small-scale industry, and internal trade but made it quite clear that all production would continue to be controlled and directed by the central authorities.

But the definitions offered by the Charter were not intended to circumscribe future changes. On the contrary, President Nasser had already stated that 'there can never be designed limits' to further transformation.[40] Certainly the boundaries of public ownership and central control have not remained at the lines demarcated in July 1961. Extensions to the power and property of the state have been made several times since then and are continuing, but so far they might be accurately described as amendments to or a tidying up of the changes inaugurated in 1960–1.

For example, Egyptian leaders evidently found the status of mixed public and private ownership provided for under laws 118 and 119 of 1961 ideologically or operationally untenable because throughout 1963 and 1964 nearly all companies partly owned by the government became fully nationalized, either for specific reasons (for example failures to renew equipment, inefficiency, exploiting consumers, &c.) or, as *al-Ahram* put it, because such steps represented 'natural continuation of the Social Revolution'.[41] No doubt the full nationalization of those assets sequestrated in 1961 and 1962 also appeared as a logical continuation of the same Revolution.[42] In addition, the government nationalized a considerable number of companies in spheres of production largely untouched by the original decree of July 1961. Thus in June 1963 the industry for the manufacture of drugs and pharmaceutical products passed into public ownership.[43] Similarly (after short-

[40] *Nasser's Speeches 1961*, p. 217.

[41] Laws 38, 51, 65, & 72, 1963; 51, 1964; *BE*, 14 Apr., 23 May, 17 June, & 12 Aug. 1963; *The Times*, 13 Nov. 1963.

[42] Law 72, 1963.

[43] *BE*, 7 June 1963 and Law 65, 1963.

lived experiments first with private and then with mixed ownership) the government found it appropriate to own and control, for purposes of planning, all the major concerns in building construction, civil engineering, road haulage, and water transport.[44] Finally, several laws tidied up anomalies whereby certain companies within a particular sector had unaccountably been omitted from the schedules of earlier measures and they extended nationalization to private family firms.[45] By the end of 1964 almost all large companies throughout every field of economic activity had been nationalized, and the public sector consisted then of enterprises both controlled and owned by the state, whereas previously many firms operated by the government had continued to be partly owned by private shareholders.

Apart from the dramatic and well-publicized extensions to the public sector, between 1961 and 1965 the government in addition curtailed still further the autonomy of producers within those areas of private ownership and enterprise left open to them. Thus, although the Charter recognized internal trade as an area for private business, during 1963 the Ministry of Supply interfered with the discretion of retail and wholesale traders, partly to facilitate the distribution of government products and partly as a response to rising prices.

Owners had also been left in possession of their houses and buildings, but in order to reduce the cost of living and as a reprisal on those who in past years had 'preferred not to invest their money in the industrial field but to block it instead in houses with high rental charges', the government applied even more stringent rent control.[46] Laws 168 and 169 of 1961 reduced rents on accommodation built after 1958 by 20 per cent and upon the bulk of houses built before that date by varying amounts equal to the tax paid by those who received rents. In January 1962 a comprehensive act made the maximum rent payable on all buildings equal to 5 per cent of the cost of the land and building plus 3 per cent for maintenance costs.[47]

Directors of larger establishments in industry and commerce

[44] Laws 63, 67, 70, & 825 of 1963 & 52 of 1964.

[45] Laws 72, 77–81, 140, 145–51, 157, 168–9 of 1963 & 2, 41, 48–51, 120–4, & 141 of 1964.

[46] INP Memo. 137, p. 21 and *UAR Yearbook 1962*, p. 275.

[47] Law 46, 1962.

which had escaped nationalization nevertheless lost still more discretion over the remuneration and working conditions for employees and the allocation of profits because the government compelled them to accord their workers the same welfare benefits and privileges as those imposed on all enterprises within the public sector. For example, under a series of laws promulgated since July 1961, the government reduced the working week to 42 hours without loss of pay and prescribed a minimum wage of 25 piastres a day for all employees over 18, and provided a more extensive and generous system of social security benefits for all workers in large-scale enterprises, public or private.[48] Larger firms were also compelled, under laws 111 and 112 of 1961, to allocate profits as follows: 5 per cent for the purchase of government bonds, 20 per cent allocated to reserves and from the remainder available for distribution to shareholders, 25 per cent had to be paid to the firms employees in ratio to their wages and salaries.[49] And in 1963, to bring themselves into line with arrangements in the public sector, the boards of all private companies were obliged by the government to reconstitute themselves to allow representation for four directors elected by their employees.[50]

THE CONTROL OF AGRICULTURE

According to the Charter (p. 63), Arab socialism excluded farmland from the domain of public ownership in favour of the redistribution of land among these without holdings of their own. Thus under an amendment to the Agrarian Reform Law of 1952, the acreage any individual might own was reduced from 200 to 100 feddans, and a further clause in the new act prevented families from acquiring or renting more than 50 feddans in addition to their existing holdings.[51] In June 1962 the sale of more than 5 feddans of land to any single individual was forbidden.[52] Penalties for evading those parts of the law which related to the control of rent and wages were made more onerous, and the

[48] Laws 133 & 175, 1961; 102, 1962; 50 & 153, 1963; & 63, 1964.

[49] *UAR Yearbook 1962*, p. 232; Law 113, 1963; *Commerce du Levant*, 23 Mar. 1963.

[50] Laws 114, 1961 & 141, 1963.

[51] Law 127, 1961 and *Nasser's Speeches 1961*, p. 308 stated that tenancy would be limited to 50 feddans.

President promised to tighten up loopholes in the original reform which had, he admitted, 'allowed some landowners through fictitious bequests and sales to continue to own up to 3,000 feddans'.[53]

But redistribution of land did nothing to solve the problem of how to ensure that farmers adopted techniques of cultivation likely to raise yields and meet the targets established for agriculture by the Plan. The Charter had rejected the nationalization of land in favour of providing 'a strong vital economy for the small land-holdings' (p. 65), and President Nasser confirmed this tenet when he told the editor of *Pravda* that 'the socialist solution for the problem of agriculture in the UAR was based on two measures': first, 'increasing the number of owners of arable land', and second, 'consolidating land ownership by co-operation and transforming the economy of small holdings into a strong one through continuous expansion of co-operation'.[54] In other words the solution to the problem of control adopted for industry and foreign trade, namely public ownership of the means of production, was not contemplated for agriculture, at least in the early years of the Plan.

But by 1965 the editor *al-Ahram*, whose articles are widely regarded as a reflection of the President's views, expressed doubts about the efficiency of smallholders and the value of private ownership in farming. Haikal focused his attention not on agriculture as a whole but upon the area to be reclaimed by the High Dam, and argued that it should be exploited directly by the state. He saw the reclaimed lands as providing the government with an opportunity for experiment denied to it throughout the rest of agriculture, bound to old institutions and traditional methods. He advocated the formation of state companies to grow fruit and vegetables for export. Such companies, Haikal considered, would be the new dynamic force in agriculture and would take full advantage of the economies of scale and mechanized techniques open to large centrally directed farms. They would provide foreign exchange and employment for thousands of labourers who would not have access to land distributed in small plots.[55]

These suggestions received a critical examination from Sayed

[52] *MRESE*, June 1962, p. 15. [53] Warriner, p. 210.
[54] *The Charter*, pp. 63–65 and *Nasser's Speeches 1962*, p. 187.
[55] *al-Ahram*, 8 Jan. 1965.

Marei, the former Minister of Agrarian Reform, who rejected collective farms on the grounds that they had failed in Russia and because state-operated farms in Tahrir Province and Abu Ghait had proved to be less efficient than privately-owned concerns. He went on to recommend the exploitation of reclaimed land by the kind of co-operatives which had developed on lands redistributed under the Agrarian Reform Laws of 1952 and 1961. In other words, Marei advocated an institutional framework which combined private ownership and some individual enterprise with a strong measure of official control over cultivation. Marei argued that the supervised co-operatives had achieved all the economies of scale and employed advanced techniques of cultivation recommended by advocates of state farms. And he dismissed the idea that Egyptian agriculture required highly mechanized production because the country suffered from a surplus, not a shortage, of labour. Marei concluded that the supervised or socialist co-operatives not only suited agricultural conditions in the Nile valley but provided a model for other countries who wished to reorganize their systems of cultivation.[56]

No doubt the outcome of this discussion will prove to be highly significant, not merely for the new lands but possibly for the whole of agriculture. But during the First Five-Year Plan the government made no move to nationalize land and has concentrated instead upon bringing its influence to bear on private cultivators in other ways. It sought, for example, to use all means of inducement available to persuade thousands of small farmers to consolidate their scattered holdings into composite plots and to adopt a whole range of new inputs and techniques of cultivation which would raise average yields throughout agriculture. As usual with farming in poor countries, knowledge of how to increase productivity had advanced much farther than useful notions on how the improved methods might be applied.

When planning began the organization of agricultural production could be divided into two sectors: the small agrarian reform area farmed by land reform co-operatives, and the great bulk of land exploited by owner cultivators and tenant farmers most of whom had joined co-operatives.

Unlike the organizations found in most Egyptian villages, land

[56] *al-Ahram*, 7, 8, & 11 Mar., 5 Apr. & 6, 7, 8, & 11 May 1965.

reform co-operatives were not voluntary associations of farmers but rather institutions within which individual owner-cultivators exercised only a limited amount of initiative.[57] As the former Minister of Agrarian Reform saw it, the advantages of such co-operatives were that they met the deep feelings of the fellahin for possession of land but at the same time ensured that ownership rights did not lead to a conflict between individual and social welfare. Absolute rights of ownership, he considered, lead to a wasteful use of land, and farmers should be 'guided' in its exploitation. Guidance took place through the co-operative. Marei made the statement that management represented the wishes of the farmers, but in fact decisions by the board as to what should be grown, the techniques of cultivation to be employed, and the overall rate of net investment by the co-operative reflected the wishes of the supervisor, appointed by and subject to the Ministry of Agrarian Reform. As Marei subsequently admitted, the government could give orders to land reform co-operatives and they had to obey.[58] The powers of the minister over co-operatives were extensive enough for some commentators to regard them as branches of the Ministry of Agrarian Reform.

The great mass of peasant proprietors, and tenant farmers who remained unaffected by the redistribution of land in 1952 and 1961, were members of co-operatives. Until 1962 these co-operatives had been organizations concerned with bulk purchase and marketing. In contrast to agrarian reform co-operatives, they had not been much involved with production itself. They will be referred to as voluntary co-operatives. Even before 1952 relations between voluntary co-operatives and the government could, however, be described as one of tutelage. They were obliged to register with the Ministry of Social Affairs, their accounts were subject to official audit, and the decisions of their elected boards liable to ministerial veto.[59] After the revolution the government actively encouraged farmers to join co-operatives which became channels of communication between them and the Ministries in Cairo. Boards of co-operatives negotiated with the Ministry of Public Works on matters related to the local irrigation system. Co-

[57] I propose to refer to them as supervised co-operatives.
[58] *al-Ahram*, 8 & 11 Mar., 5, 6, & 7 Apr. 1965.
[59] Shabanah, *Agric. Co-operative Societies*, ch. 6.

operatives disseminated information put out by the Ministry of Agriculture on new techniques and they became in fact part of the ministry's extension services. In order to obviate the 'exploitation' of small farmers by middlemen, the government encouraged co-operatives to extend their marketing arrangements as widely as possible. Through them the Agricultural Bank distributed credit, seeds, chemical fertilizers, and implements to farmers.[60] At the end of 1962 the majority of farmers still not members were compelled to join a co-operative and declare their holdings of land, livestock, and implements to its board of management,[61] while those who lived in the vicinity of an agrarian reform co-operative were obliged to join and adhere to its special arrangements for cultivation and marketing.[62]

After the nationalizations of July 1961, most of the inputs used by local cultivators were produced or distributed by the organizations within the public sector. For example, the Agricultural Bank controlled the provision of rural credit, and the distribution of chemical fertilizers. Most of the best quality seed used in Egypt was produced on farms either owned by the Ministry of Agriculture or more often by private firms under the technical supervision of the ministry. The government used its control over these intermediate products and credit to induce farmers to use the kind of seeds, fertilizers, and techniques experts thought would raise yields. To an increasing extent these inputs reached the farmer through his local co-operative society, and the public bodies concerned with agriculture dealt with boards of co-operatives and not directly with the cultivators themselves.[63]

Thus when planning began in July 1960 the cultivable land of Egypt was exploited through the combined efforts of the state, individual cultivators, and co-operatives. The government supplied vital irrigation water, credit, seeds, fertilizers, and machinery. On land reform areas the initiative allowed to individual owner-operators had been circumscribed, but for most of the agricultural sector the control of production remained effectively

[60] See below, pp. 99–100.

[61] *MRESE*, May 1962, p. 7; *BE*, 29 Jan. 1962; NBE, *Econ. B.*, iv (1962), p. 217.

[62] Law 83, 1963.

[63] *al-Ahram Econ. Suppl.* 15 June 1964, p. 48 and CBE, *Econ. R.*, ii (1963), p. 168.

in the hands of landowners, peasant proprietors, and tenant farmers, although the state brought some limited influence to bear upon their productive activities through its control over inputs and credit. But as the Plan progressed and results for the early years came in, for several reasons pressures built up for further institutional changes. First, agricultural output was not growing rapidly enough to obviate food shortages and inflation which emerged in 1963 and 1964 and Egypt became increasingly dependent upon the United States for aid in the form of wheat. Without this wheat either per capita consumption would have fallen or the government would have to divert scarce foreign exchange away from long-term capital formation towards imports of food.[64] At the same time the government disliked any degree of dependence upon a major power which rendered it vulnerable to pressure in its international relations. Next the Officers perceived that the additional output from the High Dam and other reclamation projects would take longer to appear and, given the rate of population growth, would make a much less significant impact upon Egypt's agricultural problem than they had initially anticipated. Moreover, even with the dam fully in operation, the bulk of agricultural output would continue to emanate from farms outside reclaimed lands or reform areas. Agricultural planners realized that the improved systems of crop rotation, the consolidation programme, and the reformed techniques of cultivation recommended so enthusiastically by experts had not and could not be applied at the required speed without further extensions of state control over farmers. As they saw it, the regeneration of agriculture required the continuous presence and pressure of government officials in the countryside. Plans, exhortations, even incentives were not enough.[65] If yields were to rise rapidly a new mechanism of control had to be created and by 1963 plans had crystallized to transform voluntary into supervised co-operatives.

The idea of supervised co-operatives emerged quite naturally because after a decade of experiment upon land reform estates they were considered to be a success. Voluntary co-operatives

[64] S. Naggar, *Foreign Aid to the United Arab Republic* (1964), pp. 66–71.

[65] *al-Ahram Econ. Suppl.*, 15 Nov. 1963, p. 35; *BE*, 22 Jan. & 22 Aug. 1962 & 9 Dec. 1963.

already existed throughout the countryside and the government could build upon a tradition of association among farmers going back several decades. As an ideology, co-operation evoked strong sympathy among the ruling élite. Their early manifestoes were full of patriotic appeals for co-operation between government and private producers to raise the national income. They eventually disregarded this notion for industry and trade, but retained and refined it for agriculture. Thus the Charter praised co-operatives for protecting farmers from middlemen and usurers, and it promised that the state would 'create co-operative organizations that are able to drive human efforts in the countryside to face its problems' (p. 65). Ministers conceived of co-operation in terms of a partnership between government and farmers, not as voluntary associations of farmers formed to promote their own material interests. Co-operatives, they held, suited Egyptian conditions because they respected the feelings of the fellahin for the ownership of land but at the same time avoided conflict between individual and social welfare.[67]

The rather general ideological discussion about the co-operative aspect of the 'Socialist, Democratic, and Co-operative Society' which has appeared in the press over the past three years reveals very little about what is actually happening in the countryside. Indeed, information about the organization and spread of the new co-operatives is extremely scarce. It is known that the government are proceeding cautiously because changes were initially introduced into just two provinces, Kafr Shaikh and Beni Suef, and only in the light of experience gained there, will institutional reforms be implemented throughout Egypt. Vice-President Sabry described the reorganization of agriculture in Kafr Shaikh and Beni Suef as

> A pioneer experiment. In the light of it we shall be able to organize agricultural production and to conduct agriculture along scientific lines. In short we shall be able to glimpse through it the general outlines of a socialist agricultural society.[68]

The mechanism of control introduced into Kafr Shaikh and Beni Suef duplicates that found on agrarian reform estates. It gives

[66] See remarks of Abdel Nur, Minister for Agrarian Reform, in *al-Ahram Econ. Suppl.* 1 Aug. 1964, p. 14.

[67] Marei in *al-Ahram*, 7 & 8 Mar. 1965.

[68] *al-Ahram*, 29 July 1963.

the government power to ensure that farmers cultivate their crops more scientifically and diversify output towards higher value produce, such as fruit, vegetables, meat, milk, and eggs. To assist local supervisors in guiding farmers in the use of seeds, fertilizers, and water the Ministry of Agriculture classified the soils in both governorates while the Ministry of Public Works laid down new networks of field drains connected to the public drainage canals in order that the flow of water on to and off each field could be regulated. In order to diversify output the government also distributed seedlings, young trees, calves, and improved varieties of chickens through them to the farmers free of charge. Free veterinary services and advice were also laid on. The government hoped that the purchase and use of machines by co-operatives would encourage farmers to breed cattle solely for the production of meat and dairy produce and that they would no longer use their animals for draught purposes.

Apart from raising the productivity of the land, the government used the new co-operatives to raise the productivity of rural labour. Light village industries were established within the administrative framework of co-operatives in order to provide work and income for the underemployed rural labour force. The Ministry of Industry surveyed possibilities and provided credit and organized markets for new village industries.[69]

Recently the Ministry of Agriculture proclaimed that the experiment at Kafr Shaikh and Beni Suef was a success and that plans had been formulated to introduce 'organized agriculture' into six more governorates during the Second Five-Year Plan.[70] But the ministry is perhaps unduly sanguine about the prospects for the implementation of its plans. Extensive institutional reform along the lines envisaged by the experiments at Kafr Shaikh and Beni Suef usually takes a long time to implement. Large-scale industry and commerce could be transferred overnight into the public sector, but farming poses administrative problems which have defied solution even in more totalitarian societies like China.[71] To set up supervised co-operatives will require the

[69] Min. Agrarian Reform, *The Project for Transforming Agricultural Production in Kafr Shaikh and Beni Suef* (unpubl. memo., n.d., ar.) and *al-Ahram Econ. Suppl.*, 1 Aug. 1964.

[70] *MRESE*, Jan. 1965, pp. 8 & 61 and *al-Ahram*, 27 Mar. 1965.

[71] K. Walker, *Planning in Chinese Agriculture* (1965).

creation of a bureaucracy devoted to the aims of co-operation and skilled enough to carry scientific agriculture into the villages. Upon village officials will fall the difficult task of persuading farmers to consolidate their holdings, to adopt novel methods of cultivation, to grow new crops, and to play a positive part in increasing the efficiency of agriculture. But as agents of the central power they must live and work among a people long suspicious of government and all its works. They will be intimately involved with cajoling and inducing an illiterate and conservative peasantry to employ new methods of cultivation and to diversify output. The conservatism of the fellahin should not, however, be exaggerated. During Egypt's long tradition of commercial agriculture they have shown themselves to be more adaptable and responsive to prospects of material gain than is often the case in underdeveloped countries.[72]

Nevertheless, the task facing local officials will be formidable enough; much more formidable than that previously confronted by the authorities on agrarian reform estates where a much smaller group of landless and carefully selected peasants were beholden to the government for their farms and could in any case be evicted for intransigence. Moreover the Higher Committee for Agrarian Reform operated right from the start within the framework of supervised co-operatives. Many Egyptian peasants, as small tenant cultivators, are, however, in the habit of taking instructions from their landlords, and one would expect them to be equally amenable to obeying government orders. But this class of small tenant cultivators, while numerically important, controls not more than 40 per cent of cultivable land. Throughout the countryside officials will encounter a much smaller group of owner-cultivators who farm about 60 per cent of the land and whose traditional independence and financial status will make them much less easily intimidated by authority.[73] This latter group contains the most efficient farmers found in the Nile valley, who are frequently the leaders of existing co-operative societies. If they are alienated, yields might easily fall, at least in the short run. Vice-President Sabry optimistically expected that the 'peasants would doubtless realize that the changes are for their

[72] O'Brien, in Holt.
[73] NBE, *Econ. B.*, i (1957), p. 46 and *Basic Statistics*, pp. 62–63.

own benefit.[74] Yet there are already signs in the press that the Egyptian 'kulak' class does not wholeheartedly support government policy. At the Congress of Popular Powers in June 1962 delegates indulged in a lengthy discussion as to whom might or might not be called a fellah. Some delegates wished to restrict the term to owners or not more than 5 feddans and to label other landowners 'capitalists', but eventually the term was defined to include all members of co-operatives, a definition which excluded agricultural labourers.[75] Abdel Latif Mandur, Director-General of the Organization for Co-operatives, remarked later that he wanted the boards of co-operatives reconstituted to include at least 80 per cent representation from among smallholders, but a member of parliament called upon the executive not to dissolve the elected boards of agricultural co-operatives,[76] while recently the Minister of Agrarian Reform admitted in an interview that popular forces (the Arab Socialist Union) are assisting the government to spread co-operatives by publicizing their advantages among farmers and warning the authorities about abuses and deviations.[77] How far these scraps of ambiguous evidence reflect an ideological antipathy to rural capitalists or are symptomatic of the difficulties the government is now meeting in introducing supervised co-operatives into the villages is difficult to tell.

While the shortage of suitable personnel and opposition from the richer peasants are likely to prove the most serious obstacle to the rapid reorganization of agriculture, the whole programme rests on the further assumption that government can and will create supplementary facilities to serve the new co-operatives. For example, not only must houses be erected to accommodate officials, but buildings to store seeds, fertilizers, pesticides purchased by the co-operatives from government agencies, and sheds to house the machinery owned by the co-operative have to be constructed. Mandur told *al-Ahram* in 1962 that only half of existing co-operatives possessed suitable buildings for these purposes.[78] If the trend towards diversification of output is to be reinforced, the government needs to cover all rural areas with a

[74] *al-Ahram*, 29 July 1963.
[75] *al-Goumhouriyya*, 29 May & 14 June 1962.
[76] *al-Ahram Econ. Suppl.*, 1 Dec. 1962, pp. 35–37 and *al-Ahram*, 2 June 1965.
[77] *al-Ahram Econ. Suppl.*, 1 Aug. 1964, p. 15.
[78] Ibid. 1 Dec. 1962, p. 36.

network of veterinary stations and to distribute more stock, poultry, and seedlings from its farms. Only if the Ministry of Agriculture surveys local soils and the Ministry of Public Works designs and constructs adequate field drainage will local supervisors be in a position to introduce farmers to the scientific application of seeds, fertilizers, and water. Since no strong tradition of village handicrafts exists in Egypt, the Ministry of Industry must explore the possibilities and set up rural industries before the co-operatives can begin to use their underemployed labour to manufacture saleable commodities.[79] Finally, as the state intends the co-operatives to take charge of marketing in order to eliminate all middlemen between farmers and consumers, it will have to establish facilities for gathering, sorting, classifying, storing, and transporting farm produce to urban and export markets. From time to time announcements appear in the press to the effect that the government has set up new organizations for marketing cotton, onions, or potatoes which will relieve cultivators from 'the greed or exploitation of merchants'.[80] But alternative marketing organizations, except for major cash crops, like cotton and rice, are far from extensive.

If present plans for agriculture are implemented (and their execution depends upon the co-operation of farmers, the creation of an efficient local bureaucracy, and heavy investment by the government in a whole range of ancillary agricultural services), by 1970 the institutional framework arrangements for the exploitation of Egyptian agriculture will be radically transformed. The production unit will then be a co-operative which combines a strong measure of central control with private ownership of land and only a limited amount of individual initiative. Unless further measures of land reform are introduced, the distribution of wealth and income in the countryside will, however, stay roughly as it is now, and farmers' incomes will remain proportionate to the yields from their own holdings of land. Egyptian experiments first on land reform estates and later with supervised co-operatives outside land reform areas appear to have produced

[79] Min. Agrarian Reform, *Project for Transforming Agric. Production* (ar.).

[80] *al-Ahram Econ. Suppl.*, 1 May 1962, p. 49; 1 Dec. 1962, pp. 35–37; 1 June 1963, p. 4; 15 Nov. 1963, pp. 35–36; *BE*, 13 Jan. 1962 & 27 & 31 Mar. 1963.

a fairly unique form of production unit which if successful might prove capable of adaptation in other parts of the *tiers monde*.

CONCLUSION

When comprehensive planning opened in July 1960, the Egyptian government faced the problem of how to ensure compliance from the private sector with its plans for the economy. By the end of the Plan it had solved the problem of control by enlarging the public sector to include big industrial companies, and all firms engaged in foreign trade, financial services, construction, and transport. In order to introduce a much stronger measure of central control over farming it had begun to transform agricultural institutions. These changes were accompanied by a leftward reorientation of the ruling élite's ideology, and in 1965 Egypt had emerged in theory at least as a 'Socialist, Democratic, and Co-operative Society'. Several commentators have questioned the applicability of one or other, even all, of these adjectives to the political and economic system which now exists but they can hardly deny that radical changes have occurred and that the years of the First Five-Year Plan witnessed the demise of the old private-enterprise system in Egypt.[81]

[81] For theoretical analyses of the Egyptian economic, social, and political systems see Riad, pp. 219–36 and Abdel-Malek, 'Nasserism and Socialism', in J. Saville and R. Miliband, eds., *The Socialist Register* (1964), pp. 38–52.

VII

The Socialist Economic System

THE OLD AND THE NEW ECONOMIC SYSTEMS

THE economy inherited by the Free Officers after their coup d'état in July 1952 possessed most of the salient characteristics of a free-enterprise system. Private individuals owned most of Egypt's land, minerals, houses, and productive capacity. Nevertheless a sizeable proportion of the national wealth, in the form of irrigation works, roads, railways, postal and telecommunications, schools and hospitals remained in public ownership. Ownership rights were not absolute but limited by the familiar code of civil laws designed to protect people from anti-social action by property owners. Rights to buy, sell, and bequeath property were guaranteed by law and free from state interference.

Egyptian citizens used their assets or loaned them to others for employment in production. That is, they combined land and capital with labour to produce a flow of goods and services. Similarly, the government utilized publicly-owned property and employed labour to provide society with output and services of a collective kind, such as irrigation and transport, health, education, defence, security, and justice.

Unfortunately estimates of the national wealth divided into its public and private components are not available, but production classified in this way can be broken down between the two sectors. Our tables show that at the beginning of the revolution most national output emanated from enterprises in the private sector.[1] At that time government production consisted overwhelmingly of the provision of services, such as defence, security, social welfare, irrigation, and transport. Directly or indirectly the services of the state were used by private producers in their economic activities, but government's own contribution to final output was minor.

[1] See table 16 (p. 33), col. 1. The structure of output is not a good indication of the division of wealth between public and private ownership because the capital-output ratio in the public sector was probably much higher than it was for the private sector.

The classification of an economic system based upon criteria of legal ownership reveals little about the actual organization of production. Private ownership of the means of production is not synonomous with enterprise free from intervention by the state, although historically the connexion has been strong. Nor can public ownership be equated with central control. In practice the autonomy of producers varies considerably even under identical patterns of ownership. Witness the different ways economic affairs are managed in Russia and Yugoslavia, where nearly all resources are publicly owned, and in Sweden and Lebanon which operate on the basis of private property. Comparisons between the way production is organized in different countries or contrasts between changes in its organization over time for a single society are normally made by isolating key decision-making units in an economy and analysing the freedom allowed to them by the state. Systems which afford autonomy to enterprises, permit households to consume whatever they can buy, and give workers the right to choose their own occupations and hours of work are usually described as free-market economies. Under such systems resources are allocated and output produced to accord with the preferences of consumers, as they are revealed through the pattern of relative prices, and with the desires of producers for profits.

Alternatively, in totalitarian or command economies, the state plays an important, usually the dominant part, in the allocation of resources. Labour is in some cases strongly induced and in others directed towards particular jobs and places of work. Through its overall control of the educational system the state takes very positive steps to ensure that society's requirements for skilled manpower are met. Enterprises are told what to produce and the government establishes mechanisms to see that its orders are obeyed. Of course consumers' preferences cannot be ignored but within limits they are manipulated through subsidies, indirect taxes, and the free allocation of goods and services, in order to produce a preordained pattern and distribution of output.

Before the revolution the Egyptian economy possessed most of the characteristics normally associated with *laissez-faire* free market systems of production.[2] Private purchases accounted for the bulk of total national expenditure and within broad limits

[2] For documentation of the following summary see above, pp. 46–60.

households consumed whatever they chose and could afford to buy. Their discretion to purchase meat, sugar, and vegetable oil had, however, been limited by rationing. Nor could consumers buy an unlimited range and quantity of commodities produced outside Egypt because the government enforced restrictions against luxury imports from hard-currency areas such as Germany, Sweden, and the United States in order to preserve scarce foreign exchange for more essential purposes. For the same reason the government did not allow Egyptians to invest their savings in foreign assets and compelled them to repatriate all earnings from exports.

In addition, the government acted upon the preferences of households through the price mechanism. Directly and indirectly it manipulated prices to secure certain policy objectives. Tariffs, for example, not only restrained the deficit on the balance of payments and stimulated local industry but also orientated local demand towards domestic products. Price controls and subsidies imposed upon a range of necessities such as bread, sugar, meat, tea, coffee, vegetables, and oils prevented households on low incomes from being deprived of basic foodstuffs. Even before the revolution, consumers' sovereignty had been modified by state intervention, but for the most part the structure of demand and the pattern of relative prices which reflected it represented the preferences of households and served to guide the decisions of producers.

Enterprises in agriculture, industry, and services were in general privately owned and their managers operated in order to maximize profits or at least to avoid losses. Profit was the criterion of success for any firm, farm, partnership, or individual enterprise. Failure to make profits led ultimately to the disappearance of the enterprise. Managers enjoyed considerable freedom to produce whatever they liked, in whatever quantities they thought best, using the techniques of production they found appropriate. Of course, their initiative always remained subject to the constraints of the market, the availability of finance, and the technological possibilities open to them but the amount of legal restrictions on the discretion of individual enterprises, while it had increased steadily since the First World War, was still slight.

Farmers appear to have been subjected to somewhat more

interference than any other group of producers. The government, in order to stabilize their incomes and to maximize receipts of foreign exchange, restricted the cultivation of cotton and compelled them to devote a minimum area to wheat. Farmers could not export grain or livestock and part of their wheat crop had to be delivered to the Ministry of Supply at a fixed price. If farmers associated together voluntarily in co-operatives in order to buy and sell in bulk or to take advantage of facilities for cheap credit, the accounts of the co-operatives became subject to official audit and all decisions of the board were liable to ministerial veto.

Regulations affecting enterprises in the industrial and service sectors of the economy related mainly to conditions of employment for labour and included provisions for safety regulations, health and holiday benefits, the employment of women and minors, and a minimum daily wage. But these laws applied only to larger firms because the administrative problem of extending welfare legislation to the myriad of small enterprises found in trade and manufacturing proved administratively intractable.

Traders in the export-import business operated within the system of regulations affecting nearly all transactions in foreign exchange. All earnings from exports had to be surrendered to the Central Bank, which then allocated foreign exchange in accordance with the system of priorities established by the Ministry of Economy.

Except for controls on the allocation of land and foreign exchange and the laws related to conditions of employment, producers enjoyed independence. Those who managed the thousands of enterprises which made up the Egyptian productive system decided what and how much to produce, where to buy their raw materials, machinery, and other inputs, how to combine labour and capital, where to locate the firm, when to expand or contract operations, how much to distribute in dividends or pay in wages. Each manager, faced with a set of prices for his output and for his inputs, operated in order to maximize profits.

In this free-market system government confined its activities to creating conditions within which private producers might flourish and to ameliorating some of the evils of unregulated capitalism upon the poorer classes. But the role of government was not nearly so circumscribed as these classical prescriptions might at first sight suggest. The creation of conditions within which Egyptian private enterprise could develop traditionally involved the state in a more extensive range of functions than the mere provision of defence, security, and justice. For centuries the government had exercised overall responsibility for the maintenance and expansion of the infrastructure, in the widest sense of that term, and during the post-war period public projects such as roads, railways, irrigation works, power supplies, schools, fresh water and health facilities, accounted for nearly a quarter of gross domestic fixed capital formation. In *laissez-faire* economies the bulk of investment usually reflects the wishes of private entrepreneurs for profits and the preferences of households for saving but in Egypt the state had traditionally played an important part in the crucial decision as to how much present output should be sacrificed for the sake of increased production in future.

Private producers also received considerable government support for their activities in the form of cheap credit channelled to farmers via the Crédit Agricole and to manufacturers through the Industrial Bank. The Ministry of Agriculture discovered and propagated new techniques of cultivation among farmers and the Ministry of Industry and Commerce supplied firms with technical and market information. Local industry also enjoyed a high level of protection, low rates of taxation upon its profits, rebates on the state railways, and occasional subsidies.

Consideration for the welfare of the poorer classes had prompted governments to try to protect the living standards of the urban working class in the face of inflation and to stabilize (albeit with partial success) the incomes of farmers, subject to the violent fluctuations which characterized the international market for cotton fibres. The state had made a start, but little more than a start, in building up the code of social welfare legislation now operative in most advanced industrial communities. Thus wages and conditions of employment had been regulated at least for a minority of the labour force. The provision of some kind of elementary education for the lower classes had increased steadily since the First World War. Through the Combined Centres for health and social welfare the state gave some attention to the glaring problems of illiteracy, malnutrition, and disease which characterized the lives of the mass of Egyptians who lived in villages. But, while there is no logical connexion between a system of production and the care society takes of its poor, sick, aged, and unemployed, it cannot be said that a concern for the deprived characterized the private-enterprise society of Egypt before the revolution.

Within a decade of the revolution economic organization had undergone such profound transformation that it could no longer be described as a free-market system. In theory at least Egypt now possesses a planned socialist economy, but to give content to these adjectives is difficult, partly because changes are still under way and also because information is scarce. Anything written at the present time (1965) cannot be other than tentative and impressionistic.[3] The purpose of any productive system is to use a nation's scarce resources to satisfy people's material wants. Our immediate concern is not to evaluate how well or efficiently the emergent socialist economy performs this task but rather to describe how in fact it functions.[4] First, an attempt will be made to define the sense in which the economy is planned. Then, in order to describe the system in operation, attention will be focused on three key decisions relating to production, investment, and consumption, or, more colloquially, I will try to show who decides what to produce, how, and for whom.

As an introduction it is perhaps useful to try to measure the size of the public and private sectors in Egypt. Unfortunately no figures have been issued which classify national wealth into its private and public components, but we can say that since land and houses have not been nationalized, the bulk of Egyptian property remains privately owned.[5] President Nasser put the nominal capital of the companies affected by the original nationalization laws of July 1961 at £258 million, which was about two-thirds of the total share capital of companies then registered in Egypt. Companies are not, however, synonomous with enterprises. Thousands of small-scale concerns operate in trade and

[3] A good deal of my imperfect understanding of the Egyptian economy was gleaned from conversations with managers, economists, and civil servants during my study leave in Cairo, 1962–3.

[4] The organization of this chapter has been heavily influenced by T. Scitovsky, *Welfare and Competition* (1952).

[5] Issawi, *Egypt in Revolution* (1964), p. 119 points out that before the war houses and land accounted for approximately two-thirds of the national capital.

industry without a registered capital or legal status of any kind. Presumably nearly all the £258 million of shares have now been taken into public ownership, and we might conclude that only about a third of industrial and commercial enterprises of any size or legal status remain in private hands.[6]

Figures of output emanating from public or private producers are equally scarce and the very notion of sectors which are public and private is ambiguous until the terms have been carefully defined. The budget forecast for 1962–3 provides the following breakdown, which might be compared with the national income estimate for 1953 in order to reveal the extent of change.

TABLE 6

Output from Public and Private Sectors in 1953 & Forecast Output for 1962–3

(£ million)

Sector	*1953* *Public sector*	*1953* *Private sector*	*1962–3* *Public sector*	*1962–3* *Private sector*
Agriculture	—	272.8	28.5	440.7
Industry & electricity	1.4	74.3	167.7	208.7
Transport & communications	16.6	55.0	92.9	30.7
Financial services	—	20.8	30.8	—
Trade	—	129.4	30.5	116.0
Housing	—	57.7	—	78.0
Construction	—	20.3	21.0	70.0
Public administration	110.0	—	184.0	—
Other services	—	106.3	3.9	130.4
Total Gross Domestic Product	128.0	736.6	559.3	1,074.5

Notes: The figures for 1962–3 are a planned or forecast national output. The sectoral classification (agriculture, industry, &c.) between the two estimates are not strictly comparable.

Sources: Statistics Dept, *National Income of Egypt for 1953* (*1955*) and *UAR State Budget for 1962–3* (1962), INP Memo 209.

Budget definitions are based mainly upon criteria of legal ownership, and if we wish to isolate that part of the economy under definite government *control* it is more relevant to use the

[6] NBE, *Econ. B.*, iv (1961), table 29 and Issawi, *Egypt in Revolution*, p. 60.

social accounts for 1958 which divide national output between two categories of enterprise: those employing ten workers and above and those employing less. Assuming quite plausibly that all the larger-scale enterprises can be defined as part of the public sector, the following picture then emerges.[7]

TABLE 7

Estimated Proportions of Output from Private & Public Sectors
(Per cent)

Sector	*Public*	*Private*
Agriculture	20	80
Extractive industry	88	12
Transformation industry	60	40
Building & construction	—	—
Gas, electricity, & water	100	—
Wholesale & retail trade	14	86
Financial services	100	—
Insurance	100	—
Housing	—	—
Transport & communications	52	48
Entertainment	5	95
Personal services	22	78

Notes & Sources: This is a rough estimate based on the assumption that all enterprises employing ten or more workers are now part of the public sector. Public sector means under government control but not necessarily under full state ownership. Some companies in the public are in mixed ownership (*al-Ahram*, 13 Aug. 1963). The sectoral classification and figures are from Dept of Statistics & Census, *National Income Estimates for the UAR, 1957 and 1958* (n.d., ar.). Some sectors could not be divided between large and small firms and are left blank. Other sectors are excluded entirely. The table is not intended to be comprehensive but serves as a rough guide.

Of course, it is not sensible to define agricultural output in this way, but making the further bold assumption that supervised co-operatives now cover about 20 per cent of the cultivated area, it is possible to estimate that about 40 per cent of national output

[7] The assumption certainly appears plausible for industry because the Minister of Industry said in a speech that public companies in organized industry produce 92 per cent of the output from firms employing ten or more workers (*al-Ahram*, 13 Aug. 1963).

now comes from the public sector; a situation in sharp contrast to the beginning of the revolution when the private sector accounted for 85 per cent of gross domestic product.

PLANNING

Ostensibly all productive activity now takes place within the framework of a comprehensive plan: three plans to be precise—a decennial plan, the Five-Year Plan, and annual plans. The first sets out in general terms output, employment, and investment goals for agriculture, industry, and services for the decade 1960–70. The Five-Year Plan tabulates in much greater detail targets for output and employment for all sectors and sub-sectors of the economy for 1964–5 and 1969–70 and shows the total investment in terms of local and foreign currencies needed to bring production to that level over five years. The Five-Year Plan contains commodity flow tables which measure the imports plus local production available to the country and the uses of these resources for exports, final consumption, inputs, investments, and stocks for the base year 1959–60 and as targets for the year 1964–5. Next the Plan spells out the implication of these production targets in terms of flows of revenue and expenditure for base and target years. Thus it tabulates the amounts of wages, property incomes, and taxes paid to households, enterprises, and the government for their respective parts in production and the employment of this revenue for consumption, saving, lending, payment of taxes, &c. Output, income, and expenditure encompass economic activity looked at from three distinct points of view. Articulated in figures they form the Comprehensive Plan.[8] Annual plans of the same format but in somewhat greater detail form the reference point for economic activity throughout a given period—July to July. They operate within the broad framework of the decennial and Five-Year Plans but their function is to introduce flexibility and realism into a changing economic situation.[9]

Divorced from any discussion of possibilities for their implementation and taken at face value, such comprehensive plans suggest that the volume and composition of domestic output and

[8] *Gen. Frame of 5-Year Plan.*
[9] *Ann. Plans, 1960–1, 1961–2, & 1962–3.*

imports, the allocation of resources between consumption, investment, and exports, the transfer of raw materials and intermediate products among enterprises, the deployment of labour, the level of wages, the division of income between expenditure and saving, and even the pattern of consumption are now centrally planned. Plans apparently coextensive with every sphere of economic activity and so detailed in their provisions often give the misleading impression that the economy operates within or is bound by a fully comprehensive system of regulations drawn up by the central authorities.

But Egypt's plans are not blueprints for detailed regulation of the economy. Nor are they formulated by the central authorities alone. They embody significant elements of decentralization. The crucial decision on a feasible target for Egypt's long-term economic development was, however, taken by the highest political authorities. Faced with a rapidly growing population, the government aimed to increase the rate of growth in order to raise real per capita consumption. Recommendations to the President about a possible target for national output were made by the National Planning Committee, in the light of several projections its experts made of the resources likely to be available to the country over the following two decades.[10] Other but less optimistic growth rates were put forward by the Mixed Committees on the Means of Finance.[11] Ultimately the overall target to double national income by 1970 was selected by the Presidential Council. On what basis we cannot know, but probably the decision represented a political rather than a technical choice, in the sense that the Free Officers were determined to achieve a dramatic break-through on the economic front over a short period of time.[12]

[10] NPC, *Frames for a Long-Term Plan,* Memos 44, 71, 99, 103, 124 (1958 & 1959, ar.).

[11] NPC, *Estimates of Committee on the Means of Finance* (1959, ar.), Memos 216–20. These Mixed Committees representing public organizations, private business, and independent experts had been set up in 1959 to assist the NPC in the task of building up the Plan. The Mixed Committees regarded most of the estimates of available resources by the NPC as unduly optimistic.

[12] NPC, *Doubling National Income in 10 or 20 Years* (1959, ar.), Memo. 288; *UAR Yearbook 1959*, p. 82. Dr Abdel-Rahman (Deputy Minister of Planning) suggests that the 'ambitious target' was set in the light of demographic projections (INP Memo. 76).

Given the overall goal centrally determined, the National Planning Committee broke it down into a feasible set of sectoral targets for a five-year period. 'Feasible' means that the Committee explored latent potentialities for expansion in several parts of the economy, again aided by Mixed Committees, and its suggested growth rates for industry, agriculture, and services took full account of input-output relationships between different sectors and sub-sectors. Next the National Planning Committee worked out the implications of the targets in terms of investment, savings, foreign exchange, and manpower.[13] Elements of decentralization appeared at the final stage of planning. Thus when the sectoral allocation of investible funds had been decided in the light of the macro-relationships established by the National Planning Committee, the ministries responsible for particular sectors distributed the funds made available to them among competing projects and retained full responsibility for executing its particular investment programme and for the production targets established for given sectors, subject in theory to the constraint of consistency with other parts of the Plan.[14]

Investment plans and production targets did not, however, just emanate from government departments but were often suggested by the different organizations and companies attached to them, or by private firms operating within the same sector. Most of the projects now being implemented originated in or were examined by the Mixed Committees. Many pre-date the Plan and are often schemes designed by private companies now inside the public sector. The general point to emphasize is that the selection and implementation of projects included in the Plan were and continue to be a highly decentralized process.[15]

Further, in practice the consistency constraint broke down and the macro-relationships established by the National Planning Committee to co-ordinate the allocation of resources between different sectors did not effectively restrain the choice of projects by individual departments. When the Minister of Planning attempted to cut back investment or reject projects put forward

[13] M. Imam, *Models Used in Drafting the Plan* (1962), INP Memo. 255; INP Memo. 238; N. Dief, *Some Uses of Economic Accounting in Planning Economic Development of the UAR* (1962), INP Memo. 210.

[14] NPC Memos 164 & 165.

[15] INP Memo. 63.

by his colleagues on the grounds that sufficient resources could not be made available, ministers invariably argued that the capital and labour output coefficients employed by the National Planning Committee exaggerated the skilled manpower, foreign exchange, and domestic savings required for the project in question. For reasons which are not yet clear their arguments found support within the Presidential Council, and the National Planning Committee never succeeded in enforcing its authority upon recalcitrant departments. Many projects found their way into the Plan despite its admonitions and efforts to preserve consistency with resources likely to be available.[16] The result is that the Five-Year Plan, when it emerged in July 1960, consisted of a collection of projects initiated by different government departments with an overall framework superimposed by the National Planning Committee. As a careful scrutiny of the relevant documents will show, the initial macro-frame worked out at the centre exercised only slight influence upon the sectoral plans drawn up by different ministries.[17] Egypt's First Five-Year Plan is really an amalgam of investment projects loosely co-ordinated into a single document.

If central planning means that the authorities not merely produce an integrated and detailed set of targets for most parts of the economy but seriously endeavour to compel those in charge of resources to comply with its aims, then Egypt has never experienced central planning. Given the division of power over the nation's land, labour, and capital which existed in 1959–60, the government could hardly expect to plan in this sense. As a document the Five-Year Plan is certainly comprehensive, but as implemented it is in fact an investment programme for the public sector set within a series of projections for other parts of the productive system. Much of the Plan is indicative, in the sense that its tables elucidate conditions for the achievement of the growth rate and for the volume and composition of investment established by the central authorities. That is to say the tables spell out in great detail how much additional production, employment, imports, exports, and foreign loans will be needed for success, and how commodities must flow between different parts of the economy.

[16] Sources for these statements are yet to be published.

[17] Compare NPC Memos 124, 198, 353, 429, 431, 432, 444, & 451 (1959 & 1960, ar.).

In brief, the Plan articulates in full the implications of increasing national output by 40 per cent over five years, in terms of income, expenditure, and financial flows.

The second point to observe about Egypt's Plans is that they were not formulated in order to supersede the market and price mechanisms by some alternative system of resource allocation organized from the centre. On the contrary, planners operated throughout on the assumption that markets would continue to function for the supply of raw materials, intermediate products, and labour to enterprises and also for the distribution of finished commodities among consumers. Although the Plan does contain input-output and commodity-flow tables, they were never intended to be other than sets of figures indicative of what would occur if the overall production and investment targets were met by 1964–5. Planners established output and employment targets for sectors but not for each enterprise. They assumed that producers would continue to purchase inputs on the existing markets for labour and raw materials, and that workers would remain free to offer their services where they pleased. They made no arrangements for the allocation of labour and intermediate products among enterprises. In other words, Egyptian Plans do not presume to instruct producers how to meet output targets. There is no plan which tells them how to combine land, labour, and capital. Managers are left free to operate within roughly the same system of regulated markets as prevailed before 1960. The Plan assumes that they will minimize the use of scarce factors and inputs in order to maximize profits, and in this respect it is really a set of instructions to producers and workers to react to the dictates of the market.[18]

Nor do the Plans attempt seriously to modify the price mechanism for the distribution of commodities among consumers. Consumers are left free to spend in accordance with their wishes. Moreover, Egyptian planners seem to have paid more attention to consumers' wishes than is often the case with planners elsewhere, who realistically do not ignore household preferences, but assume that the government will manipulate prices or incomes to clear the market. Apparently the Egyptian planners drew up the final bill of goods for 1964–5 by using Engel's-type coefficients derived

[18] Morshidy, pp. 48–49 & 81–85 and INP Memo. 238.

from the Family Budget Survey for 1959 and other sources.[19] Many of their proposed alterations to the structure of output are not innovations but consist in the replacement of imports by domestic substitutes. If their assumptions about the future distribution of expenditure turn out to be correct, the assortment of final output, ostensibly planned, reflects at least in a rough way the preferences of consumers.

While indicators contained in the Plan are not really targets (defined as positive injunctions to enterprises, workers, and households), they are guide-lines for public policy or goals for the work of different departments. They were intended to be something more than the set of pious hopes characteristic of many indicative plans. Planners expected that the huge addition to public expenditure would stimulate producers throughout industry, agriculture, and services to provide the complementary resources necessary for success. Moreover much of the planned investment programme was designed to set up backward and forward linkage effects throughout the economy. For example, government investment in veterinary and tractor stations, improved fertilizers and seeds, irrigation and drainage canals clearly sought to raise yields on private farms. All improvements and extensions to the infrastructure were expected to engender external economies and induce higher levels of production over a wide front, while the demands and opportunities created by the establishment of heavy industry would, planners anticipated, activate private enterprise throughout manufacturing industry. In addition, the government manipulated interest rates or issued instructions to banks in order to encourage or discourage particular types of production. Tax exemptions, import licences, and guaranteed levels of protection were also used to push private production along lines complementary to the state's own investment programme.[20] And the Plan's targets also served to guide and co-ordinate monetary, fiscal, and commercial policy implemented by different public departments.[21]

Indirect techniques of persuasion often prove ineffective in underdeveloped countries and had already been found wanting in

[19] For the discussion of consumption see NPC Memos 155, 245, 308, & 445 (1959–60, ar.).

[20] Morshidy, pp. 41, 76–77, & 82.

[21] INP Memo. 238.

Egypt. Thus once planning began the government extended its powers over the nation's resources by nationalizing all large-scale companies in industry and commerce and by initiating a policy for the establishment of supervised co-operatives throughout the countryside. Gradually it became possible for the government to exercise real command over large areas of the productive system. No doubt orders are now issued to the constituent enterprises of the public sector, but between 1960 and 1965 no obvious change appears to have occurred in the basic character of Egyptian planning despite the vastly increased potentialities for central control obtained by the authorities. Nationalized enterprises have been left free to operate more with reference to the dictates of the market than to orders from the central government. This is less true for supervised co-operatives, which are institutions designed specifically to limit the discretion of farmers, but these co-operatives are not yet widespread. On the whole, planning continues to be indicative. Detailed commands do not flow from the centre to enterprises and farmers telling them what and how to produce.

But investment is definitely planned and takes place within the framework of the medium- and long-term plans. This means that the strategy and priorities adopted in 1959–60 still guide the allocation of resources for capital formation in all parts of the economy, but the rate, phasing, and distribution of investment for any given year is accomplished with reference to an annual plan. Annual plans accord with long-term goals for development but are designed to introduce flexibility into a dynamic situation. They are used to co-ordinate the investment expenditure of all public organizations and private enterprises. Their aim is to balance multiple claims upon scarce resources in order to avoid the delays and shortages which had frustrated several programmes of public investment since the war. They also provide the central authorities with a ready means for comparing the achievements of different ministries against the funds allocated to them. Annual plans embody investment targets for every sector of the economy and detailed figures for production, exports, imports, saving, and consumption. Only the investment targets form the subject of commands from the central authorities to public departments. They alone have executive significance. All other figures are forecasts of the way the Ministry of Planning expects the economy to change over the coming year.[22]

In order to test the feasibility of continuing the investment programme at a faster or slower rate the Ministry of Planning attempts to predict the resources likely to be available for one year ahead and to reconcile different demands on scarce supplies of manpower, domestic saving, foreign exchange, &c. with its forecasts.[23] These predictions rest largely upon a series of project and progress reports submitted by other government departments at quarterly intervals throughout the year. Progress reports are questionnaires designed by the Ministry of Planning to elicit information about current developments in almost every part of the economy. They are aggregated to provide statistics on output, foreign trade, and aid, the movement of wages and prices, the flow of commodities and finance between sectors, and the level of consumption. Project reports on the other hand emanate from the officials immediately responsible for executing a particular investment project. They set out details on expenditure so far, forecast requirements for the coming period in physical and monetary terms, and contain an analysis of any difficulties retarding completion of the project. Progress reports provide a check on the activities of the authorities responsible for implementing the plans and form the basis for next year's plan. Project reports indicate if execution is on or off schedule, suggest any necessary modifications to the original targets, and enable the ministry to locate and remedy the causes of delay. In the light of this assembled information the Ministry of Planning predicts the resources likely to be available for the coming year, works out a feasible rate of investment, and co-ordinates the claims on resources by the various executive departments into a viable plan. Annual plans are thus formulated with reference to the changing availability of resources, particularly foreign exchange, and embody the experience gained over previous years.[24] Of course, the process does not operate as smoothly as the official accounts like to suggest. Ministries inevitably battle for a higher share of available funds and frequently challenge the restraints imposed by the Ministry of Planning. Ultimate recon-

[22] Min. of Planning, *Ann. Plans 1960–1 & 1961–2* (1960 & 1961, ar.)
[23] INP Memo. 63.
[24] INP Memos 141 & 167.

ciliation of claims is achieved at the highest political level, within the Presidential Committee for Planning.

Finally, the annual plan is integrated with and receives executive force from the budget. The budget itemizes and appropriates subventions for public departments on capital account. It translates the targets of the plan into flows of income and expenditure. New budgetary procedures are at present being evolved to make the traditional accounting system a more effective instrument of control over public expenditure and to allow for the kind of flexibility demanded by business activity. At the same time the integration of output targets into traditional public accounting will show the central authorities how effectively different organs of the state utilize the funds allocated to them.[25]

Investment by the private sector is also planned, not in the sense that the government can command firms outside the public sector to execute particular projects but because nearly all capital formation requires official support and is included in the annual plan. For example, extensions to manufacturing plant operated by small-scale family firms need permission from the Ministry of Industry. Building is licensed by the municipalities, and all ministries keep a close watch on activities within their spheres of responsibility in order to report on progress to the Ministry of Planning. Private capital formation can rarely elude public scrutiny because the state allocates foreign exchange and bank credit, and most capital projects require one or other at some stage of their execution. Private investment is, therefore, planned in the sense that the government can prevent businessmen from competing with the public sector for scarce resources, and it will prohibit the kind of investment considered contrary to the national interest.[26]

Given the rather tenuous relationship between planning and economic activity, the question of how the system functions cannot be answered by analysing central plans, and it remains necessary to outline how key decisions related to production, investment, and consumption are taken in Egypt.

PRODUCTION

Production consists of converting inputs of land, labour, capital,

[25] Min. of Treasury, *Draft Budget 1963–4* (1964), pp. 1 & 5 and INP Memo. 76.
[26] Morshidy, pp. 22, 41, 53, 76, 82–83.

and raw materials into finished output. Those responsible for its organization face four basic problems: what to produce, how much to produce, how to produce, and what to do with the final output. The first two decisions, often called the rate and composition of output, are self-explanatory, but the choice of technique requires further brief elucidation. Occasionally there is no choice because the process of production is technologically determined, but options usually exist for combining factors of production in different proportions. For example, a farmer may use more land and less water to grow rice and a manufacturer may replace labour with machinery. With their input mix selected, producers still have to decide where to obtain raw materials or equipment, where to hire labour and to locate the enterprise. They must also choose how and where to dispose of their output.

To describe the organization of production before the revolution is relatively easy. All four basic decisions were taken by enterprises, which operated with reference to the dictates of the market. Those who managed the myriad concerns which made up the Egyptian economic system decided the rate and composition of output, combined factors of production in the proportions they thought appropriate, hired and fired labour, located capacity, purchased raw materials and capital, sorted, transported, and sold output. The criteria which guided their operations are also simple to describe. They aimed to make profits, and therefore produced whatever would sell in the cheapest way possible. In their choice of output and techniques of production they were guided by prices determined upon relatively free markets.

Today the situation is much more complex. With the extension of state power over every part of the economy, it is difficult to locate where decisions are taken and even harder to reveal the assumptions upon which they are based. In general it can be said that the answer to the question who takes decisions varies from sector to sector, between categories of decisions, and depends upon whether the enterprise is within or outside the public sector. The indicator guiding the behaviour of producers is still profit. Generalizations about the whole system are, however, inevitably vague and the best way to comprehend its complex character is to outline the organization of production sector by sector.

Agriculture is most difficult to describe because the sector is still undergoing rapid change. At the present time the institutional arrangements for cultivating land may be classified into traditional and modern. Modern farming is conducted by supervised co-operatives, located on the lands confiscated under the agrarian reforms of 1952 and 1961 and in the provinces of Kafr Shaikh and Beni Suef, but if government plans are implemented, by 1970 similar co-operatives will be found throughout the Egyptian countryside. These co-operatives are institutions which combine private ownership and individual initiative with collective farming and some control by the central authorities.

Constitutionally supervised co-operatives may include all the tenant farmers, share-croppers, and owner operators who cultivate the land of a village. They elect a board of directors and the number of votes cast by a member depends on the size of his farm. On land reform areas, where the distribution of land is more or less equal, the principle of one man one vote applies, but throughout most of the countryside larger farmers dominate the electorate. Suggestions have been made, even officially, for reforming the suffrage based upon property, but so far no changes have been introduced.[27] To each co-operative the central authorities appoint a supervisor, a president, and their assistants. The former is an agronomist, responsible for the technical side of cultivation. He guides farmers in the use of fertilizers, seeds, irrigation water, and techniques of cultivation. The latter and his staff are accountants whose functions are to buy all the inputs used by the co-operative, to sell its crops, and distribute the proceeds to farmers.[28]

Although the division of power between the elected board and the appointed staff is constitutionally vague and the government usually insists that officials are there simply to guide or advise, most observers have concluded that power is effectively in the hands of their appointed directors responsible to ministries in Cairo.[29] Probably the board represents the view of the villagers to the officials, but it seems reasonable to assume that elected boards of land reform co-operatives will be less powerful and vociferous than those elsewhere, which include much larger

[27] *al-Ahram Econ. Suppl.*, 1 Dec. 1962, pp. 35–37 & 44–45.

[28] Min. Agrarian Reform, *Project for Transforming Agric. Production* (ar.).

[29] H. Marei, *Socialist Agriculture in the New Era* (1962, ar.), pp. 151–5; A. Goichon, 'Le plan de rénovation social de la campagne égyptienne', *Orient*, ii (1961), pp. 106–7.

farmers, not beholden to the state for their lands and who have traditionally exercised a dominant voice in local affairs.[30]

Regardless of how decisions are taken or where power really lies, the management of every co-operative aims to maximize output. In the short run the rate of output is determined by the availability of inputs which appear to be relatively fixed in supply and in the main allocated among co-operatives by the central authorities. The major inputs used in Egyptian agriculture include land, water, labour, fertilizers, seeds, pesticides, and machinery. Land is given by the boundaries of the village. If members purchase land beyond the village they join another co-operative. Water is made available by the Ministry of Public Works, and apart from natural variations in the level of the Nile, its volume can only be increased by public investment in irrigation facilities. For two reasons labour supplies are the most variable factor used by the co-operative: first, because underemployment and unemployment exists throughout the agricultural sector, and second, because the rural labour force contains a high proportion of women and children who are accessible and available for work if needed.[31] Fertilizers consist of natural manures and chemicals. The former are produced within the co-operative from its own animals, but the latter are overwhelmingly more important. Chemical fertilizers are supplied at fixed prices on credit by the Agricultural Bank. Since demand exceeds available supplies, the Bank in fact allocates fertilizers, and for any crop year the supply to a co-operative is fixed.[32] Seeds are produced within the co-operative or purchased from dealers controlled by the Ministry of Agriculture, but best quality seed, like fertilizers, is allocated by the ministry.[33] Government agencies also supply free or at subsidized prices the chemicals, equipment and veterinary services required to protect crops and livestock from pests and diseases.[34] Theoretically, the board is free to buy any number of machines for plough-

[30] Groupe d'Études de l'IDES, 'Pression démographique et stratification sociale dans les campagnes égyptiennes', *Tiers Monde*, July-Sept. 1960, pp. 314–29.

[31] *Gen. Frame of 5-Year Plan*, table 49.

[32] *BE*, 30 Jan. 1962; Marei, *Agricultural Development Programme*, pp. 7 & 11 and Law 166, 1963.

[33] *UAR Yearbook 1964*, p. 104; Marei, *Agric. Development Programme*, pp. 12 f., 18–19, 31 & 32.

[34] Ibid. pp. 45–46 and *UAR Yearbook 1963*, pp. 136–7.

ing, threshing, or field drainage it chooses but most agricultural machinery is imported and requests for foreign exchange must be vetted by the Ministry of Economy.[35] Although the mechanization of agriculture receives some priority, given the volume of claims for an extremely scarce resource, delays are inevitable and no co-operative will receive more than its share of foreign currency. The board's ability to purchase machinery is definitely limited.

Over the long run inputs used in the agricultural sector will become variable. In time foreign exchange should be available for the import of more agricultural chemicals and machinery. Moreover the Ministry of Industry is now constructing additional capacity to produce agricultural equipment and chemicals locally. The Ministry of Public Works is engaged upon schemes to extend the irrigation system and make more water available to farmers.[36] But at present all the factors of production with the exception of labour are relatively fixed in supply. This is not to say that supplies are completely inflexible. Natural manure, seeds, and second-hand machinery can be purchased on the market, but apart from these unimportant exceptions, the government does not allow any single co-operative to obtain more than its ration of selected seeds, fertilizers, machinery, and water. The board cannot bid for additional supplies in the open market; its task is to maximize output from the variable supplies of labour and relatively fixed supplies of other inputs available to the co-operatives.

Given these limitations on the volume of output, the board can maximize the value of production by allocating resources towards the cultivation of crops with higher prices. But its ability to vary the structure of output is limited: by technological restraints in the form of soil composition, the volume of irrigation water available, the rotation system, distance from markets, and above all by the skill and willingness of its farmers to depart from traditional patterns of production. The state restricts the area devoted to cotton and compels farmers to grow a minimum amount of wheat.[37] But agricultural policy aims to help the co-operatives to diversify output towards high-value produce such as milk products, meat, vegetables, and fruit. Thus government research stations provide

[35] *MRESE*, Aug. 1963, p. 19.

[36] Comité de Planification Nationale, *Cadre du Plan*, Annexe 3 and Min. Industry, *The Second 5-Year Industrial Plan* (1960).

[37] See above, pp. 47, 58, 79–80.

co-operatives with the technical information about the possibilities for horticulture in the difficult environment of the Nile valley. Veterinary units are being set up throughout the countryside to treat animals and give farmers advice about techniques in animal farming. The government are also engaged upon a programme to establish the packing, grading, and transport facilities needed to market fruit, vegetables, and meat. Finally, the Ministry of Agriculture distributes free or at subsidized prices young livestock, seedlings, trees, and new varieties of poultry from its own farms.[38]

One of the most important and frequently emphasized advantages of the new co-operatives is that their field layout has overcome the diseconomies associated with fragmented strip farming. In the traditional sector farms consist of separate holdings scattered over several fields. Apart from the waste of labour time involved in travelling between scattered plots, the proximity of different plants within a given area leads to inefficient farming and reduces productivity per feddan. Spraying, irrigation, the application of fertilizers and pesticides cannot be organized over a wide area. Diseases and pests spread between crops and excess water drains into neighbouring plots to the detriment of yields. Under the consolidated layout, universally adopted by supervised co-operatives, a farmer's holdings are relocated inside one field. Each field grows a single crop, follows a uniform scientific rotation, and can be ploughed, watered, drained, treated with fertilizer, sprayed, and harvested as a unit.[39]

Farming in the new co-operatives is a mixture of collective and individual enterprise. The board decides how to allocate land among different crops and the appropriate rotation to be followed, in the light of soil surveys and technical advice from its agronomists. Ploughing, the application of chemical fertilizers, watering, treatment against pests and plant diseases, and harvesting are generally collective activities organized by the board and utilize equipment owned by the co-operative.

Sowing, weeding, hoeing, and tending the crops are individual operations performed by the farmer upon his own land.[40] The

[38] See above, pp. 116–17 and Min. Agrarian Reform, *Project for Transforming Agric. Production* (ar.); *al-Ahram Econ. Suppl.*, 1 Aug. 1964.

[39] See above, pp. 118 and 119.

[40] See above, pp. 77 & 139 Min. Agrarian Reform, *Project for Transforming Agric. Production* (ar.).

farmer's aim is to maximize profits, and the factor supplies available to him are more variable than they are to the co-operative as a whole. He can purchase or rent more land, but the land market is now regulated to favour small units of ownership and control. Legally no family may own more than 100 feddans, lease more than 50 feddans in addition to its present holding, or sell more than 5 feddans to any single individual. And present controls upon rents and conditions of tenure undoubtedly operate to reduce the flow of land available for lease. At reduced rents and with their powers to reassume possession of a farm considerably restricted, landowners are likely to appreciate the advantages of cultivating their own lands. Farmers can also hire workers, theoretically at a minimum legal wage, but with an excess supply of labour available at any time, apart from seasonal peaks, the legal minimum cannot be enforced.[41] Cultivators can purchase natural manures, certain categories of seed, and other inputs from their fellow farmers within the village who either have a surplus or need ready cash. Nor is the division of functions between individual and collective enterprise rigid. In some co-operatives farmers retain the option of ploughing and harvesting their own plots, provided they fit into the schedules established for the whole village. Within the defined division of labour operated by the new co-operatives the behaviour of farmers approximates to the familiar model of profit-maximizing producers. That is to say, although choices related to the composition of output, the purchase and application of most inputs no longer rest with individuals, farmers nevertheless continue to employ and combine the remaining factors of production in order to maximize the difference between total costs and total revenue.

As has already been stated, the choice of technique open to a co-operative is limited by the shortages of agricultural machinery, fertilizers, chemicals, and best-quality seed, but within the narrow limits where options exist decisions are usually taken by the board. Government policy is to push new techniques and mechanized cultivation as far as possible in the hope that the use of tractors would release animals for draft work and encourage farmers to breed cattle for the production of meat and dairy produce.[42]

[41] B. Hansen, *Marginal Productivity Wage Theory in Egyptian Agriculture* (1965), INP Memo. 547.

[42] See above, pp. 116–18.

It also encourages co-operatives to construct roads, barns, hatcheries, storage buildings, and administrative offices for the village. With officials responsible to the Ministry of Agrarian Reform resident and dominant in every supervised co-operative, the government can ensure that the new institutions adopt scientific techniques of cultivation and raise the rate of fixed capital formation in the agricultural sector.

Capital-intensive techniques involve investment, which is a decision for the co-operative. While the board cannot depress real incomes of members, it possesses sufficient power to restrain rises in consumption. Certainly the marketing mechanism facilitates the accumulation of an investible surplus. Farmers retain subsistence and fodder crops but cash crops are sold for them by the co-operative. An account for each cultivator is kept at the administrative office which shows the amount received for his cash crop and on the debit side records charges made for commodities and services provided by the co-operative, such as ploughing, spraying, harvesting, threshing, and general administration, and the cost of inputs (seeds, fertilizers and pesticides).[43] The balance at the end of the year is the net cash income available for the payment of taxes, for distribution to the farmers, and for other expenditures decided upon by the board. For example, if the co-operative decides to buy a new irrigation pump or a tractor or to build a barn, the board obtains a loan from the Agricultural Bank and deducts the repayments from the money passing through its hands. The board can allocate cash to reserves, establish social security funds, or manipulate depreciation and other allowances in order to provide the finance for a predetermined rate of investment. It is interesting to observe that the new institutions also facilitate the direct taxation of rural incomes. Direct taxes upon agriculture have not so far been used to finance capital formation in Egypt, but with the spread of supervised co-operatives a mechanism is being created which will allow the state to mobilize the agricultural surplus for its industrialization programme.

Supervised co-operatives may be a portent of the future but at present they are far from widespread. The bulk of Egypt's farmers remain outside the modern sector, although even now they

[43] Min. Agrarian Reform, *Project for Transforming Agric. Production* (ar.) and Marei, *Socialist Agriculture* (ar.), p. 152.

cultivate within a much modified free-market system. For example, farmers are compelled to join the local co-operative, but these co-operatives simply bulk buy, negotiate credit, and sell cotton on behalf of their members.[44] Co-operatives purchase chemical fertilizers, best quality seeds, pesticides, and machinery from government agencies. Since the prices they pay are fixed and supplies are limited, the major inputs used by the traditional sector are also allocated between villages.[45] Water is rationed by the Ministry of Public Works and chemicals, machinery, and seeds are distributed through the co-operatives. Beyond this point the market operates. Farmers with a surplus of fertilizers, pesticides, or seeds obtained from the co-operative, or with spare natural manures or seeds produced on their own holdings sell to the highest bidder. The services of machinery and draught animals are also hired out by their owners. To the individual farmer only land and water are fixed in the short run; all other factors are variable and can be bought on the market.

In the traditional sector farmers determine the rate and composition of output and they also decide how to cultivate, the rotation to follow, and when to harvest. But for some years now the government has used all the means at its disposal to persuade farmers to diversify output towards meat, dairy produce, fruit and vegetables, and to utilize more scientific techniques of cultivation. Through the extension services and above all by its control over agricultural credit the government has been able to induce cultivators to diversify production and to farm more efficiently.[46] Moreover since 1960 the Ministry of Agriculture has been engaged upon a programme designed to persuade farmers to adopt the reformed field layout found within supervised co-operatives in order to obviate the diseconomies of fragmented holdings. According to official sources, the farmers have been impressed with the advantages in terms of higher yields and are enthusiastically consolidating their strips into composite holdings.[47]

Although the government has brought some influence to bear, ultimately key decisions are taken by farmers themselves. Guided

[44] See above, pp. 139 & 140.

[45] *BE*, 30 Jan. 1962 and *al-Ahram Econ. Suppl.*, 15 June 1964.

[46] See above, pp. 116 & 140.

[47] *al-Ahram Econ. Suppl.*, 1 Aug. 1964, p. 15; *UAR Yearbook 1964*, pp. 113–14.

by prices of inputs and outputs they decide what to grow and select their techniques of production. Investment in the traditional sector is a matter for those who own and farm the land, and unlike farmers in the modern sector they cannot be forced to save. Marketing of cotton and in some Governorates vegetables as well is, however, undertaken by the co-operative. Co-operatives have replaced landowners and middlemen as channels for the sale of cash crops, and as a result tenants' incomes have risen.[48]

Industry, like agriculture, can also be classified into two sectors. One includes all nationalized large-scale companies and the other a much greater number of small privately-owned concerns. The categories are not intended to be mutually exclusive. Not every private industrial enterprise is small and some companies in the public sector may be neither large nor owned entirely by the state.[49] For my purposes the categories private and public sectors can be defined in the above way. In terms of output the public sector is overwhelmingly more important, but the private sector employs more industrial workers.[50]

Responsibility for decisions affecting industrial production in the public sector is divided between the Ministry of Industry, 9 General Organizations, affiliated to the ministry, and 294 companies attached to one or other of the Organizations. Briefly, companies are units for production and General Organizations are like holding companies responsible to the ministry.

General Organizations are the successors to the old Chambers of Industry affiliated to the Federation of Egyptian Industry and are also modelled on the kind of public bodies set up since 1956 to supervise productive activity by the state, such as the Economic Organization and the Nasr and Misr Organizations. As early as 1953 the government compelled firms above a certain size to join the Chamber of Industry which specialized in their particular product. These chambers conducted market and technical research for constituent firms, often aided from public funds.[51] After the

[48] CBE, *Econ. R.*, ii (1963), p. 170 and *al-Ahram Econ. Suppl.*, 1 July 1962, pp. 36–38; 1 Dec. 1962, p. 38; 15 Nov. 1963, p. 35; *BE*, 4 Mar. & 31 Aug. 1963.

[49] Of the 294 companies attached to the Min. of Industry in August 1963, 28 were in mixed ownership (*al-Ahram*, 13 Aug. 1963).

[50] See tables 10 & 11. In June 1963, of 724,000 industrial workers, 284,000 were employed by the government (*MRESE*, July 1963, p. 87).

[51] Law 53, 1953 and NBE, *Econ. B.*, iv (1953), p. 291 & ii (1958), p. 103.

nationalizations of July 1961 the government completely reorganized the arrangements for industrial production by setting up General Organizations to control all companies in the public sector. Each Organization supervises companies concerned with the production of similar commodities. For example, the seventy-nine enterprises manufacturing textiles came under the General Organization for Spinning and Weaving, and there are Organizations for metallurgy, petroleum, chemicals, food, ceramics, engineering products, and rural handicrafts.[52]

General Organizations are semi-autonomous public bodies, responsible to the Ministry of Industry. They are directed by a board of nine persons, which is collectively responsible for its actions. Their membership, appointed by the President, consists usually of selected chairmen of affiliated companies, civil servants, and former directors of public enterprises. The board's task is to co-ordinate and approve the plans by member companies for investment, production, and marketing. For this purpose companies are required to submit to it their budget forecasts and final accounts. For the companies the General Organizations provide advice about marketing and technology. They negotiate loans and foreign exchange and obtain subventions from the Treasury on their behalf.[53] Relations between companies and the ministry on the one hand and the ministry and companies on the other takes place through the General Organizations. In brief, General Organizations could be described as holding companies which plan, guide, and co-ordinate the activities of constituent concerns.

The formal division of functions between the ministry, General Organizations, and the companies is set out in a number of official publications, but the actual operation of the new system cannot be really understood until case studies have been made. I will not detail their different legal powers but will attempt to show how much autonomy the basic production unit, the company, now enjoys within the public sector.[54]

Companies are managed by boards of directors, four of whom are elected by the employees. The remainder are appointed by

[52] CBE, *Econ. R.*, iv (1961), pp. 546–7. The Organizations and their affiliated companies are listed in INP Memo. 209, *UAR State Budget for 1962–3* (1962).

[53] Laws 60 & 61, 1963 and CBE, *Econ. R.*, iv (1963), pp. 411 & 439.

[54] The relevant laws are 265 & 1900 of 1960, 60 & 61 of 1963, and see *MRESE*, Jan. 1963, pp. 19–22.

presidential decree.[55] The board makes all day-to-day decisions about running the factory. For example, it establishes the internal chain of command and the layout for production, purchases current inputs, hires and dismisses labour, maintains equipment and buildings, and arranges for the sale of finished output. Companies still aim to maximize profits. Profit remains their success indicator, not output targets measured in physical or monetary terms and set out in the central plan. It is not clear, however, if a persistent failure to make profits will lead to the disappearance of the enterprise, as it does in a market economy, or whether the state will continue to subsidize unprofitable companies over an indefinite time period.

But public companies are by no means as autonomous or free to pursue the goal of profit as they were before nationalization. They are ringed with regulations which limit their initiative both in the short and long run. They must operate within a framework of administered prices, stringent controls over all transactions in foreign exchange, labour regulations, and planned investment, and refer to higher authorities on most matters pertaining to their plans for the future.

Companies are theoretically free to vary the volume and composition of their output in the short run within the limits imposed by their fixed capacity. But they must submit their annual budget forecasts to the General Organization for approval. Presumably these forecasts should accord with the targets of the annual plan. No company would be permitted, however, to restrict output in order to raise prices for its product and increase profits. Pressure from the planning authorities is directed towards the maximization of output of all commodities, and one of the avowed aims of nationalization was to eliminate monopolistic practices. No doubt the persistence of excess capacity, stock-piling, or the closing down of part or all of a plant would involve interference from authorities at higher levels than boards of companies. Lastly, under law 21 of 1958 the Ministry of Industry has the power to define the specifications for any manufactured commodity, but this power has so far been held in abeyance.

Over the long run changes in the volume and composition of industrial output depend upon the creation of new capacity, and

[55] Law 141, 1963 and *BE*, 29 Oct. 1962.

all net investment is planned. Companies certainly suggest designs for expansion to the General Organization but the option to proceed does not rest with them. General Organizations initiate and consider all investment schemes and discuss them with the Ministry of Industry. Provided the ministry agrees, the project is then offered to the Ministry of Planning for inclusion in the Plan.[56]

Limits to the expansion of output by any single company are not only set by its fixed equipment; certain other factors of production, such as skilled labour and imported materials, are also not variable in the short run. Imported raw materials and intermediate products are purchased abroad by government agencies and sold to companies at fixed prices, and it is not possible for the board to obtain more than a given share by offering higher prices, although the market may operate when companies find themselves with imported inputs in excess of their needs. Complaints of delays in the delivery of spare parts and raw materials has, however, led the government to distribute quotas of foreign exchange to the companies at quarterly intervals.[57]

Skilled manpower shortages form another bottleneck on the expansion of output by one company, not merely because labour is immobile but because the price mechanism is not allowed to operate freely. For example, no employee can be transferred between firms without the agreement of his original employer.[58] Top management is appointed at ministerial level and the government also directs certain categories of scarce manpower, such as recent graduates in engineering or chemistry, to work in particular places.[59] A company's ability to attract labour has been further hampered by the introduction of an elaborate system of job and wage classification.[60] Complete rigidity has, however, been avoided by giving boards the power to award bonuses and to allocate employees to different grades and at high or low points on a given pay-scale, provided, of course, the trade unions do not adopt a 'legalistic' attitude towards this kind of manipulation.[61]

Other inputs are allocated by the market, and the board attempts to combine factors in order to minimize costs. Again it purchases intermediate products, and hires and dismisses labour within a

[56] *MRESE*, May 1962, p. 32; *BE*, 4 Mar. 1962, and Law 95, 1965.
[57] *MRESE*, Mar. 1963, p. 49.
[58] Law 3540, 1963.
[59] See above, p. 197.
[60] Laws 1598 & 3540, 1963.
[61] *MRESE*, Jan. 1962, p. 44; Sept. 1962, p. 43 & Dec. 1962, p. 1.

framework of regulations. For example, the laws relating to the employment of women and minors, working conditions, and safety provisions are rigidly enforced throughout the public sector. Companies must pay minimum wages and provide an extensive range of fringe benefits for all employees.[62] Moreover after the government's employment drive in 1961, they have found it difficult to dismiss redundant labour,[63] while the guarantee by the government of employment for all graduates suggests that companies may be compelled to take on unwanted staff.[64] The Ministry of Industry further possesses the power to set prices for intermediate products, and it is doubtful if the ministry would permit any company to take full advantage of demand conditions by setting prices for its product as high as possible.[65] Other companies would quickly protest against the 'exploitative or inordinate' profits earned by their suppliers.

Within these limits firms seek to minimize the use of scarce factors and purchase inputs as cheaply as possible. Over the long run, finding the least-cost combination involves a choice of technique. Unless techniques are technologically determined, companies presumably have some say in questions related to their capital-labour ratios. But in general all decisions involving capital formation are taken by higher authorities within the framework of planning, already described. Companies are required to submit their investment budgets to the General Organizations for approval. General Organizations, together with the planning section of the Ministry of Industry, are responsible for the entry into or exit of companies from a particular industry. They also design and locate plant, fix the scale of operations, close down and amalgamate existing companies.[66]

It is also the companies who fix prices and arrange for the marketing of their output. The government has not yet settled upon a pricing policy for public enterprises. From time to time vague statements appear in the press to the effect that prices should be related to costs of production or that profits must be based

[62] Ibid. May 1962, pp. 27–29 & Apr. 1963, pp. 47–49.

[63] *BE*, 29 Feb. 1962 and NBE, *Econ. B.*, iii (1963), p. 59. Under Law 113, 1963, companies are required to take on skilled labour from the labour exchanges in chronological order.

[64] *MRESE*, Jan. 1965, p. 95.

[65] Law 142, 1959.

[66] Laws 60 & 61, 1963.

upon increased productivity, but the principles operative in each instance can only be revealed by further research.[67] A general striving for price stability since 1961 can be observed.[68] Moreover the Ministry of Industry possesses powers to fix prices for all manufactured commodities and intervenes to maintain the prices of basic necessities such as coarse cotton cloth and some processed foods within the reach of the poorer classes.[69] Very high profits are still regarded as anti-social, a hang-over from the days when profits accrued to a tiny group of capitalists sheltered by tariffs from external competition and who very often enjoyed a position of monopoly in the domestic market.[70] On the whole the market continues to operate and companies are guided by movements in government and consumer demand. No doubt government orders are sometimes given to produce this or that and presumably, with the high priority accorded to foreign exchange, no company would be permitted to switch from the export to the home market just because it appeared profitable to do so.

If the not implausible assumption is made that all industrial firms employing more than ten workers are now inside the public sector, the private sector might still account for 40 per cent of industrial output and 62 per cent of employment. The behaviour of private producers conforms fairly closely to the free market model. They aim to maximize profits, but because small-scale concerns are administratively difficult to control, they enjoy much greater autonomy in their pursuit of profit than companies in the public sector. To begin with, almost all the restraints upon the initiative of private concerns to vary the rate and composition of output are imposed by fixed capacity and not by government commands and regulations. Guided by the prices for inputs and finished commodities, private producers expand or restrict output, stock-pile or operate with excess capacity, and close down according to their own judgement. Officially they are encouraged to maximize output and meet the targets established for them by the Plan, but in practice they might well be prevented from increasing production either in the short or long run by the scarcity of imported machinery, spare parts, and intermediate products or,

[67] *al-Ahram*, 7 Apr. 1964.
[68] NBE, *Econ. B.*, iii (1963).
[69] Laws 152–5, 1963 and Morshidy, p. 86.
[70] Anis, pp. 676–7 & 687; NBE, *Econ. B.*, iii (1952), p. 220; *EG*, 25 Feb. 1949.

more rarely, by the shortage of skilled labour. Nationalized agencies now have complete charge of imports, and whenever competition occurs for scarce supplies between the public and private sector, priority will usually be given to the government's own companies. Only if a private producer's design for expansion accords with or is complementary to the central plan for industry will he receive the necessary building licence, bank loan, or permit for foreign exchange. Otherwise his rate of growth will be limited by his fixed capacity.

Within the limits imposed by the difficulties of obtaining imported machinery and raw materials, the choice of technique is entirely a matter for the individual enterprise. Guided by relative prices, private producers aim to combine factors of production in order to minimize costs. They purchase inputs on markets at the lowest possible prices. The government has attempted to restrict their discretion with respect to the pay and conditions of employment for labour, but provided they are small enough they can usually avoid regulation.[71] Private enterprises, unlike companies in the public sector, can attract skilled labour by offering higher remuneration. They can also 'exploit' their unskilled workers by paying less than the legal minimum and not complying with welfare legislation or with government regulations on profit sharing.[72] Evasion of the labour code is comparatively easy because a high proportion of their work force comes from within the family anyway.[73]

Private concerns can theoretically set whatever prices they like or sell to the highest bidder. Prices for certain basic necessities are, however, fixed by law and the limits to their discretion thus depend upon variations in the middleman's margin. It might also be risky for a private concern selling to public companies to charge whatever the market will bear. The atmosphere in Egypt is opposed to high rates of profit. Any private enterprise which obviously offends the prevailing social ethos runs the risk of take-over by the state.

Institutional arrangements for production in the service sector resemble closely those established for nationalized concerns in industry. Current production is carried on and managed by boards

[71] *MRESE*, Jan. 1962, pp. 40–41 & Mar. 1963, pp. 42–43.

[72] *Commerce du Levant*, 23 Jan. 1963.

[73] Presumably only the large firms in the private sector have complied with Law 141, 1963, which stipulates that boards of directors must include four representatives elected by their employees.

of companies, and is relatively free from interference by the central authorities, but future plans for expansion, particularly those which involve net investment, the formation of new companies, or the amalgamation or shut-down of existing concerns are referred to General Organizations and the appropriate ministries. The following table sets out and clarifies the formal structure of Egypt's public sector in some detail.

TABLE 8

The Organization for Production in the Public Sector

The General Organization for:	*Attached to the Ministry of:*	*No. of companies controlled*
	1. *Manufacturing and Mining*	
Mines	Industry	19
Foodstuffs		72
Spinning & Weaving		79
Chemicals		42
Building Materials & Chinaware		15
Metallurgy		8
Engineering		42
Petroleum		8
Execution of 5-Year Plan		
Handicrafts		9
Government Printing		
Military Factories	Defence	2
Medical Supplies	Health	7
Electricity	Public Works	
	2. *Agriculture*	
Agricultural Co-operatives	Agriculture	11
Agricultural Production		7
Agrarian Reform	Agrarian Reform	—
Land Reclamation		4
Desert Reclamation		—
Land Development		5
High Dam	High Dam	—
	3. *Services*	
A. *Communications*		
Railways	Communications	
Telecommunications		
Post Office		

The General Organization for:	*Attached to the Ministry of:*	*No. of Companies controlled*
Marine Transport		2
Internal Transport	Communications (cont.)	20
Suez Canal		
B. *Trade & Commerce*		
Trade		15
Promotion of Exports		
Cotton		17
Central Bank		
Banking	Economy	24
International Exhibitions		
Insurance		13
Savings		1
Consumption		23
Consumers' Co-operatives		2
Silos and Storage	Supply	8
Fisheries		3
Flour, Rice Mills & Bakeries		320
C. *Housing & Social Welfare*		
Building Contracts		73
Public Buildings		
Co-operative Housing	Housing	1
General Housing		5
Alexandria Water		
Governerates' Housing		
Social Insurance	Labour	
Insurance & Pensions		
D. *Cultural Amenities*		
Broadcasting & Television		1
Tourism & Hotels	State	5
Publishing & Printing		2
Cinema		
Theatrical Arts	Guidance	
Writing, Translation, Printing		

Sources: Adapted from Ministry of Treasury, *Draft Budgets*, 1962–63 and 1963–64. *Government and Reorganization in the UAR*, by L. Gullick and R. Pollock (unpubl. report, 1962). The distincti o between public business and public services is difficult to draw. This table employs the distinction used in the budget.

The criteria which guide the operations of public companies in the service sector cannot really be revealed until much more information is published. Until then it seems safe to observe that managers are still guided by a wish to make profits. Although profit maximization remains their success indicator, it needs to be carefully defined. In general, it can be said that the goal of almost all tertiary production by publicly-owned companies approximates to the traditional aim of government services, namely to perform a specified task or set of tasks at minimum possible cost. Their output is given and the companies' job is to minimize the use of scarce inputs. As a generalization this will pass, but it ignores some services where public companies can and do vary production by competing for a greater share of the available business. Competition seems, however, likely to be curtailed rather than encouraged by existing plans for rationalization because for the service sector the government seems to favour specialization of function. Present policy aims to avoid duplication and to confine the services of companies to given localities or to defined areas of industrial or agricultural enterprise.

For example, in 1964 the government rationalized the structure of banking so that each sector of the economy channels its entire demand for credit and loans through a single bank. Existing banks were amalgamated into five companies and the government laid down criteria for the location of branches in rural and urban areas.[74]

The prime function of banks is to provide the loans required for planned capital formation and the credit needed for the finance of production. Banks no longer distribute the assets they hold in order to maximize returns within the prevailing conventions of monetary management. Their directors have lost nearly all discretion over the composition of portfolios. Public companies or agencies will not be held up for a lack of finance and do not supplicate for bank loans and credit or negotiate over terms. Their needs are met on command from the central bank and upon terms very often decided at the centre. Because of their strategic position in the economy banks are beginning to be employed by the government as instruments of control over productive companies. Each enterprise formulates and is bound by a credit plan. Bank managers

[74] NBE, *Econ. B.*, iii (1963), p. 158; i (1964), p. 2 & xviii (1964), p. 148.

report on the financial operations of their clients in the public sector and can refuse to finance unauthorized stock-piling.[75]

Banks retain more discretion with regard to the finance of private activities but even here their initiative to vary the volume, composition, and terms of their lending is restricted. They are not permitted to provide loans for capital formation unsanctioned by the planning authorities, and the structure of interest rates for advances to the private sector is manipulated by central command. If the state wishes to encourage certain kinds of private enterprise such as co-operative housing, village handicrafts, or investment complementary to its own plans, instructions are issued to banks to provide the necessary finance cheaply. Credit for the agricultural sector used to finance the cultivation, collection, and sale of cash crops, particularly cotton, has been supplied free of interest since 1961. Two purposes lie behind this policy: first, to relieve the small farmers from the burden of interest charges, and second, to enable the authorities to influence cultivation.

Thus free credit is available only to members of co-operative societies and is used to encourage the spread of co-operatives. Officials of the Agricultural Bank, who distribute interest-free public loans, attempt to ensure that they are used in ways likely to raise yields.[76]

Except within narrow limits, banks are no longer arbiters over the flows of finance within the economy. In general they are told where to lend and what to charge. Similar instructions are issued to other financial intermediaries, such as insurance companies and investment trusts.[77] Financial organizations in Egypt operate within a circumscribed sphere of business; in brief, they are becoming specialized and do not really compete one with another for business. As public companies they are still expected to make profits. Profit remains their success indicator but their ability to vary output and increase profits, traditionally restricted, is likely to be curtailed still further by government plans for rationalization. Profits depend primarily upon their performing defined

[75] Ibid. & CBE, *Credit & Banking Developments*, pp. 22–23.

[76] See above, pp. 99 & 120–1.

[77] *MRESE*, Jan. 1963, p. 42. Insurance companies have been compelled for some years to hold 25 per cent of their assets in the form of government bonds (Issawi, *Egypt in Revolution*, p. 254).

tasks efficiently. For any scale of operations, if administrative and other costs are minimized, profits will rise.

Similar patterns of behaviour can be observed in other parts of the service sector. Public companies now transport almost all Egypt's passengers and freight, but small-scale private hauliers, river transport, and taxi services still survive here and there. Transport services are supplied at fixed prices for passengers and freight, and the companies retain initiative over their day-to-day operations. And non-price competition between road and rail and between road hauliers inside the public sector persists. Companies can increase their profits by operating more effectively and by capturing a higher share of the available demand from their rivals. Plans are, however, being formulated for the co-ordination of the transport system which will presumably eliminate competition within the public sector, although some competition might well continue between public and private companies.

Trade is divided into two sectors, wholesale and retail, and wholesale trade may be internal or external. The latter is now entirely in the hands of publicly-owned concerns which might, however, purchase goods for export from private wholesalers as well as directly from private or public producers. The government rationalized the Organization for Foreign Trade by amalgamating the companies and defining their functions. Four import companies specialize in purchasing engineering products, the other eleven firms are general export-import enterprises but operate with reference to particular regions of the world.[78]

Private concerns dominate internal wholesale trade, but the state owns several large-scale companies.[79] The task of trading organizations is to collect, transport, grade, and occasionally to process crops and manufactured commodities for domestic and export markets. For the marketing of farm produce government policy has been directed towards the replacement of middlemen by co-operatives and public companies.[80] Co-operatives are set up by farmers, with government encouragement and guidance,

[78] *Draft Budget 1963–4*, p. 4; *UAR Yearbook 1963*, p. 84; *BE*, 21 Feb. & 24 May 1962.

[79] The Minister of Economy announced in 1962 that a sixth of the capital invested in commerce belonged to companies in the public sector (*BE*, 24 May 1962).

[80] *Commerce du Levant*, 24 Aug. 1963.

to gather crops from given localities and to take them to a grouping centre for sale to a public company which then assumes responsibility for grading and transporting them to market. For Egypt's major cash crop, cotton, this system is becoming widespread, and landowners and merchants who formerly organized the marketing of cotton are being eliminated.[81] Co-operatives and public companies also market some vegetables, such as onions and potatoes and meat, and the government hopes eventually to generalize this mixture of co-operative and state trading to encompass all agricultural produce.[82]

Wholesalers deliver to retailers or to importers overseas, and retailers sell to the public. Most of the half million or so shops in Egypt are privately owned, but there is a growing public sector even in retailing which takes the form of consumers' co-operatives which the government hopes will eventually manage up to 25 per cent of the country's retail trade.[83] Consumers' co-operatives are really state shops, supervised by the Public Organization for Consumers' Co-operatives and the Ministry of Supply. Their function is to provide people 'with their requirements of food, clothes and other essential goods at reasonable prices'. They have become an instrument of the government's supply policy which aims to keep the prices of necessities stable and within reach of the urban poor.[84]

Since the summer of 1963 the government has also attempted to rationalize private retail trade in order to render shopkeepers more amenable to price controls. It is not clear how far reorganization has proceeded but the Ministry of Supply announced plans to group all shopkeepers dealing in a particular locality into a co-operative, managed by an elected administrative council responsible to the Public Organization for Consumers' Co-operatives. Eventually internal trade will be divided into sixteen branches and no merchant will be permitted to work in more than one branch.[85]

[81] NBE, *Econ. B.*, ii (1963), p. 173; *EG*, 17 & 19 Aug. & 15 Sept. 1964; *al-Ahram Econ. Suppl.*, 1 Dec. 1962, pp. 35–37.

[82] *al-Ahram Econ. Suppl.*, 15 June 1963, p. 53 and *MRESE*, Jan. 1965, p. 9.

[83] *BE*, 1 Nov. 1963.

[84] *UAR Yearbook 1960*, pp. 444 & 461; Law 267, 1960; Issawi, *Egypt in Revolution*, p. 63.

[85] *Commerce du Levant*, 10 Aug. & 16 Nov. 1963; *BE*, 5, 8, 11, 12, 14, & 17 Aug. 1963.

The criteria which underly the behaviour of trading organizations, wholesale or retail, vary between the public and private sectors. Given the total volume of trade a government concern can only increase its turnover at the expense of rivals, but competition between public companies is unlikely to persist—and competition will then occur only between the two sectors. Private traders aim to buy cheap and sell dear, but are theoretically restrained in the prices they can charge consumers because the government regulates prices for a whole range of commodities regarded as necessities. Of course, if demand consistently and appreciably exceeds supply, black markets will, and indeed have, emerged.[86] Public trading organizations are obliged, however, to adhere more closely to the government's 'fair' price policy. Price controls and subsidies have existed in Egypt since the Second World War and are designed to protect the living standards of the poorer classes during an inflationary period and to prevent local firms, sheltered from internal and external competition, from exploiting consumers. Price controls are regarded as a more efficacious alternative to income redistribution or overall wage controls.[87] And the notion now prevails in Egypt that producers, particularly farmers, should receive a reasonable price for their output and should not be 'exploited' by merchants. In fact ministers seem to regard the elimination of private middlemen as eminently desirable.[88] Notions of equity thus lie behind the prices paid by public companies in the wholesale trade to farmers and manufacturers and are at the back of prices charged by consumers' co-operatives. Their task is to bring to consumers the best quality food and goods at 'reasonable prices'.[89] In reality most of the prices charged in public shops are fixed by the Ministry of Supply.

Government trading companies thus operate within a framework of regulated prices which leaves them little leeway to buy cheap and sell dear. Nor do they compete in other ways in order to gain a higher share of the market except to a very restricted

[86] *BE*, 31 Jan. 1962 and *MRESE*, Jan. 1965, p. 96.

[87] See speeches by Vice-President for Financial Affairs in NBE, *Econ. B.*, i (1965), p. 48 and by the Prime Minister in *al-Ahram*, 10 Oct. 1963.

[88] *MRESE*, Jan. 1963, p. 4; Aug. 1963, pp. 20 & 60–61; Jan. 1965, p. 4.

[89] Note the preamble to decree 3100/1964 establishing a government organization to supply meat and milk to consumers and Min. of Treasury *Draft Budget 1962–3*, p. 61.

degree.[90] Their profits can only vary to the extent that they perform the tasks defined for them more or less efficiently. If, for a given turnover, a company is able to reduce costs for labour, raw materials, and other inputs, or, over the longer run, to adopt optimal techniques of production its profits will rise. Private traders on the other hand are free to compete with one another and with public concerns. They are less constrained by notions of fair prices and often ignore government regulations entirely. There are ways open to them to make profits not considered by trading organizations within the public sector.[91]

INVESTMENT AND SAVINGS

The investment decision is concerned with the use of resources to satisfy present or future wants. By deferring consumption a society can add to its stock of capital or body of technical knowledge in order to consume more in future. Unless additions are made to the national capital, only marginal alterations can be made to the volume or composition of total output. Net capital formation is a precondition for raising average real incomes, but it takes time to accumulate capital—time to manufacture equipment, to redeploy labour, to transform exports into imports of machinery, and time for capital to gestate and reach optimum productivity. If a society is not prepared to forego consumption now it cannot hope to enjoy higher standards of living in future.

In Egypt the decision about the rate of saving and investment, or, to put the statement another way, the decision about the volume of present consumption to sacrifice for more distant benefits, is now taken almost entirely by the state. That is to say public departments and enterprises now design and construct nearly all new capital projects while the greater part of the savings required to finance them originates from government sources. Unfortunately it is impossible to validate these generalizations with anything other than the rather dubious figures contained in the Plan Frame. By rearranging the Plan's investment and savings statistics to take account of the additions made to the public sector since 1959–60, and assuming that the figures reflect the

[90] They are at present geographically dispersed (*MRESE*, Mar. 1963, p. 51).
[91] As the Prime Minister admitted (*al-Ahram*, 10 Oct. 1963).

present situation, it is possible to guess that the state now executes approximately 85 per cent of the gross capital formation and provides 70 per cent of the savings required for its finance.[92]

Government savings include the budget surplus, net income from social and other forms of insurance, and above all the retained profits of public enterprises.[93] Within limits the state can now determine the overall rate of saving by raising taxes, cutting-back public consumption, by extending the scope of social insurance, and by instructing companies and co-operatives to increase the volume of retained profits. Although the Egyptian government has only recently started to rationalize the tax structure, since foreign trade, considerable parts of agriculture, internal trade and large-scale manufacturing and commerce are now inside the public sector, it should be relatively simple for the Treasury to impose and collect taxes upon commodities which pass through the government's hands and upon incomes and profits earned by public enterprises and employees and shareholders of enterprises it controls. The government's capacity to tax has certainly been improved by the nationalization measures and the spread of producers' co-operatives. The extension of social welfare legislation has also provided the state with an effective method of raising the rate of saving. Roughly 20 per cent of the population are covered by various forms of social insurance and plans exist to widen existing schemes to cover almost all sections of the labour force, including those employed in agriculture.[94] Contributions are levied upon employers and employees and form one of the least objectionable forms of taxation. In the early stages of their development the income from social insurance funds should exceed outgoings by a substantial margin and provide the government with finance for its investment programme.

At present retained profits represent the most important source of savings.[95] Their level in industry and commerce depends upon

[92] See tables 16 & 18 (pp. 331 & 333). A recent book (P. Mansfield, *Nasser's Egypt* (1965), p. 142) puts the share of the private sector in total investment at 17.3 per cent for 1961–2, 9.7 per cent for 1962–3, and 6.3 per cent for 1963–4.

[93] See table 18.

[94] FEI, *Yearbook 1964*, p. 11 and *MRESE*, Jan. 1963, p. 64; Sept. 1963, p. 67, & Feb. 1965, p. 67; *BE*, 24 Mar. 1963.

[95] A recent report put the distribution of domestic savings as follows: insurance and pensions, £100 m., retained profits £117 m., and personal savings £40–£50 m. (NBE, *Econ. B.*, i (1965), p. 48).

the wages and pricing policies of public companies. If the wage bill fails to increase at the same rate as output or if the prices of manufactured goods rise more rapidly than industrial costs, profits will go up. So far the government has not manipulated prices in order to find savings for its investment programme. Its aim appears to be to keep prices stable, partly because pricing policy has remained tied to the notion of 'fair' profits and partly because any move to raise prices might merely reduce total sales and revenue. Given the high level of protection and an absence of competition among local producers, the government for several years attempted to restrain the 'exploitation' of consumers by regulating profit margins. At the same time it sought to avoid depressing profits to the point which inhibited reinvestment. With private monopolies now converted into public monopolies, the fair profit policy loses its point because the government could conceivably justify the 'temporary exploitation' of consumers by reference to a high rate of investment.[96] On the other hand industry has experienced a recurring problem of finding markets since the war, and with a relatively elastic demand for manufactures the government may have decided to hold prices steady and to reap more profits by raising industrial efficiency.

If the assumptions of the Plan are a guide to policy, then the government evidently prefers to obtain more profits by allowing output to grow faster than wages, but the wage bill has not been restrained by controls over wage rates. On the contrary, the government has not seriously modified the existing free market in labour, and several recent laws have had the effect of forcing up labour costs to public companies—not only in public companies because the government has also attempted to extend labour and welfare legislation beyond the confines of the public sector.[97] For example, it raised the minimum wage payable throughout organized industry to 25 piastres a day and compelled large companies to distribute a share of profits to employees. But the potential effects of both these measures on savings should not be exaggerated because by 1962 the average wage in organized industry had already reached

[96] B. Hansen & G. Marzouk, *Development and Economic Policy in the UAR* (1965), pp. 287–90.

[97] *MRESE*, Jan. 1962, pp. 23–25; May 1962, pp. 27–29; June 1962, p. 41; *Commerce du Levant*, 23 Jan. 1963.

55 piastres a day, and all but 40 per cent of the profits ostensibly distributed to workers will find their way into social security funds.[98] However, regulations now stringently enforced relating to hours and conditions of work, medical and holiday pay, the contract of employment and other fringe benefits undoubtedly add to labour costs. And since the government initiated a drive to increase employment at the end of 1961, companies have been under pressure to increase their labour intake and have certainly found it very much more difficult to dismiss workers.[99]

On the other hand the combined effect of all these measures upon the share of income distributed as wages will be more than offset by the policy of capital deepening, pursued by private firms before nationalization and continued by public companies thereafter. Planners expected the amount of capital per worker in industry to increase between 1959–60 and 1964–5, and at the same time the share of wages in net value added to fall by 5 per cent. The selection of capital-intensive techniques, as recent advocates have pointed out, will always ensure that property incomes will rise at the expense of wages and saving at the expense of consumption.[100] Finally, since the former shareholding class has not been compensated at anything like the 'true' market value for their shares, nationalization has resulted in a drastic fall in the incomes paid to private capitalists and leaves the state with an increased surplus available for reinvestment.[101]

In the agricultural sector, the spread of supervised co-operatives is creating a mechanism for increasing the rate and the mobility of rural savings. Since the new institutions market nearly all cash crops, the officials in charge can easily decide what proportion of the co-operatives' income to invest in buildings, roads, or machinery. Moreover, with an increased flow of cash income paid to farmers and landowners passing through the hands of local officials, it should be administratively feasible for the state to collect more direct taxes from agriculture. Alternatively, since cotton and several other cash crops are sold to government agencies for resale to consumers in urban areas or overseas, the government

[98] Recent amendments transferred the investment of workers' profits to the Min. of Housing (*MRESE*, June 1963, p. 49).

[99] See above, p. 177. [100] O'Brien, in *ME Econ. Papers 1962*, pp. 107–9.

[101] See below, pp. 126, 209–10.

could tax agriculture by purchasing produce from the farmers at one set of prices, and selling at higher prices. But these co-operatives are not yet widespread and the government has so far made no attempt to increase taxes levied upon rural areas.[102] No doubt it is anxious to avoid any resistance to the spread of the new institutions. Their success in the early stages requires *positive* co-operation from the farmers, and if they are alienated by higher taxation, however well disguised, output could fall. At present the signs are that the government is being so careful to conciliate farmers that the official prices paid for some crops are higher than the prices the government receives on world markets. And the farmers have built up pressure groups around provincial Governors in order to secure higher prices for their produce. Savings and investment within the village itself may have risen with the spread of producers' co-operatives, but the mobilization of the agricultural surplus to finance Egypt's industrialization programme has hardly begun.

Egypt's rate of investment exceeds the rate of domestic saving by the deficit on income account of her balance of payments, and nearly all capital imports into the country today are on public account. Foreign borrowing by the private sector is negligible and the government conducts negotiations for credits, medium- and long-term loans, usually with other governments but with private concerns abroad as well. Most of the resources required to finance investment are thus provided by the government, but it would be an exaggeration to say that the rate of saving is now *determined* by the state. Private saving continues to be marginally important and the Egyptian government, like any other, cannot restrain consumption beyond a point. Further increases in public saving might depress private saving and thereby reduce the overall level. Even though the target of the plan was publicized in terms of doubling national *output* by 1970, the régime has raised hopes among the masses that their living standards will improve markedly in the near future; expectations that might prove politically hazardous to ignore. Nor is there now much scope to honour promises by further measures of redistribution. The wealthy have been ex-

[102] President Nasser has issued instructions that farmers must be paid 'correct' prices for their produce (*MRESE*, Jan. 1963, p. 4 and Mansfield, p. 133).

propriated and it might be dangerous as well economically inefficient to 'squeeze' the middle and professional classes much further.[103] The government must allow consumption to rise, perhaps slowly, but nevertheless perceptibly.[104] Only within limits can it determine the proportion of national resources to devote to capital formation. I need hardly point out that the constraints upon a military régime are looser than those surrounding a government subject to the sanction of periodic re-election. Certainly the Egyptian government has made no attempt to elicit the preferences of its citizens for present as against future consumption, but then there is no very convincing reason why it should.[105]

Farmers, small family firms, and households do continue to save and invest. Saving by the first two groups seems to be intimately related to possibilities for profitable investment within their own enterprises. Even household saving depends to a considerable degree upon the opportunities open in real estate. Savings by these three groups is highly volatile and, because they cannot be easily persuaded to depart from traditional forms of investment, is not a mobile source of finance.[106] With an ambitious Plan to implement, the government is obviously keen to stimulate private savings and investment and has raised interest rates on bank and post office deposits.[107] It set up national investment trusts to attract small savings, exempted their profits from taxation, designed new forms of savings certificates, and reopened the stock exchange to make fixed investment liquid to the individual.[108] Farmers, merchants, and small manufacturers are encouraged to maintain and expand their concerns by tax exemptions and offers of cheap credit.[109] To some extent the decision to forego present for future consumption is still voluntary but for several reasons

[103] For the contrary view see H. Riad, 'State Capitalism in Egypt', *Revolution in Africa, Latin America & Asia*, i/1 (1964).

[104] The Five-Year Plan provided for a rise in real consumption of 4.8 per cent per annum, but it appears that consumption has risen faster than the planned rate and the government is considering measures to restrain it during the Second Plan (NBE, *Econ. B.*, i (1965), p. 53 and *MRESE*, Jan. 1965, pp. 92–93).

[105] A. K. Sen, 'On Optimising the Rate of Saving', *Econ. J.*, Sept. 1961. pp. 480–91.

[106] NPC, Memos. 113, 138, 173, 197, & 216.

[107] *al-Ahram*, 10 Sept. 1963 and NBE, *Econ. B.*, i (1962), p. 4.

[108] Morshidy, pp. 75–76; *Budget Report 1960–1*, p. 64; *MRESE*, Jan. 1965, pp. 92–93.

[109] Morshidy, pp. 22 & 75.

developed in the next chapter, private saving and investment is unlikely to contribute more than marginally to fixed capital formation.[110]

Constitutionally the system allows for and even encourages capitalism. Profits continue to guide the actions of those in charge of resources in the private sector and presumably encourage them to convert inputs and factor supplies into output as efficiently as possible. But the persistent condition of uncertainty and ideological antipathy which still envelops capitalism in Egypt is hardly conducive to the confidence required for higher rates of private saving and investment. Reorganization of the economy has been under way for nearly five years now as one wave of nationalization and plans for institutional reform follows another. Land has been openly taken from its owners, and the compensation allowed to those whose property in industry and commerce has been nationalized or sequestrated since 1960 conceals a large element of outright confiscation.

Egypt's leaders continue to castigate the 'monopolists and exploiters' in the private sector.[111] They are openly hostile to middlemen. Egyptian socialism appears at times to be apathetic to the whole idea of private profit and the Free Officers seem to expect businessmen to be patriots, to accumulate capital, to fit in with their plans, and to behave paternalistically towards their employees, all at one and the same time. For them merely to conduct themselves like capitalists—to make profits, expand their concerns, and look after their interests—appears to be contrary to the prevailing ethos and runs the risk of take-over by the state.[112] But until conditions are created for its successful operation, the contribution of private enterprise to the growth of the Egyptian economy will continue to fall well below its optimum level.

CONSUMPTION

There remains to consider the part played by households in the Egyptian economic system. Households supply services to enter-

[110] See below, pp. 114–15 & 254–6.

[111] The Charter enjoined private enterprise 'to renovate itself and strike a new path of creative effort not dependent, as in the past, on parasitic exploitation' (p. 60).

[112] Between 1961 and 1965 several companies appear to have been nationalized on just these grounds.

prises and purchase their products. In a market economy they remain free to decide where to work and how long to work. They also decide how to distribute their incomes between saving and expenditure on the one hand and between different objects of consumption on the other. Household preferences are reflected in relative prices and guide the decisions of firms as to the volume and composition of output. Production is carried on mainly to satisfy the expressed demands of consumers and not to meet the commands of the central authority.

Today in Egypt a rising share of national outlay is undertaken by the government on behalf of its citizens. Since 1960 the share of private gross disposable income in gross national income has undoubtedly fallen while public net disposable income has risen. Given the changed distribution of income between government and households, public expenditures will naturally exert increased influence over the composition of output. As far as overall consumption expenditures are concerned, Professor Hansen's estimates show that the share of public consumption expenditure is rising.[113] In other words, total consumption by Egyptian households contains a rising proportion of services and commodities provided for them by the state. These include fresh water, health services of all kinds, welfare amenities, education, and the more traditional collective services of defence, internal security, and justice. More of the country's resources are now orientated towards meeting the needs of households as expressed on their behalf by the state.

Households no longer influence, to any significant degree, the volume of present consumption deferred for the sake of higher consumption in future. Most domestic saving has ceased to be voluntary. The government plans investment and then enforces a rate of saving upon society. In other words, the state decides the share of annual output which takes the form of capital goods, basically by controlling the share of gross national income made available to households. Households are, however, still free, and are in fact encouraged by the payment of interest, to defer expenditure from their disposable income, but their savings form only a small proportion of the total.

[113] B. Hansen, *The National Outlay of the UAR, 1937–59 & 1945–1962/3* (1963), INP Memo. 377.

Private consumption still accounts, however, for about 70 per cent of gross national expenditure and the preferences of households largely determine what is produced in Egypt. The bill of goods, or assortment of output, still conforms, at least roughly, to their wishes. While the government recognizes that consumers know best what they want and allows producers and planners to respond to their preferences, it does exercise influence on the pattern of demand through price regulations, subsidies, and indirectly by controls over the distribution of income between households.[114]

Thus consumers' preferences are not allowed to determine completely the bill of goods, and the distribution of output between households does not conform exactly to their wishes. To begin with, imports of consumer goods are strictly regulated by means of quotas and many foreign commodities defined as luxuries by the Ministry of Economy are excluded entirely. Two foods, sugar and vegetable oil, are rationed, but the principal reason why consumption departs from an *efficient* pattern is because the government continues to fix prices for a whole range of consumer goods regarded as necessities.[115] Prices for commodities like bread, meat, tea, coffee, and vegetables, &c. are set at levels which aim to bring them within reach of the lower-income groups and not necessarily at equilibrium levels which clear the market. Administered prices usually fail to reflect consumers' preferences at the margin for more of this commodity and less of that. They seldom take proper account of variations in quality.[116] At ruling prices consumers are prevented from increasing their purchases by shortages, and some families would be willing to pay higher prices in order to consume a greater volume of some goods. Alternatively, prices are sometimes set above the equilibrium levels and stocks pile up in shops, farms, and factories.

[114] Their preferences received overt recognition in the formulation of the Plan—see above, pp. 160–1.

[115] 'An economically efficient distribution of consumers' goods is one that distributes a given quantity of goods in best conformity with consumers' preferences.' This occurs when 'it would be impossible by redistribution to make anyone better off without making someone else worse off' (Scitovsky, p. 55).

[116] In a revealing interview Mr Sabry, the Prime Minister, said Egypt could ignore the question of quality at this stage of development when quantity was the overriding concern (*al-Ahram*, 10 Sept. 1963).

The press has reported both gluts and shortages.[117] Gluts are unlikely to persist over the long run because enterprises exist to make profits. Queues which indicate shortages are more evident in the consumers' co-operatives, where regulated prices are rigidly observed, than in private shops where black markets are more easily concealed. The existence of a large private sector in retail distribution ensures that the wishes of households will continue to be reflected in the movement of relative prices, but it does not follow that movements in 'illegal' prices will guide changes in the composition of output.

Black markets, queues, shortages, and such devices as key money for accommodation are likely to continue as long as the government attempts to prevent the preferences of households from exerting their proper impact on prices.[118] Present pricing policy seems in some respects redundant. It is a hangover from the past, originally designed to secure an equitable rather than an efficient distribution of goods among households. The objectives of the present policy can be better secured by operating directly on the distribution of income rather than by through the manipulation of prices.[119] Perhaps, however, the government is persuaded that controls contribute to the overall stability of the price level or is attempting to enforce a 'nutritious' diet upon its citizens.[120]

Moreover the government has never displayed any marked reluctance to redistribute income. Right from the beginning of the revolution it affected the volume and pattern of consumption through measures designed to bring about a more equal allocation of income and wealth. Agrarian reform and the expropriation of large-scale companies in industry and commerce have eliminated the concentration of wealth in the hands of a tiny group of families. Property left in private hands includes land, houses, small-scale concerns in manufacturing, and services, forms the greater share of the national capital, and is by no means widely diffused.[121]

[117] The opinion columns of *al-Ahram* are often revealing on this score.

[118] Ministerial exhortations to the public to boycott black markets are unlikely to be effective, nor will heavier penalties deter them (*MRESE*, Jan. 1965, p. 96).

[119] Hansen & Marzouk, p. 289.

[120] The government certainly believes controls contribute to price stability (NBE, *Econ. B.*, ii (1964), p. 157 and i (1965), p. 48).

[121] Y. Durells, 'Structure et développement de l'économie égyptienne', *Tiers Monde*, July-Aug. 1960, pp. 36–46.

Throughout government service salaries paid to top management and the upper echelons of the civil service have been restrained by the imposition of ceilings, while minimum-wage legislation, profit sharing, and more generous fringe benefits have raised the incomes of the minority of the labour force employed by public enterprises. The government is also trying to extend this legislation into agriculture and small private firms in industry and trade. Moreover, the reforms of 1961 rendered direct taxation more progressive. Government policy narrows the income differential between households, and its egalitarian tendency has certainly affected the pattern of demand for goods and services.

Households are also concerned with regulations relating to work as well as consumption. If workers are free to choose their jobs, have some command over their conditions of employment, and are able to opt for work or leisure, then their welfare is considered to be higher than that of workers whose rights are more limited. Under the present system the initiative of workers in these respects is still very great, but it has been marginally curtailed since the revolution. Recently graduated engineers and doctors, for example, were directed by the state to a place of employment for a period of 'national service'.[122] And the transfer of nearly all large companies into the public sector definitely circumscribed the mobility of their employees. Appointments at the managerial level are now made by the President or by the minister concerned. Managers' salaries are fixed and they are no longer free to move between companies in response to financial inducements.[123] They are compelled to reside near their place of work.[124] Workers cannot move between two companies in the public sector without permission from their original employers.[125] No doubt requests for transfer are granted but discretion has passed from the individual to the authorities. Movement is possible within the private sector and from the public to the private sector, but the latter is hardly an appealing prospect for the managerial class or an attractive one for workers since small family firms could probably not match the pay and fringe benefits offered by public companies. Legally the freedom

[122] INP Memo. 238.
[123] *MRESE*, May 1962, p. 14 and *BE*, 29 Oct. 1962.
[124] Ibid. Sept. 1962, p. 44 & June 1963, p. 48.
[125] Law 3540, 1963.

of labour to opt for work or leisure has also been restricted by recent laws, which fixed hours of work for all employees in the public companies and forbade anyone from undertaking more than a single job.[126] In the private sector employees may work as long as they please.

The command exercised by Egyptian workers over their pay and conditions of work has never been extensive or strong. Trade unions scarcely exist outside the corporate sector of industry and services. Since the revolution their membership has risen, but unions are more closely regulated than they were before 1952 and workers have lost their limited but important right to strike action. Unions have become in effect bodies which administer welfare legislation, see to it that the labour code is properly observed, and represent the grievances of their members to management. Most improvements to the status and conditions of workers do not emanate from trade union activity but come about because the state has promulgated and enforced a far-reaching code of labour legislation. The government now proudly points out that four of the nine directors who form the board of public companies are elected by the company's employees.[127] Precisely how the employees' representatives are nominated or what their powers are in the determination of company policy is not yet clear, but there are no real signs that the Egyptian government intends to emulate Yugoslavia and introduce full-scale workers' control.[128] It should also be noticed that the expansion of opportunities for free education from elementary to university levels has certainly increased the ability of new entrants to the labour force to opt for particular occupations. Positive measures of this kind are after all as important to the creation of a free labour market as the removal of legal hindrances to individual mobility.

[126] Laws 125 & 133, 1961.

[127] Law 141, 1963.

[128] All employees exercise one vote in the election (*BE*, 12 Mar. 1962). The President emphasized that the elected representatives not only have a right to be heard but their opinions must count (*Nasser's Speeches 1963*, p. 115).

VIII

The Origins of the Socialist Economic System

TEN years after the revolution of 1952 the Egyptian free-enterprise system had been effectively transformed into a centrally-controlled economy. From Mohammed Ali to the Free Officers the wheel had turned almost full circle and many of the present arrangements for the organization of production bear startling resemblance to those established by the Pasha 130 years ago. But the origins of the present Socialist Economic System should be traced to the slow movement away from *laissez-faire* after the Great War rather than to imitation of the totalitarian system of Mohammed Ali. The antecedents of many measures promulgated by the government can be found in the hesitant and inadequate efforts made by the former régime to ameliorate the evils of unregulated capitalism and to promote material progress. Historical antecedents provide us, however, with perspective and only marginally with an explanation for the rapid changes which have occurred over the past decade. The real question which faces the student of modern Egypt can legitimately be placed within a shorter time span. He can ask why did the Military Junta which seized power with so little in the way of preconceived notions about social and economic organization find it expedient, necessary, or desirable to bring about fundamental changes in the country's economic organization?

THE ROLE OF IDEOLOGY

One answer now canvassed in Egypt is that a socialist economy was implicit in the thinking or the intentions of the Free Officers right from their coup d'état of July 1952. According to the President, the ideological origins of the Socialist, Democratic, and Co-operative Society can be found in the six principles of the revolution enunciated in the early days of the revolution.[1] On

[1] *Nasser's Speeches 1961*, pp. 133, 323, & 390 and *1962*, p. 75.

examination this view seems suspiciously like *post hoc* rationalization. The six principles are in fact general and vague enough to embrace almost any kind of social organization. Neither their pre-revolution discussions nor post-revolution speeches suggest that the Officers really anticipated the kind of economic system which emerged a decade later. On the contrary, up to the Suez war their policies appear designed to create conditions within which private enterprise might flourish.

They placed few additional constraints upon producers. At the same time incentives to investors were proliferated in several government measures. A programme of public expenditure on roads, railways, electrical supplies, and irrigation canals improved the nation's infrastructure and lowered costs to the private sector. At the ideological level the Officers said everything possible to allay doubts businessmen may have had about the intentions of the new régime towards capitalism, and politically they appeared on many issues to lean more to the right than to the left. The four years after 1952 might be accurately described as the free-enterprise phase of the Egyptian revolution.

Another, more sophisticated and prevalent, explanation for the transformation of Egyptian economic organization is that change was the outcome of two revolutions: the Political Revolution of July 1952, when the Free Officers overthrew the old régime, and a Social Revolution of nine years later which wrought a profound transformation in the framework of production and the distribution of income and wealth. Thus legally the Social Revolution consisted of the nationalization decrees of July 1961 together with their more recent amendments, the extension of central control over almost all sectors of production, and several measures designed to redistribute income and wealth between social classes. According to this view, the second revolution occurred largely as a consequence of the conversion of Egyptian leaders to socialism.

Although the centrally-controlled mass media of Egypt are mainly responsible for describing the events of July 1961 as a Social Revolution and for propagating the notion that they were ideologically inspired, this official version of events derives plausibility from the fact that the prevarication and ambiguity which had characterized the attitude of Egypt's leaders towards private business during the years of Guided Capitalism ceased after July

1961. From then on they justified the nationalization of corporate industrial and commercial property with slogans drawn from the familiar canons of socialism. Their views found systematic expression in the Charter, published in May 1962, which set out to provide a comprehensive explanation for the transformation of the economic system as part of an ideology designed to serve as the basis for future developments throughout the whole area of economic and social life in modern Egypt.

The Charter offered the Congress of Popular Powers political, social, and economic reasons for the curtailment of private property and enterprise. Its explanation, set out in both general terms and within the context of Egyptian history, oscillated between praise for the virtues of socialism and condemnation of the vices of capitalism. The main political argument of the Charter can be paraphrased as follows. The existence of inequalities in the ownership of property engenders a class struggle which unless checked could lead to civil war and has certainly militated against the emergence of democracy or freedom in Egypt. On the other hand

> the socialist path, [by] providing opportunities for a peaceful settlement of the class strife and affording possibilities for dissolving class distinctions, leads to the distribution of the returns among all the people according to the principle of equality of opportunity for all . . . [and] thereby paves the way for an inevitable political development leading to liberation from the rule of the feudalist dictatorship allied with capitalism and the establishment of the rule of democracy representing the rights and aspirations of the working people (p. 61). This peaceful dissolution of class distinctions opens the gates for democratic exchange which brings the whole society nearer the age of true freedom (p. 79).

Political arguments appear, however, to be among the subsidiary reasons offered for the extension of public enterprise and the case, as presented in the Charter and also in speeches by Egyptian politicians, both for the socialist system and against capitalism was related more to advantages in terms of social justice and economic development than to gains in the form of democracy or individual freedom. The Charter began by admitting that historically capitalism had achieved rapid rates of economic growth but only on the basis of investment in colonies or, more graphically, through 'imperialist piracy', while other 'experiments of progress realised their objectives at the expense of increasing the misery of the working people, either to serve the interests of capital or under pressure of ideological application which went to the extent of sacrificing whole living generations for the sake of others still unborn' (p. 52). It went on to assert that 'mankind is now aware of the evils of imperialism' and had 'pledged itself to wipe it out' and 'the working class cannot be driven through forced labour to realise the objectives of production' (p. 83). Furthermore, throughout the underdeveloped world 'capitalism is no longer able to lead the economic drive' (p. 52) because 'the wide gap . . . which separates the advanced states and those trying to catch up no longer allows the method of progress to be left to desultory individual efforts motivated by mere selfish profit' (p. 53). In particular, Egyptian capitalists had shown themselves to be 'incapable of shouldering the responsibility of nationalist aspirations' (p. 73). They had depended upon 'parasitic exploitation' based on 'a protective trade policy which gave [private capital] benefits at the expense of the people' (p. 60) and upon a monopolistic structure of production which 'excluded every possibility of risk' (p. 73).

In brief, the Charter explicitly rejected both capitalist and Russian systems of economic organization as morally offensive and it specifically dismissed the notion that Egyptian capitalists could provide the country with real material progress and social justice. Past experience, it argued, had demonstrated their incapacity to raise the rate of growth and showed that they utilized a position, sheltered from internal and external competition, to exploit consumers and workers.

The Charter promised that the reformed productive organization would give the country both a rising standard of living and social justice. The former the Charter recognized called for 'assembling the national savings; putting all the experiences of modern science at the disposal of the exploitation of national savings [and] drafting a complete plan for production', while the latter required 'planning programmes for social action, programmes that enable the popular working masses to reap the benefits of economic action and create the welfare society to which they aspire and struggle to promote' (p. 53). Since capitalism had not and could not achieve the national objectives, the Charter assented to 'the necessity for the people's control over all the tools of production and over directing the surplus according to a definite plan', because

> efficient socialist planning is the guarantee for the sound exploitation of actually existing resources, or those which are latent or potential. At the same time, it is a guarantee for the continued distribution of fundamental services. It is also a guarantee for raising the standard of the services already now offered. It is a guarantee for extending those services to the areas which had fallen victim to negligence and inefficiency . . . (p. 54).

In other words, the economic system which emerged between 1960 and 1962 represented a response to mass demands for an efficient economy and for rapid growth combined with social justice. The new system was, moreover, the only way to meet those demands; or as the Charter puts it, 'the socialist solution to the problem of economic and social underdevelopment in Egypt . . . was never a question of free choice' but was a 'historical inevitability imposed by reality, the broad aspirations of the masses and the changing nature of the world in the second part of the 20th Century.' (p. 51).

Although the Charter does contain a number of quite specific criticisms of Egyptian private enterprise, its broad emphasis is upon ideology. That is to say, the presentation is highly general and the document consists in the main of a set of *a priori* assertions to the effect that capitalism is both morally intolerable and inefficient, while socialism alone will provide material progress and social justice. Moreover the Charter has become the reference point for explanations about recent Egyptian history. Of course it would be myopic in an age of ideology to deny the possible influence of general ideas upon the reforms introduced by the present Egyptian government. Once officially established, the socialist ideology probably exercised some independent influence of its own, either because the government felt obliged to maintain a certain consistency with the principles set out in the Charter, or because the acceptance of socialism by the régime engendered expectations and pressures among the population that promises would be kept. At the very least it hinders the ability of the government to manœuvre and makes reversals of previous policy politically hazardous.

On the other hand, because changes in Egyptian economic organization were accompanied by marked and well-publicized changes in the official ideology, this does not mean that the present economic system can be satisfactorily explained as the outcome of a revolution inspired by socialist principles. Unlike the old Bolsheviks, the Free Officers assumed power almost free from general notions about desirable patterns of economic and social organization and, with certain exceptions such as land reform, up to 1957 displayed a firm attachment to traditional forms of ownership and enterprise. Only after the Suez war did they reveal a willingness to experiment with economic organization, and even then their attempts to extend government control over the economy were not accompanied by any defined change in ideology, although one should say that their public attitude towards private business became gradually more ambiguous and suspicious. After July 1961 official ideology crystallized into a rejection of capitalism and unequivocal acceptance of socialism. The explanation in terms of ideology must logically rest upon the assumption that nine years after their coup d'état the Egyptian leaders became converted to socialism and inaugurated a Social Revolution. Apart from an obvious tendency to account for everything and nothing, for we can always inquire why the conversion occurred, the argument is unconvincing and certainly superficial.

To begin with, the impact of the 'Social Revolution' upon the mass of Egyptians has proved neither obvious nor far-reaching. Almost all the measures designed to redistribute income and property represent minor extensions or amendments to previous reforms, and none transferred income between social classes in ways novel or thorough-going enough to warrant the appellation 'revolutionary'. For example, only about 300,000 feddans were scheduled to become available for expropriation under the 1961 amendment to the Agrarian Reform Law, and presumably most owners affected by the new decree would take advantage of the clause permitting them to sell land in excess of the new maximum holding, so that the area eventually expropriated is likely to be considerably less than the possible 300,000 feddans.[2] When agrarian reform is completed, still only a minority of rural families, and they overwhelmingly 'middling peasants', will have gained

[2] Law 127, 1961 and NBE, *Econ. B.*, iii (1961), p. 278.

land.[3] These privileged beneficiaries were rewarded still further by amendments to the original agrarian reform which reduced considerably the amortization and interest charges on their land.[4]

President Nasser admitted that the provisions of the original law with respect to rent control had been evaded and that the attempt to regulate agricultural wages had also failed.[5] Agricultural labourers and their families, who formed about 40 per cent of the rural population, derived some benefit, however, from the Combined Centres set up by the government in Egyptian villages.[6]

Although reforms to the fiscal system had made it, in Dr Kaissouny's phrase, 'a socialist instrument' and income-tax rates on salaries above £3,000 were made more progressive, taxes on earnings below that level remain very high in a society where the average income is about £50 per year, while income-tax rates in the United States and Germany are still steeper than in Socialist Egypt. Another much-publicized law which limited earnings of all employees in the public sector to £5,000 a year represented a clarification of law 153 of 1957.[7] Under that statute directors of joint-stock companies could earn a maximum remuneration of £2,500 a year. But law 153 allowed a man to hold two directorships, and under the new statute he is confined to one.[8]

The reduction of house rents was certainly a 'progressive' measure, but rents had been lowered by decree twice before and the amount of income redistributed from rich to poor in the form of lower rent cannot have been substantial. Most of the gain will, moreover, accrue to middle-class tenants, because under law 168 of 1961 persons liable for higher rents will obtain a proportionately higher remission than tenants paying lower rents.[9]

The other measures which redistributed income between social classes affected only the employees of large-scale industrial and commercial enterprises. Their hours of work were reduced by the state to a maximum of 42 per week, and where this entailed a

[3] See below, p. 294.

[4] Law 128, 1961; Saab, in *ME Econ. Papers 1960*, p. 76; *Nasser's Speeches 1961*, p. 179.

[5] Warriner, p. 210 and Marei, *UAR Agriculture*, p. 54.

[6] This proportion relates to 1939 and is from Min. Agric., *Agricultural Census 1939* (1945), p. 47.

[7] Laws 113 & 125, 1961 and *BE*, 20 July 1961.

[8] *UAR Yearbook 1959*, p. 136 and *EG*, 12 Aug. 1958.

[9] The system of rent control was again revised under Law 46, 1962.

reduction in time worked, the company had to pay employees their original wage.[10] In May 1962 the government raised the minimum wage to 25 piastres a day for all employees over 18 in organized industry and commerce.[11] Finally, corporate enterprises were compelled to transfer a proportion of their net profits to their employees. The sum paid to each employee had to be *pro rata* to his wage or salary, but no one could receive more than £50 and any profits remaining after the initial distribution had to be paid over to workers whose original share fell below £50.[12]

As an obvious expression of the régime's concern for the welfare of the working class, these measures, particularly profit-sharing, received maximum publicity and reinforced the government's socialist image throughout the Arab world. It should, however, be pointed out that employees of corporate enterprises represented a privileged minority (roughtly 6 per cent of the labour force) whose pay and conditions of work already stood well above average. They had benefited more than any other section of the population from legislation designed to improve their conditions of employment and habitation, to preserve them from the worst forms of exploitation, and to reduce the uncertainties of their urban industrial environment. The body of social-welfare legislation built up by the former régime had been considerably extended both in scope and coverage and more stringently enforced since the revolution, but, to its regret, and despite efforts to do so, the government had not found it administratively feasible to extend legislation very far beyond the confines of organized industry and commerce.[13] Even at the end of 1964 the regulation of wages, housing, working conditions, health and social insurance hardly affected the majority of workers in agriculture and the non-corporate sectors of industry and trade.[14]

While the privileged employees of larger firms derived immediate and tangible benefit from the Social Revolution, their gain should not be exaggerated. They were all slightly better off

[10] *UAR Yearbook 1962*, p. 233 and Law 175, 1962.

[11] Law 102, 1962.

[12] Laws 111 & 112, 1961.

[13] On the régime's social welfare policies see *UAR Yearbook 1959*, chs. 10 & 11 and *1962*, pp. 233–4. For extensions to the laws relating to social welfare since 1960 see Laws 92 & 143, 1961; 64 & 141, 1963, & 63, 1964.

[14] At the end of 1962 about 21 per cent of the labour force benefited from social welfare legislation (*UAR Yearbook 1962*, pp. 233–4).

as a result of the law which reduced their hours of work without loss of remuneration, but probably not many enjoyed an elevation of pay under the new legal minimum wage of 25 piastres a day because in 1960 the average daily wage paid by larger firms had already attained the level of 55 piastres.[15]

Finally, although workers in corporate enterprises are entitled to a quarter of the profits made by their firms, just how much cash they will actually receive in any given year will depend on the provisions made by companies for the payment of dividends. Accounting allocations for depreciation, reserve funds, and special contingencies can always be manipulated to reduce their share of 'net profits'. Furthermore, only two-fifths of their entitlement is transferred to them in the form of cash. One-fifth goes into a welfare fund managed jointly by the company and the labourers' syndicate and the remaining 40 per cent is paid into a social security fund managed by the state.[16] Thus 60 per cent of the share of profits allocated to workers is in fact spent on their behalf. 'Saved' is perhaps a more appropriate word than 'spent' because the outgoings from social security and pension funds during their early years of growth are generally much less than their annual receipts. As early as 1953, when it reorganized the pension system for civil servants, the government recognized that welfare insurance, financed by compulsory contributions, provided at one and the same time funds for the finance of development projects and political kudos in the form of support from the bureaucracy.[17] Three years later the new government established and managed an insurance scheme for the employees of all large-scale firms in Cairo and Alexandria, financed by joint contributions from employers and workers.[18] By 1959 this same scheme had been considerably extended to cover a wider range of benefits and a greater number of workers, while the bulk of its surplus income found its way into public securities.[19]

When the plan was drafted in 1959–60, planners anticipated that net income from the various insurance funds under state control would provide up to 15 per cent of the finance required

[15] *Basic Statistics*, pp. 34–35. Larger firms, who employed 6 per cent of the labour force, means firms with more than 10 employees.

[16] Laws 111 & 112, 1961 and *Commerce du Levant*, 23 Jan. 1963.

[17] Amin, in *Ég. contemp.*, July 1959, pp. 5–11.

[18] Law 419, 1955. [19] Law 92, 1959 and *UAR Yearbook 1959*, ch. 10.

for projected capital formation between 1960–5.[20] Purely from a development viewpoint it made good sense to reconvert the profits nominally redistributed to industrial workers into social-security contributions. Consumption was thereby restrained, at least in the crucial short run, and funds were made available for the finance of the plans projects. At the same time workers became associated with the efficiency and success of their enterprises, for their immediate cash income partly depended upon the level of company profits and also because their personal efforts contributed to their future welfare benefits and pensions. Political promises that planning would produce a better future became translated in July 1961 into something more tangible and visible. Thus while these much-publicized decrees probably made only a slight difference to the current distribution of income, they certainly added to the progressive image of the Egyptian government and accorded with the requirements of sound planning.

If my analysis is correct, that the measures designed to redistribute income represent for the most part extensions to previous reforms which had no profound or immediate impact upon the overall distribution of income, then official statements to the effect that the nationalization decrees brought about a 'more just distribution of property, turned citizens into owners and lead to equality and the dissolution of class differences' also require careful examination.[21]

These claims have some substance in the sense that the nationalization and sequestration of private property between 1960 and 1964, together with the land reforms of 1952 and 1961, affected a tiny class of people who owned a disproportionate share of the national wealth. Dr Khallaf's figures indicate that in 1960 62 per cent of the shares pertaining to corporate enterprises belonged to only 9 per cent of all shareholders, and President Nasser stated in a speech that the total number of persons who lost property under the nationalization laws of 1961 and the land-reform legislation numbered about 7,300.[22] Precise measurement related to property ownership before and after the revolution is, however, not yet

[20] INP Memo. 63 and *Ann. Plan 1960–1*, p. 186.

[21] INP Memo. 137, pp. 1 & 2; *BE*, 21, 23, & 29 July 1961; Kerr, in *MEJ*, Spring 1962, pp. 127–42; *The Charter*, pp. 46, 61, 72 & 79.

[22] H. Khallaf, *Development in the Economy of Modern Egypt* (1962, ar.), pp. 407–8 and *Nasser's Speeches 1961*, p. 343.

possible, but evidence available now suggests that gross inequalities in the distribution of private wealth which previously existed have disappeared as a consequence of the expropriation of assets belonging to a very small group of aristocratic and *haut bourgeois* families.[23]

Furthermore, the expropriation of private assets in Egypt has not taken the form of compelling property owners to exchange land and property for government bonds of an equivalent capital value, a formula which leaves the distribution of wealth virtually unaltered, at least in the short run. In fact compensation paid by the Egyptian government fell way below the 'true' market value of the shares and land taken into public ownership. For example, the compensation prescribed for industrial and commercial assets nationalized in July 1961 took the form of negotiable bonds, bearing interest at 4 per cent and redeemable after fifteen years. The government fixed the price of each expropriated share at its final quotation on the Cairo Stock Exchange for 19 July 1961.[24] Share prices rose markedly during the early stages of the union with Syria in 1958, but by the beginning of 1960 prices had returned to their near average for 1956–7. During 1960 (a year marked by state control over dividend distribution and the beginnings of nationalization) prices fell rapidly, and by March 1961 the general index had fallen to its lowest point since the revolution.[25] No doubt periodic bursts of selling to anticipate possible nationalizations, a phenomenon noticed by *The Times* correspondent, were in great part responsible for this depression.[26] Unfortunately the National Bank of Egypt ceased to print a share price index after March 1961, but it does appear from a graph published by Bank Misr that after some stability during April and May, share prices began to decline very rapidly from the beginning of June, which suggests that the measures of July were not unexpected.[27] Moreover the timing of successive nationalization decrees with short gaps between the laws of June and late July undoubtedly accelerated the decline. Thus when the government blocked all dealings on the stock exchange on 19 July 1961, share prices stood at their

[23] Riad, *Égypte nassérienne*, pp. 79–81 & 84 and Abdel-Malek, *Égypte, société militaire*, p. 148.

[24] INP Memo. 137, pp. 4, 7, & 11.

[25] See table 13, p. 328.

[26] *The Times*, 21 July 1961.

[27] Bank Misr, *Econ. B.*, Sept. 1961, p. 40.

lowest level since the war.[28] Apparently the government recognized that hardship might be caused through its arbitrary system of compensation, for a month later the Ministry of Economy announced that *small* shareholders would receive additional payment for the fall in share prices.[29]

Although the Egyptian government has consistently emphasized its support for the principle of fair compensation, in March 1964 it drastically revised the whole system of payment for private property taken into public ownership. Under law 104, 1964, all land expropriated under the land reforms of 1952 and 1961 became state property without further payment of compensation. Landowners have thus received nothing except 12 years' interest on the 15-year bonds exchanged for their land. Persons whose assets and personal property had been sequestrated between October 1961 and February 1962 were paid in 4 per cent bonds of 15 years maturity up to a maximum value of £30,000, and the government compensated shareholders whose assets had been nationalized between 1960 and 1964 with similar bonds but fixed the maximum payable at £15,000.[30] Foreigners who owned property in Egypt have in most cases received virtually nothing from the state for their assets.[31] In general, our survey of the provisions made to compensate nationals reveals that they have not been paid anything like a market value for their shares. It is reasonable to conclude that, in addition to land, a considerable segment of industrial and commercial property has been, *de facto* if not *de jure*, confiscated by the Egyptian government

Land reform and the extension of public ownership seem to have been at the expense of a small group of families who formerly possessed most of the nation's wealth. Gross inequalities in the ownership of property have now certainly been eliminated, but, except in this particular sense, official arguments that nationalization has brought about a 'more just distribution of property' are still difficult to interpret.[32] Since no Egyptian citizen has added

[28] NBE, *Econ. B.*, iv (1953), p. 301 published a graph of share prices from 1947 to 1953.

[29] *BE*, 13 Aug. 1961.

[30] Information Dept., *Documents and Notes, March and April 1964* (1964) and Law 150, 1964.

[31] On foreign property see *Mideast Mirror*, 7 Aug. & 18 Nov. 1964.

[32] *The Charter*, pp. 55 & 61.

anything to his personal property as a result of nationalization, the claim can only logically apply to the long-run distribution of income which will flow from property transferred to the state. If over time the Egyptian government uses the profits accruing from nationalized assets to equalize the distribution of domestic income or directly to improve welfare of the poorer classes, then the extension of public ownership might well be described as the beginning of a Social Revolution.

Such an obvious deduction was not overlooked by Egyptian leaders, who provided for the transfer of 25 per cent of the profits of public enterprises to employees, and they also insisted that the extension of public ownership would immediately reduce 'exploitation' by the capitalist minority. President Nasser considered that the 'Socialist Framework carefully . . . wiped out the last vestiges of exploitation' and Vice-President Sabry held that 'a large public sector gave society great assurances which would enable it to prevent exploitation or domination by a minority'.[33] Exploitation was an oft-used but vague epithet applied for years past to the activities of domestic capitalists by the military régime. With the publication of the Charter its meaning became clearer. Exploitation as there defined referred to the fact that industrialists earned inordinate profits by paying low wages to their employees and from charging consumers high prices.[34]

The implications of the laws relating to profit-sharing have already been elucidated and two questions arise from the contention that the last vestiges of exploitation have been wiped out. First, to what extent did exploitation exist before July 1961, and, second, how far has the situation changed since then? Manufacturing wages in Egypt were and still are among the lowest in the world, but little about exploitation can be deduced from international comparisons of this kind because output per worker in Egypt is also very low. Moreover the productivity of Egyptian workers is not entirely a reflection of a low capital-labour ratio. Egyptian workers are also less efficient when compared with their counterparts abroad employed on the same tasks and utilizing similar productive equipment.[35] Since the Egyptian leaders have

[33] INP Memo. 137.
[34] *The Charter*, pp. 56–58, 60, & 72 and *BE*, 21 July 1961.
[35] UN, *Dev. Manufacturing*, pp. 70, 72, & 75.

explicitly rejected the Marxist definition, which describes all profits earned by the private owners of productive assets as exploitation, no clear deduction can be made and no clear conclusions drawn from the post-war fall in the share of wages in the net receipts of organized industrial enterprises because this trend reflected an upward movement in the ratio of capital to labour.[36] One might, however, argue from this same data that the industrial labour force has suffered exploitation in the sense that employers failed to pay it a 'fair' share of the rise in productivity per worker. On the other hand industrial wages appear to have increased faster than the prices of manufactured products and the cost of living during the post-war period; which at least indicates that the labour force had not been subjected to a process of 'immiserization' since 1945.[37] Nor, finally, have the newly-created public enterprises attempted to raise their employees' wages to levels which put them clearly beyond the charge of 'exploitation'. The government's new wage law was designed to secure a tolerable minimum of 25 piastres a day, not to raise the overall level of remuneration.

There appears to be more substance to the claim that Egyptian capitalists had exploited consumers because internal and external competition was weak. Industrial and commercial profits, to paraphrase the contention of Egyptian leaders, were swollen by protection against foreign commodities and the prevalence of monopoly within the domestic market. As a consequence consumers had paid higher prices, and a minority gained at the expense of the majority. Nationalization therefore represented a move towards social justice.[38]

'Monopolist' was also an epithet applied by military leaders to local industrialists almost since the inception of the revolution. Yet, to say the least, there was something inconsistent about a government castigating capitalists for sheltering behind a tariff wall it proceeded to raise even higher, and behind monopolistic arrangements it not merely ignored but in some ways fostered. Economists had recognized even before the revolution that the absence of internal and external competition among large sectors

[36] O'Brien, in *ME Econ. Papers 1962*, pp. 99 f. and table vi.

[37] The indices to support these statements are published in the *Ann. stat.* and NBE, *Econ. B.*

[38] Kerr, in *MEJ*, Spring 1962; INP Memo. 137, p. 2; *The Charter*, pp. 60 & 73; *Ann. Plan 1960–1*, p. 7; *BE*, 29 July 1961.

of Egyptian industry induced inefficiency and militated against the welfare of local consumers, but apart from the nationalization of Abboud's sugar refineries and the Cairo Waterworks, no change can be detected in the régime's policy towards monopoly. On the contrary, the new government encouraged firms to amalgamate, raised tariffs, and provided prospectors with even stronger and more enduring monopoly rights over their discoveries of minerals.[39]

But several arguments can be adduced in support of monopoly in an underdeveloped country. Monopoly may have been necessary to attract capital into industry, to the introduction of new techniques, or to realize economies of scale.[40] Monopoly also increases the share of profits in the national income, and, if Professor Lewis is correct, this engenders higher rates of saving and investment.[41] Finally, attacks on capitalists for the exploitation of consumers are not so easily or consistently sustained when both the level of protection and the pricing policies of private monopolies taken into public ownership have apparently remained unchanged.[42]

To conclude, there is little substance to the claim that since 1961 Egypt has passed through important and far-reaching changes initiated from above partly as a consequence of the acceptance of socialism by its present rulers. No doubt social revolutions are matters of degree, but my analysis of the socialist laws leads to the conclusion that up to the present time the decrees which nationalized property and redistributed income have had too slight an impact on the mass of Egyptians to warrant such an inflated title. Those who have gained most seem to have been middling peasants, the employees of corporate industry and commerce, and middle-class tenants of rented accommodation, three groups who altogether form no more than a small and privileged minority of the population. Moreover many of the 'socialist' measures represent not radical innovations but amendments and extensions to

[39] Laws 86, 1956 & 54, 1957.

[40] Naggar (*Industrialization & Income*, pp. 255–65) ignores all possible advantages of Egyptian monopolies in his thesis, but Gritly (pp. 525–6) (also without evidence) makes some of the claims listed here.

[41] W. A. Lewis, 'Economic Development with Unlimited Supplies of Labour', *Manchester School*, May 1954, pp. 139–91.

[42] Evidence about present pricing policies of nationalized industries is scarce but I know of no information that any profound changes have occurred since July 1961, although the whole subject is now under discussion in Egypt.

previous laws whose origins in some cases antedate the present régime by several decades. Other reforms had antecedents in laws promulgated by the government since 1952 but which had not previously received the accolade of socialist. For example, the nationalization of private property can be traced back to the sequestration of British and French property during the Suez war, but at that time the government employed nationalist, not socialist, arguments to support the expropriation of private property.

Nor were the nationalizations of February 1960 or of June and early July 1961 defended on socialist grounds. The government nationalized Bank Misr to ensure greater control over the private sector during the Plan. Foreign trade firms (including those pressing cotton) passed into public ownership for much the same reason. Cairo bus services were municipalized for inefficiency and the Khedivial Shipping Line was nationalized for refusing to obey government instructions. Of nationalizations which occurred before 20 July 1961, only those involving the import of tea and pharmaceutical products were defended on anything like ideological grounds. Here the Minister of Supply justified the imposition of a public monopoly because of 'profiteering' by private firms.

Lastly, the way the government proceeded to nationalize step by step first Bank Misr, then to take over half the capital of 86 companies and participate in the shares of 147 others before moving, after two and in some cases three years, to full nationalization suggests an immediate concern with control rather than with the ownership and the distribution of wealth. I conclude that the demise of private enterprise might be more plausibly and less superficially explained in terms of the culmination of a process whereby government control has been extended over the whole economy rather than in terms of an ideologically-inspired Social Revolution.

ECONOMIC CONTROL IN THE FREE-ENTERPRISE ECONOMY, 1952–7

State control has not, however, been extended steadily over the private sector since the coup d'état. It proceeded rather by a series of sharp upward steps. Even before 1952 the government had made several important incursions into the autonomy of private producers and the old order had displayed some willingness to use the state to promote economic development and social welfare. In several areas of economic policy the Free Officers continued, although with more energy and determination, along lines initiated by their predecessors, and a marked reorientation in Egyptian economic policy occurred not in 1952 but after the Suez war. At that point the régime committed the economy to comprehensive planning, to begin in July 1960, and launched almost immediately an ambitious industrialization programme. As has already been shown, the effects of this commitment upon private commerce and industry proved to be extremely far-reaching, and for agriculture its full implications have not yet been worked out.

Although the Industrialization Plan of 1957 was conceived and drawn up within the Ministry of Industry, the government certainly expected private business to co-operate in financing, constructing, and administering many of the ministry's projects, and in an attempt to channel investible funds towards its own schemes the government multiplied controls over the discretion of the private sector. For example, it curbed investment in real estate, and as the Central Bank attempted to conserve scarce foreign exchange for planned development projects, private exporters and importers found themselves operating within a tightening and more wide-ranging system of regulations. State control over the credit policies of financial institutions increased under the Banking and Credit Law of 1957 and as a result of the Egyptianization of several major foreign banks during the Suez war. Through the Economic Organization and Bank Misr the government put strong pressure upon firms to participate in its projects, and in February 1960 the Bank was nationalized in order to ensure that Misr companies definitely complied with government instructions.

By 1960 the government had assumed almost complete responsibility for capital formation and proposed to organize and execute the bulk of projects contained in the Plan for 1960–5. The Plan was comprehensive in the sense that it laid down detailed targets for both private and public sectors. When the Plan opened in July 1960 the private sector still provided the bulk of the country's output, foreign exchange, and domestic savings, and the failure of firms and individuals to accommodate their patterns of production, investment, and saving to the designs of the National Planning

Committee could seriously frustrate the government's own investment programme and jeopardize the success of its ambitious and well-publicized target of doubling the national income over the following decade. But, despite the importance of the private sector, the government made no serious effort to consult businessmen about the content of the Plan or to secure their co-operation for its implementation. Private producers could certainly be prevented from contravening public policy, but their positive compliance with the planner's directives remained much more problematical. Incentives and indirect techniques of persuasion had not, moreover, operated very effectively in the past, but experience with the Economic Organization and Bank Misr showed that at least the larger firms could be controlled if the state owned sufficient shares to appoint a majority of nominees to their boards of directors. Thus by 1960 the nationalization of corporate property and the extension of further controls over agriculture and small-scale enterprise appeared almost as a logical next step for a government committed to comprehensive planning and ambitious development targets.

Perceived in historical perspective and placed within the context of a commitment to planning, the demise of free enterprise seems to require little further explanation. Nationalization and the curtailment of private initiative in the economic field simply form part of a process whereby the present régime extended its control over the economy. But this hypothesis prompts rather than answers questions. After all, there was nothing inexorable about the process. When the Free Officers seized power they were not committed either to central planning or to changing the basis of the economic system of production. On the contrary, their early actions and pronouncements show them as favouring the notion of trying to make capitalism work, and apart from land reform their economic policies from 1952 to 1956 can be described as orthodox economic liberalism. To account for the changes which have occurred in Egyptian economic organization, it seems necessary to ask why a reorientation of policy took place after Suez? What were the underlying economic and social forces which impelled the régime to assume more and more responsibiilty for development? Why did the present government, after a short trial of four years, abandon its conviction that the nation's economic progress could, in general, be left to private enterprise, in favour of comprehensive planning conducted by an enlarged public sector and tighter controls over farmers?

While Egypt's economic problems received more attention from the new government than they had under the monarchy, development does not appear to have been of prime concern to the Free Officers during the early years of their rule. Their top priorities seem to have been the consolidation of power, the creation of a new political system, the evacuation of the canal zone, and Egypt's relations with foreign powers.[43] Only gradually did the economy attract more and more of their attention. As the Officers assumed full responsibility for national welfare, the need to alleviate the appalling poverty of their fellow citizens became more obvious, and a Military Junta seeking widespread support no doubt found it expedient to pay close attention to the welfare of the masses. During the 1950s all states and international agencies displayed greater concern than ever before with poverty, and few political leaders remained immune from this world-wide pressure and publicity to raise living standards for their people. Moreover, in their quest for non-alignment and independence in relations with other states, the Free Officers became impressed with the advantages of moves towards autarky. Egypt's dependence on the outside world for arms was demonstrated to them in 1955 and its vulnerability to economic sanctions was made obvious during the Tripartite Aggression.[44] To diversify exports and to develop local sources for steel, arms, engineering products, and capital equipment must have seemed the only viable and lasting basis for genuine independence.

Finally, the Suez war and the events surrounding it ended whatever hopes the Junta had of attracting substantial amounts of western aid and private foreign capital into Egypt. Until 1956 'orthodox' policies towards domestic business reflected, in some part, the Officers' anxiety to assure western governments and investors of the continued stability of the Egyptian economy.[45] They made it easier for foreign investors to repatriate their earnings

[43] Vatikiotis, chs. 4, 5, & 6.

[44] President Nasser admitted that Suez pushed the Egyptians into depending upon themselves more (*Nasser's Speeches 1959*, p. 401).

[45] *BE*, 1 May 1954 & 26 May 1955.

on capital invested in Egypt and revoked a nationalistic decree of 1946 which prevented aliens owning more than 49 per cent of the share capital of any Egyptian company.[46] Despite all blandishments by the Junta, the inflow of capital between 1952 and 1956 remained negligible.[47] Nationalization of the canal, the purchase of arms from Czechoslovakia, and the sequestration of British and French assets made it useless for the government even to try to placate the fears of western politicians and investors. Egyptian business then lost a safeguard from state interference on account of the national need to attract foreign capital.

After Suez not only did the Junta give economic development a higher priority but policies from 1956 indicate that it had lost confidence in the ability of the private sector to achieve material progress at a pace and along lines considered desirable. Thus the state began to circumscribe the autonomy of private business and to invest in spheres of activity traditionally left to capitalists, and the government made more determined attempts to channel private investment into officially approved directions. No doubt the response from the private sector to patriotic appeals and to the plethora of incentives offered to it by the Military Régime during the free-enterprise phase of the revolution were in great part responsible for the reorientation of policy. Although the Junta announced ambitious plans for agriculture in the form of vast reclamation projects such as the New Valley and the High Dam, the emphasis of their development policy lay clearly upon industrialization. To encourage private investment in the industrial sector the government had raised tariffs, lowered taxes, cheapened finance, reformed company law, and increased private profits by a variety of fiscal and monetary devices. Foreign exchange had been more carefully conserved for development purposes. The state had embarked upon an expansive programme of capital formation to improve every part of the nation's infrastructure. The Officers hoped that given the right incentives private enterprise would raise the rate of investment, particularly in the industrial sector. Yet from the government's point of view the overall performance and response from private business and investors can only be called disappointing.

[46] *UAR Econ. Features*, pp. 18–19. This decree was reimposed in 1958.
[47] M. Messayer, *L'Égypte à travers le chemin du développement* (1962), p. 207.

The scattered and somewhat dubious statistical evidence now available indicates that the absolute level of fixed capital formation by the private sector after 1952 was consistently and appreciably lower than in the four years preceding the revolution.[48] Since so many of the new incentives were designed to encourage industrialization, it is regrettable that no figures exist which can be used to estimate private investment in the manufacturing sector. However, the statistics show that, except for one year (1955–6), gross *industrial* investment (public and private) appears to have risen only slightly before 1957.[49] National Bank and other reports often deplored the slow movement of funds into industry during the early years of the revolution and some further support for the complaints is provided by figures of net annual additions to the statutory capital of corporate industrial enterprises, which (except in 1955 and 1956) exhibited no significant tendency to rise after 1952.[50] Lastly, what does emerge unequivocably from investment statistics is that, in absolute terms, an increased volume of investible funds flowed into real estate after the revolution.[51] Despite the restrictions of 1956, investment in residential buildings continued to increase until 1959, supporting Dr Hamdi's observation that the Egyptian capitalist class often displayed an inexplicable antipathy towards industrial shares.[52]

The failure of private investors to respond enthusiastically to exhortations and incentives from the government is one of the more important factors behind the inadequate performance of the Egyptian economy during the years which followed the revolution. In real terms the annual average increment to Gross National Product from 1945 to 1952 was £44 million. For the years 1953 to 1957 the increment averaged only £27 million. Or to express the statistics another way, the rate of increase of national product slowed down from an annual average rate of 3·5 per cent during

[48] Table 14 (p. 329) shows that fixed capital formation by the private sector for 1948, 1949, 1950, and 1951 was at an average annual level of £113 m. For 1953, 1954, 1955, and 1956 the level was £77 m. Both figures are expressed at constant prices.

[49] See table 12 (p. 327). The rise in 1955–6 government investment was mainly responsible for the rise in 1955–6 (NBE, *Econ. B.*, ii (1957), p. 157).

[50] See table 15 (p. 330) and ibid. ii (1956), p. 109. Breakdowns of the figures show that public funds raised total investment in 1956 (NBE, *Econ. B.*, ii (1957), p. 157).

[51] FIE, *Ann. 1958–9*, p. 25.

[52] Hamdi, p. 157.

the last years of the former régime to 2·6 per cent after the revolution. Throughout the post-war period the Egyptian population has been rising at between 2·5 and 2·9 per cent per annum, and the consequence of this slower rate of increase of national product was a roughly constant per capita income from 1953 to 1957.[53]

From 1948 to 1956 the index published by the National Bank of Egypt shows that the production of field crops failed to show any upward trend.[54] Before Suez the efforts of the Junta to raise yields or to extend the cropped area has no obvious effect on the volume of field crop production. For industry the record appears more satisfactory in that the annual average increment to manufacturing output was higher after 1952 than it had been under the former régime, but the annual average rate of growth of industrial output from 1953 to 1957 fell slightly below that achieved from 1947 to 1951.[55] After the revolution production was rising, but at a slightly slower rate despite the more strenuous efforts made by the new government to force the pace of industrialization. In short, stagnation continued.

Why private enterprise failed to respond more enthusiastically to the appeals and incentives directed at them by the Junta is an important question which, without surveys on the attitudes of the Egyptian business class, remains in large part unanswerable. Certain features of the environment private investors and entrepreneurs found themselves operating in after the revolution can, however, be elucidated to provide at least the beginnings of an explanation. In general, it should be observed that the economic and political climate prevailing in Egypt from 1952 to 1957 cannot be described as providing the kind of atmosphere most conducive to private investment.

Economically the early years of the revolution coincided with the downswing of the trade cycle. For several years after the war the incomes of Egyptian farmers and landowners had risen as a result of the rapid rise in the prices of raw materials on international markets, and their ability to purchase the services and commodities

[53] The figures are a trend-line average from data in INP Memo. 335.

[54] See table 19 (p. 334). The index does not include animal products.

[55] The annual average increment (trend line value) from 1945 to 1951 was 6·1 points and from 1953 to 1957 8·2 points. The annual average rate of growth from 1947 to 1951 was 7·3 per cent and from 1953 to 1957 the average rate was 7·1 per cent—see table 19.

of local commerce and industry increased *pari passu*. Investment in industry, agriculture, commerce, and housing responded to the stimulus exerted by the rising world demand for Egyptian cotton and the reopening of international trade after the war years. Industrialists replaced obsolete and worn-out equipment, while the rents of landowners and the profits of merchants flowed into real estate as the urbanization of Egypt pushed up the demand for houses. The upswing reached its peak during the Korean boom of 1950–1 and thereafter the terms of trade moved against Egypt.[56] The relative decline in agricultural incomes, coupled with some acceleration in the rate of growth of population, made the prospects for further rapid expansion appear less optimistic. Moreover the deflationary financial and fiscal policies pursued by the new government during its early years of office did nothing to stimulate local demand, and industry found itself with idle capacity.[57]

Nor was the political atmosphere conducive to optimism. After all, a revolution in the political system had occurred in July 1952. The Free Officers seized power following years of civic disorder, attacks on property, and a collapse of political leadership.[58] The propertied classes naturally waited to assess the stability of the Military Régime before committing their savings to fixed and slowly gestating investments. Their caution is not difficult to understand, because it took the Junta over two years of struggle with other political groups as well as factions within its own ranks to consolidate power.[59] And the displaced and often imprisoned members of the former political élite had been closely connected not merely with landlords but also with the *haute bourgeosie*, who owned and controlled most of industry and commerce.[60] During these years the Officers pursued foreign policies which risked direct military intervention from France and Britain. In 1955 they purchased arms from a communist state. One year later France, Britain, and Israel invaded Egypt.[61]

Despite repeated assurances by the Officers about the future of free enterprise in Egypt, their willingness to experiment with

[56] See above, pp. 18, 19 & 32.

[57] *EEPR*, Suppl. on Industr. Production, July 1957 and GB, *Report of UK Trade Mission*, pp. 32–39.

[58] Safran, pp. 185, 194, & 200–5.

[59] Vatikiotis, ch. 4 and Wheelock, chs. 1–3.

[60] Riad, *Égypte nassérienne*, pp. 77–84.

[61] Cremeans, pp. 147–54.

public enterprise and occasional radical utterances from some members of the Revolutionary Council probably evoked apprehension among a business class which had lived for many decades in an environment of *laissez-faire*, while agrarian reform must have reduced the willingness of landowners to improve their property and may even have had a discouraging psychological effect on investors throughout the economy. More tangibly the reform lowered the share of national income accruing to a group with a higher than average propensity to save and invest. Its precise influence cannot be measured, but it seems reasonable to argue that land reform had some adverse effects upon capital formation by the private sector, at least in the short run.[62]

If the Junta expected, in Colonel Nasser's phrase, an 'Industrial Renaissance' to emerge from the offer of fiscal and financial incentives, their hopes were unrealistic.[63] Similar policies had been tried over several decades by the previous governments and further elevations of tariffs and even cheaper credit could not have made very much difference to decisions by entrepreneurs and investors,[64] while experience in other countries might have warned the government that lower taxes on incomes and profits are weak incentives during the early phases of industrial development, when the rate of return on capital before or after tax is not usually very high anyway, and as far as reinvestment is concerned, tax exemptions only benefit firms making large profits.[65]

Nor should the Junta have expected its well-publicized programme of improvement to Egypt's infrastructure to stimulate much private investment in directly productive activities. Public expenditure on roads, railways, power supplies, and irrigation facilities had risen steadily since the war and the new government simply extended and implemented more rapidly the Five-Year Plan drawn up by the former régime in 1947.[66] Moreover Egypt was not nearly so deficient in social capital as many other poor countries. Its long participation in the international cotton

[62] Ghonemy, 'Investment Effects of Land Reform', *Ég. contemp.*, 1954, pp. 1–15.

[63] *BE*, 26 May 1955.

[64] See above, pp. 5–56 & 62.

[65] W. A. Lewis, 'The Industrialization of the British West Indies', *Caribbean Econ. R.*, May 1950.

[66] See above, pp. 33, 60 & 62 and PCDNP, *Report 1955* (ar.), pp. 257–94 & 342–401.

market had led to the creation of a fairly well developed system of transport, power supplies, and financial institutions. While further improvement to those facilities certainly seemed necessary, it was not likely to achieve the spectacular economic results which so often follow from the creation of an infrastructure in poor countries.

To the new government the term 'Industrial Renaissance' really implied the orientation of investment towards novel and complex lines of manufacturing. My analysis in Chapter 1 suggests that the strategy adopted by the Officers for industrial growth was, moreover, based upon a sound appreciation of past developments and future prospects for the industrialization of Egypt.

By the early 1950s Egyptian industry had completed what might be called the primary stage of industrialization. During this stage an industrializing country replaces most of its more simple manufactured imports with domestically produced substitutes. Foreign competing manufactures are excluded by tariffs or other protective devices, and such industries as textiles, clothing, footwear, manufactured foodstuffs, household utensils, and furniture capture the home market. Most of these industries are of low capital intensity and utilize relatively simple production techniques. Usually they are based upon raw materials from the local agricultural sector. Their market has often already been explored and established by importers.

Of course the model simplifies, but it focuses attention on salient features of Egyptian development. From 1930, when Egypt first secured control over her external tariff and instituted a protective policy towards domestic industry, the growth of textile production, foodstuffs, beverages, footwear, manufactured tobacco, and leather products accelerated. The Second World War helped local manufacturers still further by effectively excluding foreign goods from Egypt and by adding the demand of troops stationed in the area to the domestic market.[67]

Stimulated by tariffs and war, rapid development took place in consumer-goods industries, accompanied by a declining share of foreign competing products in aggregate consumption. Unfortunately available information is insufficient to chart the process of import substitution but fragmentary figures now published paint

[67] See above, pp. 13–18.

in part of the picture. Thus in 1932 Egypt imported 22,500 tons of cotton goods, eighteen years later the quantity had fallen to 5,000 tons. Over roughly the same time-span output of cotton yarn rose from 3,000 to 50,000 tons and production of fabrics from 93 million metres in 1938 to 225 million metres by 1950. Soap imports fell by 44 per cent in a decade while domestic production rose by 55 per cent. In 1928 251,000 tons of cement were imported but ten years later no foreign cement was used in Egypt.[68] Comparisons between 1930 and 1950 of quantities imported of prepared cereals and vegetables, cooking oils and fats, manufactured tobacco and beverages reveal a decline in purchases overseas of processed foodstuffs.[69] According to Professor Bonné, by 1939 Egyptian manufacturers already met almost all local demand for sugar, alcohol, cigarettes, milled cereals, glass, shoes, cement, soap, and furniture.[70]

At mid-century, after two decades of protected development, Egypt seems to have achieved self-sufficiency in processing food produced by its agricultural sector and in the manufacture of cotton yarn and cloth. Food, beverages, tobacco, and textiles dominated industry. Yet industry still contributed little to national output or employment and production was orientated towards the home market.[71] Less than 10 per cent of manufactured output was exported, most of it cotton cloth and yarn; but, unlike Britain in the early nineteenth century or Hong Kong today, Egypt did not apparently have the capability of capturing a substantial share of world trade in cheap textiles. Nor was the Egyptian economy endowed with the kind of skills and resources which could produce commodities enjoying a rapidly growing demand on world markets.[72] Outlets for Egyptian industrial products had to be found locally; but the size of the domestic market remained relatively small and dependent upon the level of family incomes. While industry remained a small sector of the economy, the multiplier effects of industrial investment were unlikely to raise appreciably the demand for manufactured commodities. The mass

[68] NBE, *Econ. B.*, ii (1951), pp. 16–18.

[69] Statist. Dept., *Ann. Statements of Foreign Trade*, 1931 & 1951.

[70] A. Bonné, *State and Economics in the Middle East* (1948), p. 297.

[71] See above, p. 19.

[72] *Analyses of Egypt's Balance of Trade and Cotton Exports*, by P. Bög (1958), NPC Memos 7 & 9.

market for the consumer-goods industries consisted of the majority of Egyptian families who obtained their livelihood from farming. That market could expand if the prices of manufactured commodities fell or if incomes rose as a result of increased productivity in agriculture or, finally, as a consequence of an upward movement in prices of its principal cash crop, raw cotton, on world markets. For reasons discussed in Chapter 1, neither industrial nor agricultural productivity appeared likely to change significantly in the short run, nor in 1952 could the Egyptian government reasonably expect any substantial improvement in the nation's terms of trade.

As the National Production Council perceived, almost the only clear way forward was again through import substitution. Not, however, in simple consumer goods, where industry had already reached the margin, but a pattern of development which replaced, wherever possible, imported consumer durables, intermediate producers' goods, and capital equipment with domestic substitutes. The trade statistics for the early 1950s showed that possibilities for further import replacement along these lines were considerable, and several other arguments strongly commended this strategy to the new government. Clearly the local market existed and possibilities for its future expansion could be easily investigated. A growing deficit on the balance of payments called for urgent correction through the transfer of resources towards producing at home commodities Egypt could no longer afford to buy overseas. Moreover, as long as the capital goods sector remained small, any development programme would all too quickly run into a problem of rising imports. Given the high opportunity cost of foreign exchange, social returns from import replacement were likely to be higher than from the alternative use of resources to promote exports of primary produce, subject to falling prices on world markets. Mounting public expenditure on improvements and extensions to the infrastructure and also upon arms did not afford anything like maximum possible stimulus to Egyptian industry because a high proportion of government spending took the form of imports. The construction of productive capacity to meet predictable state demand seemed an obvious way for industry to expand. Finally, the promotion of heavy industry would probably induce investment in other parts of the economy. For example, the proposed steel mill would purchase bricks, electricity, and transport services and provide an accessible local input for a host of metallurgical products, and the projected plant for rubber tyres would purchase cotton and flax from Egyptian farmers. Most new investments, the Council anticipated, would set up similar backward and forward linkage effects throughout industry and also with the agricultural sector.[73]

The Junta quickly realized that the state would have to take the lead in the establishment of new industries and set up the National Production Council to plan and execute projects in such sectors of manufacturing as steel, heavy chemicals, electrical and railway equipment, rubber tyres, petroleum, and jute. It was certainly the policy of the Council to associate private capital and enterprise with all its ventures, but despite the provision of incentives and exhortations from the government, the response of private investors and the contribution of entrepreneurs to the challenge of a new industrial era so clearly presented by the Council seems to have been slight. The government, it seems, provided major impetus behind the growth of a producer-goods sector after the revolution. Most new projects were designed and established by the National Production Council. The Council also undertook the negotiations with foreign companies and governments for credits, equipment, and technical advice necessary to set up novel, expensive, and complicated forms of manufacturing. It also made arrangements with the Central Bank for the allocation of foreign exchange, for loans from the Industrial Bank, and tax concessions from the Treasury. Only limited information is available on how the new projects were financed, but the evidence for steel, railway equipment, electric cables, fertilizers, and jute suggests that the major component of domestic finance came from public sources.[74] Moreover a study by the Industrial Bank shows that the government provided 74 per cent of capital invested in joint-stock companies operating in heavy industry, and founded between 1954 and 1958. According to this same study, private investors in

[73] The arguments in favour of the industrialization strategy adopted by the Egyptian government are set out in PCDNP, *Report 1955*, pp. 17, 20, 26, 174–6, & 192–4 and continued in *Industry after the Revolution*, pp. 9–10, 90–92, & 101–7.

[74] PCDNP, *Report 1955* (ar.), pp. 2, 174–6, 186, 199, & 202; *UAR Econ. Features*, pp. 42, 48–49; *UAR Yearbook 1959*, pp. 160, 162, & 165.

industry opted overwhelmingly to place their savings in companies concerned with food-processing or textiles.[75]

Through their work on the National Production Council the officers came into direct contact with the Egyptian investing and entrepreneurial class. No doubt they quickly became aware of the difficulties of persuading this class to depart from traditional and deeply-rooted patterns of investment. And furthermore, as their experience with designing and administering new projects grew, so did their confidence to embark upon more ambitious plans for state enterprise.

To be fair to the private sector, the new pattern of industrialization called for the building up of enterprises requiring managerial and technical knowledge very different in kind from that found among those who managed textiles or food-processing firms, where the product and techniques of production are relatively simple. Steel mills are, for example, more difficult to establish and run than cotton mills or jam factories. In general, producer-goods industries need more engineers, chemists, and other technicians for almost all branches of their administration; skills which were in short supply in modern Egypt. For economic and technological reasons the scale of production was large, which meant a heavy capital commitment. Opportunities for cautious experiments on a minor scale were not feasible in the new industries. To investors the gestation period seemed longer, the risks appeared greater, and returns more liable to fluctuate, than in the consumer-goods industries. Private enterprise had some limited experience with heavy industry but not enough to develop it at a rapid rate and thereby obviate the need for government participation in planning and finance of the new projects.

Yet part of the explanation for their failure to inaugurate a 'Second Industrial Revolution' must be laid at the door of Egyptian entrepreneurs and investors themselves. Their efforts in developing food-processing and textile manufactures might well be described as adept and laudatory, but they appear unprogressive in face of the admittedly more difficult task of building up heavy industry. Without proper surveys and sociological studies, very few, and merely hypothetical, reasons can be

[75] R. Hassan, *Financing Industry in the 5-Year Plan* (1961, ar.), pp. 5–6 & app. 1 & 2.

suggested for their apparent lack of enterprise.

To begin with, the Egyptian investing class remained small.[76] According to Hassan Riad, the ownership of industrial capital was heavily concentrated in the hands of a small minority of families who originated, not like their counterparts in Europe from the *Tiers État* (artisans, small traders, and clerks), but from the landed aristocracy itself. Egyptian capitalism developed from the wealthy groups in society linked closely to foreign capital and enterprise. It did not emerge as a dynamic force from lower down in the class structure, and this fact may help to account for its conservatism and unwillingness to take risks outside a narrow range of obviously profitable industries.[77] Its preferences were for land, houses, and industry in that order.[78] Within the industrial sector investors displayed a conservative attachment to more traditional forms of manufacturing and a marked propensity to favour projects yielding quick returns.[79]

As for industrial entrepreneurs and managers, they too were a small and closely-knit community, of recent origin. Early promoters of industry in Egypt were nearly all Europeans. During the inter-war years from among Egyptian merchants and landowners there had emerged a class of native entrepreneurs who successfully emulated the pioneering ventures of foreign enterprises in the Nile valley. By mid-century Egyptians owned and managed most industrial firms. Their technical competence was not outstanding but they possessed considerable commercial skills. They preferred high profit margins on a small turnover.[80] Entrenched behind tariffs, they displayed no great interest in efficiency and no tendency to venture outside traditional spheres of manufacturing enterprise.[81]

Published comment suggests that the Egyptian investing and entrepreneurial class, which had displayed commendable vigour in developing, over a short span of two decades, a flourishing consumer-goods sector, possessed few of the characteristics required to inaugurate and carry through a second industrial

[76] Khallaf, *Dev. in the Economy* (ar.), pp. 407–8.
[77] Riad, *Égypte nassérienne*, pp. 74–84.
[78] Hamdi, pp. 157–8 & 258.
[79] Hassan (ar.), p. 5 & *UAR Econ. Features*, p. 37.
[80] Gritly, pp. 373–7 & 502; UN, *Dev. Manufacturing*, pp. 56 & 83.
[81] Naggar, *Industrialization & Income*, p. 255.

revolution in heavy industry. Perhaps more enterprise could have been evoked if the government had listened to the advice of the Federation of Egyptian Industry and guaranteed profits on all new projects.[82] Alternatively the new régime might have stimulated private investment by adopting the 'revolving fund' or Japanese pattern of industrial development. Under this system (now operating in parts of Asia and Latin America) projects are planned, financed, and, for a time, managed by the state. When these projects are going and obviously profitable concerns, the government sells out to private investors and utilizes the proceeds to launch another pioneering venture. Although mooted, for political reasons state-engendered capitalism of this kind was never seriously entertained by the Officers.[83] Investors' incomes were already swollen by tariff protection and monopolistic arrangements; guaranteeing profits or selling the upper classes risk-free outlets for their savings were just not feasible policies for a régime which attempted to present its coup d'état to Egyptians, and the rest of the Arab world, as a progressive revolution.

ECONOMIC CONTROL IN THE MIXED ECONOMY, 1957–61

The reorientation of economic policy occurred after the Suez war. At that point the Junta had consolidated power over the state machine and had effectively destroyed all centres of organized opposition in Egypt. It had compelled the British government to evacuate the canal zone and successfully resisted the Tripartite Aggression of 1956. From a new position of internal and external security the government appeared willing to accord more priority to the problem of economic and social development. Faced with rates of development in industry and agriculture which they regarded as inadequate and with a growing problem of unemployment, the Officers concluded that bold policies were essential to raise living standards and make Egypt economically more powerful.

Moreover, as they saw it, private enterprise had not responded enthusiastically enough to exhortations and incentives over the past four years and they drew the conclusion that the time had

[82] FIE, *Ann. 1952–3*, p. 3.
[83] NPC Memo. 185 and *EEPR*, Feb. 1957, p. 37.

come for the state to assume a much greater degree of responsibility for the initiation and promotion of economic growth. Thus the Junta committed the economy to comprehensive planning, to begin in July 1960. For agriculture it centred policy upon the High Dam but hoped that the efforts of the Agricultural Bank would achieve some immediate improvement in yields throughout the countryside. For industry the Officers adopted the strategy suggested by the National Production Council and launched immediately an ambitious programme with an emphasis upon heavy industry. They also accepted the view that the innovator and prime mover of any 'Industrial Renaissance' in Egypt must be the state. Thus only 22 per cent of all capital formation suggested by the Plan of 1957 was located in the more traditional sectors of manufacturing such as food-processing and textiles. The Plan assumed, however, that this investment would be undertaken by the private sector, while the state would take almost complete responsibility for the finance and execution of the remaining projects in petroleum, minerals, metallurgical products, and chemicals.[84]

Over time these commitments enlarged the area of public enterprise, engendered a whole range of controls over the autonomy of private producers, and relegated private enterprise to a subordinate place in the long-term development of the Egyptian economy. But until 1961 the Junta attempted to promote development and force the pace of industrialization without altering the institutional framework of private ownership. Apparently the government hoped to assume responsibility for fixed capital formation and at the same time to guide or persuade the private sectors to comply with its plans simply by using whatever direct and indirect controls appeared necessary and feasible.

Given the assumption that investment priorities would be decided from the centre, the government's first task was the negative one of preventing the use of investible funds for any but approved purposes. Hence it took steps to curb house building by means of licences and rent fixing. Foreign exchange and bank credits were tightly controlled and allocated only for projects sanctioned by the government. Even in the agricultural sector officials began to exercise close supervision over farmers who

[84] *Industry after the Revolution*, p. 165; *UAR Econ. Features*, p. 75, and S. Amin, in *Ég. contemp.*, Jan. 1960, p. 10.

demanded credit from the Agricultural Bank. But more positive control or pressure from the centre could only be exerted upon larger companies, particularly companies of the Misr group, and here the government attempted to make managers distribute less in dividends and invest more profits in the projects of the Industrial Plan.

To these extensions of central control the government added tax incentives and a continuous barrage of exhortation designed to evoke patriotism among businessmen and investors. Private enterprise was assured repeatedly that it had a real part to play in the industrialization of Egypt and was enjoined to co-operate with the government in building up the new economy.[85] There is no reason to believe that Egyptian statesmen were not sincere in their appeals. On the other hand their attitudes and actions towards private business after 1957 appeared far from conducive to the successful promotion of a mixed economy. This was not a simple matter of antithesis between public control and private freedom. As India and other examples show, to function effectively private enterprise should be allowed clearly demarcated spheres of activity. Entrepreneurs must be allowed opportunities to display initiative. Private enterprise can develop while subject to wide ranging controls, if it knows in advance the nature of the regulations within which to operate and provided also this legal framework does not change too rapidly. Investors must be ensured of some modicum of social approval, for they are unlikely to behave well when subject to public disapprobation just for making profits. Finally, capitalists are likely to co-operate more enthusiastically with government plans for development when they have been properly consulted in their formulation, particularly in the setting of investment and production targets which they are expected to meet.

Few of the conditions for the successful functioning of a mixed economy were really present in Egypt between 1957 and July 1961. To begin with, the government never demarcated publicly and clearly spheres of industrial activity for purely private enterprise. By implication the Industrial Plan left light and traditional manufacturing to the private sector and assumed that heavy industry would be the preserve of the state, but the Plan drew no definite

[85] *Nasser's Speeches, 1959*, pp. 385 & 401.

boundary and the amorphous public sector which emerged after the Suez war blurred whatever distinction may have implicitly existed. Until then public enterprise had operated within fairly well-defined fields of activity such as transport, petrol refining, and the new pioneer heavy industries: steel, metallurgical products, fertilizers, railway equipment, rubber tyres, and chemicals. During the Suez war the Officers sequestrated British and French property, and shares in banks, insurance companies, trading enterprises, cement, cigarette, light metals, spinning, weaving, and dyeing firms passed into public ownership. Originally enemy property was 'Egyptianized', a term which suggests that the Junta contemplated its eventual transfer to Egyptian capitalists, but evidently the President himself decided against selling the shares.[86] At the beginning of 1957 the former British and French assets together with all other government shares in industry and commerce were centralized under a single authority, the Economic Organization, which was also empowered to establish new companies in whatever lines of production its board thought appropriate, and the Organization could also buy the shares of any existing company.[87] Through the Economic Organization the state not only exercised closer control over all companies in which it possessed an interest but it operated over a wide area of the economy including trade, finance, and light manufactures.[88] At numerous points businessmen found that state companies competed in activities which had hitherto been the sole preserve of private enterprise. Unfortunately their reactions were never published but one can perhaps detect their anxiety in oft-repeated assurances from the government that the Economic Organization aimed simply to 'collaborate, co-operate, and to reconcile public and private economic activity'.[89]

Landowners never received an explicit guarantee from the government against further redistribution of land and rent control, while amendments to the original Agrarian Reform Law almost certainly engendered uncertainty and inhibited investment in the

[86] Ibid. *1961*, p. 379.

[87] *UAR Econ. Features*, pp. 66–68 and Economic Organization, *Yearbook 1958–9* (ar.), pp. 13–27.

[88] *UAR Econ. Features*, p. 67.

[89] *UAR Yearbook 1959*, p. 96; *1960*, p. 182; *Budget Reports 1957–8* & *1960–1*, pp. 13 & 69; *BE*, 13 Jan. 1960.

improvement of farms or the private reclamation of land. For example, the original law permitted companies engaged in reclamation to retain land above the maximum 200 feddans for a period of twenty-five years, but an amendment of 1957 compelled them to sell 25 per cent of their holdings to the Ministry of Agrarian Reform. Opinions were mooted in government circles about the need to reduce still further the maximum area of land an individual might own, and a step in this direction was taken in 1958 when a decree limited family ownership to 300 feddans.[90]

It cannot seriously be maintained that the comprehensive controls imposed on the economy after 1956 allowed entrepreneurs and investors much scope to display whatever talents they possessed for initiative and enterprise. Industrial investment had to fall within the pattern prescribed by the Industrial Plan, a plan private business had played no part in formulating. Law 21 of 1958 prevented managers of large industrial firms from expanding, limiting capacity, or changing the location of plant without reference to the Ministry of Industry. The minister was also empowered to define specifications and fix prices for manufactured commodities. At the same time officials of the Agricultural Bank interfered more and more with the discretion of farmers.

Nor can it be argued that the Egyptian investing and business classes received that measure of political and social approval necessary to encourage their effective participation in developing the economy. Egypt's leaders and press seemed unable to decide whether capitalists were villains or heroes of their new society. On the one side the government lauded their past achievements, emphasized their continuing importance, and assiduously sought their collaboration.[91] On the other they were warned against 'opportunistic individualism, exploitation and monopoly'.[92] More was plainly hoped for from businessmen than mere expansion and profits. The Free Officers expected them to be men of integrity, patriots as well as agents of economic growth. It was a difficult transition to make for men from whom traditionally society had

[90] Law 84, 1957 and Warriner, pp. 192–3.

[91] *Budget Report 1957–8*, p. 13; *Nasser's Speeches 1958*, p. 186 and *1959*, pp. 185–6, 258, 358, & 401; *Industry after the Revolution*, p. 93; *UAR Yearbook 1960*, p. 113; *EG*, 11 July 1960.

[92] *Nasser's Speeches 1958* and *1959*, pp. 403 & 357, 401; *EG*, 6 Dec. 1957 & 13 Aug. 1958.

demanded nothing save a modicum of taxes. They were allowed little time to adapt, or indeed given little encouragement, because the Junta so frequently displayed an implicit or explicit lack of confidence in Egyptian capitalism. Industry before the revolution was described by the Minister of Industry as 'misdirected in industrial knowhow' and he charged it with having 'failed to study the market or its trends'.[93] Consequently the minister felt 'capitalists could no longer be left free to invest their capital in industries they liked or great harm would befall the public welfare'. The presumption of Law 21 of 1958 was clear: managers could not be trusted to run their companies without referring all major questions of policy to the Ministry. Law 114 of the same year implied that company directors paid themselves too much and did too little work because it precluded directors from holding more than two jobs or earning more than £2,500 a year and laid down an age limit for retirement of 60.[94]

Probably no better indication exists of the underlying attitude of Egyptian leaders towards private enterprise than the way in which they formulated their development plans. When both the Industrialization and Five-Year Plans were drawn up, the private sector had overwhelming control over Egypt's productive resources. The achievement of planned production and savings targets depended upon the co-operation of private managers and investors. Yet for the Industrialization Plan of 1957 businessmen seem not to have been consulted at all. Their part in formulating the Five-Year Plan in 1959 and 1960 was negligible but exaggerated by the government. Their admonitions advocating a cautious approach to investment and careful market studies were ignored entirely.[95]

From the winter of 1959–60 onwards the anti-capitalist atmosphere in Egypt hardened. Its deficiencies both as a social and economic system received more and more publicity. Thus continuous discussion took place in official circles and in the press on the need for further measures of social reform to reduce inequality in income and wealth.[96] One editor considered owners

[93] *Industry after the Revolution*, pp. 4–5.
[94] *EG*, 12 & 13 Aug. 1958.
[95] NBE, *Econ. B.*, iii (1958), pp. 230–1 and ii (1958), p. 105.
[96] *The Socialist, Democratic and Co-operative Society* (1959, ar.), NPC Memos 188, 303, & 333–5.

had 'abused their freedom' and that government attempts 'to secure co-operation from the over-privileged business group had failed', and another pointed out that

> the large profits obtained by industrial companies are the result of policies of the planned economy and of the great sacrifices which the latter places on the general public in the form of higher prices for commodities in the local market in order to strengthen these companies and to guarantee a market for their goods within the country and abroad.[97]

Ministers castigated investors for their failure to risk capital in new industries, and Vice President Boghdadi, when he introduced the Five-Year Plan to the Congress of National Union in 1960, inveighed against the 'wastes of competition and inefficiencies of the market system'.[98]

How in fact private enterprise performed under the conditions of 'Guided Capitalism' unfortunately cannot be measured. Apart from the minor dislocation of the Suez war, the years from 1956 to 1961 appeared economically more conducive to private investment than the early phase of the revolution. Agricultural prices picked up and remained more or less stable after the sharp fall which followed the Korean boom. The wider deficit on the budget and increased development expenditure by the government stimulated local demand, while the union with Syria in 1958 widened the market still further. Gross fixed capital formation and production certainly rose more rapidly after 1956, but the figures are not separated into their private and public components.[99] Dr Amin suggested that the level of gross private investment for 1957 and 1959 remained on average lower than from 1954 to 1957, but only slight reliance can be placed upon his compilations.[100] Despite government efforts to divert domestic savings towards industry, private investment in buildings continued to rise until effectively checked in 1959, and the figures relating to the reinvestment of profits by joint-stock companies do not indicate rapid expansion by large-scale firms, because from 1955 to 1959 the proportion of

[97] *EEPR*, Apr. 1960, pp. 17–18; *al-Ahram Econ. Suppl.*, Jan. 1960, p. 3; *EG*, 17 July 1960; *General Frame of 5-Year Plan*, p. viii; *Ann. Plan 1960–1*, p. 7.

[98] *BE*, 2 Feb. 1960 and Boghdadi, pp. 8–9.

[99] See tables 12 & 13 (pp. 327–8).

[100] Amin, in *Ég. contemp.*, July 1959, pp. 14–18.

gross profits retained by them actually fell.[101] There is nothing in the evidence to suggest that the accelerated growth of agricultural and industrial production after 1956 originated from a higher rate of private investment. On the contrary, the comments and scattered figures published by the National Bank support the contention that improved performance of the Egyptian economy during these years was due almost entirely to efforts by the government.[102] The efforts made by the Officers after 1956 to elicit the co-operation of the private sector seem half-hearted and tactically inept. They obviously preferred to promote development by the direct use of state power rather than through the protracted process of negotiation and compromise which is integral to any system of planning in a mixed economy. Understandably, but, for its own interests foolishly, private business failed to respond to the government's plans with sufficient enthusiasm to obviate the need for further extensions of central control over the economy.

PROBLEMS OF CONTROL AND THE FIVE-YEAR PLAN, 1960–5

Comprehensive planning provided both the occasion and the need for further controls over the private sector. While the Five-Year Plan was not nearly so unrealistic as the Industrialization Plan of 1957, its prime aim to raise national product by 40 per cent between July 1960 and July 1965 was ambitious. This target had been chosen by the Presidential Council in 1959, against expert advice from the Ministry of Planning, as part of a longer-term goal of doubling national product over a single decade.[103] 'Doubling in a decade' soon became one of the most publicized and acclaimed of government promises. President Nasser and his ministers felt deeply committed to the Plan, which they saw as the most important instrument for the transformation of Egypt into a 'Socialist, Democratic, and Co-operative Society'.[104] No doubt as politicians they appreciated how difficult it would be to gloss

[101] FIE, *Ann.*, *1958–9*, p. 25. The falling share of gross profits retained by the organized business sector was revealed in sample studies of company finances by the NPC: Memos 4, 32, & 134 (1959, ar.).

[102] NBE, *Econ. B.*, ii (1957), p. 157 and ii (1958), p. 94.

[103] Preparatory work on the plan by the NPC took place on the assumption that the long-range target would be to double per capita production over two decades (see NPC Memos 71, 99, 103, 124, & 292 of 1958 & 1959, ar.).

[104] Dept. Information, *Reports & Statements by Ministers.*

over the failure of an economic policy reduced to so simple a slogan. They were determined to succeed. Although the government had arranged to undertake most investment planned for the years 1960–5, the achievement of targets still depended to a considerable degree upon the performance of the private sector. When the Plan became operative in July 1960 not more than a quarter of gross domestic production originated in the public sector.[105] The government expected the public sector to grow more rapidly than the private sector, but if targets were realized four-fifths of the planned addition to national income from 1960–5 would still come from private sources.[106] The plan for industry emphasized heavy industry, where output was expected to increase by 210 per cent over five years, while industry which remained the province of private enterprise was expected to grow by only 37 per cent. Nevertheless, because of the absolute size of light traditional manufacturing, planners anticipated that 81 per cent of the overall additional to industrial output would emanate from the private sector.[107] Approximately half of the planned rise in agricultural output had to come from improvements to the productivity of land cultivated by farmers over whom the government exerted only slight influence. If the private sector failed to achieve these production targets, the whole success of the Plan would be placed in jeopardy, but the problem of how those who controlled resources could be made to realize the pattern of investment and the structure of output established for them by the National Planning Committee raised questions about the whole institutional framework of the economy as it existed at the opening of the Plan.

The inherent contradiction in the Junta's attempt centrally to plan an economy dominated by private enterprise not particularly amenable to their inducements or exhortations can perhaps be seen most clearly in relation to the provisions made for financing capital formation. Planners anticipated that between one-fifth and one-third of required finance would come from aid and foreign loans to the government.[108] While complete figures are not yet

[105] See table 10 (p. 325). I have included in this ratio an estimate of production by Misr companies which were nationalized in Feb. 1960.

[106] See table 10.

[107] See table 10 and Hassan (ar.), pp. 6–7 & app. 3.

[108] A. Hosny, *Financing Capital Formation in UAR* (1962), INP Memo. 211, and *Budget Report 1960–1*, p. 63.

available, the annual plans for 1960–1 and 1961–2 reveal that the National Planning Committee also expected roughly 70 per cent of the required domestic savings during those years to emanate from private sources.[109] The important role allotted to private savings reflected the assumption that further increases in taxation were not a feasible way of financing the Plan. It is also a measure of the significance the Egyptian government has consistently attached to the principle of containing deficit finance within limits which avoided the dangers of real inflation.[110]

How planners proposed to enforce the specified savings rates upon the private sector and to mobilize private finance for their purposes were never adequately explained. Yet several memoranda submitted to the National Planning Committee had revealed how difficult it would be to raise the overall rate of saving and to channel investible funds into government projects. For example, household savings, which are the smallest part (26 per cent) of private savings, formed only 2 per cent of disposable income.[111] Most personal savings were directly invested in housing; and only about a fifth took the form of bank deposits and post office savings accounts.[112] Despite all government efforts to encourage it, households invested little directly in industry.[113] Furthermore, for several reasons the attainment of the ambitious savings targets established for households appeared on the face of it unlikely. Not only was per capita income low, but there was a trend towards greater equality in its distribution, a trend which the government had promised to reinforce. Controls upon rents and housebuilding probably reduced the inclination to households to save and invest, and if their propensity to save was sensitive to the distribution of profits, the government's attempt to block dividends in 1959 may well have strengthened their antipathy towards risking capital in industry. Most banks and insurance companies had recently passed

[109] See table 18 (p. 333). By the closing year of the Plan a greater share of domestic finance was expected to come from the enlarged public sector.

[110] *Government Savings and the 5-Year Plan* (1959, ar.), NPC Memo. 147 and NPC Memo. 113; Hassan (ar.), p. 10 and *Budget Report 1961–2*, p. 92.

[111] INP Memo. 211, p. 10, and *Ways of Increasing Household Saving* (1959, ar.), NPC Memo. 197. Savings figures used by the NPC were very dubious but they can be used to map out the elements of the problem which confronted the Committee in 1960.

[112] NPC Memo. 113 and INP Memo. 211, p. 17.

[113] INP Memo. 211 and Hassan (ar.), app. 1.

under direct government ownership and control, which may have engendered some reluctance by the Egyptian middle classes to deposit their savings with financial institutions.[114] Finally, the whole political environment in 1959 and 1960 made their response to government schemes designed to increase savings through investment trusts and higher returns on post office deposits highly problematical.

Similar difficulties faced the planners with respect to the non-organized business sector: a sector which included individual and family enterprises, farms, professional partnerships, and small private companies in trade, industry, and agriculture. It accounted for 72 per cent of all local production; [115] 80 per cent of property income which accrued to the private sector in 1959–60 originated in small-scale non-corporate enterprises and most of it was consumed.[116] Rates of saving for the non-organized business sector were directly related to possibilities for investment within the enterprises. If the possibilities and prospects for expansion appeared limited, savings and investment by proprietors fell in favour of higher consumption. The Planning Committee realistically recognized that savings by this sector were volatile and not easily mobilized.[117]

Thus by elimination the National Planning Committee arrived at retained profits of corporate business as the only source of private saving really amenable to central control. The Committee anticipated that a rising share of private production and hence savings would originate from corporations during the Plan period.[118] But the willingness of large companies to reinvest more of their gross profits was certainly not evident from their dividend policies, which indicated that the ratio of retained to gross profits had declined in recent years.[119] In 1959 the government attempted to restrain the distribution of profits but failed owing to the

[114] There seems, however, to be no marked change in the annual additions to savings deposits with commercial banks or to post office savings accounts after 1956: see *Budget Report 1961–2*, p. 57.

[115] NPC Memo. 138. [116] *Ann. Plan 1961–2*, pp. 186–7.

[117] NPC Memo. 113.

[118] See table 18 (p. 333) and *Methods of Estimating Savings Expected to be Generated in the Organized Business Sector* (1959, ar.), NPC Memo. 134.

[119] *Production Appropriation and Capital Accounts of the Organized Business Sector* (1959, ar.), NPC Memos 4 & 32 and NBE, *Econ. B.*, ii (1957), pp. 88–101; ii (1959), pp. 85–105; iii (1960), pp. 264–87.

opposition from the companies. Moreover, as savings by households were probably sensitive to any such limitation of dividends, the policy of profit restraint would probably reduce the level of household savings and might thereby offset possible additions to total private savings by corporations. Finally, the problem of how company profits could be utilized for purposes decided by the state appeared insoluble without further controls over the companies. In general, retained profits had been used within the companies themselves for the purchase of equipment and stocks of raw materials, and by definition were not likely to be a particularly mobile source of investible funds.[120] This much the government had already recognized when it compelled large companies to invest 5 per cent of their gross profits in Treasury bonds, but further steps along the same lines might have inhibited private investment throughout industry and reduced the overall level of domestic savings.

To conclude: from 1957 the state assumed more and more responsibility for the promotion of long-term development. As they endeavoured to force the pace of industrialization and raise productivity in the agricultural sector, the Free Officers came up against the existing institutions of private ownership and enterprise. Their attempt to plan comprehensively an economy dominated by private producers revealed clearly to them the apparent incompatibility between the Plan's ambitious targets and the means open to the state for the achievement of success. Exhortations, incentives, and indirect controls would not and could not ensure that the private sector complied with the patterns of production and investment established for it by planners. In every case which entailed an incompatibility between ends and means the government almost invariably reacted by increasing the power of the state rather than adopting the alternative path of negotiation and compromise. Hardly ever was the Military Junta diverted from its chosen aims by the presence of traditional patterns of ownership and control over productive resources. As soon as contradictions emerged, the Junta simply altered the institutional and legal framework in order to make the economy amenable to control from the centre.

[120] M. Mohammed, *Role of the Banking System in Mobilizing Private Savings* (1958, ar.), NPC Memo. 21 and NPC Memos 4 & 32.

IX

Efficiency and Equity in the Socialist Economic System

THE CENTRALIZED MARKET ECONOMY

THE economy which has now emerged is officially designated as a planned, socialist, and co-operative system. On the other hand hostile commentators have disparaged it as both communism and state capitalism. But to find or coin a term which embraces the complexity of economic institutions found in Egypt is a fruitless quest. 'Socialist' is not a really adequate term. Socialism is about distributive justice and the care a society takes of the old, sick, young, and deprived, and should not be perverted into a descriptive category for a particular type of economic organization.

Institutionally the Egyptian economy is a mixture of primitive capitalism, public and state enterprise, managerial capitalism, consumers' and producers' co-operatives, and it also contains elements of syndicalism.[1] Primitive capitalism embraces the myriad of owner-operated concerns found in agriculture, small-scale manufacturing, and trade. Managerial capitalism used to be the dominant form of organization in industry, financial services, and wholesale trade but now includes a few private companies managed on behalf of shareholders which still survive here and there. The predominant form of organization throughout these three sectors is something midway between an agency of the state and an autonomous public enterprise. Its exact status is not yet clear, but productive concerns inside the public sector appear to enjoy a considerable measure of independence. Moreover four from the nine directors heading public companies are not appointed by the state but are elected by their employees. Egypt's public sector is certainly not one vast factory employing a unified labour force, transferring intermediate products among its constituent cells, and selling final output as a monopolist. Strong

[1] Precise definitions of these forms can be found in P. Wiles, *The Political Economy of Communism* (1964), ch. 1.

traces of autonomy for the individual enterprise seem to have survived and are built into the system.

Co-operatives are found in trade and agriculture. For trade, co-operatives are not the kind of consumers' associations found in western Europe but are really state shops and wholesale enterprises. In agriculture there are two kinds of co-operatives—voluntary and supervised. The latter, which will be predominant by 1970, is a hybrid form containing elements from the Soviet kolkhoz and the Danish-style co-operative. It has combined ministerial direction, local initiative, and individual enterprise to produce a unique form of agricultural organization. Traditional co-operatives are the more familiar voluntary associations of farmers concerned to buy and sell in bulk.

Perhaps the most striking feature of Egypt's economy is its institutional diversity. Almost all possible forms of organization are represented, but most of the recent innovations such as public companies and supervised co-operatives did not arise spontaneously but have been created by government decree. How long the régime will continue to experiment pragmatically with different institutional forms, or whether they will be persuaded that socialism demands a specific kind of economic organization is difficult to say. At present the signs are that the government listens to advice from anyone and is equally prepared to experiment with the designs of business efficiency experts from the United States, with Russian-style state farms and workers' control from Yugoslavia.[2] Pragmatism endures as the 'philosophy of the revolution', and no doubt Egypt will evolve an institutional framework suited to its own aspirations and environment. Meanwhile to attempt to categorize the present system with catch phrases drawn from the political vocabulary of western or eastern Europe is not appropriate.[3]

To epitomize the system in operation is equally difficult.[4] Enterprises produce within such an intricate framework of plans,

[2] At present managerial consultants from the United States are investigating the Egyptian steel industry on behalf of the government (*MRESE*, Feb. 1963, p. 17).

[3] I find Professor Issawi's 'socialist nationalism' and Dr Riad's 'state capitalism' equally unconvincing (Issawi, *Egypt in Revolution* and Riad in *Revolution, Africa, Latin America and Asia*).

[4] The following summary is based upon ch. 7.

regulations, and markets that to expose the criteria underlying their behaviour must be the task of deep and careful research. At present we can observe that the rate and composition of investment is determined by the central authorities. Egyptian planning consists of a public investment programme set within a framework of production, consumption, and savings targets for the economy as a whole. It is a mixture of indicative and command planning. Enterprises are not instructed to meet physical targets and do not, in general, receive requisitions of inputs from the centre. Planners assume that managers will react to the price movements and will purchase their labour and production requirements on markets. Profit remains as the success indicator of all enterprises, public and private. But capital formation is planned in the sense that virtually no investment takes place without permission from the government. Moreover ministries intervene with the market mechanism to ensure that investment targets are met and the whole programme keeps roughly on schedule. Finally, centralized allocation does occur for some key inputs such as imported equipment, raw materials, and intermediate goods, agricultural chemicals, selected seeds, irrigation water, and certain categories of skilled labour.

Producers do not, on the whole, operate within free markets. The government interferes pervasively and continuously with the price mechanism to achieve the ends of economic and social policy; to secure, in other words, the coincidence of private and social profit. For example, the prices of 'necessities' are fixed in order to affect the distribution of income in urban areas. Profit margins for almost all producer goods are regulated to avoid the exploitation of consumers and to encourage enterprises to use particular inputs such as domestic steel and fertilizers. Minimum wages have been set for agricultural and industrial workers and pay-scales are now legally established for all employees in the public sector.

Nor does the government stand completely aloof from the process of production, particularly in the agricultural sector where the new co-operatives were designed to give officials power to determine both the allocation of land among different crops and to influence the techniques of cultivation as well. In organized industry the labour code has made it difficult for managers to dismiss redundant labour, and their choice of production methods is always conditioned by the availability of foreign exchange.

Profit may be the success indicator of Egyptian enterprises, but the economy cannot be described as a modified free-market system. Output does not really emerge as the result of the autonomous decisions of atomized production units co-ordinated through the price mechanism. Decisions relating to investment and the allocation of key inputs are centralized and prices are not determined by the free play of demand and supply. In operation Egypt's productive organization stands between the command economies of eastern Europe and the modified market systems of the west. Perhaps the term 'centralized market economy' is roughly applicable to its unique amalgam of institutional forms and operational arrangements.

THE INSTITUTIONAL FRAMEWORK

Is the new economic system efficient? Inefficiency obviously existed under the former system and few of its underlying causes have been eradicated by nationalization and planning. The relevant inquiry is whether or not efficiency is likely to be promoted or hindered by recent institutional changes. At present this question may be posed, defined, and analysed into its components, but certainly not answered. Economic reorganization is too recent for historical evaluation and information is not available to conduct any of the empirical tests which must form the basis for a proper appraisal of Egypt's economy. My answer can only be in terms of probabilities, tendencies, and predictions.

Efficiency is concerned with the effective use of scarce resources to satisfy people's wants. An economy is technologically efficient if it converts given factor supplies into the maximum volume of output or if it produces a given output with the least possible input of resources. And the goods made available must also conform to the wishes of the community. Unless consumers' preferences are respected and the right assortment of commodities and services are produced, over the right time period the system cannot be described as economically efficient. To begin, I propose to analyse technological efficiency in the public sector, agriculture, and in the private sector. Then I will consider the problem of prices. Dynamic efficiency and the question of consumers' sovereignty will be deferred until the end of the chapter.

Managers of state enterprises effectively control production in the public sector but they share responsibility with General Organizations and ministries. Managers hire and dismiss labour, purchase inputs, determine the process and layout for production, maintain buildings and equipment, fix the level for inventories, arrange for the delivery of intermediate and finished goods, and suggest new techniques and lines of production to their superiors. What are the pressures and inducements which prompt them to perform these tasks efficiently? Can they be compelled or persuaded to avoid waste, select the best input-mix, fire redundant labour, care about quality, and be constantly on the look-out for ways of minimizing costs? Efficiency will ultimately depend upon the quality of men the government appoints to run its companies. As a result of the nationalizing decrees and the establishment of new enterprises, the personnel of Egypt's managerial élite has changed quite radically in recent years. Many of its former members have been replaced by state appointees, but in the absence of proper sociological studies the characteristics of the new men cannot be properly analysed. To a considerable extent managers of public companies were recruited from the private sector and the civil service, and to a lesser degree from the army and universities. Informed impressions are that the old bourgeoisie has been superseded by people with administrative experience or technical skills, many of them promoted from middle-management within the nationalized companies themselves.[5] No serious suggestions have been made that the boards of public enterprises are now packed with friends or relatives of the régime. Management is perhaps today more than ever a career open to the talents. If anything, the government appears over-impressed with formal degrees and certificates and pays inadequate attention to possibilities for the promotion of promising recruits lower down the hierarchy. The rapid expansion of vocational education in sciences and management studies is constantly expanding the numbers of people with relevant qualifications, but whether they will possess the requisite qualities is another matter. Unfortunately, despite continuous efforts, the régime has not yet created a cadre devoted

[5] *BE*, 17 May & 29 Oct. 1962.

to the ideals of the revolution which might have been the obvious source for the recruitment of managers. In time the Arab Socialist Union may provide Egypt with a dedicated élite comparable to members of the communist parties of China and eastern Europe.

In the absence of a devoted cadre, the Egyptian government has realistically tried to establish the kind of institutional arrangements conducive to efficiency. Undoubtedly the most important device for this purpose has been the retention of profit as the success indicator for public enterprises.[6] Since managers cannot increase profits by restricting output but only by cutting costs, profits are an even better index of efficiency than they are in capitalist economies characterized by imperfect competition. Ministers usually announce to the press increases in profits made by companies under their jurisdiction as proudly as corporation executives in the United States, and no doubt quickly call to account managers whose profits fall below the levels achieved in previous years.[7] Profit statistics provide General Organizations and ministries with an immediate check on the activities of public companies. Very high rates of profit might prompt ministries to reduce prices in accordance with the government's fair price policy, while low profits or losses could lead to an investigation into the efficiency of the enterprise.

Pressures also exist within the company pushing managers to seek higher profits. The incomes and fringe benefits of their employees are partly dependent on their share of the profits, and since the workers are entitled to elect four representatives to the board, managers should be prevented from leading too quiet a life. Presumably they would not wish to, because while their incomes are fixed, the government awards bonuses to those who contribute to the fulfilment of the Five-Year Plan and their status and promotion in the hierarchy depends to some extent upon being efficient.[8]

Managers also run their enterprises within a system of regulations designed to provide their superiors with the means of checking and evaluating their performance. For example, they are required to render detailed forecasts and final accounts to the

[6] Interestingly enough, some of the more old-fashioned Egyptian Marxists have criticized the government for the retention of the profit motive.

[7] *MRESE*, Jan. 1963, p. 27.

[8] *BE*, 6 Aug. 1963.

General Organizations and through them to the ministries. All investment decisions and applications for foreign exchange are vetted by higher authorities, and in future public companies will be required to adhere to a credit plan enforced on behalf of the state by banks.

On the face of it the framework of rules surrounding the public sector both promotes and inhibits efficiency.[9] On the one hand persistent negligence can hardly escape detection and, provided ministers are ruthless enough, could easily be eliminated. Moreover the system should achieve some economies of scale. For example, General Organizations have centralized certain functions, such as investment, research, exploration of markets, negotiations for loans and credit, previously undertaken independently by the separate companies. They co-ordinate the work of similar enterprises and can thus readily compare relative performances of companies under their charge and remedy defects in their methods of production. General Organizations will be able to survey production over a field wider than the single company and economies or new techniques found to be successful in one part of industry can be readily duplicated elsewhere. General Organizations investigate and correct bottlenecks common to an entire industry and can bring to the notice of the ministries concerned deficiencies in power and transport, delays in the deliveries of raw materials, and persistent shortages of skilled labour.[10]

On the other hand ministries and General Organizations may interfere too frequently and over too wide a front with the day-to-day operations of constituent companies. Managers may not be given enough authority over their subordinates or sufficient autonomy to fulfil their responsibilities. They may feel impelled to refer too many decisions upwards and protracted delays will inevitably occur and hamper the flow of production. Examples of over-centralization have been reported in the press but it is too early to say whether such faults are or will become general. Two American experts in public administration warned the Egyptian government against assimilating economic enterprises to civil service procedures, and the government appears to have heeded

[9] These rules and regulations have already been described in ch. 7.

[10] Many of these points are not spelled out in the law but are implied or underly the new organizations.

their advice by establishing a flexible and decentralized chain of command for the public sector.[11] Ministers cannot interfere directly with companies but must operate through General Organizations which should be more in touch with the everyday problems of economic enterprises. Attempts have certainly been made to avoid the conventional procedures of Egyptian bureaucracy, and the régime is obviously keeping an open mind about appropriate administrative arrangements for the public sector.

At the same time encroachments continue to be made on the prerogatives of management. For example, the procedures set up for the import of raw materials, spare parts, and machinery are frequently exposed in the press as cumbersome. Recent laws relating to the pay and job classification for employees in public enterprises certainly appear to be assimilating the industrial and commercial labour force to civil service procedures and must reduce the initiative formerly enjoyed by companies to bargain with labour and to operate their own wage and promotion systems.[12] Moreover the new regulations completely ignore the proposals of economists to institute piece-rates throughout industry, although managers retain some power to grant bonuses and incentive payments in addition to time rates if they wish. Managers frequently complain how difficult it is to dismiss redundant or unproductive labour since the government's drive to reduce unemployment in 1961.[13] Few are enthusiastic about elected representatives on the boards and privately some describe their presence as a nuisance.

On the other hand the labour code contains elements which should raise the productivity of workers. Their health and skills should be improved by the new provisions for training and social services.[14] High turnover rates will certainly be reduced by law 3540 of 1963, which prevented the movement of employees between public companies without permission. Workers, who share in the profits and elect representatives to the boards of directors, should develop an interest in promoting the efficiency of their companies. The government has, moveover, introduced a system of annual reports for each employee which are intended

[11] *Government & Reorganization in the UAR*, pp. 48–49.
[12] Laws 1598 & 3540, 1963.
[13] Mansfield, p. 150.
[14] Law 63, 1964.

to provide a rational basis for promotion within and between grades.[15] Lastly, it cannot seriously be argued that the government is squeezing consumption to a point where Egyptian workmen become indifferent to higher money income. All the signs are that their consumption horizons are continually expanding.

Whether on balance the framework of institutions and regulations established for the public sector promotes or retards the efficiency of industry and commerce depends, of course, upon how they work in practice. The formal system of motivations, checks, and balances and the chain of command seems, however, not to be one which justifies the rather dire predictions of Professor Issawi.[16]

For the agricultural sector the reformed institutional framework at present covers only a small portion of cultivated land, but since supervised co-operatives should be general by 1970, I propose to analyse their efficiency.[17] Supervised co-operatives are institutions which combine private ownership and some individual initiative with a strong degree of central control over agriculture. Although their performance has never been measured on *a priori* grounds, it should be possible to begin an appraisal.[18]

To a considerable extent their efficiency will depend upon the quality of the officials sent to the villages to take charge of co-operatives. This job is more exacting than that held by factory managers who head a fairly well-defined chain of command and who possess sufficient powers to discipline their subordinates. In villages the authority of supervisors and their assistants, paid by and responsible to the ministries in Cairo, will depend more upon their powers of persuasion and the recognition by farmers that their expertise is relevant and useful. Of course, ultimately local officials possess sanctions to make farmers obey. For example, on agrarian reform estates owners can be evicted for incompetence, and throughout agriculture the allocation of essential inputs such

[15] *MRESE*, Dec. 1962, p. 1.

[16] Issawi, *Egypt in Revolution* and my comments on this book in 'An Economic Appraisal of the Egyptian Revolution', *J. of Development Studies*, Oct. 1964, pp. 106–11.

[17] I am assuming that the suggestions for collective farms made by the editor of *al-Ahram* in April 1965 will not be implemented.

[18] The appraisal is based upon the evidence already presented in ch. 6, pp. 137–47 and ch. 7, pp. 166–71.

as water, fertilizers, high quality seed, and credit are under state control and could be withheld from farmers who obdurately refuse to co-operate. On the other hand supervisors who resort frequently to sanctions have failed in their job of managing an institution which is nominally a co-operative. Moreover to lose the respect of the farmers while continuing to reside among them would impose an intolerable strain upon even the most authoritarian persons, particularly in Egypt where social disapproval exercises a subtle but potent check upon all in positions of command. Anyone who has talked to village officials quickly realizes that while their formal powers may appear considerable, they must also work with the farmers.

Ideally supervisors of co-operatives require technical competence in agronomy, a sense of purpose, and powers of persuasion. How far the government has appointed suitable personnel one cannot say. For the agrarian reform estates the ministry managed to recruit a body of competent officials devoted to their jobs, but with the spread of supervised co-operatives the government will probably have to rely upon less dedicated men. For this exacting task the Egyptian government has not yet been able to create the kind of devoted cadres found on Chinese communes.[19] The Officers still hope the Arab Socialist Union will in time provide them with a militant *avant garde* for work in the villages, or alternatively that the actual experience of working in co-operatives will engender an enlightened rural leadership from among farmers themselves.[20] Meanwhile village officials are being recruited from established civil servants of the Ministries of Agriculture and Agrarian Reform. The latter ministry managed to recruit and train a class of competent and dedicated men, and some are now available for work outside reform areas. Inevitably many of the men sent to villages will lack expertise or experience or both. Fortunately graduates from agricultural colleges and the Institutes for Co-operation are now coming forward at least in small numbers, and recently a lively discussion has taken place about the content

[19] It is perhaps a sign of the régime's failure to create such a cadre that the Ministry of Agrarian Reform placed the construction of suitable accommodation for officials among the preliminary tasks for the new co-operatives (*al-Ahram*, 14 Jan. 1965).

[20] A. Abdel-Malek, 'La réforme agraire en Égypte', *Développement et Civilisations*, June 1965, pp. 22–27.

of education appropriate for work in villages.[21] Qualified people have traditionally displayed a marked reluctance to reside and work outside towns, and the government must be prepared to pay higher salaries in order to attract good quality local officials. Alternatively it could experiment with periods of national service in villages for graduates with appropriate qualifications. The task of regenerating the countryside needs bold measures to break down the dual economy and society which obviously exists in Egypt.

Pressures upon supervisors and their assistants to perform their functions efficiently come from their superiors in the ministries and from the local farmers themselves. Farmers can report cases of incompetence to the ministry and, provided their voices are heard, local officials should be discouraged from laziness and negligence. Probably it would be an excellent idea, as Sayed Marei suggested in a recent lecture, to make farmers directly responsible for the payment of the salaries of officials who manage co-operatives. Alternatively remuneration could be tied in some way to the profitability of the co-operative. Under these conditions pressures towards efficiency would be reinforced and they might prevent the inflation of a village bureaucracy.[22]

Theoretically the division of functions between ministries, local supervisors, and farmers appears on the whole conducive to efficiency. Supervisors are responsible to Cairo, but work with an elected board of farmers. They possess expertise in agronomy and should soon acquire knowledge of local conditions. Through them the government will implement its agricultural policies which seek to raise yields per feddan and to diversify output towards more valuable crops, horticulture, and animal farming. Supervisors will be admirably placed to disseminate scientific techniques and methods of cultivation among farmers and they will become the pivotal point in Egypt's agricultural extension services. If they remain in a locality and acquire a good reputation, they could become a trusted and useful guide to the farmers.

At least the centralization of administrative functions such as the purchase of inputs and the sale of cash crops in the hands of specialists will leave farmers with more time to devote to their own

[21] *al-Ahram, Econ. Suppl.*, 15 Nov. 1963, pp. 38–39.

[22] Apparently the tendency is for central government to take over responsibility for the payment of local officials and services (ibid. 1 Dec. 1962, p. 37).

skill of cultivating land, while the control exercised by boards of co-operatives over the flow of receipts and payments creates possibilities for higher rates of investment throughout agriculture. On the other hand the possible diseconomies of centralization should not be overlooked. If, for example, officials fail to buy seed on time or are tardy in selling perishable crops, the entire co-operative suffers a loss. Inefficiencies at higher levels are even more serious, as in 1961 when the Ministry of Agriculture failed to deliver pesticides and about a third of the cotton crop was lost to the cotton worm. And directives from Cairo on methods of cultivation or upon the allocation of investment funds may not be in the interests of efficiency. The present policy of pushing mechanization does not appear to be based upon a proper analysis of the costs and benefits involved and may aggravate the under-employment problem.[23] Farmers and supervisors need to enjoy sufficient autonomy to resist directives from the centre which are clearly not relevant to their locality and cannot be justified on economic grounds. Provided decisions remain decentralized, the present arrangements should work well.

The division of individual and collective functions for the cultivation of land appear at first sight admirably designed to promote efficiency. Supervised co-operatives should circumvent many of the diseconomies traditionally associated with small-scale and fragmented holdings in Egyptian agriculture. Their consolidated field layout, apart from obviating the deleterious effects on yields which resulted from strip farming, should achieve economies in the use of water, fertilizers, and pesticides. Equipment such as tractors, threshers, sprayers, hatcheries, barns, and storage buildings will be owned by the co-operative and will avoid the waste of resources involved in the duplication of under-employed fixed capital among thousands of small farmers. Finally, if the co-operative spirit prevails, the board should be able to organize underemployed labour for the creation of fixed capital, such as roads, schools, social centres, and farm buildings, which would benefit the village as a unit.

The division of cultivation into collective and individual processes ensures that village land is ploughed, watered, fertilized, and sprayed scientifically. Collective harvesting circumvents the

[23] See above, p. 13.

seasonal shortage of labour. At the same time the retention of private ownership and individual initiative in the sowing and tending of crops provides incentives to efficiency which are so often lacking in collective forms of agriculture. Discussions are now under way about the possibilities for centralizing the control—not the ownership—of all livestock possessed by members of the co-operative.[24] Specialization of this kind could improve the yield and quality of meat and dairy products.

In general, provided local farmers become properly associated with the collective operations of the co-operatives and are vigilant about their profits, the new institutional arrangements for Egyptian agriculture could well push yields per feddan much nearer to their optimum levels.

PRIVATE ENTERPRISE

The government has devoted thought to the creation of an administrative framework for its own productive enterprises and to the reform of institutions in agriculture, but it has paid scant attention to the establishment of conditions for the efficient operation of Egypt's not inconsiderable private sector in industry, housing, internal trade, and other services. Private enterprise could, as the Charter suggests (p. 72), invigorate public companies through competition. Alternatively it might serve to obviate bottlenecks, delays, and shortages which inevitably appear in any planned economy. Moreover with an ambitious growth rate to achieve the government is obviously concerned to encourage private savings and investment. If, however, private enterprise is only tolerated until such time as its functions can be taken over by the state, if private production is subjected to constant interference, compelled to work within too rigid a framework of price controls, credit regulations, and labour laws, and kept on tenterhooks regarding further nationalization or rationalization measures, then it is unlikely to operate in the best interests of society as a whole. Since 1957 the government's attitude to private business can certainly be characterized as one of antipathy. It has still made no real attempt to create conditions for the successful operation of a mixed economy and has never scrupled to interfere with private producers, whatever the effects on production might be.

[24] *al-Ahram Econ. Suppl.*, 15 Nov. 1963, pp. 40–42.

Entrepreneurs and managers in charge of private concerns have not been replaced by nominees acceptable to the state. In fact their ranks may have been revitalized by some of the managerial talent dismissed from their former positions as a result of the nationalization decrees. But the government has attempted to reform the management of private firms by obliging boards to admit elected representatives from among their employees and to adopt the provisions for profit sharing now operating in private companies.[25] Both may be useful devices to promote efficiency whenever ownership, public or private, is separated from control. But in many owner-operated concerns with a small labour force they could have the opposite effect. Small capitalists usually require no prompting to maximize profits and their drive may wane if they are required to share the control and profits of their enterprise with others. Some line should be drawn between areas where the new institutions are relevant and where they might impede efficiency.

Even before 1961 the discretion of private producers with respect to their methods of production and investments had been limited by government regulations, and since then their initiative has perhaps been too rigidly circumscribed. Planners are naturally anxious to avoid competition for scarce resources and attempt to guide all private investment into channels complementary to their own schemes. Decisions to commit resources towards capital formation usually require either definite permission from the ministry concerned, or foreign exchange in order to import the necessary machinery and raw materials. Most investments also require construction or bank credit. Bank loans, foreign exchange, and construction are controlled by the central authorities. Thus private investors and enterprises may design and suggest projects but ultimately their ability to implement them requires official sanction and support. Private firms are likely to be given a lower priority than their rivals in the public sector, and the government is unlikely to interrupt its own production and investment programme if it can be avoided at the expense of private producers.[26]

[25] Law 141, 1963 and *MRESE*, Mar. 1963, pp. 42–43.

[26] The private sector has already complained about discrimination (*al-Ahram*, 10 Sept. 1963 and Mansfield, p. 143). In 1963 private building stopped because of a cement shortage (*BE*, 8 Aug. 1963).

As far as labour is concerned, private firms are in a favoured position. Unlike their counterparts in the public sector they can pay high managerial salaries and bid for skilled labour in the market. Moreover they can often avoid regulations with respect to minimum wages and fringe benefits for their employees. Perhaps the overall effect of the priority accorded to public companies in the allocation of foreign exchange and capital equipment will be to push private producers into labour-intensive techniques and lines of production. If they can utilize under- or unemployed labour by developing an intermediate technology and leave production with a high capital or foreign-exchange content to public companies, then over time an efficient division of labour between the two sectors could emerge. But to encourage this development the government should refrain from promulgating measures likely to raise wage rates above their scarcity levels.[27]

At the present time one of the most important obstacles to the efficient operation and vigorous growth of private enterprise is precisely the government's failure to demarcate and abide by some division of function between the two sectors. Although the Charter publicly demarcated its sphere to include land, housing, internal trade, and small-scale light industry, the government has never really respected any line drawn between public and private activity, given businessmen much opportunity to display initiative, or provided the kind of security essential for private investment.

For example, while Egypt's leaders insist that land nationalization is not contemplated, Haikal's recent advocacy of state farms for lands reclaimed by the High Dam casts doubt upon Arab Socialism's belief in the private ownership of land.[28] Nor has the government issued any guarantees against further measures for the redistribution of land. On the contrary, agrarian reform is still publicly discussed, and the current reorganization of agriculture almost certainly inhibits improvements by landowners to their farms.[29] The decision related to the purchase and formation of fixed capital required for farming is now passing rapidly from individual cultivators into the hands of new organizational units—

[27] Present policy is, however, to extend wage and welfare legislation as widely as possible.

[28] See above, pp. 137–9.

[29] Abdel-Malek, in *Développement et Civilisations*, June 1965.

supervised co-operatives—and is becoming subject to a strong degree of government influence. The traditional division whereby the state supplied land and water and farmers provided all other capital needed for agriculture in the Nile valley is breaking down. Landowners and farmers will obviously defer investment until private and collective functions inside the new institutions are more clearly separated. Why, for example, should they buy tractors and irrigation pumps, or lay down field drainage, if the new co-operatives will shortly provide such facilities and if their present holdings are relocated into a single field under the consolidation programme?

Trade has also been subjected to considerable interference as a result of the Ministry of Supply's endeavours to 'socialize' internal distribution, and shopkeepers have complained against discrimination by state wholesale companies.[30] Wholesale trade in agricultural produce is also in the process of transformation. The government's avowed aim is to eliminate middlemen between farmers and consumers by establishing a new structure of co-operative marketing. In several governorates co-operative societies have already assumed responsibility for the collection, storage, and transportation to cities and ports of cotton fibres, onions, potatoes, and poultry. Merchants are being slowly pushed out from wholesale trade.

Housebuilding, the other traditional outlet for private saving, now appears a very unattractive proposition despite a rising demand for accommodation. Over the past seven years the government has applied stringent and, as far as investors are concerned, increasingly unfavourable controls over house rents in order to redirect savings towards activities regarded as socially more beneficial. Rents now stand well below their 1958 level, and were recently reduced still further because the President received a flood of complaints against 'high' rents.[31] At the same time public investment in low-cost housing has not been sufficient to obviate a growing shortage of accommodation in the cities and ministers often appeal to the private sector to build more houses.[32] One efficacious way to promote private saving and investment

[30] *al-Ahram*, 10 Sept. 1963.
[31] *MRESE*, Feb. 1965, p. 70.
[32] Ibid. Jan. 1965, p. 95 and Mansfield, p. 140.

would be for the government to lift the controls on rents, and allow those with capital to invest it in something they formerly regarded as safe and profitable.[33]

PRICES

Managers of public enterprises seek to increase profits by producing at the lowest possible cost. Total costs measure the total value of the resources purchased to produce a given output. If managers can produce that output with a smaller input of raw materials, intermediate products, land, labour, and capital costs will fall and profits will rise. Resources should then be released for production elsewhere and the economy will move towards the Paretian optimum, where there are no possibilities for increasing the output of one commodity without reducing the production of another. In Egypt markets still operate for the allocation of inputs among enterprises, and managers calculate costs in terms of prevailing prices. But unless the prices they employ reflect the social-opportunity costs of the various inputs transformed into output, their endeavours to maximize profit will not result in optimal efficiency for the economy as a whole. Prices thus have an allocative function and make it possible to distribute resources in such a way that the final assortment of goods is produced at least cost. If, however, prices are 'distorted' and the prices of produced or original factors of production are not scarcity prices, a combination of inputs that minimizes costs for the enterprise will not release resources to create output elsewhere. Private and social interest can thus diverge even when nationalized enterprises behave according to the rules of market socialism.

Prices are not just relevant to the current operations of existing enterprises but are also employed by the planning authorities in decisions related to capital formation and future production. Planners conduct cost-benefit analyses in order to determine which projects are likely to contribute most to national output for a given expenditure of real resources. They are involved in the allocation of investment funds among sectors, between projects, and with the choice of technique, of scale, and of location for

[33] Even now the bulk of private investment is in houses (*MRESE*, Feb. 1965, p. 70).

different projects within sectors. Their concern is to obtain a given output from the minimum input of investible resources or to obtain maximum returns from a specified quantity of resources. In all their decisions calculations of costs and benefits are made in terms of prices. If they employ prices that do not indicate the real costs of the resources involved, the allocation of investment will not be optimal and greater benefits could have been obtained from an alternative allocation of the same volume of real resources.

Professor Hansen has emphasized that at the centre of the efficiency problem in Egypt is not the quality of managers or even the institutional arrangements for production in the public sector, but the question of prices. Distorted prices he considers to be a more potent cause of inefficiency than all the delays and blunders of bureaucrats. Unfortunately almost nothing is known about the pricing rules adopted by ministries and public enterprises, but there is certainly no evidence to suggest that they are based upon correct criteria. Professor Hansen's analysis, which is focused mainly on the question of consumers' efficiency, shows that the government's fair-price policy encourages the production of a bill of goods not in line with consumers' preferences and leads to shortages and black markets. He argues that this policy, designed to restrain rises in the prices of 'necessities' and to obviate the 'exploitation of consumers by private monopolies', is redundant now that the bulk of industry and wholesale trade are in the public sector. Nationalization has created possibilities for a more rational price structure and allows for alternative methods for redistributing income. The infringement of consumers' sovereignty is now more questionable.[34]

But even if the final bill of goods remains determined by the government, technological efficiency could still be encouraged if the prices of raw materials, intermediate goods, and factors of production were scarcity prices. If existing prices promote a distribution of resources among enterprises and alternative uses such that the output of any one commodity can only be increased at the cost of lowering the output of another, then prices reflect opportunity costs and enterprises will be prompted to economize on the use of scarce factors and will minimize real costs of production. Government intervention has, however, militated against

[34] Hansen & Marzouk, pp. 286–90.

the formation of scarcity prices and serves to push the economy away from optimum efficiency. Such intervention is often in the interest of equity, and one could argue that it sometimes accelerates long-run development. Equally there is no doubt that government policy frequently conflicts with the requirements for efficiency at any point of time. Examples are numerous but their precise effects cannot be measured. Given the absence of data, I can only describe policies which tend to push factor and product prices away from their scarcity levels.

Government intervention in the labour market has been concerned to establish minimum wages for industrial and agricultural labourers and to fix ceilings for the salaries of managers. It has also limited the discretion of public enterprises to establish their own wage structures and to bid away labour from each other. The likely effects of these measures are to raise wage rates for unskilled labour above its scarcity levels and to restrain the pay of managerial staff and skilled workers at artificially low levels. Enterprises will be prompted to economize on the use of the former and will neglect to exploit the potentialities of labour-intensive techniques. They might be more wasteful in their use of skilled labour.

Another example concerns rents of agricultural land, which are fixed at low levels in order to bring about a redistribution of agricultural income between farmers and owners. As a result the mobility of land will be reduced because at low rents owners will prefer to cultivate it themselves. More important, land will not be leased by farmers, to the point where the revenue obtained from the increased value of output covers the price paid to the landowner. More efficient farmers will be prevented from offering higher rents and society loses the additional putput they could extract from a given feddan. Furthermore, land is an extremely scarce factor of production and rent control might weaken the incentive to substitute labour and chemicals for it in the production of crops and also remove pressure on farmers to reallocate land to more labour-intensive produce, such as vegetables and dairy produce. On the other hand very high rents may act as a disincentive, and the transfer of an increased share of output to cultivators could prompt more efficient farming.

Raw materials, intermediate goods, and capital equipment purchased outside Egypt are imported by state trading organizations and distributed by the government. Total imports at any time are limited by supplies of foreign exchange, part of which is used to buy consumer goods. How scarce supplies are allocated between producers' and consumers' goods has not been revealed by the planning authorities, but presumably a low priority is given to the latter.

Capital imports are for the replacement of obsolete or depreciated equipment or for the net investment. Investment will be considered in the next section. Here my concern is with the allocation of foreign exchange for the purchase of imported raw materials, intermediate goods, agricultural chemicals, spare parts, replacement equipment, &c. Information on this question is again almost non-existent, but it appears that the price mechanism has been superseded by some kind of rationing system based upon centrally determined priorities, which are no doubt influenced by bargaining between different ministries, each concerned to obtain the maximum possible for the enterprises under their command. Enterprises, including farms and co-operatives, obtain their imported requirements at international prices. With a present exchange-rate policy which may be 'rational' from a balance-of-payments viewpoint, international prices reflect the scarcity values of imports on world markets and not their opportunity cost within the domestic economy. Enterprises cannot obtain more than a predetermined share of imports by offering higher prices in Egyptian currency to state trading companies. Flexibility could exist if the government permitted managers with excess foreign exchange to sell it on the open market, but it has stamped out such practices.[35] The government naturally tries to avoid interruptions to the flow of production although shortages and delays inevitably emerge. Recently the press reported cases of private businessmen who attempted to bribe officials concerned with exchange control.[36]

The general point to observe is that the amount of foreign exchange available to meet the demands of producers is limited, but is not distributed among them by the price mechanism. Any other system offers no rules for its rational allocation, provides no real incentive to enterprises to economize in the use of an extremely scarce resource, and is unlikely to be efficient, in the

[35] Law 95, 1963.

[36] Mansfield, p. 197.

sense that no reshuffling of imported producers' goods could increase output. Professor Hansen's point that prices in the foreign trade sector are most out of line with the optimal conditions for consumers' efficiency applies equally well to technological efficiency for producers.[37]

PLANNING AND CONSUMERS' SOVEREIGNTY

My general conclusion is that efficiency in current production is impeded by government regulations and pricing policies. My next question concerns the long-run efficiency of the economy and may be phrased in the following manner. Given the overall rate of saving and the selection of output streams for the future, is the present allocation of investment among the alternatives, chosen largely by the government, likely to maximize the rate of growth of production? In other words, is investment distributed so that the production over time of any single commodity could only be increased at the expense of a reduction in the flow of some other commodity?

To a considerable extent the allocation of investment depends on the pattern of production chosen for the target year of the plan. Given a bill of goods, the allocation of investible resources is in a large part technologically determined. For example, if planners decide to increase the steel content of domestic production by 1970, then a defined share of the foreign exchange available to Egypt between 1965 and 1970 must be used for the import of blast furnaces. Again, if the Ministry of Public Works decides to build a multi-purpose irrigation project, then the allocation of predetermined proportions of the supplies of cement, mobile generators, and skilled engineers must be devoted to the task of its construction. Furthermore, part of the allocation of capital funds available to Egypt is made abroad in countries which offer it aid or loans on favourable terms. Such offers are frequently tied to particular projects, designed and ready for execution, and the Egyptian government is merely presented with the option of acceptance or refusal.[38] In general, choice is limited but it does exist. Usually there are alternative ways of producing a selected commodity. Decisions have to be made between capital- or labour-intensive techniques, between different types of raw materials,

[37] Hansen & Marzouk, pp. 291–4. [38] *Ég. industr.*, Feb. 1961, p. 6.

between places for the location of plant, and between alternative scales of operation. The more efficiently these choices are made, the more the rate of growth will increase.

Investment allocation thus depends partly on the production targets chosen by planners and partly on the criteria they employ to choose projects and techniques for the achievement of targets. A rational allocation of investible resources presupposes an efficient selection of production targets. By the latter economists usually mean a bill of goods in conformity with the preferences of consumers. At this point it seems appropriate to discuss the whole question of consumer sovereignty as it relates to Egypt. It has already been noted that rationing and controls preclude consumers' wishes from being reflected in the movement of prices and that prices do not signal their wishes to producers at all accurately. Professor Hansen has emphasized that the present violation of consumer sovereignty cannot easily be justified now that the bulk of the economy is under direct central control. He also points out that tariffs set high enough to make the internal prices of imported consumers' goods reflect their social-opportunity cost would be a more efficient device for the allocation of scarce foreign exchange than completely to ignore consumers' desires to purchase foreign goods by the imposition of physical quotas on imports.[39]

In the present context my interest is, however, mainly concerned with the respect paid by planners to the wishes of consumers in selecting output targets for the Five-Year Plan. Respect for consumers' preferences implies that planners, in fixing the overall rate of domestic saving, should take into account the time preferences of households for present against future consumption, and in selecting the bill of goods for the target year of the Plan they should predict and meet the wishes of consumers. Both conditions are related, because the time preferences of households will be reflected in the division of future output between consumers' and producers' goods. In Egypt virtually no attempt was made to elicit household preferences about the rate at which they wish to substitute present for future output. The system permits the government to determine the level of saving for the community and it did so unilaterally. Is the system, therefore, irrational and inefficient?

[39] Hansen & Marzouk, pp. 287–9 & 292–4.

In terms of the definitions employed by classical welfare economics, the answer must be yes. But few economists would now support the proposition that a country's rate of saving should be determined by the preferences of households. Several have castigated time preference as irrational and as a failure to perceive that consumption in future is objectively just as satisfying as present consumption. People's desires and needs, they argue, are in a process of continuous expansion, and future increments to consumption may yield greater satisfaction than consumption now.[40] But in Egypt the present high propensity to consume seems reasonable enough. Real incomes are at subsistence levels and extra food, clothing, and shelter now must appear eminently more desirable than deferred consumption. Life expectancy is low and Egyptians realize that they may not survive to enjoy the future. Moreover technical progress, changes in the terms of trade, increased donations of aid may render it possible to obtain the same output in future at lower cost, while present sacrifices may not, because of war or inefficient allocation of investment funds by the planners, yield the promised benefits.

On the other hand the community does apparently want higher standards of living which can only be achieved at the cost of some sacrifice, and the government should not be too circumscribed by the dictates of the present generation. It has some responsibility towards future generations as well. Carried to its logical conclusion, respect for the time preference of households implies that the government invests only savings loaned to it voluntarily, which means that the overall rate of investment is determined by a small minority with a surplus over their present consumption requirements. In other words, investment would be a function of the distribution of income. Alternatively the government could follow the suggestion, made by Professors Eckstein and Krutilla, that tax revenues should only be invested to the point where returns on its marginal investment project are just equal to the community's rate of discount on future consumption. Their preference for present over future consumption can, they argue, be calculated from the rates of interest they pay on hire-purchase loans. For example, if people are willing to borrow at a rate of interest of 10 per cent in order to consume now, that rate expresses their

[40] M. Dobb, *An Essay on Economic Growth and Planning* (1960), pp. 15–28.

valuation of current consumption and should be used to discount returns on investment by the government. Only projects with a positive return net of discount should be implemented.[41]

But their recommendation applied to Egypt would hand over the determination of the level of savings and ultimately the growth rate of the economy to a minority who happen to be rich enough to enjoy the privilege of hire purchase. Decisions about the national rate of growth are really quite different from individual decisions about raising money for the purchase of consumer durables. In the former case people are participating in a political process concerned with the future of their country, and there is no reason to suppose that they would express the same view about the distribution of national income over time as they would about the distribution of their personal incomes.[42]

In Egypt the government's problem is, therefore, to select a rate of savings which satisfies the general aspiration for development and at the same time permits per capita consumption to rise above its present meagre level. The rate at which average real consumption will rise is partly determined by the rate of growth of population, by political considerations and attention to efficiency. The latter is important because unless consumption horizons expand, the incentives for the labour force to work harder will be impaired and output may be reduced. Over the Plan period, 1960–5, consumption has been permitted to rise at a rate which hardly justifies the charge that the Egyptian government is imposing an intolerable sacrifice on the present generation for the sake of its richer successors.[43] The Charter explicitly rejected the kind of forced capital accumulation achieved in communist societies, and so far this promise appears to have been honoured.[44]

Given a rate of investment that is selected by the central authorities, the question next arises as to how far its allocation

[41] O. Eckstein & J. Krutilla, *Multiple Purpose River Development* (1958), pp. 79–88. Their recommendation relates to the USA.

[42] Sen, in *Econ. J.*, Sept. 1961.

[43] During the Five-Year Plan, 1960–5, real consumption was expected to rise at 4.8 per cent per annum (*Gen. Frame of 5-Year Plan*, sect. 10). The signs are that consumption may have risen at an even faster rate.

[44] The Charter, p. 52. Professor Frisch, in his advice to the NPC, advocated discounting future returns by some kind of social preference function (*The Preparation of a Draft Investment Plan for Egypt* (1959), NPC Memo. 25).

accords with the wishes of consumers. Looking at the structure of output for the target year of the Plan, we observe a division into capital goods, intermediate goods, exports, commodities and services supplied for the government, and consumers' goods. The distribution of total output between capital and all other goods is determined by the rate of investment selected by planners. Commodities and services supplied by the government include defence, security, and justice, public administration, health, education, social welfare, and other forms of collective consumption. The level of this kind of output and its claim upon productive resources is fixed by the government according to a political assessment of social needs. As two former Deputy Ministers of Planning observed, 'the importance of the social milieu by the creation of a suitable social and cultural environment are explicitly recognised and, therefore, strongly emphasised'.[45] Between 1960 and 1965 the government planned to devote an increasing amount of resources towards raising the health, education, and welfare standards of the population, particularly the poorer classes. Thus an increased share of total consumption will take the form of services provided by the state for its citizens, and since the government has, at the same time, reformed the tax system in a progressive direction, this expenditure should contribute to the achievement of one of the most frequently emphasized goals of the Plan, namely to diminish inequalities in the distribution of income.[46]

Output targets for 1964–5 also reflect other aspects of the strategy underlying the Plan. For over a decade Egyptian economic policy has been directed towards the achievement of long-term equilibrium in the balance of payments. Limitations on the capacity to import equipment and other producers' goods has for many years represented a key constraint on the rate of growth. Increased supplies of foreign exchange not only provide the means to augment fixed capital, but since additional earnings from exports raise incomes throughout agriculture, they impart a general stimulus to domestic demand as well.[47] When planning began

[45] INP Memo. 76.

[46] *Gen. Frame of 5-Year Plan*, p. v and *Ann. Plans, 1960–1 & 1961–2*, pp. 7 & 3.

[47] INP Memo. 210 and *Analyses of the Balance of Payments* (1959, ar.), NPC Memos 44, 62, & 219.

in 1960 the deficit on income account showed every sign of further deterioration and planners paid very close attention to possibilities for import substitution and export promotion.

Import substitution appeared to them the obvious way forward, particularly in cases where unexploited natural resources offered the country comparative advantages over rival products from abroad. The market had been pioneered by foreign goods and future demand could be predicted with some certainty. Moreover projects involving import substitution often attracted loans and credits from overseas. Past industrialization had proceeded successfully by replacing simple manufactures in the home market, but this kind of import substitution had reached the margin. As the National Production Council recognized in 1955, further industrial progress depended upon the replacement of imported consumer durables, intermediate goods, and capital equipment by domestic substitutes.[48] If Egypt wished to mitigate the foreign-exchange restraint on future investment programmes, capacity needed to be created in the capital goods sector.[49] Finally, moves towards a lessening of dependence on foreign loans and aid naturally commended themselves to a régime attempting to play a positive and independent role in world politics.

Export promotion involved selecting lines of production in which Egypt seemed to enjoy some long-run comparative advantage. For example, the Mixed Committees of Planning set up to appraise projects for the Plan considered that agriculture should diversify output towards fruit, vegetables, flowers, rice, and the very finest grades of cotton fibres for export markets. Diversification possessed the additional merit of rendering the economy less vulnerable to a downward trend or sharp fluctuations in the price of cotton, its dominant export crop, on international markets.[50] For manufactured exports the National Planning Committee sought to process local raw materials for sale on world markets in a finished or semi-finished condition. The Ministry of Industry hoped, for example, that most of the country's raw cotton would in time be transformed into yarn or cloth before being exported. Net earnings of foreign exchange would thereby increase and the

[48] PCDNP, *Report 1955* (ar.), pp. 18–19, 26, 193–4, & 234–5.
[49] M. Ibrahim, *A Rough Outline of Planning in Egypt* (1959), NPC Memo. 548.
[50] NPC Memos 251, 252 & 261.

processing of raw materials would absorb underemployed labour.[51] The strategy underlying the Plan was thus heavily influenced by Egypt's situation in the world economy and can be elicited from the changes planners hoped to bring about in the balance of payments and in the structure of imports and exports.[52]

Other considerations also affected the allocation of investible funds between broad sectors of the economy. For example, rapid population growth upon a limited area of land had made it imperative to create opportunities for production and employment outside agriculture. Industrialization is unquestionably the only long-term solution to Egypt's population explosion; hence the emphasis of the Plan is upon the development of industry. Within the industrial sector the country had achieved virtual self-sufficiency in simple manufactures, and present investments are designed to create capacity for the manufacture of capital equipment, intermediate goods, and consumers' durables. Basic industries, the Ministry of Industry argued, would make the country militarily more secure and would exploit indigenous resources such as oil, phosphates, coal, iron ore, copper, zinc, gypsum, and manganese. Thus the ministry had given 'absolute priority to strategic and basic industries on which existing industries depend and which pave the way for the creation of new schemes'.[53] Notice here and in comparable statements the government's concern to create conditions for sustained growth over time. Planners seem to believe that the new industries would set up, in Hirschman's terminology, backward and forward linkage effects with consumers' goods manufactures and with agriculture which would accelerate long-run growth and reduce Egypt's dependence on foreign countries for supplies of capital equipment.[54]

Although industry received the lion's share of investible funds and the Plan aimed to increase its relative contribution to national product, agriculture was not neglected. Agricultural investment was directed, however, towards the extensive margin; that is, to a small number of giant reclamation projects such as the High Dam, the New Valley, and Liberation Province. Most of these schemes

[51] *Report of Committee on Spinning and Weaving* (1959, ar.), NPC Memo. 230.

[52] *Gen. Frame of 5-Year Plan*, pp. 1 & 82 & table 90 and NPC Memos 219 & 220.

[53] *UAR Yearbook 1960*, pp. 97–99, 257, 268–9, 333, 335 f.

[54] INP Memos 76 & 238.

were designed and under execution before the Five-Year Plan began in July 1960 and were included as a matter of course. Moreover nearly all of the foreign exchange required for their execution is being supplied through loans and foreign aid, and this alone provided the planning authorities with sufficient reason for undertaking them. Only a minor proportion of investment in agriculture is along the intensive margin and has been allocated to basic research into soils, seeds, fertilizers, animal and plant diseases, &c. But above all this category of expenditure is directed towards persuading and inducing farmers to allocate their lands to more valuable crops and to cultivate more scientifically. It is also used to finance the programme of institutional reform now being implemented in the villages. Such investment is not capital-intensive and its benefits cannot easily be measured.[55] Finally, planners recognized that the persistent growth of population had created a serious and worsening problem of underemployment in villages and unemployment in towns. Some investment, for example in village handicrafts, aimed specifically towards its alleviation.[56]

My somewhat general discussion of the strategy underlying Egypt's First Five-Year Plan reveals that in addition to consumers' preferences, social-welfare policy, income redistribution, strategic considerations, the balance-of-payments problem, employment objectives, and the promotion of long-term growth all played a part in the allocation of investment among competing alternatives and in the selection of output targets for the Plan. What precise weight planners attached to consumers' preferences is difficult to discover. They did make some attempt to predict and meet the pattern of demand for 1964–5 but their methodology seems fairly crude and the final bill of goods was certainly adjusted to serve other objectives.[57]

Welfare economics defines a rational or efficient pattern of production as one in conformity with consumers' wishes. Are we then to criticize the Egyptian Plan for its obvious violation of consumer sovereignty? In the context of investment programmes for an underdeveloped country, it appears arbitrary to deny the accolade

[55] Comité de Planification Nationale, *Cadre du Plan*, pp. 195–203.

[56] *Gen. Frame of 5-Year Plan*, p. viii and *Cadre du Plan*, p. 217.

[57] NPC Memos 155, 245, 308, & 445 and INP Memo. 255.

of rationality to any of the goals established by the government just because they happen to conflict with consumers' choice. Dr Dief, a former Deputy Minister of Planning, observed that 'planned development consists of purposeful change of the volume and structure of production. In order to choose among strategies it is necessary to estimate the consequences of each as a supplier of the greatest stimulus to change'.[58] Such emphasis upon long-run growth is also reflected in several presidential speeches and in the Charter with its focus on the future. Growth, not choice, is the impetus behind planning in Egypt, and as Professor Wiles strongly argued, the two are not always compatible. Delicate adjustments designed to satisfy consumers may act as a brake on development, particularly where some violation of consumers' sovereignty is probably necessary in order to reap economies of mass production. As he puts it: 'responsiveness to changes in consumer demand, not necessarily to changes in long run scarcity relationships . . . has little to do with technical progress or growth and may even directly hinder them'.[59] Perhaps in fact he overstates his case. Carried to its logical absurdity the argument could imply that resources should be allocated to a very small number of commodities with high ratios of output to capital. Growth is not an end in itself and should ultimately be directed to the satisfaction of the desires of the community. The conflict is not inevitable, and unless more than cursory attention is paid to the wishes of households, their incentive to produce may be impaired and growth itself hindered. But the point is valid, particularly in poverty-stricken societies like Egypt where few informed observers would question the priority given to growth and to the restoration of equilibrium in the balance of payments. Moreover present plans do not constitute a blatant violation of consumers' sovereignty and the Egyptian government has given no attention to the establishment of 'rational' norms for consumption, measured in terms of proteins, calories, or cubic capacity for accommodation and the like. In fact in some quarters planners have been criticized for paying too much attention to consumers' wishes, especially where the import of household durables is concerned.[60] Efficiency defined as conformity to the preferences of consumers for present

[58] INP Memo. 210. [59] Wiles, pp. 212–13.
[60] Abdel-Malek, in Saville & Miliband, p. 44.

against future consumption and for a particular selection of output seems to have diminished relevance to the problems of low-income societies like Egypt.[61]

THE ALLOCATION OF INVESTMENT

Given the government's concern for growth, military strength, and a healthy balance of payments, technological efficiency still remains highly relevant, even if the prescriptions of welfare economics with respect to consumers' sovereignty receive a low priority. Over time Egypt's leaders aim to achieve the maximum possible growth, security, and autarky from a given volume of investible resources, and the task of their economic advisers is to design an optimum programme for the attainment of these politically decreed ends. Resources can be allocated more or less efficiently in terms of diverse goals. If, for example, a reshuffling of investment funds would lead to a higher rate of growth, more security, and a smaller deficit in the balance of payments over the long run, then the chosen allocation is inefficient. When no further reallocation could increase the performance of the productive system, in terms of one or more of the various goals, then efficiency has been achieved. In this sense welfare economics and their extensions into linear programming are germane to the problems of poor and rich countries alike and provide us with a method for evaluating the pattern of investment allocation in Egypt.[62]

Investment planning in Egypt proceeded by the allocation of investible funds (resources) among different departments of state

[61] In a telling simile the present Minister of Finance once likened the Egyptian economy to an old car. The government's task was, he considered, to get it going and to worry later about an appropriate speed and direction.

[62] H. Chenery, 'Comparative Advantage and Development Policy', *American Econ. R.*, Mar. 1961, pp. 31–33. In this context I find it difficult to understand the contentions of Professor Wiles that 'rapid growth diminishes the harm done by violation not only of consumer sovereignty but also of rational allocation in general' and 'that a certain increase in growth is worth any amount of minor allocation errors' (Wiles, p. 217). No doubt rapid growth inevitably engenders a certain waste of resources which must be written off as the costs of development and that the real costs of over- or under-investment in particular branches of the economy will be diminished if demand increases as a result of growth. But surely the aim of rational allocation is to minimize waste and thereby increase growth. I fail to see that any rate of growth, however rapid, excuses a misallocation of resources, or that technological efficiency defined in a dynamic sense conflicts with growth.

responsible for particular sectors of the economy, while the choice of projects and techniques of production selected to achieve sectoral production targets remained the responsibility of the ministries involved. Macro-allocation was supervised by the Ministry of Planning, and departments were required to submit their projects to it in order to maintain consistency with the overall constraints of the Plan. Efficiency criteria for the allocation of investment are the same at the macro- (cabinet) or the micro- (ministerial) level, but I propose to consider the two decisions separately.

Formally an efficient allocation of investible funds is attained when the addition to the social product from the marginal unit of expenditure is the same for all sectors of the economy. In other words, no further reallocation between sectors could increase social output for the end year of the Plan.[63] The social marginal product criterion, as this rule is called, raises innumerable problems connected with the valuation of real costs and returns from different investment expenditures which need not detain us here since sectoral allocation in Egypt was not determined with reference to formal efficiency criteria. In almost all planned economies, the levels of capital formation for different parts of the economy is the result of political bargaining among ministries, based ultimately upon some general agreement about the more obvious priorities. Unfortunately little published information exists on the procedures used for macro-planning in Egypt. It seems to have been a very *ad hoc* and improvised affair. The picture which emerged from my interviews with officials of the National Planning Committee is as follows. Given the politically-determined rate of growth, which also determined the distribution of output between capital formation and consumption, the National Planning Committee worked out a feasible pattern of production for consideration by the Supreme Economic Council. The Committee projected consumers' demands, public consumption, investment, and exports for 1964–5 and 1969–70. The structure of final output automatically included several projects already under construction or future projects, tied to aid or foreign loans, such as the High Dam, while the level of collective services, defence, education,

[63] A. E. Kahn, 'Investment Criteria in Development Programmes', *QJ Econ.*, Feb. 1951, pp. 38–61.

health, social security, &c., was determined politically. Next, export projections were undertaken by commodity groups and consumers' demand was estimated by the application of rather crude Engel's-type coefficients. From a given set of provisional targets for final demand which could be met either from domestic production or imports, the National Planning Committee considered the implications in terms of real flows between sectors with the aid of an input-output table. The table showed how domestic output and/or imports for different sectors needed to expand by 1964–5 in order to meet projected deliveries for private and public consumption, investment, and exports. At this stage planners calculated Egypt's probable capacity to import (equal to exports plus foreign loans and aid, minus capital and interest repayments overseas) and they explored potentialities for meeting the gap in the requirements for foreign exchange by import substitution.[64] Of course, in these calculations the coefficients utilized were crude and a feasible programme did not emerge immediately but involved repeated adjustments to the pattern of final output and constant exploration of different methods of meeting targets. But finally the real product flows assumed a completed form and were articulated into financial accounts to form the frame of the Five-Year Plan.[65]

The point to notice is that planners and ministers did not proceed in quite the way implicit in recent discussions of investment criteria. Their task did not involve selection from among a large number of self-contained and competing projects but rather consisted of limited modifications to the pattern of final output. Once a few key targets and priorities had been selected the pattern of investment followed more or less from the feasibility tests of the National Planning Committee. At the macro-level the emphasis remained upon consistency and the avoidance of supply bottlenecks and the Egyptian government made no attempt to perform the difficult, perhaps impossible, task of calculating the

[64] This is my understanding of the procedures used for planning in Egypt and is based upon interviews with officials of the NPC in 1962–3 and G. Eleish, *The Uses of the Input-Output Model in Development Planning* (1962), INP Memo. 168. See also INP Memos 210, 238, & 255 and NPC Memos 44, 71, 75, 76, 82, 98, 99, 218, 219, & 220.

[65] N. Dief, *Defining the Aims of Production and Investment in the First 5-Year Plan* (1959, ar.) and *National Budget in Relation to the 5-Year Plan* (1959, ar.), NPC Memos 124 & 181.

optimum allocation of investment.[66] They should not be criticized for that because precise measurement of costs and benefits seldom takes place at the macro-level, and the economic benefits from many forms of social expenditure, such as defence, health, education, welfare services, and local administration, are extremely difficult to measure. Appraisal of investment between sectors must realistically be limited to broad questions of strategy and overall consistency.

Egypt's development strategy predated the Plan, and in conception at least much of it predates the revolution. But since 1952 the Permanent Councils for National Production, various ministries, and latterly the National Planning Committee have been engaged in exploring potentialities for development. As a result, compared with many poor countries, the quantity and quality of information about Egypt's economy is quite remarkable. Population and manpower projections, surveys of natural resources, input-output tables, national accounts, forecasts of imports and exports, detailed appraisals of the infrastructure, and long-run growth studies provided the National Planning Committee with a body of data adequate enough for the formulation of broad economic and social priorities. The distribution of investment between sectors may not be optimal but serious misallocation is unlikely because several possible paths for development have apparently been investigated. Further, the range of alternatives open to Egypt was never very wide. The country's resource endowment does not appear bountiful and the government is exploiting or plans to exploit almost all known deposits of minerals over the next few years. Given the rate of population growth, the exhaustion by the High Dam of possibilities for expansion along agriculture's extensive margin, and the limited opportunities for increases in yields, industrialization was obvious and unavoidable.

Within the industrial sector sufficient capacity had already been created to satisfy predictable increases in domestic demand for the more simple manufactured commodities. The obvious way forward seemed to be along the frontier of import substitution for producers' goods and consumers' durables. Perhaps, however, Egyptian planners have given too much emphasis to import

[66] They received plenty of advice on how this might be achieved from Professor Ragnar Frisch—see his NPC Memos 17, 19, 21, & 25 (1959 & 1960).

replacement and paid inadequate attention to possibilities for export promotion, but the latter implies a drive to improve the efficiency of existing industries. The Plan is almost silent on prospects for expansion through improvements in efficiency, probably on the mistaken premise that the industrial tradition is too short to expect Egyptian industry to be vigorously competitive. But is thirty years really so short a time for infant industries to grow up? Nor is it clear that the right imports are being replaced. At times the Ministry of Industry appears obsessed with the creation of basic industry almost for its own sake, and the ministry's publications suggest the influence of vulgar Marxism with its emphasis on necessary stages of industrial development.[67] Again, exports might be a more efficient way of transforming local resources into steel, heavy chemicals, and engineering products. One wonders how many years it will be before these industries can stand foreign competition. Over the long run no commodity should be produced locally which can be imported at lower real cost, and exports should be pushed to the point where marginal cost equals marginal revenue. While Egypt's planners certainly had the balance of payments in the foreground of their thinking, it is not obvious that they attended closely enough to Egypt's long-run comparative advantage.[68]

Ministries received an allocation of investment funds but the choice of methods for the achievement of output targets was left to them. An efficient allocation of funds presupposes that each ministry considered alternative ways of meeting targets and selected projects, techniques, scales of production, and locations which minimized the use of scarce resources. If they performed their tasks correctly, the contribution made to the social product by any included project should be greater than from any excluded project. Appraisal of the procedures used by ministries for the allocation of investment funds requires information about the criteria applied and the data utilized to measure costs and benefits of different projects. Unfortunately almost nothing has been

[67] *Industry after the Revolution*, pp. 90–92 and *UAR Yearbook 1960*, pp. 335–6.

[68] Furthermore Professor Frisch advised the government against too strong a concentration on the balance-of-payments equilibrium, but he recognized that the question of foreign indebtedness is a political decision (R. Frisch, *Optimal Investments Under Limited Foreign Resources* (1959), NPC Memo. 53).

published about the methods used to select projects, and it is therefore impossible to judge how far any particular selection departed from the rules for an optimum allocation of resources.

We might tentatively conclude that the attention lavished upon project appraisal by the Mixed Committees and the National Planning Committee in 1959 should prove sufficient to avoid complete technological failures, and the delegation of decisions about projects and techniques to the ministries closely involved with particular sectors of the economy should also preclude the kind of gross mistakes which sometimes result from over-centralization. Probably all the projects included in the Plan are at least feasible. Moreover the Egyptian government received plenty of advice from Professor Frisch and others about the methodology for project evaluation.[69] The advice seems to consist basically of variants of the social marginal productivity criterion outlined by Professor Kahn in 1951. The social marginal product for any given amount of capital invested equals its gross annual returns minus gross annual costs, including interest and amortization changes, over the sum invested. Social marginal product obviates the disadvantages of other criteria—e.g. the capital-turnover rule, of allowing for only a single restraint, or the scarcity of capital or foreign exchange—which ignores the fact that several inputs are scarce and the maximization of returns on any one may not lead to optimum efficiency.[70]

Most of the difficulties involved in the application of the social marginal productivity criterion are related to its quantification. For example, benefits from investment in education, health, social service, transport, fresh water supplies, military installations, and the like can only be measured very roughly, but the most formidable problems concern the pricing of both costs and benefits.[71] Returns from a project should reflect benefits to a society as a whole and may need adjustment to take account of external economies. If the investment brings under-utilized capacity or unemployed labour into production, the social product from the

[69] J. Tinbergen, *Summary of Answers to Questions* (1958), NPC Memo. 187.

[70] Chenery, in *QJ Econ.*, Feb. 1953, pp. 77–94.

[71] It is wrong to suppose they cannot be measured at all, and as Professor Frisch told the Egyptian government, measurement should be used to push forward the frontier to where qualitative judgments must be applied (NPC Memo. 53).

project will be greater than its private product. The same is true if it increases the supply or cheapens the cost of inputs used by other companies. Spill-over effects of this kind make it very difficult to measure the real gains from any single project and it may be necessary to group projects in order to take full account of external economies.[72]

In the same way prices used to measure costs should reflect the opportunity costs of the inputs employed. Supply prices if they are set at scarcity levels will encourage planners to employ factors in the proportions available to the economy as a whole and their choice will then maximize output over time. Such prices would represent the value of the marginal product to be obtained from a given input. If factor and input prices do not represent their real values, a combination of factors and inputs, however, carefully designed to minimize money costs for a given project, will not minimize costs in terms of resources. In Egypt market prices do not reflect at all accurately the opportunity costs of productive resources. Prices of producers' goods have been distorted by taxes, tariffs, and direct controls. Wages have been raised and rents lowered by legislation, while exchange and interest rates have been kept at artificially low levels by government policies which, however sensible from other points of view, make the task of project appraisal more complex. Just how far any particular price deviates from its scarcity value is impossible to discern, but it is perfectly clear that current prices are imperfect indicators for the measurement of the real costs of resources employed in investment projects.

Even if current prices provided a somewhat better measure of opportunity costs, they are not entirely relevant to a plan designed to bring about important modifications in the structure of production. When the Plan is completed existing scarcity relationships will alter, perhaps considerably. For example, investment in technical education will augment the supply of skilled labour and, unless demand increases proportionately, its wage rate should fall. Imports will probably grow faster than exports over the Plan period and make foreign exchange even more scarce and valuable. The relevant prices for the calculation of costs and benefits are

[72] O. Eckstein, 'Investment Criteria for Economic Development', *QJ Econ.*, Feb. 1957, pp. 57–64.

those which indicate scarcity values over time—or what Professor Tinbergen calls shadow prices.[73] Shadow prices are the prices that will prevail when the investment programme has been carried out and new equilibrium levels have been established in factor and product markets. The derivation of shadow prices thus involves forecasting future demand and supply for factors and inputs, not merely within the domestic economy but, for a country like Egypt where imports account for about 20 per cent of gross domestic product, planners need to take account of world markets as well. Prediction of this kind is inordinately complex, but is the kind undertaken in any economy, planned or unplanned, and must be attempted if a rational allocation of investment is to be achieved.[74]

In all, some 1,400 projects were eventually included in the First Five-Year Plan. Just how many were subjected to the kind of detailed cost-benefit analysis recommended by the government's economic advisers is impossible to discover.[75] Several, like the High Dam itself and extensions to the steel industry, appear to be acts of political faith accompanied by only cursory evaluation of costs and benefits.[76] Practice no doubt varied from ministry to ministry but where attempts were made to appraise projects scientifically, Egypt's planners were fortunately not hampered by ideological preconceptions about incomes from property. Interest and rent remain as operative categories and were used to measure the real cost of capital and land. On the other hand there is no evidence to suggest that shadow prices were widely used. On the contrary, there seems to have been a tendency to employ current prices, uncorrected even for taxes, subsidies, tariffs, and controls of various kinds.[77]

I found no examples of the allocation of capital to projects with high output to capital ratios which boost the short-run rate of

[73] J. Tinbergen, *The Design of Development* (1958), pp. 39–43, 82, & 86.

[74] For the methodology of shadow price derivation see A. Qayum, *Theory and Policy of Accounting Prices* (1960).

[75] In one of his memos to the NPC Professor Frisch mentioned that in 1959 a 'national profit rate' had been calculated for 200 projects (*The National Profit Rate on an Investment Project* (1959), NPC Memo. 10).

[76] Almost all the analyses of the costs and benefits from the Dam and the steel industry seem to have been undertaken ex-post their acceptance by the government. These projects are, however, tied to foreign loans and their inclusion can be justified on that ground alone.

[77] Hansen & Marzouk, pp. 303–8.

growth and the reputation of the ministry concerned at the expense of longer-run efficiency. Many of the projects included in the Plan are characterized by high capital-output ratios and long gestation periods. The time horizon of Egypt's planners does not appear unduly long or short. One potential source of inefficiency was the absence of a lengthy list of projects. Several officials interviewed considered that choice of alternatives was not the essence of the problem but rather detailed scrutiny of a limited number of schemes in order to avoid obvious technological blunders. But unless project designs are available in abundance, a rational allocation of capital is impossible and their scarcity could eventually reduce the overall rate of investment.

Finally, the bias in favour of capital-intensive techniques is very obvious. The Charter dismissed the advocates of more labour intensity in the following words:

> We must put aside the assumption which says that using modern instruments does not give a full chance of work, on the grounds that modern machines do not need large labour power. This conception may prove sound at the beginning, but it is not valid in the long run. For modern instruments are capable of enlarging the base of production quickly. This opens new horizons of industrialization, and so gives wider chances of labour as a result (p. 68).

Officials at the Ministry of Industry appeared uninterested in capital-labour ratios, and the Ministry of Agriculture is promoting the use of tractors and threshing machines to replace labour and draught animals,[78] while the work of the manpower planning unit of the National Planning Committee appears to have exercised no influence on the choice of projects by different departments of state. Its prime concern was, moreover, with skilled manpower and the expansion of technical education to meet the needs of the new industries. Proper research into the current and potential utilization of manpower in Egypt began in fact after the inauguration of the Five-Year Plan.[79] Information on and interest in the employment problem is definitely scant.

Yet the failure to utilize optimum techniques or to bring idle

[78] Dr Amin has calculated the costs and benefits for each technique and it is perfectly clear there is no justification for tractors or threshing machines at the present time (Amin, pp. 142–50).

[79] The current surveys of the ILO and the INP should provide a more rational basis for manpower planning during the Second Five-Year Plan.

resources into production represents a source of inefficiency. Unemployed labour is not, however, without an opportunity cost because when employed and paid wages, total expenditure will rise and resources will be diverted from capital formation or from production for export in order to produce food, clothing, or shelter formerly provided by the relatives of the unemployed. The lower the elasticity of supply for labour and the higher the wage, the greater will be the cost of bringing underemployed labour into production. But provided its contribution to output exceeds real consumption, labour should be employed.[80] The migration of unemployed agricultural workers to towns results in the diversion of resources to house building and other forms of social capital. If opportunities for employment could be created in the countryside, investment funds would be released for the creation of more productive capacity. And unemployment constitutes a growing social problem and conflicts with the expressed ideal of the government to redistribute income to the least fortunate classes in the community. Without work the very poor derive little benefit from the Plan. The government has publicly acknowledged the gravity of open unemployment in towns and underemployment in the countryside. In 1961 it compelled factories to take on workers in order to alleviate the problem, and managers now find it almost impossible to dismiss redundant labour. Recently the Ministry of Social Affairs drew up schemes for generous unemployment insurance.[81] Why, one could ask, in the face of a serious employment problem and a rapidly growing population have planners and ministers paid inadequate attention to possibilities for utilizing more labour-intensive techniques? Why make the controllers of highly mechanized factories take on surplus labour or divert funds to unemployment insurance when labour might be used productively? Are there not possibilities for adopting some of the ideas put forward in Cairo by Professor Raj only a few years ago?[82]

Part of the answer to these questions is that the government has chosen to develop industries for which the technological possibilities for substituting labour for capital are limited. Egypt's development strategy may be rational from other points of view,

[80] I. Little, 'The Real Cost of Labour', *QJ Econ.*, Feb. 1961, pp. 1–15.

[81] Law 63, 1964 and *BE*, 9 Mar. 1964.

[82] K. Raj, *Employment Aspects of Planning in Underdeveloped Countries* (1957).

but it is not likely to make serious inroads into the employment problem.[83] Planners also consider that the low quality of the labour force and the shortage of managerial talent capable of exploiting surplus labour hinders the establishment of the kind of small-scale manufactures found to be successful in other poor countries.[84] An even flow and quality of production, particularly for the export market, is best secured, they argue, by using machinery. Egypt, planners insist, has no tradition of handicrafts and the marked reluctance of managers and technicians to reside in villages impedes the spread of rural industries. Finally, echoes of the argument put forward several years ago by Professors Galenson and Leibensten can be detected in their thinking. This argument favours capital-intensive techniques because they reduce the share of net output accruing to labour and maximize returns to property, now owned by the state. Since savings from wages are negligible while property income is almost entirely reinvested, capital intensity promotes higher rates of net capital formation and long-run growth.[85]

All these arguments, apart from the last, are valid up to a point. Galenson's model in which all wages are spent and all profits are reinvested seems more applicable to situations where the government or capitalists cannot extract the reinvestible surplus except by using techniques which reduce the amount of income accruing to labour. Now that the bulk of large-scale industry and commerce is publicly owned, the government can obtain the surplus through taxation, by manipulating prices and wage rates, or, more palatably, through schemes of social insurance. In Egypt there is no longer any obvious conflict between techniques which maximize the short- and the long-run rates of growth because the savings problem can be solved by other means. None of the other arguments against labour-intensive technology really excuse the neglect of Egypt's most abundant resource or the government's preoccupation with highly mechanized and modern technology. Egypt possessed a tradition of handicrafts and small-scale manu-

[83] I have dealt with this question in my paper 'Industrial Development and the Employment Problem', *ME Econ. Papers 1962*.

[84] They neglect to point out that many of the controls now imposed on the private sector hinder the 'exploitation' of surplus labour.

[85] W. Galenson & H. Leibenstein, 'Investment Criteria, Productivity and Economic Development', *QJ, Econ.* Aug. 1955, pp. 343–70.

factures which flourished as recently as the Second World War, when larger firms could not import machinery. After the war it declined in face of competition from imports and more mechanized factories, but the tradition could perhaps be revived. The Japanese and Indonesian examples demonstrate what can be achieved provided the government is willing to help.[86] Rural and small-scale industries need technical advice based upon careful research into a technology appropriate to their needs and level of development. To operate competitively they also require credit and transport and marketing facilities suitable for a structure of dispersed small producers. Of course, no recommendation to subsidize inefficient concerns over the long run will promote efficiency but at present the possibilities for aiding and developing this kind of activity in Egypt are only just beginning to be explored. And officials of the Ministry of Agrarian Reform who have resided in villages believe that it is feasible to use under-employed agricultural labour to build health centres, schools, roads, and the like within village boundaries, particularly if the new producers' co-operatives obtain the support of the peasantry.[87] For centuries rural labour has been mobilized for the maintenance of and extensions to the irrigation system; surely its horizons can now be widened to include other forms of social capital?

Lastly, the choice of products and technique for the modern sector could be reviewed in order to take more account of the employment problem. There is no case for developing highly mechanized manufactures which compete with existing small-scale concerns. At this stage of development planners are better advised to concentrate on lines of production not feasible upon a small scale or with labour-intensive techniques. If possible they should avoid projects which extinguish traditional producers in such simple manufactures as clothing, furniture, and food-processing because redundant labour will not be readily absorbed elsewhere. Why not devote funds into research designed to make such firms as efficient as possible in the short run? If and when labour scarcity emerges, capital-intensive techniques will become

[86] T. Herman, 'The Role of Cottage and Small-Scale Industries in Asian Economic Development', *Economic Development & Cultural Change*, July 1956, pp. 356–70.

[87] Current plans for the new co-operatives include schemes for rural manufactures and village capital formation.

relevant to all branches of the economy and can be readily applied. Even within modern capital-intensive industries auxiliary processes such as sorting, handling, loading, and cleaning can be performed manually and need not be mechanized. But in Egypt there is a definite tendency to regard mechanization as an end in itself when it is merely a means to greater efficiency.

THE SOCIALIST, DEMOCRATIC, AND CO-OPERATIVE SOCIETY

Unlike previous chapters, which were largely descriptive, the present argument is prescriptive in its emphasis. I have employed the norms of welfare economics in order to try and evaluate, within the limits of scanty information, the efficiency of the present economic system. Economists have, however, often been warned against appraisals on grounds of efficiency alone because it leads to the impression that they consider efficiency more important than equity and freedom.[88] As Professor Samuelson rightly says:

> At some point welfare economics must introduce ethical welfare functions from outside economics. Which set of ends is decidedly not a question of economics. We should dispel the notion that by a social welfare function is meant one unique and privileged set of ends. Any set of ends is grist for the economist's unpretentious deductive mill and he can be expected to reveal that the prescribed ends are incomplete and inconsistent.[89]

For Egypt the ends of economic and social action prescribed by the government are to create a 'Socialist, Democratic, and Co-operative Society'. First proclaimed at the end of 1957, these goals are now part of the constitution and have become one of the most frequently reiterated slogans of the ruling élite.

Unfortunately the insistence by Egypt's leaders that the adjectives socialist, democratic, and co-operative must be understood in an Arab or Egyptian sense while at the same time failing to define and develop these emotive words in any but the most vague terms may render them tautologous. Socialism, democracy, and co-operation are in danger of meaning what the régime chooses

[88] Scitovsky, p. 62.

[89] P. Samuelson, 'A Comment on Welfare Economics', in B. Haley, ed. *A Survey of Contemporary Economics* (1952), p. 37.

instead of being ideals or measuring rods against which its performance can be tested. For Egyptian development, a social-welfare function should not imply one set of ends, but the difficulty is to define precisely what the ends of policy are. Perhaps wisely, Egypt remains without a clearly formulated national ideology, and any appraisal of its revolution must to some extent be in terms of ends imported from outside the country. Moreover the advice to take the ends of policy as given is perhaps unnecessarily relativist. Would many economists really be prepared to design an 'efficient' programme for an underdeveloped country aimed specifically to occasion much greater inequality in the distribution of income and wealth? Comments upon the Egyptian revolution should certainly take full account of the local aims in their local context, but equally there seems to be no very good reason to abandon the ideals of European liberalism and socialism for the vaguely formulated doctrines of a Military Junta. And any national régime which employs the vocabulary of alien ideologies must be prepared to be judged, partially at least, by their standards, even if it does take the precaution of prefixing them with the adjectives Arab or Egyptian. I propose to use the words 'socialist, democratic, and co-operative' in ways comprehended both inside and outside Egypt.

Democracy is decidedly the most intangible of the three. In the Charter the word is defined both negatively and positively. Its negative aspect resides in a thorough-going rejection of Egypt's political structure before the revolution as a sham democracy of constitutional façades which maintained the power of a privileged class. When the Charter went on to outline conditions for a 'true democracy', it included the familiar catalogue of freedom of speech, of criticism, and of the press, but also insisted strongly on the tenets of positive liberalism, namely that democracy demanded some measure of economic equality in order to eliminate the possibility of political domination by an economically powerful minority. Gross inequality in the distribution of wealth and income, the Charter emphasized, engenders a violent class struggle which precludes democracy, while

> the removal of such clash will pave the way to peaceful solutions to class struggles. It does not remove the contradictions in the rest of the social classes, but it creates a chance for the possibility of resolving

them peacefully, namely by means of democratic action (p. 46).[90]

But few observers would argue that free criticism of government, either by the mass media or by individuals, exists to any significant degree in contemporary Egypt. Nor are citizens allowed to organize themselves into groups or parties for the purpose of influencing or opposing government policy. Economic conditions for a viable democracy have been created, though it is much too early to say whether or not the recently established political institutions, designed to give concrete expression to promises contained in the Charter, are democratic.

The Charter recognized the sovereignty of the people and promised it would be expressed through elected assemblies at every level of government, national and local. 'To apply democracy, the authority of popular councils should have authority over all production centres and over the machinery of local or central administration' (p. 86). On the functions of popular councils the Charter remained vague. Nor did it supply much detail about conditions for membership and election except to say they would be based upon free elections and should contain at least 50 per cent representation from workers and peasants who formed the majority of the people (p. 47). Fortunately the provisional constitution of March 1964, which is the direct outcome of deliberations on the National Charter, is explicit about the legal framework of Egypt's present political system. This constitution provides for a presidential system of government with strong checks upon executive power by a sovereign elected assembly.

Members of the National Assembly were elected by universal suffrage under secret ballot. Voting was compulsory. Candidates for election had to be thirty years old and members of Egypt's only political party, the Arab Socialist Union. They are to be re-elected every five years and meanwhile possess full parliamentary immunity. Two candidates represent each of the country's 350 constituencies, but at least one must be a fellah or a worker.

According to the constitution the National Assembly is the supreme power in the state. It can initiate laws and ultimately insist on their promulgation, if necessary over the President's veto. No tax or loan can be raised without its consent. Presidential decrees are subject to approval by the Assembly. Government

[90] See also Kerr, *MEJ*, Spring 1962.

reports are discussed by members, who also have the right to question ministers. If the Assembly withdraws confidence from any minister or the government as a whole, his resignation must follow.

The President is nominated by the National Assembly and the nomination is referred to the electorate for a plebiscite. His powers are to appoint and dismiss Vice-President and ministers and to establish 'the general policy of the State in all the political, economic, social and administrative domains' and supervise its implementation. He can initiate and veto laws passed by the Assembly, but must ultimately give way if they are passed by a two-thirds majority. He can dissolve the Assembly but must call fresh elections within sixty days.[91]

Assemblies or popular councils also exist at other levels of government. They have been partly appointed and partly elected. At the Governorate level the council includes 11 *ex-officio* members, including the Governor, appointed by the central government, 5 active members of the Arab Socialist Union, and 4 members elected by secret ballot. City councils consist of 6 *ex-officio* representatives, 5 active members of the Arab Socialist Union, and 20 members elected by secret ballot. Village councils include 28 elected members, 2 members of the Arab Socialist Union, and 6 appointed representatives.[92] Although the Charter promised that 'local government should gradually but resolutely transfer the authority of the state to the people, for they are in a better position to feel their own problems and find the proper solutions', it is not yet clear how much additional power has been devolved upon the localities.[93] Their functions are described as 'the establishment and administration of public utilities and welfare services within the locality'. On the other hand they are 'required to operate within the general laws and regulations of the State and will conform to the policy set by the Ministry concerned'.[94] Localities seem to have played little part in the formulation of the First Five-Year Plan, but provisions are being made for their

[91] *The Constitution, 1964.* This constitution is provisional and is valid until the National Assembly elected in March 1964 draws up a permanent constitution.

[92] Law 24, 1960 and *UAR Statist. Pocket Yearbook 1952–61*, pp. 170–6.

[93] *The Charter*, p. 47.

[94] *Statist. Pocket Yearbook 1958*, p. 173.

participation in the Second. Nor is the division of power between officials and the councils clear. On the face of it local assemblies are less democratic in their composition than the National Assembly.

In Egypt democratic participation theoretically extends to economic enterprises and farmers' co-operatives. In factories and firms owned by the state, employees elect 4 from the 9 members of their boards of directors. How candidates are nominated is not known, but the President has insisted that their voices on the board should be effective.[95] Egypt's public sector has thus advanced some way in the direction of the kind of syndicalist organization now operative in Yugoslavia.

Until case studies are published nothing very definite can be said about Egyptian co-operatives or about the 'co-operative' aspect of the Socialist, Democratic, and Co-operative Society. 'Co-operative', like 'democratic', remains an elusive term, but its meaning might best be understood in the context of a brief consideration of the institutions referred to in Egypt as co-operatives.

Co-operatives are found in housing, internal distribution, and agriculture. In housing and retail trade co-operatives are state organizations which aim to supply good quality food and accommodation to consumers at 'fair' prices. For wholesale trade co-operative organizations have been set up by the government in order to eliminate 'exploitative middlemen' between farmers and consumers. In all three cases co-operatives represent the institutional expression of the government's attempt to raise the living standards of the urban poor. Agricultural co-operatives are overwhelmingly more important, and all farmers are now members of co-operatives. At present two types exist in agriculture—voluntary associations of farmers of the traditional kind which buy and sell or negotiate credit; and supervised co-operatives which regulate the process of production in addition to buying and selling in bulk for their members. Supervised co-operatives have developed since the revolution, initially in areas redistributed under the agrarian reforms of 1952 and 1961, but present policy is to generalize them over the entire countryside.

According to the Charter, co-operatives are 'democratic organisations capable of spotting and solving the problems of the

[95] *Nasser's Speeches 1963*, p. 115.

farmers' (p. 48). They have also been described as the 'cells of socialist agriculture', whose task is to change the mentality of the farmer, to enlighten him, to make him a better farmer and to broaden his cultural and social horizons.[96] As productive enterprises Egypt's co-operatives seem admirably designed to achieve the aims of agricultural policy, namely to diversify output and raise productivity. But as institutions which express the traditional ideals of co-operation (voluntary and democratic participation of farmers through associations formed to promote their interests as they perceive them), they have a long way to go. In this sense the new co-operatives are a departure, not merely from an alien ideal, but from the co-operative tradition as it developed within Egypt between 1907 and the present time.

Membership is no longer voluntary, decisions do not appear to be taken democratically, and for good or ill farmers own but no longer fully control their own farms but cultivate in accordance with a wider or national interest, as perceived by the government. Some ministers insist that farmers are not enlightened enough to manage their own affairs and that they should be compelled to cultivate scientifically and raise agricultural output. Others are circumspect when faced with this criticism and insist that co-operatives are run democratically by elected boards of farmers with only 'assistance or guidance' from the agronomists who are appointed, paid by, and responsible to the agricultural ministries in Cairo.[97] In the absence of case studies, nothing very dogmatic should be asserted about the division of powers between elected boards and appointed officials, but most observers are of the opinion that authority over farming is passing rapidly into the hands of government officials. The experience on land-reform areas and in the provinces of Kafr Shaikh and Beni Suef suggests that co-operatives have become an alternative to land nationalization, and are semi-public institutions through which the influence of the state is brought to bear upon the process and composition of production.[98] Moreover recent views published in *al-Ahram* warned the government not to turn co-operatives into public organizations or to

[96] *al-Ahram Econ. Suppl.*, 1 Dec. 1962, pp. 35–37; *al-Ahram*, 29 July 1963, and *al-Goumhouriyya*, 29 May & 16 June 1962.

[97] This seems to be the view of Sayed Marei (*al-Ahram*, 8 Mar. 1965).

[98] This became very obvious from the discussion between Sayed Marei and Hassanan Haikal in *al-Ahram* at the beginning of 1965.

discourage the spirit of co-operation among farmers.[99] Other authorities laid great stress on sending the kind of supervisors to the villages, who could work with the farmers and lead them to the point where they could manage their own co-operatives.[100] Supervisors might, as the Director-General of the Organization of Co-operatives suggested, eventually withdraw from producers' co-operatives, but at present they represent the extension of state control over agriculture.[101]

On paper the Egyptian constitution, with its provisions for universal suffrage, a sovereign assembly, carefully balanced division of powers between the executive and elected arms of the government, and its homage to the principle of decentralization, deserves to be termed democratic, by almost all the usual tests applied to that elusive adjective. Constitutions are, however, frequently not worth the paper they are written upon, and the real test of any political system lies in its operation or practice.

Since the revolution of 1952 Egypt has operated under three constitutions, and the constitutions of 1956 and 1958 made almost the same kind of legal provisions for the exercise of political power as the present document.[102] Yet no serious political commentator has been prepared to argue that the Assembly elected in 1957 and dissolved a year later, or the National Union which technically operated between 1958 and 1961 exercised any real political authority or ever provided an effective check on the power of the ruling élite.[103]

After their coup d'état in July 1952 the Free Officers not only suppressed political parties of the old régime but brought under control all other independent associations which could possibly challenge their authority. Gradually organized groups such as trade unions, co-operatives, professional syndicates, students, religious leaders, and eventually all large-scale economic enterprises passed under the domination of the state, until no groups

[99] *al-Ahram Econ. Suppl.*, 1 Jan. 1962, p. 19.

[100] Ibid. 15 Nov. 1963, pp. 35–39.

[101] Ibid. 1 Dec. 1962, pp. 35–37.

[102] 1956 constitution (*Mideast Mirror*, Jan. 1956) and *UAR Yearbook 1960*, pp. 8–47.

[103] Wheelock, pp. 54–55 & 67–72; Abdel-Malek (*Egypte, société militaire*, pp. 118–20) describes this assembly as fairly free and suffused with the democratic spirit, but he provides no examples of its checking the exercise of executive power.

existed capable of mediating between the state and society or between the individual and his rulers. The pre-emption of all organized political, social and economic activity not only increased the power of the state but, as Professor Vatikiotis has convincingly argued, was accompanied by the centralization of power within the state apparatus itself. The Free Officers seized office as a group and during the early years of the revolution leadership remained collective. But with the emergence of a 'strong man' and under conditions of rapid economic change engendered from above, power passed inevitably into the hands of the President. Action, decision, and the drive for modernity were more readily achieved under aegis of a highly centralized command. Within the hierarchy the President found his power sustained and supported by two groups—the army, which is the ultimate basis for his authority, and a cadre of technocrats appointed by him to positions of authority in a vastly enlarged bureaucracy. This latter group, together with the old civil service, are necessary for the modernization of Egypt. Their skills give them authority and their allegiance is to the President.[104]

For several years Egypt has been ruled by a highly efficient and benevolent dictator, assisted and no doubt occasionally checked by his loyal cadre of officers, technocrats, and civil servants. The proclamation of the Charter and the provisional constitution of 1964 suggest that the existing power structure is in the process of being democratized and that the President is going to share authority with an elected National Assembly and will devolve power upon local authorities, also elected.

But the powers of these elected bodies will depend very much upon whether or not their members are prepared to take the Charter at its face value and exercise real criticism of the government. Will assemblies develop into the sovereign authorities in Egypt, or will they degenerate into mere debating chambers with no real place in the government of the country? Will they, as the Charter hoped, protect the leadership from the assumption that 'the great problems of national development can be solved by . . . bureaucracy and administration' or from becoming 'a new class that

[104] This section relies heavily upon P. Vatikiotis, 'Some Political Consequences of the 1952 Revolution in Egypt', in Holt; and Abdel-Malek, *Égypte. société militaire*, pp. 363–7.

has replaced the old and has taken over its privileges' (pp. 89–90).

It is undoubtedly premature to answer these questions, but it is noteworthy that during its brief life the National Assembly of 1957 successfully exposed corruption in Liberation Province and failed in its attempt to modify the policy for higher education.[105] In general, however, its deliberations were never treated seriously by the government. The present National Assembly, elected in March 1964, has subjected some ministers to close questioning and has been instrumental in amending the policy for higher education.[106]

Over the long term the effectiveness of the National Assembly and its local counterparts will depend upon the quality and independence of their members. Until now the régime has consistently refused to allow parties to emerge and offer candidates for election. All candidates must be members of Egypt's sole political party, the Arab Socialist Union. Like the Marxist parties of Russia and eastern Europe, the Arab Socialist Union runs parallel to and interlocks with the structure of the state at every level of government, including public enterprises. For example, its committees operate at factory, village, town, district, provincial, and national levels. On paper the internal structure of the party appears democratic, in that its executive committees at all levels are appointed by and carry out the decisions of elected conferences of party members.[107]

The difficulty is to discern what precisely the functions of the Arab Socialist Union are or will be in the country's present political system. The Charter describes its functions very vaguely as 'the driving force behind the possibilities of the revolution and the guardian of the values of true democracy' (p. 46). As the successor to the National Union it can be deduced that one of its prime tasks will be to screen candidates acceptable to the government for election to the nation's assemblies. At present the higher echelons of the party are appointed or controlled by the ruling élite, and men unacceptable to the government will not be permitted to stand for election. Members of legislative assemblies who owe their positions to a government they constitutionally

[105] Wheelock, pp. 67–68.
[106] Mansfield, p. 206.
[107] I assume that the structure of the National Union is the same as the Arab Socialist Union (*UAR Yearbook 1960*, pp. 28–29 and Mansfield, p. 200), Election works on the principles of democratic centralism.

control are unlikely to be vociferous in their criticism of its policies, nor will they provide an effective check on the exercise of executive power. On the other hand they may still develop in time a corporate independence of their own and, if they obtain the support of the wider public outside, the assembly may eventually wield real power. After all majority parties in the western democracies are not simply vehicles of acclamation for their leaders, although they sustain them in office. Evidently the President was disturbed at the extent to which 'undesirable' elements managed to join the National Union between 1958 and 1961, despite careful screening by the government.[108] No doubt he is anxious to avoid any but the most loyal supporters from infiltrating into the Arab Socialist Union. But can the ruling élite call into a being a mass organization designed to see that its policies are properly implemented, to act as a channel of communication between the masses and Cairo, to supply a cadre of administrators and leaders for towns and villages and candidates for the assemblies, and at the same time retain their absolute freedom to initiate policy? The loyalty of mass organizations is usually conditional upon something other than blind obedience to the wishes of their leaders. As Rousseau says, 'the strongest is never strong enough to be always master unless he transforms strength into right and obedience into duty'. In Egypt, where men participate in politics with reluctance and are not easily swayed by vaguely formulated ideals of a golden future, the continued existence of a mass party presupposes that its members will obtain some say in how decisions are made at the top. Otherwise the Arab Socialist Union will degenerate into a hollow bureaucracy perfunctorily obeying its paymasters. It will not provide the régime with the revolutionary impetus and mass support that it sincerely seeks to acquire. Egypt will remain a country without a viable political system where, in the words of the Charter, 'the accumulation of great powers in few hands indisputably leads to the passage of real power to those who are not in fact responsible before the people' (p. 90).

Perhaps the socialist aspect of the 'Socialist, Democratic and Co-operative Society' is more amenable to analysis. Not only has Egyptian socialism been more fully defined than co-operation and

[108] *Nasser's Speeches 1962*, p. 383.

democracy, but socialism is usually about equality and the care a society takes of its young, old, sick, and deprived. Provided data are available, a government's achievements in these respects can, to some extent, be measured.

Socialism in Egypt has, however, been defined to embrace much more than the redistribution of income and social welfare, which are its essential tenets in western European thought. In Egypt the discussion has centred around economic organization, questions of ownership and long-term growth, while the ends of the new economic system have received rather less emphasis. For example, in the Charter and in speeches by the ruling élite socialism seems largely synonymous with a public sector and central planning. The enlarged public sector in industry and commerce emerged mainly as a consequence of the nationalization decrees promulgated between 1960 and 1964, which their authors describe as having 'eliminated feudalism, eradicated monopoly capitalism, liberated society from exploitation by a minority' (p. 73), turned all citizens into owners, and created conditions for rapid economic development through planning.[109]

No one would deny that the nationalization of corporate property in industry and commerce, together with land reform, brought to an end a situation whereby the ownership and control of Egypt's productive resources were vested in the hands of a tiny minority of the population. Equally there is no doubt that much of private industry and certain areas of commerce operated under conditions of monopoly and in that sense exploited consumers. Finally, nationalization has made it easier for the government to raise the rates of domestic savings and investment and to control and plan the economy. Provided the loss of output, regarded by some commentators as a likely consequence of the transfer of enterprises from the private into the public sector, does not exceed the addition to output accruing from the higher rate of investment there is no reason to suppose the Egyptian government will not be able to emulate other centrally-planned economies and enforce higher rates of saving and investment than would have been achieved under the old private-enterprise system.[110] Furthermore,

[109] See also *Social Laws and Decrees*, pp. 1–3.

[110] I have argued elsewhere that there is no reason to suppose the waste of output will increase as a result of nationalization.

the government has increased the share of investment devoted to technical research, and its emphasis on building up a capital-goods sector will increase the potential of the economy for growth over the long run.[111]

Thus if socialism is defined to mean a large public sector and high rates of investment by the state, then Egypt has qualified as a socialist society. But there is no logical connexion between this kind of socialism and the distribution of income or the care a government lavishes upon the least fortunate members of society. In fact it is compatible with a high degree of inequality and a blatant disregard for social welfare. Revenue from nationalized assets may simply be used to finance increased military expenditure or be transferred in one form or another into higher real incomes for state bureaucrats and managers, who thus succeed to the privileges and standards formerly enjoyed by dispossessed capitalists. One recent analysis of the contemporary Egyptian scene concluded that a new privileged class has already emerged and that extensions to the public sector have produced not socialism but state capitalism.[112] Dr Riad's assertions are not supported by anything like the evidence required to substantiate them. The Free Officers are certainly aware of the dangers of creating a 'new class'. Presumably that is why they have placed a ceiling on salaries for all state employees.[113] Moreover they have not neglected to include in their definition of socialism a more just distribution of income, the reduction in class differences, and a commitment to provide a wide range of social services.[114] Unfortunately data necessary for the appraisal of their actual achievements in these respects has either not been published or processed. Obviously the present régime is more concerned to mitigate inequality and provide social services than its predecessor, but to verify meaningfully and empirically what it has accomplished is difficult. Most observers seem content merely to tabulate the socialist measures promulgated by the Officers without analysing their effects or

[111] Dobb, pp. 64–76, demonstrates the formal conditions under which this will pertain.

[112] Riad, in *Revolution in Africa, Latin America & Asia*, i (1964) and *Égypte nassérienne*, pp. 85–89 & 219–43.

[113] *MRESE*, June 1963, p. 48.

[114] *The Charter*, pp. 51, 61, 72, 76, & 89; *Ann. Plan 1960–1*, p. 7; *Nasser's Speeches 1961*, pp. 140–9 & 308–10; *BE*, 20 & 21 July, 16 & 29 Sept. 1961.

pointing out that many represent extensions to welfare legislation introduced by the former régime, which displayed some concern for the least fortunate groups in Egyptian society long before 1952.[115]

Undoubtedly the most original and extensive redistribution of wealth and income accomplished in Egypt since the revolution has occurred within the agricultural sector. According to the most recent official figures, 944,000 feddans were expropriated and will be redistributed under the Agrarian Reform Laws of 1952, 1957, 1961, and 1962. This land has been expropriated from a tiny minority of approximately 5,000 owners who received virtually no compensation. By the autumn of 1965, 647,000 feddans had been handed over to 273,000 families and, assuming that the remainder is allocated in plots of 3 feddans, by the time the present programme is completed, approximately 372,000 families will have gained land. Thus the reform will eventually redistribute about 18 per cent of the cultivable area and benefit 27 per cent of the 1,363,000 families who derive their livelihood from agriculture.[116]

In addition to the direct redistribution of land, the government also fixed maximum rents and regulated leasehold and share-cropping agreements in favour of tenants. Opinions differ as to the effectiveness of this legislation on actual rents paid by farmers, but few observers consider that it is without influence, although there seems to be considerable regional variation between Governorates and between small and large landowners.[117] Its unmeasurable effect is to transfer income from landowners to tenants. Government policy also aims to substitute co-operative organizations for private merchants for the internal distribution of farm produce. Ministers proclaim this will eliminate the 'exploitation' of farmers by middlemen, but its precise influence cannot be assessed until prices paid by state trading organizations are compared with those paid by merchants. There is some indication that farmers still prefer to deal with the latter. Finally, all cultivators obviously

[115] See above, pp. 49–53.

[116] Abdel-Malek, in *Dévelopment et Civilisations*, June 1965, p. 22; ownership and control of land have also been more equally distributed because many owners sold land to anticipate reform. Furthermore, no owner is now allowed to sell more than 5 feddans to any one person and no farmer may lease more than 50 feddans.

[117] Warriner, pp. 39–40 & 210; Saab, in *ME Econ. Papers 1960*, pp. 79–8 and B. Hansen, *Distributive Shares in Egyptian Agriculture* (1965), INP Memo. 597.

gained from the law of 1961 which made loans from the Agricultural Bank interest-free.

While the direction of the redistribution of agricultural income has in general been from richer to poorer groups, the reduction of rents, the elimination of middlemen, and the abolition of interest charges by the Agricultural Bank affords greater benefits to those who cultivate, borrow, and sell on a larger scale than to smaller and less affluent farmers. Moreover the selection of owners for land redistributed under the agrarian reforms did not favour the most impecunious families in the countryside but was biased, on efficiency grounds, towards existing tenants or those considered likely to be competent farmers.

While it is impossible to imagine anything remotely comparable being implemented by the old régime, this should not obscure the fact that agrarian reform has not been extensive. Most rural families are untouched by it and remain either landless or with insufficient land to produce anything more than the most meagre subsistence. If rumours that the government plans to lower the limit for ownership to 25 feddans are correct, then a further million feddans will become available for redistribution, and over half of all families at present engaged in agriculture could become beneficiaries of land reform. But at present the government appears to be in no hurry to introduce further reforms. Instead its efforts are being concentrated upon the introduction of supervised co-operatives throughout agriculture, and any attempt to combine that programme with redistribution of land might produce an upheaval in the countryside profound enough to lower output. Moreover, while the dispossession of aristocratic landowners proved to be relatively easy, the political effects of expropriating a much larger class of medium owners, many of whom farm their own lands, could endanger the stability of the régime. Evidently some Free Officers have publicly expressed antipathy to lowering the ownership limit beyond 100 feddans, and a recent attempt to introduce a bill into the National Assembly providing for a maximum holding of 10 feddans was rejected by the steering committee as contrary to the spirit of the Charter.[118]

Measures which directly alter the distribution of income outside

[118] Abdel Malek, in *Dévelopement et Civilisations,* June 1965, p. 35. The information about the bill I owe to a prominent member of the Assembly.

the agricultural sector include controls upon rents for accommodation, minimum-wage legislation, and the introduction, in 1961, of profit-sharing. Minimum wages were also fixed for agricultural labour, but proved to be unenforceable, and no law compels farmers to share profits with their labourers, who are probably the poorest class in Egypt. For industry and commerce the laws related to wages and profits are administratively impossible to enforce beyond the bounds of the public sector and the remaining large-scale private enterprises, which means that only a minority of the working force benefit from them. Their effects upon the money incomes of those eligible under the law should not be exaggerated. When the legislation came into effect few workers in organized industry and commerce received less than the prescribed minimum wage of 25 piastres a day. It provided a cushion for the wages of the unskilled and did not attempt to push wage rates above their market levels or to redistribute income from property to labour. As a group, industrial and commercial workers probably gained more from the regulations making it difficult for their employers to dismiss redundant labour. Cash benefits from shared profits will be small because the definition of profit can be manipulated by managers in order to retain additional funds for reinvestment. More important, the bulk of profits paid to workers is utilized to finance their social-security benefits and pensions. Rent controls have certainly been instrumental in transferring income from a rich minority who own houses to their poorer tenants. Again, blanket reductions in house rents of the kind now implemented tend to favour the more as against the less affluent tenants and operate against those seeking to rent accommodation for the first time. On examination Egypt's Social Revolution appears to have favoured an 'aristocracy of labour' who work in large-scale industry and commerce, middling peasants, and the urban middle class.[119] In terms of direct redistribution between social classes, the Free Officers have introduced progressive but hardly radical measures. With the expropriation of a tiny class of property owners who owned a disproportionate share of the nation's wealth, gross inequalities are no more, but of itself this has brought no immediate improvements to the very poorest classes of Egyptians, such as agricultural

[119] See above, pp. 135–6, 177 & 189–90.

workers and those who labour in small concerns in industry and services. Perhaps their lot can only be improved by economic growth. Egyptian socialism has certainly done little to alleviate it so far.

Some redistribution of income has also occurred indirectly through the provision of free or subsidized collective services financed by progressive taxation. Any appraisal of Egyptian socialism must analyse the social-welfare legislation actually implemented by the Free Officers, particularly as their proclamations and development plans do not neglect to promise universal health insurance, free education, the right to work, and security against old age, sickness, and unemployment.[120] Once again data are neither plentiful nor processed sufficiently to permit anything more than a cursory survey.

The available facts, presented in table 9 below, suggest that the régime's record is far from unimpressive. Public expenditure on

TABLE 9

Government Expenditure on Social Services

Sector	1950–1		1955–6		1959–60		1962–3	
	£ *m.*	% *GNP*	£ *m.*	% *GNP*	£ *m.*	% *GNP*	£ *m.*	% *GNP*
Education & research	22·2	2·2	35·3	3·3	51·4	3·7	96·1	5·8
Health	7·3	0·7	10·9	1·0	9·0	0·7	28·8	1·8
Social, religious, cultural	38·0	3·9	52·6	4·9	44·9	3·3	32·5	2·0
Supply services	12·4	1·3	6·7	0·6	9·5	0·7	47·8	2·9
Total	79·9	8·1	105·5	9·8	114·8	8·4	205·2	12·5
Total GNP	984·0		1,072·0		1,372·0		1,634·0	

Notes: GNP and government expenditure are measured in current prices. The figures for 1962–3 are estimates. The GNP total for 1950–1 is the average of GNP for the calendar years 1950 and 1951.

Sources: (*a*) for GNP: INP Memo. 335 and Min. of Finance & Econ., *UAR State Budget for 1962–3;* (*b*) for govt expenditure: Issawi, *Egypt in Revolution*, p. 278 and *UAR State Budget 1962–3*.

120 *The Charter*, p. 76 and INP Memo. 76.

social services—defined to include personal and public health, education, cost-of-living subsidies and pensions for the sick, the unemployed, the old, and the dependants of fatally injured or disabled workmen—has risen by 70 per cent since 1952.[121]

In relative terms the proportion of Gross National Product devoted to social services has risen from 8·1 to 12·5 per cent and the most significant rise has been registered in the field of education. With a limited natural endowment Egypt is devoting resources towards the improvement of her most abundant resource, manpower. The government's emphasis has been upon primary education, and in 1960–1, 63 per cent of the age-group 6–12 years were undergoing instruction compared with 45 per cent a decade earlier.[122] Education at the secondary and higher levels is not yet free but the fees have been drastically reduced, particularly for vocational training.[123] Education is not simply an agent for economic development but is probably the most important vehicle for social mobility now operating in Egypt. The status and material standards of poor and illiterate families will rise with their children's advancement up the educational ladder.[124]

Given the very poor health and low life expectancy of the majority of Egyptians, the expenditure on public-health services, particularly in rural areas, does not appear outstanding. Vaccination, inoculation, and propaganda for hygiene certainly affect a much wider section of the community than at mid-century, and fresh piped water will be available to almost the entire population by 1970.[125] The numbers of hospital beds per head of population have fallen slightly but the number of doctors per capita has risen rapidly since 1952.[126] The government is, however, open to criticism for not allocating more expenditure to villages, which contain the most appalling poverty and disease.

In 1947 the former régime inaugurated a programme of

[121] This calculation neglects to deflate additions to monetary expenditure for changes in price. Deflation might reduce the rate of increase by 10 per cent.

[122] *Basic Statistics*, p. 175.

[123] Issawi, *Egypt in Revolution*, p. 98.

[124] In 1960 only 45 per cent of all males and 16 per cent of all females aged 10 and above were literate (*Basic Statistics*, p. 175).

[125] Between 1956 and 1960 consumption of piped water rose 26.5 m. cubic centimetres, to 101.9 m.

[126] *Basic Statistics*, p. 193 and Mansfield, p. 111, says the number of doctors was 1 per 4,000 people in 1951–2 and in 1964 it was 1 per 2,000 people.

Combined Centres for rural Egypt. The aim of these centres was to combine under a single administration doctors, nurses, teachers, agricultural extension experts, and social workers. Peasants and their families would receive free medical care and advice on family planning and farming, and would be subjected to propaganda for personal hygiene through the centres.[127] Apparently they are in general effective and popular. In 1947 the government estimated that a minimum of 863 units would be required to cover the countryside, but by the end of the Plan only 373 will have been established.[128] The shortage of experts willing to work in villages is the major impediment to their rapid extension, but the government should be prepared to offer high salaries or if necessary to use its coercive power to direct young graduates, as it does already for doctors and engineers.

Social-security schemes have been redefined to include more of the hazards of modern living and extended to embrace wider sections of the community. Before the revolution the middle and upper classes arranged their own insurance through private companies but the government had compelled large firms to compensate their employees for accidents incurred at work, obliged them to pay for sick leave, and to award indemnities to those workers who lost their jobs through sickness. In 1951 the state introduced a scheme of its own to provide pensions for the dependants of deceased or disabled workmen.[129] Under the present government the scale of benefits have been made much more generous and workmen are today covered not only for death, sickness, and disability but are eligible for free medical care, unemployment pay, and old-age pensions as well, while recently their dependants were included in a comprehensive health insurance scheme.[130]

Although the government has promised to extend social security to the whole population, at present public provision does not encompass much more than civil servants and the employees of

[127] Information Dept., *The Collective Units* (1954, ar.) and *Social Developments under the New Regime.*

[128] Issawi, *Egypt in Revolution*, pp. 107–8 and see above, pp. 50–51 & 155.

[129] Min. Social Affairs, *Social Welfare in Egypt*, pp. 61–63 & 109; see also above, pp. 75 & 76.

[130] Laws 91 & 92, 1959; 143, 1961; 63 & 113, 1964; *MRESE*, May 1962, p. 29; June 1962, p. 41; Apr. 1963, pp. 47–49; Feb. 1964, p. 67.

public and the larger private companies. According to a recent estimate for 1963, about 775,000 workers in industry and services participated in social insurance. If we add to this total 429,000 civil servants, it appears that approximately 1,204,000 workers from a total labour force of 6,599,000 are covered by the government's provisions for social security.[131]

Distinct advances have been made since 1952, but it is clear that the majority of the labour force are still not protected by the state against the consequences of sickness, disability, unemployment, death of the bread-winner, and old age. Social security is not only confined to a minority of the population but government schemes play little part in alleviating the poverty and distress of the least affluent groups in Egyptian society. It would be unfair not to mention the costs and administrative problems involved in the extension of social services beyond the limited and privileged strata at present succoured, but until they are widened to include the most deprived members of the community, they hardly warrant the accolade of socialist.

Finally, to be redistributive social-welfare services should be financed by progressive taxes. This is not the case in Egypt, where the finance is provided by the firms and to a more limited extent by the workers themselves. For example, for retirement pensions employers and employees contribute an amount equal to 5 per cent of the wage.[132] Payments for accident and disability insurance are made by the firm only, and under the new health scheme covering workers and their dependants, employers contribute 6 per cent and employees 1 per cent of their wages.[133] Workers also contribute the bulk of their share of profits to social-security funds. Presumably the extra costs incurred by firms are passed on as higher prices, and social security is ultimately financed by consumers in general.

Not only is the finance of social security relatively unprogressive, but the tax system as a whole does not attain very high standards of equity. Only a small proportion of tax revenue is collected directly from levies upon income or wealth. Earned incomes are rated more highly than unearned, and rents from land largely

[131] FEI, *Ann. 1964*, p. 11 and *Basic Statistics*, pp. 36 & 41.

[132] Law 92, 1959.

[133] Issawi, *Egypt in Revolution*, p. 198.

escape taxation, while the exemption level for the progressive income-tax appears to have been set at too high a level for such a poor society.[134] No doubt such anomalies are a legacy from the past, but until further reforms are implemented the tax system does not deserve to be called 'a socialist fiscal instrument'.[135]

CONCLUSION

Egypt's ruling élite is attempting to build a 'Socialist, Democratic, and Co-operative Society'. Its achievements since the coup d'état of 1952 and more obviously since the proclamation of these goals in 1957 are not unimpressive. Few would deny that progress has been made, particularly in the sphere of social justice, but its extent should not be exaggerated. Egypt still possesses a highly centralized and autocratic political system. At all levels of government, central and local, as well as in organizations controlled by the state, such as trades unions, farmers co-operatives, and public enterprises, decisions are seldom taken democratically. Through the Arab Socialist Union the Free Officers hope to encourage more participation in politics and are seeking to establish a viable set of political institutions. Gross inequalities in income and wealth have been eradicated but redistribution has so far done little to alleviate the material conditions for the mass of poverty-stricken Egyptians. If new privileged groups have emerged in Egypt it is not really among the ruling élite and their entourage, as some writers suggest, but among factory workers, medium peasants, beneficiaries of land reform, and the urban middle class. Until the effects of social and economic policy are more diffused, the régime's dedication to socialism will remain mainly ideological.

[134] Hansen & Marzouk, pp. 265–7.

[135] The words are those of the Minister of Treasury quoted in *BE*, 16 Sept. 1961.

X

Conclusion

THE economy inherited by the Free Officers at their coup d'état in July 1952 certainly cannot be described as a flourishing concern. Poverty, malnutrition, and disease faced them at every turn. Looking back they could see little sign that average real income had risen since before the Great War. 'Stagnant' is an appropriate epithet for the Egyptian economy at mid-century, not because total output had remained stationary but because it had risen more slowly than population.

In fact farm production, the dominant component of national output, had grown at a commendable pace over the present century but still not rapidly enough to prevent farm output per capita and per man employed in agriculture from falling steadily. The factor behind this trend was a continuous decline in the amount of land available to each cultivator, not offset by rising yields per feddan. As a reaction to the shortage of land and water Egyptian farmers, with some encouragement from the government, attempted to raise the productivity of their plots. They reallocated land to more valuable crops and employed more scientific techniques of cultivation. As a result average yields did increase, but the use of fertilizers, selected seeds, and pesticides did not proceed rapidly enough to compensate for the overall shortage of land. Moreover, as the government brought sub-marginal land into cultivation and the ratio of cropped to cultivated area increased, the fertility of the soil became impaired and the farmers found it progressively more difficult to maintain average yields. A large part of the massive application of fertilizers reflects their attempt to preserve the fecundity of land subjected to the deleterious results of too much water and multiple cropping.[1] No doubt the conservatism of Egyptian farmers and landowners formed a real obstacle to improvement, but the preconditions for the widespread application of new techniques, namely the reform of tenurial institutions in ways which gave more incentives to the cultivators and the con-

[1] O'Brien, in Holt; see also above, pp. 5–8.

solidation of scattered holdings into a composite plot, were changes too revolutionary even to be considered by the old order.

Agricultural productivity obviously needed to be raised, but Egypt's development strategy pointed inescapably towards industrialization. In order to meet the growing pressure of population upon a relatively fixed area of land, productive capacity and opportunities for employment had to be created outside the primary sector. For about two decades before the revolution the government provided private manufacturers with every incentive to expand. Output grew very rapidly, but by 1950–2 the industrial sector had reached a kind of impasse which manifested itself in the downturn of those years. The symptoms of crisis consisted of a slower rate of growth, mounting stocks, and unemployment. Its causes were both cyclical and secular. On the demand side the sharp decline in cotton prices on world markets after the Korean boom lowered purchases by farmers. Without the Korean war the rapid growth rate for Egyptian industry would probably have declined sooner. Industrial expansion had been based on the replacement of imported consumer goods by domestically-produced substitutes, and over two decades local manufacturers had developed sufficient capacity to satisfy domestic demand and to meet predictable increases in that demand. After the 'once-and-for-all' period of import replacement the pace of industrial advance inevitably became conditioned by the growth of local incomes and the income and price elasticities of demand for manufactured commodities. Since industry remained a small sector of the economy, the effects of the growth of industrial incomes upon demand for industrial products also remained slight. The mass market was in villages, but real per capita incomes in the agricultural sector appeared unlikely to rise rapidly enough to impart much stimulus to further industrial expansion.

Egyptian industry could still grow if it succeeded in cutting costs and prices. Room certainly existed for improvements in efficiency, but none of the surveys on Egyptian industry conducted during the early 1950s suggested that many firms could stand competition from overseas, let alone compete on world markets. Egypt's infant industries had received protection for two decades but had not grown into healthy adolescents. Of course, twenty years is a short period for a country to establish an industrial base.

Moreover responsibility for the relatively low level of efficiency cannot be ascribed entirely to those who controlled industrial enterprises. First of all, the government could be criticized for not providing industry with cheaper transport, better marketing facilities and power supplies—not too strongly, because the country possessed an infrastructure well above the standard normally found in low-income societies. But the government might legitimately be blamed for its failure to expand education, particularly technical and managerial studies, because shortages of skill and low levels of literacy certainly lowered the productivity of the industrial labour force. Next, industrial managers could, with some justification, excuse their high costs on the grounds that the low productivity of the agricultural sector maintained the prices of many industrial raw materials at uncompetitive levels. Here is another vicious circle characteristic of many over-populated countries. Egypt needed to industrialize because of diminishing returns on the land, but industrial progress was hampered by the inefficiency of local farms. Thirdly, mechanized industry had existed in Egypt for too short a time and upon too limited a scale to undermine a whole complex of cultural and sociological obstacles to its own rapid development. The rural character of the industrial labour force, antipathy among the educated to work at the bench, the nepotism of managers, the irrational preference among the middle class for imported commodities, and the inexplicable reluctance of investors to depart from traditional patterns of investment in land and real estate, all served to impede the efforts of industry to raise efficiency and would disappear only with the definite establishment of an industrial tradition.

But not all the deficiencies of industry could be blamed upon outside factors. Manufacturers had not designed a structure of shares or pressured for a body of company law which would have induced the maximum flow of investment into industry. Many firms paid far too little attention to training their workers and instituting systems of wage incentives and welfare benefits in order to reduce, within narrower limits, the labour bottlenecks which resulted from absenteeism and high rates of turnover. And the ratio of capital to labour which existed in the larger firms suggested that their engineers were perhaps over-impressed with modern technology and failed to exploit the almost unlimited supplies of cheap labour available in Egypt. Finally, their scale of operations indicated a desire to reap monopoly profits rather than a concern to minimize costs.

Several possibilities existed for reducing costs but the chances that industrial efficiency would be raised substantially in the short run seemed remote. Protection, the persistence of a sellers' market during the war and post-war periods, and the monopolistic structure of Egyptian industry, while conducive to the establishment of infant industries, had not encouraged a high regard for efficiency. Significantly Egyptian industrialists reacted to the crisis of 1950–2 by calling on the government for still more protection, lower taxes, and guaranteed profits. They did not promote schemes for the rationalization of industry in order to make it more competitive.

Given the problem of demand, the prospects for Egyptian industry seemed to depend on raising the level of efficiency and exporting more manufactured commodities. The other way forward appeared to be along the line of further import replacement. Egypt still imported most of her consumer durables and intermediate and capital goods. Markets thus existed, future demand could be predicted, and several subsidiary arguments commended the strategy still further. For example, natural resources such as iron ore and potash could be exploited by the establishment of steel and fertilizer plants. New industries would save foreign exchange which not only possessed a high opportunity cost but, as the terms of trade moved against Egypt's primary exports, became more expensive to earn on world markets. If the country possessed its own capital-goods sector, its development programmes became less vulnerable to shortages of foreign exchange. Government expenditure upon development projects and armaments would stimulate local industry and employment and not constitute a 'leakage' into imports. Finally, the backward and forward linkage effects set up by heavy industries would induce investment throughout the economy.

Although the strategy of diversifying industry seemed sensible enough, the difficulties of establishing sophisticated forms of manufacturing appeared unlimited. Unlike consumer goods, the new industries required heavy investment which gestated slowly. Possibilities for cautious experiment on a small scale did not exist.

They needed to be carefully planned and called for large inputs of scarce foreign exchange, skilled labour, and managerial expertise.

Thus when the Free Officers seized power in July 1952 they found themselves confronted with a daunting array of economic and social problems. They observed an accelerated decline in the cultivated area per person and concluded that their government needed to reclaim land and to encourage local farmers to cultivate more efficiently. They also realized that productive capacity and opportunities for employment had to be created outside the primary sector. They appreciated that rapid industrialization involved the formation of fixed capacity not merely within manufacturing itself but in sectors serving industry such as power, transport, marketing, and finance; that it required the diversification of industrial output to take advantage of opportunities for import replacement, and that industrialization implied that the average efficiency of existing enterprises had to be raised if sales of manufactured commodities were to increase upon local and world markets.

The Officers did not bring to power any firm notions how Egypt's economic problems should be tackled or any ideological preconceptions about the kind of social and economic system they wished to adopt. On one side their attitudes evinced an antipathy for the 'monopolists, corrupt capitalists and exploiters' of the former régime. They successfully resisted a demand for a return to party and pressure-group politics and thereby destroyed the blatant influence previously exercised on departments of state by property owners and businessmen. Their agrarian reform terminated the power of a small group of families in the countryside. On the other hand they leaned, politically speaking, to the right. Militant trade unionists and communists were among the first to be executed and imprisoned by the new régime and workers lost their limited rights to strike action. The Officers maintained good relations with the United States, publicly expressed support for free enterprise, and insisted that they were not socialists. And during the early phase of the revolution the struggle to consolidate power against several rival contenders (politicians of the old order, communists, and Muslim Brothers) naturally occupied more of their attention than the long-term development of Egypt.

Against this ideological and political background, it is perhaps not surprising to find very clear signs of continuity in the economic and social policies pursued during the early stages after the revolution. The Officers certainly brought energy and determination to the promotion of economic growth. They appeared less reluctant than their predecessors to use the state to plan, finance, and manage the new heavy industries, and the trend away from *laissez-faire* soon became more obvious. Nevertheless, over the whole area of economic and social activity change appears less than radical. Policy rested upon the traditional premise that the task of government was to create conditions within which private enterprise might flourish. Moreover in the formulation of policy the Officers often consulted representatives of organized business. Industrialists, merchants, and bankers became members of the Permanent Councils set up to study and recommend policies for economic and social development. The government diligently sought their support and co-operation. Finally, the techniques used to stimulate industrial growth seem much the same as those employed before 1952. Thus the new government raised tariffs even higher, took greater care in the allocation of foreign exchange among competing projects, reformed the capital market in order to facilitate the flow of savings into industry, lowered or waived taxes upon new investment, offered firms larger amounts of cheap credit, and continued the programme of extensions and improvements to the country's network of roads, railways, and power supplies.

Agrarian reform was certainly radical and the new institutional arrangements for farming expropriated land eventually provided a model for changes throughout agriculture. The new government also allocated more funds for research into seeds, fertilizers, and soils, and the extension cadres of the Ministry of Agriculture persisted with the difficult task of persuading farmers to adopt scientific techniques of cultivation. In the early years of the revolution the reform affected only a small area, and the government's efforts to raise agricultural output remained centred on the extensive margin. It approved several imaginative schemes for land reclamation, such as the High Dam and New Valley, and invested heavily in improvements to the existing irrigation network.

In the field of social welfare the Free Officers instituted new programmes of social insurance for the employees of larger firms. This small group of workers also benefited from the more generous regulations affecting their pay and conditions of employment, but the mass of the population remained outside the scope of social policy. Although public expenditure upon social services, including education, rose in absolute terms, expressed as a proportion of gross national income it showed no great tendency to increase.[2]

Neither radical changes in the economic and social system nor much extension of state power over private producers followed the revolution. For at least four years, continuity predominated over change and Free Officers operated not upon but within the existing framework of laws and institutions. They co-operated with private enterprise and encouraged it to develop the economy with, it must be added, much more determination and imagination than the old order. The years 1952–6 might be called the free-enterprise phase of the revolution.

After Suez, innovation in economic and social policy becomes obvious and soon gathered sufficient momentum to culminate in the establishment of a socialist economy four years later. Because the nationalizations of July 1961 represented such a dramatic break with the past and were accompanied by marked changes in ideology, several observers of modern Egypt have concluded that a social revolution occurred then. But nationalization represented little more than a change of ownership; modifications to the free market economy occurred long before 1961.

In 1957 the Free Officers committed the country to comprehensive planning, to begin three years later, but they launched immediately upon an interim industrialization programme, and the part played by the state in promoting long-term growth increased substantially. By 1960 the government had already assumed responsibility for nearly all capital formation, whereas before 1952 it had undertaken less than a quarter of total investment. Instead of obtaining the co-operation of the private sector for its plans, the government used all possible authority to channel investment along lines it thought appropriate for the future development of Egypt. By the end of 1958 most new investment came in some way under government scrutiny and control. Crucial

[2] INP Memo. 377.

decisions about the structure of future production and the rate of domestic savings ceased to be the responsibility of private individuals.

State control over net capital formation was not, however, accompanied by much additional control over current production. Although the Ministry of Industry obtained extensive powers to regulate private firms, they remained unused. The sequestration of British and French assets and the nationalization of the Suez canal increased the government's power over transport and financial services. In agriculture the Crédit Agricole exploited the medium of cheap credit in order to promote co-operatives and to encourage farmers to grow their crops more efficiently, but the Officers had realized that institutional reforms were needed if they intended to tackle seriously the problem of raising average yields. As a start, the ministries concerned with rural affairs had concentrated upon spreading co-operatives. Grouped together farmers at least became more open to pressure from the central authorities. Apart from new investment, the freedom of entrepreneurs to decide what to produce, how to organize production, where to buy labour and raw materials, and the prices to charge consumers had not been substantially modified by 1960. In other words, the system continued to operate pretty well on traditional free-market lines.

But with the derogation of private enterprise to a subsidiary role in the long-term development of Egypt, there occurred a perceptible hardening in the attitude of the Free Officers towards those who formerly had more complete charge of the economic system. They took much less trouble than before to consult representatives of organized business about their plans. They refused to sell 'Egyptianized' British and French assets to private capitalists.[3] After Suez the government displayed a willingness to use the state to do very much more than create a favourable environment for private enterprise. While ministers appealed for co-operation and the word 'partnership' was constantly on their lips, they also admitted that capitalists would be 'guided' or

[3] President Nasser admitted later in a speech that when Egyptian businessmen had asked for the foreign property, 'on that day I said to Kaissouny all these companies will go to the public sector. We shall not allow capitalists to increase their domination by taking the companies under sequestration' (*Nasser's Speeches 1961*, p. 379).

'directed towards collaboration if necessary'. Finally, discussion opened around President Nasser's promise of December 1957 to build up a 'Socialist, Democratic and Co-operative Society'.

His promise became translated into action when the Five-Year Plan for Economic and Social Development began operations in July 1960. The Plan set out detailed investment, saving, production, and consumption targets for every part of the economy. Its ambitious aim, to double real national income over a decade, received great publicity throughout the Arab world, and Egyptian leaders became deeply committed to its success. But their promise comprehensively to plan an economy over which they exercised only limited control seems surprising unless they expected the private sector to comply faithfully with directives from the central authorities. Ministers naturally appealed for co-operation and the Minister of Planning warned private producers against deviation. Yet the Officers could hardly have hoped for an enthusiastic response from businessmen. After all, they had been consulted only in the most perfunctory manner about the form and content of the Plan, while the whole political atmosphere in Egypt from the beginning of 1960 onwards became markedly anti-capitalist, and before the Plan opened the government found it necessary to nationalize Bank Misr in order to extend control over organized industry.

Even with Misr companies in the public sector the problems of control posed by central planning remained formidable. The government could more or less determine the level and pattern of capital formation, but the whole investment programme could have been seriously jeopardized by the failure of private producers to meet targets established for them by the Plan. The public sector was still small and private farmers, merchants, and industrialists remained responsible for producing the bulk of additional output expected to emerge between 1960–5. Planners also thought that household savings, the retained profits of business corporations, and the reinvested surplus of farms and small family firms would provide most of the domestic savings required to finance planned capital formation. If local enterprises and households failed to comply with their designs, inflation and supply bottlenecks could arise and reduce actual achievement well below target levels.

How in practice the government proposed to persuade or induce the private sector to participate in the Plan was never specified, even though the normal policy instruments, including fiscal and monetary techniques, had been tried in Egypt and found wanting. Moreover the government made no serious attempt to elicit the positive co-operation of private producers. After just a year of comprehensive planning in the mixed economy and nine years after their coup d'état, the Free Officers, not unexpectedly, nationalized the bulk of corporate enterprise in industry and foreign trade. The first wave of nationalizations were, however, considerably less than wholesale and created companies of mixed public and private ownership in light industry and commerce. Land, housing, internal trade, and transport were hardly affected by the measures of July 1961, although the government did redistribute more land and imposed rigid controls on the rents of accommodation. Later the Officers decided to abolish mixed ownership and to extend the public sector into all spheres of activity, including internal trade and transport, building and civil engineering. Furthermore, the Ministry of Supply announced plans for the rationalization of wholesale and retail trade, and, as a result of successful experiments in Kafr Shaikh and Beni Suef, the agricultural ministries began to establish supervised co-operatives throughout the countryside. By 1970, when these programmes are completed, the Egyptian economic system will become a command economy. The Free Officers will then have created the economic controls so conspicuously lacking at the beginning of the First Five-Year Plan. They will be in a position to plan comprehensively.

Within a decade of the revolution Egyptian economic organization had undergone such profound and rapid transformation that it could no longer be described as a free-market system. Why the transformation occurred cannot be fully answered until we know more about the inner workings and motivations of the political élite who rule Egypt, but the beginnings of an explanation can be attempted. Looking at the changes in historical perspective leads to the observation that the connexion between state and economy has been close throughout most of Egypt's recent history. It was intimate under Mohammed Ali, who in the first half of the nineteenth century ruled over an even more centralized and regulated economy than the system which has emerged today.

After 1850 the command economy established by the Pasha disintegrated and evolved gradually towards a free-market *laissez-faire* system of production. By the Great War, markets almost entirely free from state intervention had emerged for land, labour, capital, and for the sale of industrial and agricultural commodities. In commercial policy the country embraced free trade and permitted almost unrestricted capital movements across its frontiers, but the state retained overall responsibility for the upkeep and extensions to the irrigation system, roads, railways, and ports.

Our historical survey also reveals that between 1914 and the revolution, under the impetus of two world wars and the Great Depression, successive governments began to retreat slowly from the position of *laissez-faire* in economic policy. A concern to mitigate the incidence of wartime inflation upon the living standards of the urban working class led the government to impose controls upon food prices. The endeavour to stabilize the incomes of farmers faced with fluctuations in returns from their leading cash crop, cotton, on world markets during the Great Depression involved the state in the organization of price support and buffer-stock policies. At least some members of the former régime regarded urban and rural poverty as problems which required action by the central authorities. To alleviate poverty the Ministry of Social Affairs encouraged the formation of co-operatives and constructed welfare centres in some villages. The same ministry enforced the code of legislation governing wages and working conditions for a minority of the labour force employed in large-scale industry and commerce. Finally, the whole problem of Egypt's long-term economic development began to receive serious attention from the government. Plans were made, and partially implemented, to improve the nation's infrastructure. Through its extension services the Ministry of Agriculture disseminated scientific methods of cultivation among farmers. The government had perceived that the way forward for Egypt was through industrialization and gave private industry all possible aid to expand. Tax concessions, cheap credit, subsidies, railway rebates, and above all tariffs helped to make the two decades after 1930 a period of impressive industrial advance. By 1952 successive national governments had pushed the state away from the marked *laissez-faire* position it held in 1914, but the contrast with 1914 was not obvious, and on the eve of revolution the part played by government in the nation's economic affairs remained fairly restricted.

For about four years after their coup d'état of July 1952 the Free Officers continued to promote development and social welfare along the lines initiated by their predecessors in office. Perceptible changes in economic policy occurred not in 1952 or in 1961 but after the Suez war. The reorientation of economic policy to embrace central planning and state control over capital formation thus preceded the Officers' conversion to socialism, and cannot be plausibly explained in ideological terms. The nationalization and other decrees of July 1961 came more as the logical outcome of the extension of state control over the economy and a commitment of planning than as the fruit of an ideologically-inspired social revolution. The impact of the July decrees upon the mass of Egyptians hardly warrants so grandiose a description.

To demonstrate that ideology proceeded from institutional change rather than the reverse and to describe the present system as resulting from the extension of state control over the economy raises rather than settles problems. Why did the Free Officers find it necessary or desirable to increase the power of the state over the economy after 1956? Why did they not continue with their existing policy of trying to create conditions for the success of private enterprise? Finally, what impelled them to nationalize all large companies and radically reorganize the arrangements for farming?

My answers to these questions began with the observation that the Free Officers came to power devoid of notions about how the economy should be organized, and at a time when they were preoccupied in consolidating power over their rivals, and with the evacuation of the canal zone it is hardly surprising to find they took the line of least resistance and continued with traditional economic policies.

During the early years of its rule the new government refrained from direct intervention with the economy and preferred to give private enterprise every possible inducement to expand. But businessmen and investors failed to invest enough to make any obvious impact on the rate of growth. In an unfavourable economic and political climate their enthusiastic response to tax exemptions, cheaper credit, higher tariffs, and improvements to the infrastructure always seemed improbable anyway. Such incentives had already been carried a long way by the previous régime and were unlikely to be effective at the margin. Moreover the government's strategy for industrial development consisted of attempts to divert private capital towards heavy industry, where investments were slow to gestate, where cautious experiment upon a minor scale was not feasible, and where the risks appeared much greater than for alternative investments in land, real estate, and light industry. The Egyptian investing and entrepreneurial class was small, cautious, and not given to risking capital outside narrow and well-tried spheres of activity, unless the government was prepared to guarantee profits.

After the Suez war, government interest in development became more pronounced. The Officers appeared determined to achieve real and obvious progress over a short period of time. Moreover they realized that their economic policies had to go beyond the creation of a favourable environment for private enterprise. The rather negative response of the private sector to inducements and appeals implied that the state had to take the lead in pushing the economy forward. Thus between 1957 and 1960 the government gradually appropriated responsibility for capital formation and used every conceivable form of pressure and inducement to impel the private sector to comply with its plans for development. It prevented savings from being channelled into real estate and other types of capital formation with a low social priority. It hoped private business would follow the lead given by the public sector and respond to its appeals and incentives. On the other hand the government never created the conditions for the successful operation of a mixed economy. No line was drawn between spheres for public and private enterprise. Landowners received no guarantee against further measures of expropriation. Merchants and industrialists were no longer consulted about the régime's plans for economic development and never received that social and political approval necessary to dispel their fears for the future of private enterprise in Egypt. Thus although the economic climate became more favourable, government policy engendered insecurity among the business community, particularly after 1959 when ministers and press became overtly hostile to capitalism.

In 1960 the government introduced a Five-Year Plan which

revealed clearly the incompatibility between its ambitious aims and the division of power over the nation's economic resources. The Plan consisted of a programme of public investment, but its success depended upon the realization of production and savings targets by the private sector. Unless these targets were achieved the whole Plan would have been jeopardized. By 1961 the Officers had little confidence in the ability or the willingness of private enterprise to follow the lines mapped out for it by the National Planning Committee. Rather than risk the success of the Plan, to which they were deeply committed, they preferred to nationalize those parts of the economy amenable to central control. Nationalization brought foreign trade and the bulk of industrial production inside the public sector and gave the state direct power over the principal source of domestic savings, namely the profits of organized industry and commerce. For agriculture the government proceeded more cautiously to spread producers' co-operatives throughout the countryside.

Given the impatience of the Officers for rapid development and the understandable but nevertheless short-sighted caution of private business, the transformation of Egypt's economic system can be adequately explained without recourse to ideology. Ideology followed rather than determined events, except in one sense. Private enterprise could perhaps have been induced to force the pace of development if the Officers had guaranteed profits or emulated the Japanese pattern of development, whereby the government establishes enterprises and then sells them to native entrepreneurs as going and profitable concerns. But the Officers were not prepared to go beyond the kind of nurturing practised by the former régime. After all, they did try to obtain mass support for their coup by presenting it as a progressive revolution. Providing the bourgeoisie with risk-free outlets for its savings went against the grain. Furthermore, their failure to create conditions for the successful operation of a mixed economy resulted in part from an unwillingness to negotiate and compromise with those who owned and controlled Egypt's economic resources. No doubt the close links between these groups and the deposed political order played a part in their antipathy. Rumour has it that during the Suez war representatives of the Federation of Egyptian Industries petitioned the President to negotiate with the enemy powers, a step not calculated to increase the confidence of the Officers in private business. Their whole political outlook was against compromise, and in nearly every case of incompatibility between ends and means the Officers reacted by increasing the power of the state. Hardly ever was the Junta diverted from its goals by the presence of traditional power structures in economic or in other fields.

The system which replaced the old private-enterprise economy is usually referred to as a planned socialist economy. To describe in a phrase how production is organized and resources allocated is, however, extremely difficult, but perhaps the term centralized market economy is more revealing than vaguer adjectives like planned and socialist. Institutionally the system is marked by diversity. Almost all forms of economic organization from family farms to giant public corporations contribute to national production, while the bulk of the nation's wealth, including land, houses, and the assets employed by all small-scale enterprises, remains in private ownership. No doubt it is risky at this point of time and with the poverty of information at my disposal even to attempt to analyse the new system, let alone appraise its efficiency and equity, but it seemed useful to isolate key decisions and key decision-makers in order to reveal something about its inner workings.

Ostensibly decisions about production continue to be decentralized and are made by those who control factories, farms, and firms providing services. Managers determine the rate and composition of production. They combine land, labour, capital, raw materials, and other inputs required in order to produce commodities and services. They sell their products to each other or to consumers. Moreover the criterion underlying their behaviour is the traditional one of profit maximization. Profit remains as the success indicator for all Egyptian enterprises, public and private. Profits are increased when resources are allocated to the production of commodities for which demand by consumers is rising and when costs of production are kept as low as possible.

Superficially it looks like the old system, but what has changed since 1952 is the institutional and legal framework within which managers operate. In agriculture, for example, by 1970 farmers will produce the bulk of output within the framework of producers' co-operatives. These co-operatives, developed under the present régime, are a unique amalgam of centralized direction, local supervision, and individual initiative. Directors of co-operatives aim to maximize profits from the fixed and variable factors of production available to the co-operative as a whole. Land, irrigation water, chemical fertilizers, pesticides, best-quality seed, and imported farm machinery are allocated among co-operatives at fixed prices by the central authorities. For any crop year directors are unable to obtain more than a rationed quantity of these scarce inputs, which they combine with the more variable supplies of labour, animal fertilizers, and lower-quality seed in order to produce output. They determine the composition of output, presumably with reference to movements in relative prices, but are subject to legal constraints upon the area of land allocated to cotton and wheat. Their choice may also be influenced, to some extent, by government propaganda and inducements in favour of horticulture and animal farming. Directors also decide upon the rotations and broad techniques of cultivation to be followed, influenced again by the information on improved techniques disseminated through the extension services of the Ministry of Agriculture.

Cultivation is a mixture of collective and individual processes, with ploughing, irrigation, the application of chemical fertilizers and pesticides, and harvesting under the first heading, while sowing, weeding, and tending crops are at the discretion of the farmers. Farmers are free to apply additional fertilizers, pesticides, and all the labour time they choose upon their parcels of land. They aim to maximize yields from their own plots. Cash crops are sold through the co-operatives usually at prices fixed by the government, although free markets operate for certain produce. Returns are divided according to net cash income from each holding, calculated after costs for services provided by the co-operative have been deducted. From the co-operative's net income, funds are allocated for investment, designed to raise its capacity to provide services. In future government policy aims to increase the rate of capital formation in agriculture and the marketing arrangements adopted by producers' co-operatives give officials ample opportunity to purchase machinery, build new farm buildings, and to construct roads, &c.

For industry and services two sectors exist, public and private. Public enterprises operate within a framework of rules and institutions designed to render them amenable to central control and at the same time to allow them sufficient autonomy and flexibility to conduct their day-to-day operations efficiently. Their management, which constitutionally consists of boards of directors including representatives elected by the employees, aims to maximize profits. In the short run capital is given but managers purchase raw materials, intermediate goods, and labour on markets and combine variable with fixed inputs in order to produce a flow of commodities or services for sale to consumers or to the government. Theoretically the rate and composition of output is their concern, but they are required to submit annual budget forecasts to their superiors in General Organizations who supervise all public companies producing homogenous products or services and are in turn responsible to a Ministry. No doubt General Organizations would prevent any company from indefinite stock-piling or from the restricting of output in order to raise prices. They might also have the power to reject proposals to launch a new product or alter the quality and composition of existing commodities.

Managers organize production, but imported raw materials, intermediate goods, and spare parts are rationed among companies by the central authorities. The price mechanism does not function for the allocation of foreign exchange. Nor does it operate for skilled labour or managerial personnel whose wages and mobility are regulated by law. In fact, for labour, managers are compelled to pay minimum wages and afford a defined range of fringe benefits. Thus inputs are not purchased nor labour hired on free markets, but managers seek to combine factors allocated to them or purchased at regulated prices in order to produce a given output at minimum cost.

Managers also arrange for the distribution and sale of finished output through public or private trading organizations. All services performed for public enterprises, such as wholesale distribution, export-import business, transport, and banking, are becoming more closely interlocked with production itself. As far as its own companies in the service sector are concerned the government appears to be encouraging a functional approach, whereby banks for example specialize in the provision of credit for particular groups of enterprises or import companies deal in a defined range of commodities. Competition is not encouraged and companies seek to perform their specialized services at the lowest possible cost.

Private enterprises in production or services operate ostensibly within the same framework of laws as public companies, but they are not part of a chain of command stretching from ministries through General Organizations to the enterprises. Provided they obey the rules established for the employment of labour and price controls, they are left alone to determine their output and production methods. Moreover as small-scale concerns outside the institutional framework for the public sector, private firms can more easily evade price controls and other regulations and thus continue to enjoy almost complete autonomy in current production.[4]

Long-run modifications to the structure of output or the methods of production involve choices of technique and capital formation. Investment decisions affecting the public or private sectors no longer come within the province of individual companies. Managers might advise, suggest, and request, but increases in capacity for a given company or the creation of new enterprises are matters for higher authorities. Investment is planned.

As a document the First Five-Year Plan suggests, however, that almost all economic activity is centrally planned, but as implemented Egyptian planning includes no more than investment expenditure by the public and private sectors and the allocation of foreign exchange. Other targets contained in the Plan are indicative and serve to elucidate the overall conditions required for the achievement of the investment programme. And the formulation of that programme was neither highly centralized nor a very scientific process. Probably its major function has been to articulate a set of priorities and to provide guide-lines for previously unco-ordinated fiscal, monetary, foreign exchange, and investment policies implemented by separate departments of state.

At present the economy appears to be operating without the Second Five-Year Plan, due in July 1965, and planning is really expressed throughout the annual plans and the budget, which attempt in a rough and ready manner to co-ordinate the policies

[4] The recent attempts by the Ministry of Supply to reorganize the framework for internal distribution demonstrates that the government is not satisfied with the degree of control it can exercise over traders and shopkeepers.

and reconcile the claims of different departments upon forecasted supplies of foreign exchange and investible funds.[5] The process of reconciliation appears to be the traditional one of political bargaining among ministers, but one can say that, as a direct consequence of planning, it is now based upon a more realistic appraisal of the resources likely to be available over the coming fiscal year, and it also operates within the framework of a predetermined and agreed set of priorities for the long-term economic and social development of Egypt.

No doubt it is premature even to ask if the socialist economic system is likely to be more efficient or equitable than the old, but at least the preliminary outlines of an answer have been offered.

Efficiency in the sense of attention and the preferences of consumers for present as against future consumption and for a particular pattern of final output appears likely to diminish. Institutional changes in the economic system occurred largely to render it possible for the state to force the rate of growth, and the government is not likely to be deterred by the prevailing high propensity to consume. Provided the imposed rate of domestic saving is not intolerable or an obvious source of inefficiency, there is no convincing reason why it should defer greatly to the time preference of the present generation. Less attention is also likely to be paid to the wishes of consumers for a particular bill of goods. Physical controls upon imports imply that their desires are virtually ignored in the determination of purchases abroad. Price controls and rationing prevent, to some extent, the movement of relative prices from signalling the wishes of consumers to producers. But as a method of redistributing income, price controls are redundant because nationalization has created possibilities for more direct techniques of income redistribution.

Significant modifications to the structure of current production have been made by planners, and in 1960 they attempted to forecast the pattern of future demand by consumers, but how far their rather crude predictions actually influenced the bill of goods selected for the final year of the Plan is difficult to assess. Under the Plan investments funds are directed to creation of a capital-

[5] Theoretically the Second Five-Year Plan began operations in July 1965. My sources tell me that it will be a Seven-Year Plan which is not yet on paper (Oct. 1965).

goods sector, to the restoration of equilibrium in the balance of payments, to the stabilization of agricultural incomes, and to the provision of collective services, such as defence, education, and social welfare, as well as to the satisfaction of consumers. Above all the selection of targets for 1964–5 was designed to remedy persistent obstacles to rapid economic development. Where choice conflicted with growth, no doubt the desires of consumers was and will probably continue to be disregarded. In the new economic system they are respected but are certainly not sovereign.

Under the former economic system managers of relatively independent farms and firms, motivated by profits and guided by the movement of relative prices, performed the task of converting available resources into output. Will the new institutional arrangements and regulations for production prompt those who now control resources to perform their task more efficiently? Is the new system conducive to a better selection of techniques for production, a closer attention to ways of avoiding waste, a more ruthless attitude towards redundant labour and obsolete equipment; in short, a greater concern with ways of reducing costs? If so, the present institutional arrangements will push the economy closer to optimal efficiency where no possibilities exist for increasing the production of any single commodity without reducing the output of another. Of course, time alone will provide answers to these questions, but on *a priori* grounds there seems no reason to expect public enterprises in industry and services or producers' co-operatives in agriculture to be less efficient than the organizations they have replaced.

The quality of the new managerial élite appointed by the government is not obviously inferior to the old. Profit has been retained as their success indicator and the drive to maximize profits might be reinforced by the presence on their boards of directors of representatives elected by employees or farmers, who also have an interest in profit. Prices continue to guide their decisions and competition is as strong (or rather as weak) as it was under the old system. Finally, ministries and General Organizations are perhaps more strategically placed to detect and remedy negligence and inefficiency than powerless assemblies of shareholders or absentee landowners.

Constitutionally the present arrangements for production leave a considerable measure of autonomy to the men on the spot, managers of firms and supervisors of co-operatives. Centralization and the assimilation of business to civil service procedures has on the whole been avoided. At the same time the administration of industry, agriculture, and services has advanced in the direction of greater specialization and seems admirably designed to achieve economies of scale. On the other hand the forces of centralization and the vices of bureaucracy are strong in Egypt and may operate to nullify the sensible constitutional arrangements for the conduct of production. In fact recent labour legislation will reduce the mobility of labour and the operation of an efficient wage system for the allocation of labour among enterprises in the public sector. Nor has the government lavished proper attention upon creating conditions for the successful operation of Egypt's not inconsiderable private sector, but it appears intent upon imposing irrelevant regulations and frustrating controls over the activities of small-scale producers and traders. They might be allotted spheres of activity and left alone to make profits. Perhaps then they will do more to utilize the country's growing supply of under- and unemployed labour.

Even if the new institutional arrangements work well and managers are assiduous in their efforts to minimize costs, unless the prices of the factors they employ reflect their scarcity values to society as a whole, efficiency will not be promoted. 'Distorted' prices are probably the most potent cause of inefficiency in Egypt's economic system. Distortion arises principally from government regulations designed to affect the distribution of income, such as minimum wage legislation, controls upon rents, profits, and prices. No doubt many of these rules promoted more equality in the distribution of income, particularly under the former free-enterprise system when tariffs, the absence of competition, and the weakness of trade unions gave firms opportunities for the exploitation of consumers and workers. Equally it seems that the present system has created administrative possibilities for the redistribution of income through progressive taxation and social-welfare expenditure, that is by methods which do not impair the efficiency of the price mechanism as an allocator of resources to anything like the same extent.

Lastly, the question of efficiency should be posed in a dynamic sense. The new system will probably maintain higher rates of saving and investment than the old, but how closely will the allocation of investment funds approximate to the optimum? To answer this question information is required about the criteria employed by planners in allocating resources between sectors of the economy and the factors which influenced their choice of techniques, scale, and location for particular projects. At the sectoral level their emphasis appears to be upon consistency and the avoidance of bottlenecks rather than on the achievement of an optimum distribution of resources. Decisions are made in terms of broad priorities and do not rest on the measurement of benefits which might accrue from the reallocation of marginal units of investment between sectors. Optimal allocation is almost never attempted at this level and appraisal must realistically be confined to rather general remarks about priorities. Since Egypt's resource endowment is far from bountiful the range of choice open to planners was never very wide. They appear to be proceeding along the more obvious lines, and the general strategy is certainly based upon an extensive survey of the possibilities. Perhaps their preoccupation with import substitution and heavy industry is doubtful, but few economists have questioned the priority accorded to industrialization in general or the need for Egypt to achieve a more satisfactory balance on her international payments account.

What seems more open to criticism is the selection of projects by different ministries. While the scrutiny of Mixed Committees should avoid any obvious technological failures, there is no evidence that ministries applied proper methods of appraisal to the task of selecting projects and techniques of production. In general, the government displays a bias in favour of capital intensity which is often quite unwarranted. Labour is the country's most abundant resource, and with a worsening problem of underemployment in the countryside and growing urban unemployment, more attention and resources should be devoted towards utilizing labour.

The new economic system promises to produce higher rates of growth. There is no reason to suppose that it will be any more inefficient than the old. After all the régime has not destroyed a dynamic and competitive system of private enterprise, but has rather replaced managerial capitalism, engendered by the state, which operated largely under monopolistic conditions, with semi-autonomous public companies. Profits still motivate the actions of those who control resources and prices continue to guide their actions. Also there is no question that the new system is considerably more equitable than the old. Glaring inequalities in the distribution of wealth and income have been removed. Social welfare schemes now operate to protect at least a section of the working force from the hazards of an industrial and urban environment, while recently the régime has shown itself aware of the need to associate wider sections of the populace with the making of decisions at all levels of government. It has set itself high ideals—no less than the construction of a Socialist, Democratic and Co-operative Society.

Much has been accomplished but there is a tendency to underestimate difficulties and to mistake plans for achievements. Unwarranted inequalities in the distribution of power and income persist. We may agree with Richard Tawney that

> inequality of power is inherent in the nature of organized society since action is impossible unless there is an authority to decide what action shall be taken and to see that its decisions are applied in practice. Some measure at least of inequality of circumstance is not to be avoided, since functions differ, and differing functions require different scales of provision to elicit and maintain them.

But Tawney goes on to say that

> inequality of power is tolerated when the power is used for a social purpose approved by the community, when it is not more extensive than that purpose requires, when its exercise is not arbitrary, but governed by settled rules and when the commission can be revoked if its terms are exceeded. Inequality of circumstance is regarded as reasonable, in so far as it is a necessary condition of securing the services which the community requires in so far as . . . it is grounded in differences in the power to contribute to, and share in, the common good.[6]

Power in Egypt is on the whole utilized for social purposes approved by the community, but its exercise is arbitrary. Some of the remaining differences in income and wealth are perhaps not really necessary to secure services which the community requires. Present inequalities in power and circumstances continue to offend not only the conditions for a just society articulated so well by Tawney, but the ideals expressed by Egypt's leaders themselves.

[6] R. Tawney, *Equality* (1931), pp. 118–19.

Statistical Appendix

TABLE 10

Net Value Added, by Sectors

(£ million)

Sector	*1953*		*1959–60*		*1964–5**	
	Private sector	*Public sector*	*Private sector*	*Public sector*	*Private sector*	*Public sector*
Agriculture	272·8	—	390·5	9·4	479·5	32·2
Industry & electricity	74·3	1·4	258·1	15·3	474·9	65·4
Transport & communications	55·0	16·6	30·8	66·7	33·8	83·7
Financial services	20·8	—	10·7	2·5	9·0	9·6
Trade	129·4	—	213·8	0·1	266·2	0·5
Housing	57·7	—	71·6	1·4	81·6	2·4
Construction	20·3	—	52·0	—	51·0	—
Government administration	—	110·0	—	137·3	—	178·2
Other services	106·3	—	114·5	2·8	142·0	3·7
Total gross domestic product	736·6	128·0	1,142·0	235·5	1,538·0	375·7

* Plan targets.

Notes: The division of value added in the public sector for 1953 between industry and electricity and transport and communications is an estimate based on the assumption that the share of profits between the two sectors is equivalent to the ratio of wages between them. The figures for 1964–5 are the original targets for the Plan expressed in 1959–60 prices. The figures for 1953 and 1959–60 are expressed in current prices. The term 'public sector' is that used by the Plan and covers enterprises partly owned but effectively controlled by the state as well as enterprises fully owned and controlled. Government administration embraces the traditional functions of government: defence, security, justice, financial administration, and social services.

Sources: Statist. Dept., *National Income of Egypt for 1953* (1955), pp.2, 10, & 20; *Gen. Frame of 5-Year Plan*, tables 18, 64, 76, 81, & 91.

TABLE II

The Working Force, by Sector

(000)

Sector	*1947*		*1959–60*		*1964–5**	
	Private sector	*Public sector*	*Private sector*	*Public sector*	*Private sector*	*Public sector*
Agriculture	—	—	4,060	160	4,306	354
Industry & electricity	—	—	595	37	802	44
Construction	—	—	170	—	159	—
Transport & communications	—	—	92	127	85	141
Housing	—	—	14	2	20	—
Trade	—	—	590	20	700	—
Financial services	—	—	21	—	18	12
Other services	—	—	527	5	630	8
Government administration	—	515	—	483	—	581
Total	5,962	515	6,069	834	6,720	1,140

* Plan targets.

Notes: The working force includes all persons participating in production, employers and employees. The division of the working force between the private and public sectors for 1959–60 and 1964–5 has been calculated on the assumption that the average wage paid by government and private enterprise is the same for each sector. Figures for 1964–5 are the original targets for the Plan. Figures for 1947 are not available by sectors but the figure for government administration is the category 'Public and Social Services' in *Statist. Pocket Yearbook 1960 & 1961*, p. 13. The figures exclude military personnel.

Sources: 1947: from ILO, *Yearbook of Labour Statistics 1959*, table 4; 1959–60 & 1964–5: *Gen. Frame of 5-Year Plan*, tables 49–54.

TABLE 12

Domestic Fixed Capital Formation, by Sector

	1952–3	*1953–4*	*1954–5*	*1955–6*	*1956–7*	*1957–8*	*1958–9*	*1959–60*	*1960–1*	*1961–2*
Agriculture & land reform	6·9	5·5	6·0	8·7	12·5	14·5	16·3	16·7	20·7	31·8
Irrigation & drainage	6·8	9·3	9·3	9·3	7·1	6·7	8·5	8·6	12·2	22·3
High Dam	—	—	—	0·5	0·4	0·5	1·2	4·2	9·5	10·3
Industry	29·5	27·2	33·6	49·2	31·1	35·6	47·8	49·3	67·0	99·9
Electricity	5·8	11·3	7·3	9·5	9·3	7·7	6·7	6·2	5·5	13·0
Transport, communications & Storage	19·1	19·2	23·6	24·5	15·5	23·5	27·0	30·0	67·2	71·1
Suez canal	—	—	—	—	4·0	5·0	6·0	5·8	5·9	11·2
Housing	37·7	46·0	50·0	52·0	50·0	48·0	40·0	31·1	18·2	42·1
General Service Organization	2·9	2·7	4·6	5·1	6·4	7·7	10·4	7·5	7·7	13·8
Educational services	4·1	5·0	5·1	6·0	6·5	7·3	8·2	7·8	6·7	11·4
Health services	1·3	1·4	1·5	1·5	1·6	1·7	1·8	1·2	0·5	3·3
Social services	0·5	0·5	0·5	0·5	0·6	0·6	0·6	0·9	1·1	1·3
Other services	4·0	4·3	4·7	5·3	6·0	6·6	6·9	2·1	3·6	23·4
Total	118·6	132·4	146·2	172·1	151·0	165·4	181·4	171·4	224·8	354·9

Notes: All figures normally excluded investment in stocks. The figures for 1952–3 to 1959–60 are at current market prices. The figures for 1960–1 and 1961–2 are at constant 1959–60 prices. The figures for 1961–2 are Plan targets for that year. This series was prepared by the Ministry of Planning. The figure for 1959–60 does not agree with the Plan Frame total (recorded in table 16) which is probably a better estimate.

Source: Dept of Statist. & Census, *The Revolution in Ten Years* (1962, at.), table II.

TABLE 13

Development Expenditure by Government for Fiscal Years 1950/1—1959/60

(*£ million*)

Sector	*1950–1*	*1951–2*	*1952–3*	*1953–4*	*1954–5*	*1955–6*	*1956–7*	*1957–8*	*1958–9*	*1959–60*
Agriculture	0·6	1·0	0·6	1·4	9·4	12·4	10·8	3·7	6·4	13·8
Irrigation & drainage	5·4	7·5	4·7	9·7	5·5	6·9	5·7	5·3	7·9	6·7
High Dam	—	—	—	—	—	0·5	0·4	2·8	2·6	13·2
Industry	7·5	1·3	1·4	4·6	6·0	7·9	8·5	5·1	17·4	49·4
Electricity	1·8	4·8	3·1	14·5	7·3	8·8	7·7	9·3	8·3	9·0
Transport & storage	5·5	9·6	6·6	8·8	11·5	13·4	17·4	15·9	16·2	19·6
Housing & public utilities	1·9	3·1	3·2	5·1	11·2	20·9	9·5	9·5	8·6	7·0
Defence, security, & justice	0·3	0·5	0·1	0·1	0·3	1·1	0·2	0·5	0·6	0·2
Services	7·9	6·7	4·9	3·4	5·7	15·8	6·4	6·9	9·6	8·4
Total	30·9	34·5	24·6	47·6	56·9	87·6	66·6	59·0	77·6	127·3

Notes: Development Expenditure is equal to sums spent under the Development Budgets, 'new works' in the Ordinary Budget and development expenditure in the annexed budgets.

Source: NBE, *Econ. B.*, iv (1961), pp. 408–9.

TABLE 14

Availability & Use of Resources, 1946–56

(£ million)

	1946	*1947*	*1948*	*1949*	*1950*	*1951*	*1952*	*1953*	*1954*	*1955*	*1956*
1. Total available resources	718	755	916	941	1,024	1,098	1,051	964	1,014	1,095	1,132
2. Public gross fixed investment	11	12	15	18	19	26	28	35	44	57	49
3. Public consumption	50	55	75	99	108	118	128	124	138	152	170
4. Private consumption	604	612	720	712	779	831	808	729	748	783	832
5. Private gross investment	53	76	106	112	118	123	87	76	84	103	81

Notes: The figures are expressed in 1954 prices. Investment figures are gross and include some changes in stocks. The investment series were taken from NPC Memo 40A (1957.) Changes in stocks have been added to private fixed investment.

Source: INP Memo 377.

TABLE 15

Statutory Capital of Organized Enterprises

Year	*Net annual increase in statutory capital*			*Registered statutory capital of commercial & industrial enterprises* (£ m.)	*Paid-up capital of joint-stock enterprises* (£ m.)
	Industrial enterprises (£ m.)	*Commercial enterprises* (£ m.)	*Total* (£ m.)		
1951	2·1	7·0	9·1	175·4	120·8
1952	2·2	9·4	11·6	183·1	121·9
1953	1·1	6·2	7·3	190·5	141·0
1954	3·6	6·3	9·9	201·3	147·3
1955	9·7	5·0	14·7	215·7	146·9
1956	23·4	5·1	28·5	246·7	172·9
1957	7·2	8·5	15·7	259·9	191·5
1958	11·1	5·7	16·8	286·3	200·4
1959	18·1	5·9	24·0	297·5	229·1
1960	44·1	5·8	49·9	336·1	235·1

Sources & Notes

'Net annual increase in statutary capital of industrial and commercial enterprises' means net additions made to nominal or legal capital by the organized sector of industry and commerce—that is by firms affiliated to chambers of commerce and industry. Smaller-scale enterprises are excluded. Statutory capital is simply the capital registered with the Ministry of Economy. It does not equal either paid-up capital or the current value of assets employed by a firm. These figures are published by the FIE *Ann.* and NBE, *Econ. B.* There are inexplicable but slight variations from one publication to another. The figures reported in the table have been copied from *Annuaires 1958–9*, p. 386 and 1962 statist. app., p. 72.

'Registered statutory capital of commercial and industrial enterprises' is the total registered capital of firms described above. Unfortunately I have been unable to locate a set of aggregated figures consistant with the annual changes. Published by Ministry of Economy, in *Economic Progress in the UAR.*

'Paid-up capital of joint-stock enterprises' represents equity shares paid in full. It excludes reserves and interest-bearing loans. Paid-up capital does not represent the value of fixed capital or other reserves of capital employed by a firm. Joint-stock companies form the most important part of Egyptian organized and registered enterprise. These figures have been copied from the *Yearbook of Joint Stock Companies* and were communicated to me privately by Dr A. Tanamli.

All three series are extremely dubious indicators of capital formation by organized business but in the absence of other figures they can at least be compared with qualitative evidence and other economic indicators now available.

TABLE 16

Gross Domestic Capital Formation, by Sector

Sector	*1959–60* (*£ m.*)	*1960–1* (*£ m.*) (*Planned*)	*1961–2* (*£ m.*) (*Planned*)	*1964–5* (*£ m.*) (*Planned*)
Private business	19·5	40·4	60·8	128·0
Households	9·0	9·0	6·4	9·0
Total private sector	28·5	49·4	67·2	137·0
Government business	95·3	170·2	209·8	117·4
Government administration	80·1	85·8	85·9	96·8
Total public sector	175·4	256·0	295·7	214·2
Total gross domestic capital formation	203·9	305·4	362·9	351·2

Notes: All figures are expressed in 1959–60 constant prices. The figures for 1960–1, 1961–2, and 1964–5 are Plan Targets. All figures include depreciation and changes in stocks.

Sources: Gen. Frame of 5-year Plan, tables 80, 83, 85, & 89 and Min. of Planning, *Ann. Plan for 1960–1* & *1961–2* (ar.), tables 80, 82, 85, & 89.

TABLE 17

Planned Investment by Public & Private Sectors, 1960–1 & 1961–2
(£ million)

Activity	*Public sector*	*Private sector*	*Public sector*	*Private sector*
Agriculture	30·6	4·5	27·4	4·4
Irrigation & drainage	16·1	1·0	21·1	1·2
The High Dam	10·3	—	10·3	—
Industry	58·3	18·5	85·8	14·2
Electricity	7·2	1·7	13·0	—
Transport, communications, & storage	54·9	8·0	69·0	2·2
Suez Canal	14·9	—	11·2	—
Building & construction	13·9	21·2	17·0	25·1
Public utilities	12·8	0·1	13·8	—
Services	20·2	1·0	24·7	14·8
Total	239·2	56·0	239·3	61·9

Notes: All figures are expressed in 1959–60 constant prices. Investment means net investment but includes the cost of land. It refers to investment in projects began before the opening of the Plan Year and new projects commencing during the Plan Year.

Sources: Min. of Planning, *Ann. Plans 1960–1* & *1961–2* (ar.), Sect. 1.

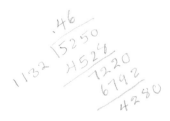

TABLE 18

Sources of Domestic Savings, 1954 to 1964

(£ million)

Sector	*1954–5*	*1959–60*	*1960–1 (Planned)*	*1961–2 (Planned)*	*1964–5 (Planned)*
1. *Private Sector*					
Retained profits, private organized business	52·5	38·7	54·5	138·6	93·7
Retained profits, non-organized business	32·7	25·6	25·7	22·6	41·0
Household savings	12·1	22·7	77·0	66·6	80·0
Total private saving	97·3	87·0	157·2	227·8	214·7
2. *Public Sector*					
Government budget income account: surplus or deficit (+ or −)	—	+12·0	−5·8	−73·6	+5·5
Retained profits of public enterprises	—	67·6	75·0	128·7	143·6
Net income from social insurance	—	14·4	20·5	24·2	27·8
Total public saving	15·9	94·0	89·7	79·3	176·9
Total domestic saving	113·2	181·0	246·9	307·1	391·6
Foreign aid and loans	—	22·9	58·5	59·9	−40·4

Notes: All figures are expressed in 1959–60 prices. Profits of public enterprises transferred to the Budget account have been recorded as retained under public savings. The figures for 1954 and 1959–60 are actual figures. The rest are Plan targets. The figures for 1964/5 are as planned in 1959–60. All other planned figures are calculated about one year before they are published. Public enterprises are enterprises controlled by the government. Misr companies are not included in the figures for 1959–60, 1960–1, or 1964–5. 'Private organized business' is corporate enterprises registered under law 26 of 1954. In 1964–5 planners expected a surplus of £40.4 m. on current account the balance of payments which would be utilized to repay foreign loans.

Sources: The Egyptian National Accounts for 1954 (1958, ar.), NPC Memo 90; *Gen. Frame of 5-year Plan*, tables 74 & 75; Min. of Planning, *Ann. Plan 1960–1*, p. 204 & *1961–2*, pp. 186–7.

TABLE 19

Indices of Industrial & Agricultural Production

Year	*1* *Manufacturing industry*	*2* *Manufacturing industry*	*3* *Manufacturing industry*	*4* *Agricultural production*	*5* *Agricultural production*
1945	71		64		
1946	75		68	100	
1947	80		72	101	
1948	90		81	113	
1949	98		88	116	
1950	100		90	116	
1951	105	95	95	110	
1952	105	98	98	119	96
1953	113	100	100	120	92
1954	122	107	107	132	102
1955	133	177	117	128	103
1956		125	125		107
1957		132	132		115
1958		143	143		117
1959		149	149		121
1960					

Notes: Index 1 is a quantum index covering manufacturing production. Index 2 is a base weighted quantum index of manufacturing production. Indices 4 & 5 cover all agricultural production. Both are base weighted indices, weighted according to the contribution of produce to net value added in agriculture for 1934–8. The base of comparison is 1934–8=100 for index 4 and 1952/3–1956/7=100 for Index 5. Both indices refer to fiscal years: thus 1947=1947/8.

Sources: Index 1: NPC Memo. 86. Index 2: NBE, *Econ. B.*, statist. sect. Index 3: spliced index from indices 1 & 2. Indices 4 & 5: FAO *Yearbooks.*

TABLE 20

Changes in Industrial Output per Employee

Year	*Total employees* (000)	*Index of employment*	*Index of manufacturing output*	*Index of output per employee*
1947	279	100	72	100
1950	244	87	90	143
1952	265	95	98	143
1954	265	95	107	157
1956	257	92	125	189
1957	274	98	132	188
1959	308	110	149	188
1960	318	114	—	—

Notes: Total employees refer to firms employing 10 or more workers. The figures have been adjusted to include the labour of proprietors and unpaid family labour.

Sources: Nos. of industrial employees from UN, *Dev. Manufacturing*, p. 103 and *Statist. Pocket Yearbooks*, *1958*, *1960*, & *161*, table 34. Index of manufacturing output is cited in table 8.

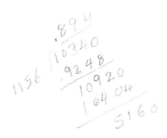

TABLE 21

Gross National & Per Capita Product, 1945–60

Year	*Gross national product at 1954 prices* (*£ m.*)	*Total population* (000)	*Per capita product at 1954 prices* (*£*)
1945	702	18,460	38·0
1946	735	18,792	39·1
1947	767	19,068	40·2
1948	866	19,494	44·4
1949	916	19,888	46·1
1950	934	20,393	45·8
1951	959	20,872	45·9
1952	980	21,473	45·6
1953	970	22,003	44·1
1954	997	22,557	44·2
1955	1,027	23,063	44·5
1956	1,046	23,643	44·2
1957	1,080	24,179	44·7
1958	1,139	24,666	46·2
1959	1,207	25,324	47·7
1960	1,284	25,948	49·5

Notes: This series has been calculated by averaging fiscal-year figures in table 8 of INP Memo 335 into calendar years and by adjustment to present GNP at 1954 constant market prices.

Sources: INP Memo 335, tables 4 & 8. Population figures and mid-year estimates from FIE, *Ann.*, Sect. 2 and UN, *Yearbook of Demographic Statistics*, Sect. 4.

TABLE 22

Index of Share Prices

(1946 = 100)

Year	*Banks insurance*	*Industrial commercial*	*Buildings & hotels*	*Land*	*General*
1951	74·7	90·3	67·9	92·1	83·6
1952	60·0	66·9	52·5	65·1	62·7
1953	62·2	58·0	51·5	57·3	57·1
1954	67·8	76·7	64·6	60·8	70·8
1955	61·4	81·4	63·6	49·0	70·1
1956	57·3	83·2	52·4	41·2	66·2
Mar. 1957	55·3	80·0	47·5	40·1	63·1
June 1957	55·3	79·7	47·9	39·2	62·9
Sept. 1957	50·9	76·8	42·1	31·9	57·9
Dec. 1957	57·6	81·9	42·7	36·3	61·9
Mar. 1958	55·0	80·7	40·0	39·0	60·8
June 1958	55·2	82·4	38·4	36·7	60·6
Sept. 1958	58·1	91·7	41·4	41·4	66·6
Dec. 1958	58·0	114·5	45·1	43·7	77·1
Mar. 1959	58·2	115·1	49·7	45·7	79·3
June 1959	53·2	98·9	42·8	38·5	68·5
Sept. 1959	54·0	102·6	45·2	39·5	70·8
Dec. 1959	57·1	100·2	44·2	39·5	70·1
Mar. 1960	54·9	92·9	41·4	37·0	65·2
June 1960	49·8	86·5	38·0	31·8	59·7
Sept. 1960	49·9	81·9	38·7	31·1	57·9
Dec. 1960	48·7	77·6	35·4	29·9	54·8
Mar. 1961	49·7	78·2	34·4	30·8	54·3

Source: NBE, *Econ. B.*, statist. sect.

Bibliography

1. *Egyptian Official Publications**

Bank Misr. *Economic Bulletin.*

Banque Belge en Égypte. *Revue économique trimestrielle.* Quarterly.

Central Bank of Egypt. *Economic Review.* Quarterly.

— *Credit and Banking Developments.* 1962.

Central Statistical Committee. *Basic Statistics.* 1962.

Comité de Planification Nationale. *Cadre du Plan, 1960–5.* 1960.

Department of Statistics & Census. *al-Thawra fi ashr sanawat.* 1962.

— *Uslub taqdir al-dakhl al-qaumi fi'l-gumhuriyya al-arabiyya al-muttahida (misr) an sanatey 1957 wa 1958.* n.d.

Economic Organization. *al-Kitab al-sanawi al-am al-thani, 1958–9.* 1959.

Federation of Egyptian Chambers of Commerce. *al-Gumhuriyya al-arabiyya al-muttahida, baadh al-mathahir al-iqtisadiyya.* 1958.

— *UAR; Some Economic Features.* 1958.

Fédération des Industries Égyptiennes. *Annuaire.* Annually.

Federation of Egyptian Industries. *Égypte industrielle.* Monthly.

Government and Reorganization in the UAR. Unpubl. report by L. Gullick and R. Pollock. 1962.

High Dam Authority. *al-Mathahir al-iqtisadiyya li-mashru al-sadd al-aali.* 1962.

Higher Committee for Agrarian Reform. *Replies to the United Nations Questionnaires relating to Egyptian Agrarian Reform.* 1955.

Industrial Bank. *al-Taqrir al-sanawi li-sanat 1956.* 1956.

— *The Development of Industrial Credit in Egypt.* 1956.

Information Dept. *The Charter.* 1962.

— *The Constitution, 1964.* 1964.

— *Documents and Notes.* Monthly.

— *The Egyptian Revolution in Three Years.* 1955.

— *Goals of the Egyptian Revolution.* 1955.

— *The Permanent Council for Public Welfare Services.* 1955.

— *President Nasser's Speeches and Press Interviews.* 1958, 1959, 1961, 1962, 1963.

* All published in Cairo. For memoranda of the National Planning Committee and Institute of National Planning, see below, pp. 340 & 341.

— *Reports and Statements by Ministers to the Congress of National Union*. 1960.
— *Social Developments under the New Régime*. 1954.
— *Socialist Laws*. 1961.
— *UAR Yearbooks*. 1959, 1960, 1962, 1964.
L'Institut de l'Assurance de l'Épargne des Travailleurs. *Rapport, 1956*. 1957.
Institute of National Planning. *Monthly Review of Economic and Social Events*. 1962–5.
Ministry of Agrarian Reform. *Muthakkara an mashru tanzim al-intaj al-zirai fi muhafazatay Kafr al-Sheikh wa Beni-Suef*. n.d.
— *Statutes of Zaafaran Cooperative*. 1955.
Ministry of Agriculture. *Agricultural Census, 1939*. 1945.
— *al-Amal al-zirai wa'l-istishari fi misr*. 1945.
— *Nahwa al-ishtirakiyya al ziraiyya*. 1962.
Ministry of Commerce & Industry. *The Companies Law*. 1954.
Ministry of Economy. *Economic Progress in the UAR*. 1960.
Ministry of Finance. *Return on State and Prospect of the Cotton Crop*. Monthly.
Ministry of Finance & Economy. *Budget Report, 1957–8*. 1958.
— *Census of Industrial Production, 1945*. 1947.
— *Census of Industrial Production, 1950*. 1953.
— *Ihsa al-intaj al-sinai li sanat 1954*. 1956.
Ministry of Industry. *Industry after the Revolution and the Five-Year Plan*. 1957.
— *The Second Five-Year Industrial Plan*. 1960.
Ministry of Planning. *al-Khitta al-sanawiya li-sanat 1960–1, 1961–2*. 1960 & 1961.
— *General Frame of the 5-Year Plan for Economic and Social Development, July 1960–June 1965*. 1960.
Ministry of Social Affairs. *The Labour Department*. 1957.
— *Social Welfare in Egypt*. 1950.
Ministry of Treasury. *Budget Project, 1961–2, 1962–3, 1963–4*.
National Bank of Egypt. *Annual Reports*, 1947–56.
— *Economic Bulletin*. Quarterly.
— *National Bank of Egypt, 1898–1948*. 1948.
Permanent Council for the Development of National Production. *Taqrit*. 1955.
The Permanent Council of Public Services. *The Population Problem in Egypt*. 1955.
Statistical Dept. *Annuaire statistique*. Semi-annually.
— *Annual Statement of Foreign Trade*.

— *Census of Industrial Production, 1957 & 1959*. 1958 & 1962.
— *Census of Population, 1917, 1920, 1927, 1947, & 1960.*
— *National Income of Egypt for 1953*. 1954.
— *Statistical Pocket Yearbook*. Annually.

2. *Other Official Publications*

FAO. *Yearbook of Food and Agricultural Statistics*. Rome, annually.
France, Institut National de la Statistique et des Études Économiques. *Égypte*. Paris, 1950.
Great Britain, Board of Trade. *Overseas Economic Surveys: Egypt*. London, 1933, 1935, 1937, & 1951.
— *Report of Mission to Egypt, Sudan and Ethiopa*. London, 1955.
— Parliamentary Papers: *Reports by the Consuls-General on Finances, Administration and Conditions of Egypt*. 1884–1921.
United Nations.* *Demographic Yearbook*.
— *The Development of Manufacturing Industry in Egypt, Israel and Turkey*. 1958.
— *Economic Developments in the Middle East, 1956–7*. 1957.
— *Economic Development in Selected Countries*. 1947.
— *Statistical Yearbook*.
United States, Dept. of Labor. *Summary of the Labor Situation in Egypt*. Washington, 1955.

3. *Institute of National Planning Memoranda*

63 *Planning for Balanced Social and Economic Development*, by I. Abdel Rahman. 1961.
76 *Social Aspects of Development Planning in the UAR*, by I. Abdel Rahman & N. Dief. 1961.
137 *Social Laws and Decrees Issued in January 1961*. 1962.
141 *The System of Follow-up of the First Five-Year Economic and Social Plan*, by N. Dief. 1962.
167 *Development Programming and Public Budgeting in Egypt*, by I. Abdel Rahman. 1961.
168 *The Uses of the Input-Output Model in Development Planning*, by G. Eleish. 1962.
209 *UAR State Budget for 1962–3*. 1962.
210 *Some Uses of Economic Accounting in Planning Economic Development of the UAR*, by N. Dief. 1962.
238 *Comprehensive Planning in the UAR*, by I. Abdel Rahman. 1962.
255 *Models Used in Drafting the Plan*, by M. Imam. 1962.
259 *A Production Function for Egyptian Agriculture, 1913–55*, by M. Imam. 1962.

* All published in New York.

335 *The National Income of Egypt, 1939–52*, by B. Hansen & D. Mead. 1963.
377 *The National Outlay of the UAR, 1937–59 and 1945–1962/3*, by B. Hansen. 1963.
547 *Marginal Productivity Wage Theory in Egyptian Agriculture*, by B. Hansen. 1965.
597 *Distributive Shares in Egyptian Agriculture*, by B. Hansen. 1965.

4. *National Planning Committee Memoranda*

4 *Tahlil nataij hisabat al-intaj wa'l-takhsis wa ras al-mal.* 1959.
7 & 8 *Analysis of Egypt's Balance of Trade and Cotton Exports*, by P. Bög. 1958.
10 *The National Profit Rate on all Investment Project*, by R. Frisch. 1959.
11 *Tatawwur al-tijara al-kharijiyya fi'l khamsa wa'l-ishrin sana al-sabiqa.* 1958.
11 *Nashat sharikat al-tamin.* 1959.
21 *Daur al-nizam al-masrafi fi taqbiyat idkharat al-qita al-khas.* 1958.
24 *Adhwa ala mashakil al-kiyas al-kammi li'l l-amala wa'l batala.* 1958.
25 *The Preparation of a Draft Investment Plan for Egypt*, by R. Frisch. 1959.
29 *al-Tatawwur fi mizaniyet mizan al-madfuat li'l-iklim al-misri 1947 September sanat 1958.* 1959.
32 *Tahlil nataij hisab ras al-mal li-sanat 1961.* 1959.
44 *Taqdirat al-natij al qaumi.* 1958.
44 *al-Tatawwur fi'l-mizan al-tijari li'l-fatra 1954–58.* 1959.
53 *Optimal Investments Under Limited Foreign Resources*, by R. Frisch. 1959.
61 *al-Arqam al-kiyasiyya li-intaj wa tijaret misr al-kharijiyya 1945–54.* 1957.
62 *Taqdir mawarid al-bilad min wassail al-dafaa al-ajnabiyya khilal al-sanawat 1960–64.* 1959.
68 *The Economic Significance of the High Dam*, by A. Meguid. 1959.
71 *Mashru itar khitta tawilat al-ajal li'l-iqlim al-misri min 1959 ila 1979.* 1958.
86 *Ihsaat an al-tijara al-kharijiyya wa'l-intaj wa'l-dakhl wa'l takwin al-rasmali.* 1959.
86 *Statistics of Trade, Income, Production and Capital Formation*, by I. Abdel Rahman. 1959.
99 *Itar al-khitta al-amma li'l-tanmia al-iqtisadiyya li'l-iqlim al-misri fi'l gumhuriyya al-arabiyya al-muttahida (1957–58).* 1958.
103 *al-Taqdir al-awwali li-imkaniyat al-intaj khilal al-khitta.* 1958.

113 *al-Taqdirat al-mabdaiyya li-hajm al-idkharat al-mahalliyya al-mutuawaqqaa li'l-istithmar li'l tanmia fi'l-sanawat 1959–63 fi'l-iqlim al-misri.* 1958.

121 *al-Ittijahat al-amma li-numuw al-iqtisad al-misri fi'l-rubu qirn al-madi*, by A. Sherif. 1959.

124 *Tahdid ahdaf al-intaj wa hudud al-istithmar fi'l-khitta al-khamsiyya al-aula wa'l-khitta al-ishriniyya.* 1959.

135 *Tariqat taqdir al-idkharat al-muntazar en tatawwalad fi qita al-samal al-munazzam al-khas khilal al-fatra min 1959 ila sanat 1963.* 1959.

138 *Taqdir al-idkharat al-mutawwalida* (*milhaq*). 1959.

147 *Qiyas hajm mudakharat al-qita al-am fi'l-khitta al-khamsiyya 1959–63.* 1959.

149 *Tahlil al-mizaniyya wa'l-siyasa al-maliyya li'l-sanawat al-khams al-mathia wa'l-muqbila, 1954–64.* 1959.

151 *Wadh al-khitta wa jadwal al-intaj wa'l istikhdam.* 1959.

155 *al-Majmuat al-aula min al-bayanat al-lazima li-taqdir ihtiyajat al-istihlak fi'l-khitta al-khamsiyya.* 1959.

163 *Taqrir al-lajna al-fariyya li-idkharat al-qita al-munazzam.* 1959.

164 & 165 *Draft Reports on Egyptian Planning*, by J. Tinbergen. 1957.

173 *Taqdir al-arbah al-muhtajiza fi majmuat al-mashruat ghair al-munazzama.* 1959.

181 *al-Mizaniyya al-qaumiyya li-sanat 1963 wafqan li-tafsil al-khitta al-khamsiyya al-aula.* 1959.

185 *al-Nawahi al-maliyya li'l-khitta.* 1959.

187 *Summary of Answers to Questions*, by J. Tinbergen. 1958.

197 *Wassail tanmiyya wa ziyadet al-mudkhirat fi'l-qitaa al-aili.* 1959.

198 *Taqdir al-mawarid al-idkhariyya al-idafiyya al-nashia an tanfidh mashruat al-khitta.* 1959.

201–10 *Taqarir al-lajna al-fariyya li'l naql.* 1959.

216 *Taqrir awwali an taqdir al-idkharat li'l-qita ghair al-munazzam wa'l-aili khilal al-sanawat 1959–63.* 1959.

217 *Taqrir lajnat al-arbah ghair al-muwazaa.* 1959.

218 *Taqrir mabdai an al-waridat al-murtaqiba khilal al-sanawat al-khams al-qadima 1959–63.* 1959.

219 *Taqrir mabdai an mawarid al-bilad min wassail al-dafaa al-ajnabi khilal al-sanawat al-khams al-qadima.* 1959.

220 *al-Taqrir al-nihai li-lajnat al-masail al-maliyya.* 1959.

221–30 *Taqarir lajnat al-sinaat.* 1959.

231 *Taqrir lajnat al-kahraba.* 1959.

232 *Taqrir lajnat al-tadrib.* 1959.

233 *Taqrir lajnat al-raisiyya li'l-sinaat wa'l quwa'l-kahrabaiyya.* 1959.

234 *Taqrir lajnat dabt al-nil.* 1959.
235 *Taqrir lajnat al-sadd al-aali.* 1959.
236 *Taqrir al-rai wa'l sarf.* 1959.
237 *Taqrir lajnat al-miyah al-jawfiyya.* 1959.
238 *Taqrir lajnat al-quwa al-kahrabaiyya al-maiyya.* 1959.
239 *Taqrir lajnat mashruat rai al-sahari.* 1959.
240 *Taqrir al-lajna al-raisiyya li'l-rai wa'l-sarf-wa'l-miyah al-jawfiyya.* 1959.
245 *Taqrir al-lajna al-fariyya li-tanmit al-istihlak adad* 1959.
246 *Taqrir al-lajna al-fariyya li'l-sukkan wa'l-quwa al-amila.* 1959.
249–63 *Taqarir lajnat al-ziraa.* 1959.
264 *al-Taqrir al-thani li-lajnat al-masail al-maliyya.* 1959.
265 *Taqrir an-iadet taqdir al-muddakharat li-sharikat al-tamin was-sanduq al-tamin wa'l-maashat wa muasasat al-tamin wa'l-idkhar li'l-ummal khilal al-khams sanawat al-qadima.* 1959.
288 *Hal yumkin al-isra fi'l tanmiyya bi-mudaafat al-dakhl al-qaumi fi 10 sanawat badalan min ishrin sana?* 1959.
292 *Hisab muaddalat mukhtalifa li-mudaafat al-dakhl al-qaumi fi'l-iqlim al-junubi.* 1959.
303 *Ahammiyyat al-takhtit fi'l-riaya al-ijtimaiyya.* 1959.
308 *Maudva al-istihlak fi'l-khitta.* 1959.
333–5 *Nahwa mujtama ishtiraki dimukrati taawauni.* 1959.
353 *al-Tawfiq bayna mukhtalaf al-ahdaf fi'l-khitta.* 1959.
429 *Tahlil al-tatawwur al-iqtisadi fi sanat 1959 wa darurathu ka-asas li'l-mizaniyya al-qaumiyya li-sanatey 1960–61.* 1960.
431 *al-Tarabut fi itar al-khitta al-amma.* 1960.
432 *Murajaat arqam al-tijara al-kharijiyya al-warida fi itar al-khitta al-khamsiyya.* 1960.
444 *Mulahazat ala mudhakkarat al-sayyid wazir al-ziraa wa'l-islah al-markazi bi-shan murajaat itar al-khitta–qita al-ziraa wa'l-rai.* 1960.
445 *Murajaat itar al-khitta bi-wasitat wazarat al-tamwin.* 1959.
451 *Nataij tahlil al-tadaffuqat al-maliyya fi am 1958 al-namt al-tamwil fi'l-qita al-khas.* 1959.
548 *A Rough Outline of Planning in Egypt*, by M. Ibrahim. 1959.

5. *Books and Articles*

Abdel-Malek, A. *Égypte, societé militaire.* Paris, 1963.
— Nasserism and Socialism, *in* J. Saville & R. Miliband, eds., *The Socialist Register.* London, 1964.
— La Réforme agraire en Égypte. *Développement et Civilisations*, June 1965.

Ali, A. R. *al-Bunuk al-tijariyya fi misr.* 1961.

Amin, G. *The Food Problem and Economic Development in Egypt.* Ph.D. thesis, London Univ., 1964. (Published in London, 1966.)

Amin, S. Le Financement des investissements dans la province égyptienne de la RAU. *L'Égypte contemporaine*, July 1959 & Jan. 1960.

Ammar, A. *A Demographic Study of an Egyptian Province* (*Sharqiya*). London, 1947.

Amr, I. *al-Ard wa'l-fallah.* 1958.

Anderson, J. Law Reform in Egypt, *in* P. Holt, ed., *Political and Social Change in Modern Egypt.* London, 1967.

Anis, M. *A Study of the National Income of Egypt.* Cairo, 1950.

Arminjon, P. *La Situation économique et financière de l'Égypte.* Paris, 1911.

Artin, Y. *The Right of Landed Property in Egypt.* London, 1885.

Audsley, M. Labour and Social Affairs in Egypt. *St Antony's Papers*, iv, 1958.

Baer, G. Egyptian Attitudes Towards Land Reform, *in* W. Laqueur, ed., *The Middle East In Transition.* London, 1958.

— *History of Landownership in Modern Egypt.* London, 1962.

Barawi, R. & Ulaish, M. *al-Tatawwur al-iqtisadi fi misr fi'l-asr al-hadith.* 1945.

Barawy, R. *The Military Coup in Egypt.* Cairo, 1952.

Berger, M. *Military Élite and Social Change: Egypt since Napoleon.* Princeton, 1960.

Bertier, F. L'Idéologie sociale de la révolution égyptienne. *Orient*, ii, 1958.

Boghdadi, A. *Speech to the National Union, 4 July 1960.* Cairo, 1960.

Boinet, A. L'Accroissement de la population en Egypte. *Bulletin de l'Institut égyptien*, vii, 1886.

Bonné, A. *State and Economics in the Middle East.* London, 1898.

Cameron, D. *Egypt in the Nineteenth Century.* London, 1898.

Chenery, H. The Application of Investment Criteria. *Quarterly Journal of Economics*, Feb. 1953.

— Comparative Advantage and Development Policy. *American Economic Review*, Mar. 1961.

Cleland, W. A Population Plan for Egypt. *L'Égypte contemporaine*, May 1939.

Crabités, P. *Ismail the Maligned Khedive.* London, 1933.

Cremeans, C. *The Arabs and the World.* New York, 1963.

Cromer, Lord. *Modern Egypt.* London, 1908.

Crouchley, A. A Century of Economic Development. *L'Égypte contemporaine*, Mar. 1939.

— *The Economic Development of Modern Egypt.* London, 1938.

Darling, M. Land Reform in Italy and Egypt. *Yearbook of Agricultural Cooperation, 1956.*

Dobb, M. *An Essay on Economic Growth and Planning.* London, 1960.

Dorra, A. L'Industrie égyptienne. *L'Égypte contemporaine.* Nov. 1943.

Douin, G. *La Mission du Baron Boislecomte en Égypte et la Syrie en 1833.* London, 1927.

Durelles, Y. Structure et développement de l'économie égyptienne. *Tiers Monde,* July-Aug. 1960.

Eckstein, O. Investment Criteria for Economic Development. *Quarterly Journal of Economics,* Feb. 1957.

— & Krutilla, J. *Multiple Purpose River Development.* New York, 1958.

Eman, A. Le Financement de l'industrie en Égypte. *L'Égypte contemporaine,* Mar. 1945.

Fahmy, H. The Technique of Central Banking in Egypt. *Middle East Economic Papers,* 1954.

Fahmy, M. *La Révolution de l'industrie en Égypte 1800–50.* Leiden, 1954.

Fawzi, M. *Nawaj.* 1958.

Fikry, A. *The Economic Development of Egypt since 1876.* London, 1918.

Galatoli, A. *Egypt in Mid-Passage.* Cairo, 1950.

Galenson, W. & Leibenstein, H. Investment Criteria, Productivity and Economic Development. *Quarterly Journal of Economics,* Aug. 1955.

Garzouzi, E. *Old Ills and New Remedies in Egypt.* Cairo, 1958.

Ghonemy, M. R. Investment Effects of Land Reform. *L'Égypte contemporaine,* 1954.

— *Resource Use and Income in Egyptian Agriculture.* Unpubl. Ph.D. thesis, North Carolina State College, 1953.

Gindi, G. & G. Tajir. *Ismail d'après les documents officiels.* Cairo, 1946.

Girgis, F. *Dirasat fi tarikh misr al-siyasi mundhu'l-asr al-mamluki.* 1958.

Goichon, A. Le Plan de rénovation sociale de la campagne égyptienne. *Orient,* ii, 1961.

Gritly, A. *The Structure of Modern Industry in Egypt.* Cairo, 1947.

— *Tarikh al-sinaa fi misr.* n.d.

Group d'Étude de L'IDES. Pression démographique et stratification sociale dans les campagnes égyptiennes. *Tiers Monde,* July-Sept. 1960.

Hamdi, M. *A Statistical Survey of the Development of Capital Investment in Egypt since 1880.* Unpubl. Ph.D. thesis, London Univ., 1943.

Handley, W. The Labour Movement in Egypt. *Middle East Journal,* July 1949.

Hansen, B. & Marzouk, G. *Development and Economic Policy in the UAR.* Amsterdam, 1965.

Harbison, F. & Ibrahim. I. *Human Resources for Egyptian Enterprises.* New York, 1958.

Hassan, R. *Tamwil mashru al-sanawat al-khams li'l-sinaat.* 1961.

Herman, T. The Role of Cottage and Small-Scale Industries in Asian Economic Development. *Economic Development & Cultural Change*, July 1956.

Heyworth-Dunne, J. *Egypt; the Co-operative Movement.* Cairo, 1952.

Hindi, M. Tanzim al-dawra al-ziraiyya wa atharuhu al-iqtisadiyya fi ziyadet al-intaj. *Agricultural Economics*, Sept. 1962.

Khallaf, H. Financing Economic Developments in Egypt. *Middle East Economic Papers*, 1955.

— *al-Tajdid fi'l iqtisad al-misri al-hadith.* 1962.

Lacouture, J. & S. *Egypt in Transition.* London, 1958.

Lahita, M. *Tarikh misr al-iqtisadi fi'l-usur al-haditha.* 1944.

Laqueur, W., ed. *The Middle East in Transition.* London, 1958.

Levi, I. Le Commerce extérieur et l'industrialisation de l'Égypte. *L'Égypte contemporaine*, Dec. 1939.

Lewis, W. A. Economic Development with Unlimited Supplies of Labour. *Manchester School*, May 1954.

— The Industrialisation of the British West Indies. *Caribbean Economic Review*, May 1950.

Little, I. The Real Cost of Labour. *Quarterly Journal of Economics*, Feb. 1961.

Lloyd, E. *Food and Inflation in the Middle East.* Stanford, 1956.

McCoan, J. *Egypt under Ismail.* London, 1889.

Mansfield, P. *Nasser's Egypt.* London, 1965.

Marei, S. *Agrarian Reform in Egypt.* Cairo, 1957.

— *The Agricultural Development Programme for the Egyptian Region of the United Arab Republic.* Cairo, 1962.

Marei, H. *al-Ishtirakiyya al-ziraiyya fi ahdiha al jadid.* 1962.

— *UAR Agriculture Enters a New Age.* Cairo, 1960.

Mattison, B. Rural Social Centres in Egypt. *Middle East Journal*, Autumn 1951.

Mengin, F. *Histoire de l'Égypte sous le gouvernement du Mohammed-Ali.* Paris, 1823.

Messayer, M. *L'Égypte à travers le chemin du développement.* Lausanne, 1962.

Morshidy, A. *Planning Economic Development in the UAR.* Unpubl. report for UN. Cairo, 1963.

Mouriez, F. *Histoire de Mehemet Ali.* Paris, 1858.

Mustafa, A. The Breakdown of the Monopoly System in Egypt after 1840, *in* P. Holt, ed., *Political and Social Change in Modern Egypt.* London, 1967.

Naggar, S. *Foreign Aid to the United Arab Republic*. Cairo, 1964.

— *Industrialisation and Income*. Unpubl. Ph.D. thesis, London Univ., 1951.

Nahas, J. *Situation économique et sociale du fellah égyptien*. Paris, 1901.

Nasif, E. Le Problème des prix en Égypte. *L'Égypte contemporaine*, May 1947.

Nasser, G. Abdel. *The Philosophy of Revolution*. Cairo, 1954.

O'Brien, P. An Economic Appraisal of the Egyptian Revolution. *Journal of Development Studies*, Oct. 1964.

— Industrial Development and the Employment Problem in Egypt, 1945–65. *Middle East Economic Papers, 1962.*

— The Long-Term Growth of Agricultural Production in Egypt, 1821–1962, *in* P. Holt, ed., *Political and Social Change in Modern Egypt*. London, 1967.

Penrose, E. T. Economic Development and the State. *Economic Development & Cultural Change*, 1963.

Prest, A. *War Economics of Primary Producing Countries*. Cambridge, 1948.

Qayum, A. *Theory and Policy of Accounting Prices*. Amsterdam, 1960.

Quni, M. *Tatawwur misr al-iqtisadi fi'l-asr al-hadith*. 1944.

Radi, M. *The Structure of the Cotton Market in Egypt*. Unpubl. M.Sc. (Econ) thesis, London Univ., 1957.

Rafi, A. R. *Asr Ismail*. 1932.

— *Tarikh al-haraka al-qaumiyya wa tatawwur nizam al-hukm fi misr*. 1929–30.

Raj, K. *Employment Aspects of Planning in Underdeveloped Countries*. Cairo, 1957. (National Bank of Egypt Memorial Lectures.)

Rashad, I. The Cooperative Movement. *L'Égypte contemporaine*, May 1939.

Riad, H. *L'Égypte nassérienne*. Paris, 1964.

— State Capitalism in Egypt. *Revolution in Africa, Latin America & Asia*, i/l.

Rivlin, H. *The Agricultural Policy of Mohammed Ali*. Harvard, 1961.

Saab, G. Rationalisation of Agriculture and Land Tenure Problems in Egypt. *Middle East Economic Papers, 1960.*

Saaty, H. *Industrialisation in Alexandria*. Cairo, 1959.

Sadat, A. *Revolt on the Nile*. London, 1957.

Safran, N. *Egypt in Search of a Political Community*. Cambridge, Mass., 1961.

Said, G. The Cotton Problem. *L'Égypte contemporaine*, Oct. 1951.

— Productivity of Labour in Egyptian Industry. *L'Égypte contemporaine*, May 1950.

Samuelson, P. A Comment on Welfare Economics, *in* B. Haley, ed., *A Survey of Contemporary Economics*. Stanford, 1952.

Saville, J. & Miliband, R. *The Socialist Register*. London, 1952.

Scitovsky, T. *Welfare and Competition*. London, 1952.

Sen, A. K. On Optimising the Rate of Saving. *Economic Journal*, Sept. 1961.

Shabana, Z. *al-Iqtisad al-taawuni al-zirai*. Alexandria, 1961.

Sherbini, & A. Sherif. Marketing Problems in Egypt. *L'Égypte contemporaine*, July 1956.

Soliman, A. *L'Industrialisation de l'Égypte*. Lyons, 1932.

Tadross, H. Recent Developments in Egypt's Balance of Payments. *Middle East Economic Papers*, 1957.

Tanamli, A. Agricultural Credit and Cooperative Organisation. *L'Égypte contemporaine*, Oct. 1962.

— Évolution de l'économie rurale égyptienne dans les cinquante dernières années. *L'Égypte contemporaine*, Oct. 1960.

Tawney, R. *Equality*. London, 1931.

Tinbergen, J. *The Design of Development*. Baltimore, 1958.

Vatikiotis, P. *The Egyptian Army in Politics*. Indiana, 1961.

Walker, K. *Planning in Chinese Agriculture*. London, 1965.

Warriner, D. *Land Reform and Development in the Middle East*. London, 1962.

Weir, J. An Evaluation of Health and Sanitation in Egyptian Villages. *Journal of the Egyptian Public Health Association*, iii, 1952.

Wheelock, K. *Nasser's New Egypt*. Pennsylvania, 1960.

Wiles, P. *The Political Economy of Communism*. Oxford, 1964.

Wilmington, M. The Middle East Supply Centre. *Middle East Journal*, Spring 1952.

Newspapers

al-Ahram. Daily.

al Gumhuriyya.

al-Ahram al-Iqtisadi. Bi-weekly.

Bourse égyptienne. Daily.

Egyptian Gazette. Daily.

Index